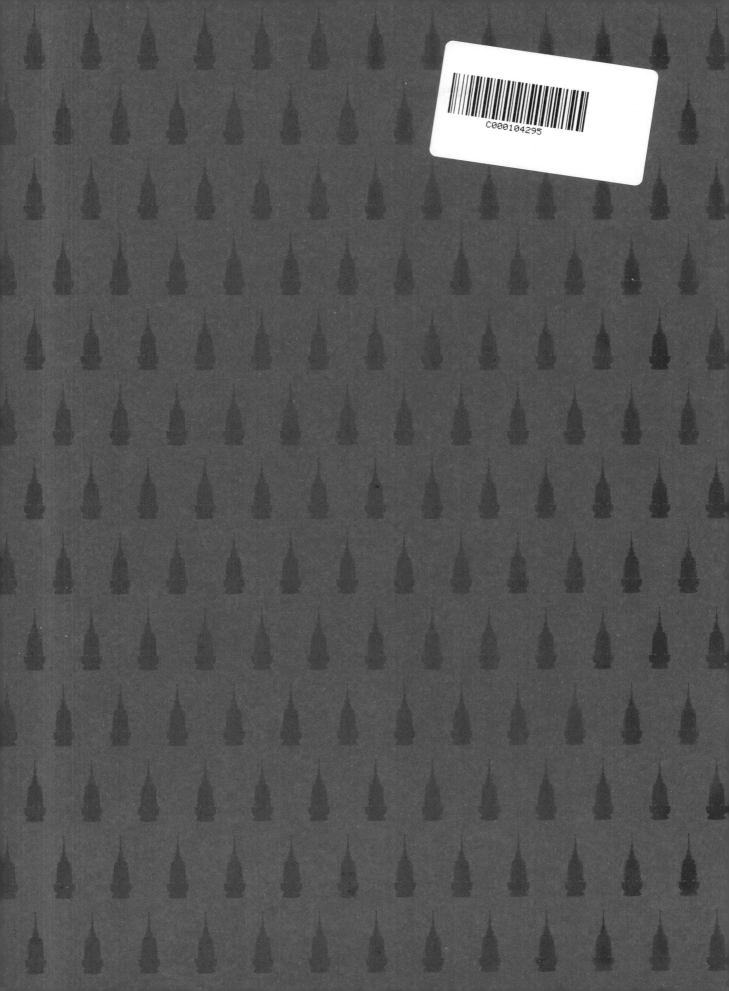

KING BHUMIBOL ADULYADEJ

A Life's Work

KING BHUMIBOL ADULYADEJ

A Life's Work

Thailand's Monarchy
In Perspective

edm EDITIONS DIDIER MILLET

EDITIONS DIDIER MILLET

PUBLISHER
Didier Millet

GENERAL MANAGER
Charles Orwin

EDITORIAL DIRECTOR
Douglas Amrine

EDITORIAL CONSULTANT
Francis Dorai

MARKETING DIRECTOR
Antoine Monod

STUDIO MANAGER
Annie Teo

PRODUCTION MANAGER
Sin Kam Cheong

First published in 2011 by Editions Didier Millet
Reprinted in 2012

Singapore Office
121 Telok Ayer Street, #03-01, Singapore 068590
Tel: 65-6324 9260 Fax: 65-6324 9261

Thailand Office
Suite 707, Panavongs Bld., 104 Surawong Rd, Bangkok 10500
Tel: 66-2-238 1570 Fax: 66-2-236 7242

Email: edm@edmbooks.com.sg   www.edmbooks.com

Colour separation by SC Graphic, Singapore   Printed by Sirivanata Interprint Public Co., Ltd., Thailand
ISBN 978-981-4260-56-5

This book was made possible thanks to the generous support of the following organisations:

Ministry of Foreign Affairs

ไทยพาณิชย์ SCB · SCG · Bangkok Bank

THAI Smooth as silk · ptt Group · ThaiBev · TOYOTA

BOON RAWD BREWERY CO., LTD. · RAIMON LAND ...developing a better environment · King Power KING OF DUTY FREE

Bangkok Post · FOUR SEASONS HOTEL Bangkok · BANGKOK public relations

Acknowledgements

The publishing team is grateful to the following individuals for their assistance and advice:
Khunying Ambhorn Meesook, Amnat Barlee, Anake Nawigamune, Anthony Davis, Apinan Poshyananda, Arsa Sarasin, Ar-tara Satraroj, Aravinda June Tanskul, Prince Bhisatej Rajani, Bob Hawke, Busarakham Nilavajara, Chai-anan Samudavanija, Catherine Faulder, Chaiyut Sanamwong, Charles Mehl, Chayaphan Bumrungphong, Chirayu Isarangkun Na Ayuthaya, Christopher Szpilman, C.J. Hinke, Denis Gray, Gris Chungsiriwat, Hasan Basar, Hubert Viriot, Jill Saunders, Jirasak Wattanawong, Kantana Noysoncharoen, Kasem Watanachai, Kateprapa Buranakanonda, Kittipong Kittiyarak, Kraisak Choonhavan, Kwanrudee Maneewongwatthana, Lachie Thomson, Khunying Maenmas Chavalit, Manrat Srikaranonda, Martin Cross, Morgan J. Thanarojpradit, Nanda Krairiksh, Nelson Hilton, Nicholas Farrelly, Nicholas Koleszar, Norbert Eschborn, Paddy Dickson, Pathorn Srikaranonda, Patthraporn Noomphan, Peter Cummins, Peter Schoppert, Piti-Sithi Amnuai, Polapatr Suvarnazorn, Poonnatree Jiaviriyaboonya, Poranand Poosawang, Priyanut Piboolsravut, Richard Butler, Ronald Renard, Rusarin Smitabhindu, Sasipar Yansithi, Simon Makinson, Simon Wallace, Siriluk Howsopchoke, Somsri Chungsiriwat, Songkram Supcharoen, Soodrak Chanyavongs, Suchit Boonbongkarn, Suleeporn Bunbongkarn, Sunathee Isvarphornchai, Supakorn Vejjajiva, Swalee Siripol, Sylvana Foa, Teera Ramasootra, Thartri Likanapichitkul, Tom Whitcraft, Vimla Tritasavit, Voramas Raksriaksorn, Wathana Sukarnjanaset, and special thanks to Pipatra Choomkamol of Immediate Thailand and the staff at the EDM Kuala Lumpur, Singapore and Paris offices.

We also appreciate support offered by the personnel at the following organisations:
Bangkok Post Information Centre, Bangkok Post Library, Center of Academic Resources at Chulalongkorn University, The Chaipattana Foundation, Chao Pho Luang Upatham School (Chiang Mai), Chulalongkorn Memorial Hall, Court Astrologers and Brahmin Priests Division (Bureau of the Royal Household), Crown Property Bureau, Faculty of Medicine at Siriraj Hospital, Hua Hin Royal Rainmaking Centre, Huai Hong Khrai Royal Development Study Centre, Huai Sai Royal Development Study Centre, Hup Krapong Cooperative Community Project, Information Division of the Office of His Majesty's Principal Private Secretary, Klai Kangwol School, Ministry of Foreign Affairs, National Archive of Thailand, National Library of Thailand, The Office of His Majesty's Principal Private Secretary, Office of the Royal Development Projects Board, Phra Dabos Foundation, Pranburi Irrigation Project, Privy Council Chambers, Public Works Department of the Bangkok Metropolitan Administration, Queen Savang Vadhana Foundation, Rajaprajanugroh Foundation, Rajprachasamasai Institute, Relief and Community Health Bureau of the Thai Red Cross Society, The Royal Chitralada Projects, The Royal Elephants Museum, The Royal Irrigation Department, Royal Project Foundation, S.F. Group, Siam Cement Group, Siam Commercial Bank, The Siam Society, Siriraj Medical Library, Suan Somdet Phra Srinagarindra Baromarajajonani Project, The Supreme Artists Hall, Thai Junior Encyclopaedia Project, Thailand Information Center and Thammasat University Libraries.

Finally, we would like to extend our profound gratitude to our friends and families.

CONTENTS

Foreword

His Majesty King Bhumibol Adulyadej of Thailand succeeded to the throne on 9 June 1946. He left the kingdom shortly afterwards to complete his university education in Switzerland.

At his coronation on 5 May 1950, King Bhumibol made a promise to the nation: "We shall reign with righteousness, for the benefit and happiness of the Siamese people." Since that historic day, the king has conscientiously upheld this commitment.

King Bhumibol Adulyadej: A Life's Work provides an account of the king's life and work. The book strives for balance, objectivity, accuracy and readability so that it may stand the test of time, helping any reader, today or in the future, to understand Thailand better and to learn more about its head of state, the world's longest-reigning monarch.

The introduction, A History of Kings, provides an overview of the salient underpinnings of the Thai monarchy within a historical context, while The Life relates the remarkable story of the king from his birth in 1927 to the present day. The second part of the book, The Work, gives focus to the king's efforts to promote development in Thailand—a cause to which he has dedicated his working lifetime. Indeed, it is through King Bhumibol's work in healthcare, education, agriculture and rural development—including his pioneering drug crop substitution programme—that the king has carved such a meaningful role for Thailand's constitutional monarchy. The final part of this book, The Crown, offers insights into the Thai monarchy as an institution. It includes historical and factual profiles of both the Crown Property Bureau and the Privy Council. It also presents objective surveys of the law of *lèse-majesté* and the process of succession, as well as a section on the royal traditions that form part of Thailand's cultural heritage.

The concept for *King Bhumibol Adulyadej: A Life's Work* originated from a strong belief that these subjects are of timely interest to a widening audience. The book's Editorial Advisory Board brings together notable experts on the monarchy, history, law, agriculture and sustainable development. The editors and contributing writers, among them respected academics and journalists, worked independently to draft the volume in its entirety. The role of the board was to critique the manuscript for accuracy, balance and relevance.

This dialogue between Thai experts, many of whom have enjoyed decades of personal interaction with the king in their official capacities, and the mostly international editorial team proved to be very productive, enlightening and spirited. Differing opinions and perspectives were exchanged freely and forthrightly to achieve the finished volume.

The book's quality, however, is for readers to judge. Our hope is that, by reading the passages that follow, you will gain a better understanding of Thailand and its monarchy, as well as deeper insight into His Majesty King Bhumibol's lifelong work in fulfillment of his promise to the people.

Anand Panyarachun
Chairman of the Editorial Advisory Board

The Royal House of Chakri

King Buddha Yod Fa Chulalok Maharaj
(Rama I, r. 1782–1809)

King Buddha Lert La Nabhalai
(Rama II, r. 1809–1824)

King Pra Nang Klao
(Rama III, r. 1824–1851)

King Mongkut
(Rama IV, r. 1851–1868)

King Chulalongkorn
(Rama V, r. 1868–1910)

King Vajiravudh
(Rama VI, r. 1910–1925)

King Prajadhipok
(Rama VII r. 1925–1935)

King Ananda Mahidol
(Rama VIII, r. 1935–1946)

King Bhumibol Adulyadej
(Rama IX, r. 1946–present)

Picture captions for opening pages. Page 5: *King Bhumibol on his coronation day, 5 May 1950.* **Page 7:** *Suphannahong, or Golden Swan, at sunset on the Chao Phraya, the River of Kings, opposite Wat Arun, the Temple of Dawn. The spectacular main royal barge dates from 1912 in the reign of King Vajiravudh.* **Page 8:** *King Bhumibol waves to well-wishers during a visit to Germany on the world tour in 1960 that took him on state visits to a dozen countries.* **Page 10:** *King Bhumibol passes one of numerous sitting Buddha images that gaze across the Thail landscape. In an overwhelmingly Buddhist nation that has received people of many faiths, the king is the defender of all religions.* **Following pages:** *King Bhumibol rides a mule during a visit to the remote northern highlands in the 1960s. The king's upcountry travels have taken him to every one of Thailand's more than 70 provinces using all means of travel imaginable.*

A Note on Style

Many visitors to Thailand soon discover there is no universally accepted official system for the transliteration of Thai words into Latin script. Some Thai words are rendered in Western languages according to quite precise systems which are nevertheless open to various criticisms from different quarters. Others are transliterated on a more ad hoc phonetic basis. This all results in considerable variety, confusion and cheerful disagreement.

The Western spellings of the names of Thai individuals are wherever possible reproduced in this book as they themselves have decided they should be written. For other words, particularly place names, the transliteration system of the Royal Institute is used in the interests of achieving some degree of consistency—but with some exceptions. For example, the more common spelling of Ratchadamnoen Avenue in Bangkok and the more archaic spelling of Ayudhya, the former capital, are used.

For monarchs of the Royal House of Chakri, we refer to the first three kings as Rama I, Rama II and Rama III. After the first three kings, the remaining six monarchs of the Royal House of Chakri are referred to in English by their most often used and recognisable names—King Mongkut (Rama IV), King Chulalongkorn (Rama V), King Vajiravudh (Rama VI), King Prajadhipok (Rama VII), King Ananda (Rama VIII) and King Bhumibol (Rama IX). King Vajiravudh only introduced the system that numbers the kings of the Royal House of Chakri as Ramas around 1920. He declared himself Rama VI—and retroactively gave the titles to his ancestors.

In the interests of clarity and brevity, this book follows the Western convention of usually using only one name for a royal personage, for example Queen Victoria or Emperor Hirohito. Contrary to common practice in Thailand, the book minimises the use of honorifics, such as His Majesty, His Royal Highness, His Serene Highness or His Highness. This once more is in the interests of brevity and clarity.

King Ananda Mahidol is most often referred to in this book as King Ananda. The charitable foundation which bears his name today is, however, called in English the Anandamahidol Foundation. The father of King Ananda and King Bhumibol was Prince Mahidol Aduldej, Prince of Songkla. The spelling of Aduldej differs from the spelling of Adulyadej in King Bhumibol's name, and the spelling of Songkla differs from the usual spelling of Songkhla, the province in Thailand's far south. Adding to the great potential for confusion, some names change during the course of people's lives as their ranks and titles become more elevated. For example, King Ananda and King Bhumibol's mother, Princess Sri Nagarindra, the princess mother, was the mother of two kings but never a queen. Indeed, she started life as a commoner named Sangwan. She received a courtesy title and became Mom Sangwan upon her marriage to Prince Mahidol in 1920. Her title as the princess mother of King Ananda was not bestowed on her by him until the late 1930s, and was later elevated further. For narrative purposes, in such instances, people are named as they were at the time being described irrespective of whatever rank or title they may have ascended to in later life.

Thai royal and noble titles typically denote a person's relationship to the king and stem from an ancient and complex hierarchical system. A few of the more prevalent titles appear in this book and customarily denote either birth titles of extended royal family members, titles conferred in recognition of achievements or women who have married into royal lines. Great-grandchildren of a king, for example, may use the title mom rajawongse. Khunying, sometimes translated as dame or lady, is a conferred non-inheritable lifetime title for a married non-royal woman. Thanphuying is the highest conferred non-inheritable lifetime title for a non-royal woman. Thunkramom is an informal way of referring to a prince or princess, with the word chai or ying added on the end according to whether they are male or female, respectively. The title mom has several possible implications—either a female commoner married to a prince as in the case of Mom Sangwan, or, either a former prince who has had his title stripped or a mom rajawongse who has been conferred with a higher title.

These style arrangements are not intended to be polemical and make no claim to being definitive. Their purpose is simply to make the narrative as accessible as possible to an intelligent English-speaking readership which cannot be expected to understand the difficulties and pitfalls of transliteration from Thai—or for that matter nuances of hierarchy and protocol, some of which date from ancient Siamese times.

The Editorial Advisory Board and editorial team apologises in advance to anybody who may not agree with the style choices in the pages that follow, but hope that they will find any decisions they consider errant at least consistently so.

A HISTORY OF KINGS

The Siamese monarchy is one of the most enduring of all monarchies in a region once full of them. From the 13th century until 1932, when absolute monarchy was replaced with constitutional monarchy, Siamese kings ruled. From 1932 until today, they have reigned.

This span of more than 750 years, however, has not been seamless. Behind the narrative commonly presented in Thai textbooks of four successive Siamese kingdoms—Sukhothai (c. 1249–1378), Ayudhya (c. 1351–1767), Thon Buri (1767–82) and Rattanakosin (1782–present)—lies a more complex history of competition, warfare, consolidation and transformation. Indeed, hundreds of rulers have controlled city-states and kingdoms of varying sizes within the area that is now called Thailand. Since the mid-1800s, Siamese monarchs have engaged with Western powers and ideas that have transformed the politics of Thailand and the region. In the 20th century, monarchies around Southeast Asia and the world were toppled. Yet nothing has changed the fact that the Siamese choose to place a king at their head.

What is the Siamese conception of monarchy, how has it evolved and why has it prevailed? The answers to these questions began to take form long before the current dynasty, the Royal House of Chakri, assumed power or the borders of Siam were drawn.

__Left__ Beneath a nine-tiered umbrella, King Bhumibol presides over the opening of parliament at the Ananta Samakhom Throne Hall in 1979.

Early Siamese Kings

Archaeology shows that the area of modern Thailand has been inhabited for several thousand years. But language and much else that has shaped the national culture arrived with the Tai people, who migrated south from China between the 8th and 12th centuries. Experts in cultivating rice and distinguished by their common language and unique houses built on stilts, the Tai settled the hills and then the low-lying plains of the Chao Phraya valley, where they farmed and fished, planted orchards, hunted game, tended cattle, created many crafts and practised small commerce.

As their numbers and wealth increased, Tai families banded together to protect against external threats, forming small fortified communities known as *mueang*. As these settlements expanded they became more complex. The ruler of a *mueang*, typically the head of its most successful family, would be charged with arbitrating disputes, distributing land and securing labour, among other duties.

These small communities existed in the shadows of the great Indianised empires of Pagan to the west and Angkor to the east. By the 13th century, however, both Pagan and Angkor were in decline and Tai rulers expanded their territory, creating alliances with and taking charge of neighbouring *mueang*. In time, these *mueang* developed from small city-states into larger confederations, spread over wider territory. These networks, such as those radiating from Lanna (modern-day Chiang Mai) and Sukhothai, are regarded by modern Thais as the first truly Siamese kingdoms. Their paternalistic rulers, called *pho khun* (father-rulers) in chronicles from the time, are widely accepted as the first Siamese "kings".

Through the mixture of animist, Hindu and Buddhist beliefs present at the time, early Siamese kings found ways to legitimise and glorify their rule. In this era, the Hindu model of kingship had reached its pinnacle in the Khmer empire of Angkor (c. 802–1431). In Angkor, the kings, led by Brahman priests and steeped in ritual, identified themselves with the pantheon of Hindu gods. The king was a god-like figure at the head of an extremely hierarchical, cosmologically ordered society. He rarely revealed himself to his subjects. When the king did appear, his subjects would prostrate themselves and place their foreheads on the ground. The king was so far above ordinary men that any address to the sovereign was made not to his person but to "the dust beneath the dust of his feet".

Theravada Buddhism, meanwhile, had been present in the Chao Phraya valley since at least the 5th century. When the animist Tai arrived, they embraced the religion, especially during the 12th century when a Buddhist revival spread east from Sri Lanka. Their preference for Buddhism would have a significant impact on the unique style of kingship that the Siamese kings created. While the sophisticated social structure and elaborate court rituals and customs of Angkor would strongly influence the Siamese conception of monarchy, it was the Buddhist ideal that was to become the defining paradigm of Siamese kingship.

Above *A painting on cloth depicts an episode from the Vessantara Jataka Buddhist tale in which Prince Vessantara demonstrates his charitable nature to the people.*

The Buddhist Ideal of Kingship

Borrowing from the ancient Pali canon, Theravada Buddhism posits its own cosmological order of heavens, hells and an earthly realm, on which man is initially led astray by desire and greed, and human society exists in chaos. But by selecting a king, a man of remarkable charisma, wisdom and skill, order is created. "The main function of the king," writes historian Frank Reynolds, "was of course to constitute the central pinnacle—the bond between the divine and the human, around and below which the Thai civil order took form. The king was closely associated with the figure of Indra, the great God who ruled in the heavenly realm, which was located at the peak of Mount Meru, the central mountain of the Thai Buddhist cosmology. As Indra ruled and maintained the order of *dhamma* [Buddhist teachings] in his domain, so the Thai monarch was to rule and maintain order in his earthly kingdom."

The Buddhist canon—and early Siamese texts like the *Trai Phum*—describe in detail the qualities of a king based on his unique role as "the bond between the divine and the human". He cannot be a monk, or some kind of high priest in the Western sense, because he must govern and occupy himself with worldly affairs, like leading his people into battle for instance. Similarly, he is not an ordinary man. Only merit accrued through many past lives could lead to circumstances where a person becomes a king. Certainly he is a devout practitioner of the faith because his central duty is to preserve and promote the *dhamma* to his subjects.

Even to this day, Thais refer to the monarch by many special names, including *phra chao yu hua*, which translates as God Upon Our Head and signifies his supreme right of leadership over his subjects; *chao chiwit* (Lord of Life) because the fates of his subjects can be determined by him; *phra chao phaen din* (Lord of the Land), signifying that the king possesses all the land in the realm and was responsible for its fertility and prosperity; *phra maha kasat* or Great Warrior, charged with protecting the realm; and *dhammaraja*, referring to his role in promoting justice, virtue, wisdom and the teachings of the Buddha. This last title, which translates as "righteous ruler", is particularly emblematic of how Buddhism defines kingship. In an excerpt from one tale, for example, the Buddha says to King Pasenadi:

"The ruler ought to rule his country under the principle of righteousness with

Above *A sitting Buddha image at Wat Mahathat in Sukhothai historical park. The Siamese conception of kingship is inspired, in part, by Buddhist tales and teachings that instruct rulers to draw authority from the merit of their actions.*

earnestness and carefulness in all royal duties treating his subjects as parents treat their own children ..."

And in another text from early Buddhist literature, the Buddha says: "A righteous ruler is one who honours, reveres, esteems and relies only on righteousness. With righteousness as his standard, as his banner, as his power and sovereignty of governing, he righteously works for his political principles and policy ... watching over and protecting the kingdom. He does so with regard to the scholars, the army, the businessmen, the householders, town and country folk, the recluses, the beasts and birds alike." In return, the subjects of the king do not question his sovereignty. The king is accepted during his lifetime as an incipient Buddha (Bodhisattva) or Cakravartin (Universal Emperor).

A Buddhist monarch as a result carries tremendous responsibility. He is bound to observe the Ten Virtues of the King (*dosapit rajadhamma*). They include *dana* (generosity), *sila* (moral conduct), *pariccaga* (self-sacrifice), *ajjava* (honesty and integrity), *maddava* (gentleness), *tapa* (perseverance), *akkodha* (freedom from hatred, ill-will and enmity), *avihimsa* (causing no harm to others), *khanti* (patience, forbearance and tolerance) and *avirodhana* (steadfastness and justice).

A king who follows these moral precepts ensures order and happiness in his kingdom. Those who ignore them lead the kingdom into chaos. As former professor of philosophy Siddhi Butr-Indr wrote, citing the words of the Jataka: "When a wicked unrighteous ruler reigns, water turns into blazing fire, safety into fear, refuge into bane, the people are neglected and left to rely upon themselves each for their own survival in states of 'laissez faire' and finally of 'barbaric anarchism'." The king's own fate is also at stake, the monarch's own happiness and suffering inextricably linked to that felt by his people.

The Buddhist rules of kingship thus act to check the potentially unmitigated power of the king and present him with a clear social contract. As sovereign, he is accorded tremendous respect and power, but he enjoys this status only because his subjects, believing in his worthiness, assent to it. As a result, the individual personality and abilities of the "Great Elect" (*mahasammata*, as he is sometimes called) become a significant variable in determining the strength of his reign. A good king who fulfils the expectations of the Buddhist ideal can command enormous reverence and authority. A bad king rules weakly.

Legendary Sukhothai

Children attending state schools in Thailand are taught that the Sukhothai kingdom (c. 1249–1378) was the first independent state founded by the Siamese people. They are told its first king helped break the yoke of Hindu Angkor and that its reach once spread as far north as Luang Prabang (in modern-day Laos), as far south as Nakhon

Si Thammarat province (in peninsular Thailand) and all the way to Hongsawadi (in modern-day Myanmar, formerly Burma). Most importantly, they learn that the kings of Sukhothai ruled paternalistically according to the Buddhist ideal. Indeed, this history is inextricably linked to the contemporary Siamese conception of kingship.

Much of this history was disseminated by the military governments of the 1930s as part of a nationalist movement. It was formalised, however, during the early 20th century reign of the sixth king in the Royal House of Chakri, King Vajiravudh (r. 1910–1925), who sought to define the origins of the native Siamese and engender patriotism among them. King Vajiravudh promoted in a stone inscription dating from the Sukhothai era the perfect Magna Carta for Siam. Sukhothai Inscription One was discovered in 1833 by the future King Mongkut while he was still a monk and then brought to Bangkok. Dated 1292 from the reign of King Ramkhamhaeng, it is the first record of the Thai alphabet and the earliest of several inscriptions from the kingdom of Sukhothai which detail the lineage, deeds and achievements of its rulers. Most significantly, it depicts the kingdom as an open and prosperous society ruled by a just and righteous monarch:

"In the time of King Ramkhamhaeng this land of Sukhothai is thriving. There are fish in the water and rice in the fields. The lord of the realm does not levy toll on his subjects for travelling the roads; they lead their cattle to trade or ride their horses to sell; whoever wants to trade in elephants, does so; whoever wants to trade in horses, does so; whoever wants to trade in gold and silver, does so. When any commoner or man of rank dies, his estate—his elephants, wives, children, granaries, rice, retainers and groves of areca and betel—is left in its entirety to his son. When commoners or men of rank differ and disagree, [the king] examines the case to get at the truth and then settles it justly for them. He does not connive with thieves or favour concealers [of stolen goods]. When he sees someone's rice he does not covet it, when he sees someone's wealth he does not get angry ... He has hung a bell in the opening of the gate over there: if any commoner in the land has a grievance which sickens his belly and gripes his heart, and which he wants to make known to his ruler and lord, it is easy; he goes and strikes the bell which the king has hung there; King Ramkhamhaeng, the ruler of the kingdom, hears the call; he goes and questions the man, examines the case, and decides it justly for him. So the people of this *mueang* of Sukhothai praise him."

In recent decades, there has been controversy over the authenticity of this inscription. While most historians believe that it is either the actual work of King Ramkhamhaeng or produced by a later Sukhothai king to glorify the dynasty, a few argue that the inscription is a forgery produced by King Mongkut, who they say hoped to convince encroaching Western powers of Siam's rich and long history. The king translated part of the inscription and presented it to British emissary John Bowring in 1855 after which its significance faded until the reign of King Vajiravudh.

Whichever view one takes on its origins, Sukhothai Inscription One is a pivotal historical document that has, as scholar Michael Wright notes, "taken on a sacred character, symbol of the nation, first constitution, enshrining the essence of all that 'Thainess' meant". Inscription One establishes a tradition of kingship based on Buddhist ideals that contrasts with the Hindu concept of divine kingship. Its story of the bell, for example, shows that even Siamese kings of yore have been accessible and responsive to the needs of their subjects. Kings of the present dynasty beginning with Rama III carried on this practice, placing a drum outside the palace gates, while 20th-century successors King Vajiravudh and King Prajadhipok assigned a gentleman-at-arms to receive written petitions from the people at the palace gates.

Inscription One, however, is not the only evidence that Sukhothai kings were inspired by Buddhism. The great monuments and art preserved from this time focus on the image of the Buddha and clearly attest to the vitality of the religion. Buddhist statues and relics gained through conquests were enshrined in temples. The dynasty's last four kings assumed the title of Maha Dhammaraja (The Great Dhamma King). Other, less controversial chronicles record the ruler's merit-making or donations to monastic institutions and highlight his pious and merciful character. In the 1357 Sukhothai Inscription Three from the reign of King Lithai (Maha Dhammaraja III), for example, the monarch describes his study and command of the central Buddhist canon the *Tipitaka*. He also presents himself as a worldly figure who knows how

Above left *The Wheel of Law symbolises Buddhist teachings and the spiritual transformation that occurs by following them. A Thai king, who is duty-bound to dispense the teachings to his subjects, is considered a Cakravartin ("one through whom the wheel turns").* **Above right** *Sukhothai Inscription One tells of King Ramkhamhaeng and the prosperity created by his benevolent rule in the 13th century.*

Above *A depiction of Ayudhya painted by the Dutch, who first settled there in the 17th century. One of the largest in Asia at the time, the impressive city was crisscrossed with waterways, and was home to many Buddhist temples.*

to catch and ride elephants, build irrigation ditches and weirs, and is the master of recreational games, astrology, science and military affairs. The *Trai Phum* text, believed to date from his reign, defines the Buddhist cosmology and establishes a vast moral hierarchy and the role of king within it.

Regardless of the righteousness and achievements of its rulers, the kingdom of Sukhothai proved rather short-lived. By the mid-1400s, its power had waned and it had become, like many other states of the era, a tributary to an emerging kingdom to the south: Ayudhya.

Uneasy Reigns

Initially a river port the Chinese referred to as Hsien (which the Portuguese then translated into Siam), Ayudhya was located at the confluence of three rivers near the seat of the former Angkor outpost of Lop Buri. Its outstanding economy fuelled its rise. Unlike Sukhothai, Ayudhya had access to the sea and would grow over the 14th and 15th centuries into a prosperous trading centre. By its golden age in the 16th and 17th centuries, Ayudhya's reputation had spread as far as Europe. Chinese, Japanese, Indian, Arab, Persian, Malay, Dutch, French and English traders all settled outside its walls. Hearing that the Siamese tolerated other religions, Jesuit and other Catholic missionaries came to proselytise in the midst of the many Buddhist temples. Royal barge ceremonies, court dramas and festivals featuring Chinese opera, acrobatics and puppet shows were staged. With an estimated population of nearly 500,000, the capital was one of Asia's largest cities when it was sacked by the Burmese in 1767.

Building, protecting and regulating such a kingdom, however, required manpower and laws. The kings of Ayudhya codified a highly original, hierarchical and bureaucratic system that placed all but the nobles, monks and foreign traders into a rigid framework known as *sakdina*. Titles and numerical units were allotted to every member of society, from top to bottom, rigidly defining his or her position in the hierarchy. Slaves, for example, received a *sakdina* of five units while the highest ministers received 10,000 units. This system persisted into the late-1800s.

In Ayudhya there was no standing army or official salaries. Instead, manpower and land were the key forms of capital that defined the *sakdina* system. By the 17th century, an estimated two thousand people and their families formed a nobility that controlled the entire population of Ayudhya under the unseen gaze of the king. The common people (called *phrai*) owed up to six months a year in service to the crown. Typically, they would be sent into battle or worked in construction or mining, or were engaged in digging canals, making bricks or building temples. Some fled to the forests. Enemies captured during warfare were resettled in the capital and became slaves.

The kings sat at the zenith. There were 34 of them during the Ayudhya era and numerous dynasties. There were warrior-kings whose bravery in battle is celebrated to this day. Others are now infamous despots or usurpers who gained the crown through murder. Several reigns lasted less than a year. Once Ayudhya had established itself and prospered, kingship became increasingly ritualised. Through Brahmans, who held eminent positions in the court, the kings associated themselves with the pantheon of Hindu gods. Some remained almost entirely hidden from view in an inner sanctum of the palace. When they did appear in public—a rare occasion—their subjects were prohibited from looking at them. To address royalty, an elaborate language known as *rajasap*, which is used to this day, was developed from the Khmer court tradition. Foreign traders referred to the deified status of the king in their correspondences. The Frenchman Abbé de Choisy, who came to Ayudhya in 1685 during the reign of Louis XIV, contended that, "The king has absolute power. He is truly the god of the Siamese: no one dares to utter his name."

The popular historical view of Ayudhya's kings is that they strayed from the path of Buddhist kingship and fashioned themselves in the Hindu-style of *devaraja* (divine rulers). Some historians explain this departure from the Sukhothai ideal as owing to geography. Ayudhya's proximity to the Khmer outpost of Lop Buri may have exposed its original rulers and inhabitants to ancient Khmer customs and Hindu influences. Kingship in Ayudhya was undoubtedly shaped by the increasingly sophisticated challenges and threats from both within and outside the kingdom. Warfare, conquests, disease and fire took a heavy toll. To cite just one example, in 1569, a dispute over auspicious white elephants triggered a successful invasion by the Burmese—the Ayudhya king was famed for possessing seven white elephants but refused to relinquish any. It would take a decade and many battles led by King Naresuan before the Siamese would be able to reassert control.

Internally, competition for the throne, which had accrued enormous wealth, was intense. Succession laws were unclear. Intrigue was rife. When a king died, bloodline was a significant determinant of the heir but so too was clout. Hoping to advance their own status and gain the spoils of increased manpower for themselves, factions of nobles surrounding the court lobbied in the name of rival heirs. Foreign traders and monks patronised by high princes also exerted influence over the selection. The losers in the succession dramas often lost their lives, and their entire families and allies were violently purged.

In the 1540s, the court official Khun Worawongsa usurped the throne through an elaborate plot hatched with the help of a consort of the king. When the king died and the consort became regent, she placed a child on the throne. The boy was then murdered, making Khun Worawongsa king, but not for long. Forty-two days into his reign, a group of nobles created a ruse, inviting the king and his queen to view a recently captured elephant renowned for its size. While travelling by boat, they were ambushed and beheaded, their heads placed on spikes. With such inherent dangers, it is little wonder many kings of Ayudhya sought refuge in the palace.

Contact with the West created other challenges. King Narai's close relationships with foreigners engendered xenophobia during his reign (1656–88). Famous for sending missions to Louis XIV's France and for promoting an Anglo-Greek trader named Constantine Phaulkon to become his closest adviser, the king expressed (or

Above A painting depicts Louis XIV of France granting an audience at Versailles in 1686 to the delegation of Siamese ambassadors sent by King Narai.

feigned) interest in both Catholicism and Islam. After King Narai fell ill in 1688, Phaulkon was charged with treason and put to death. The king himself passed away soon after, and both his line and Western influence fell from favour. In a matter of months, all of King Narai's possible heirs had been murdered. French traders and soldiers, and many other foreigners, abandoned Ayudhya.

Through all of the upheavals, however, the throne remained the locus of legitimate and sacred rule. The palace was the unquestioned seat of power and Buddhism, the widely practised religion of the people, continued to play a key role in upholding and regulating the kingship. In chronicles from the time, monks praised kings who ruled fairly according to the *dhamma*, and criticised those who were greedy or otherwise set a bad example to the laity. Like the kings of Sukhothai, the rulers of Ayudhya constructed enormous temples to make and demonstrate their merit, enshrine Buddhist relics and commemorate their illustrious ancestors. The dynasty that followed King Narai oversaw a revival of Buddhism, but like the reigns of many kings of Ayudhya, this was also cut short.

Devastation and Resettlement

In the 1760s, the Burmese began a campaign of invasions that devastated the city-states of the central plains, climaxing with the sacking of Ayudhya in 1767. The Burmese were bent not on expanding their territory but destroying their eastern rival and its vassals. Campaigns into the north destroyed Lanna, Lampang, Sukhothai, Nan and Luang Prabang and, in the south, Ratchaburi, Phetchaburi and Chumpon. When forces finally infiltrated the capital of Ayudhya, they turned the once grandiose city to rubble and ash. The vanquishers carted away people and property, and torched centuries-old texts, records and temples, leaving the artistic, intellectual and physical architecture of the kingdom in tatters. The king at the time is said to have escaped to the forest where he starved to death.

In a chronicle, a monk described the general scene: "Some wandered about, starving, searching for food. They were bereft of their families, their children and wives and stripped of their possessions and tools … They had no rice, no fish, no clothing. They were thin, their bodies wasting away. They found only the leaves of trees and grass to eat … They grew thinner, and their flesh and blood wasted away. Afflicted with a thousand ills, some died and some lived on."

The Burmese campaign across the former network of Ayudhya was so cataclysmic that many towns were not properly resettled for many decades. Yet within only six months, a new capital emerged downriver at the port of Thon Buri, founded by a man of common birth and Chinese blood who was the former provincial governor of Tak, a northwestern outpost of Ayudhya. An excellent military tactician and charismatic leader, King Taksin, as he was known, rapidly expanded his power base.

While King Taksin's success in re-establishing stability and territory was remarkable, his alliance with the former nobility and military commanders was tenuous.

Having fallen into disarray, the Buddhist clergy posed another challenge to King Taksin. One band of monks led by a self-proclaimed priest-king named Ruan had even turned to banditry, vice and violence, sacking the city of Phitsanulok before being subdued by King Taksin. The king's attempt to reform the monkhood led to his undoing. Declaring himself a *sotapanna*—an enlightened being nearing nirvana—the king subjected monks to lectures and humiliated those who failed his tests. In 1782, when a small rebellion formed against an unpopular tax collector appointed by the king, the revolt led by disgruntled nobles and officials turned into a coup against King Taksin. Having returned home from a campaign in Cambodia, the king's own top general, Chao Phraya Maha Kasatsuk (formerly known as Chao Phraya Chakri), was offered the throne and accepted it. Following the protocol regarding the taboo on spilling royal blood, King Taksin was placed in a velvet sack and killed by a single blow to the back of his neck with a sandalwood club.[1]

The First Chakri

The timing of the founding of the Royal House of Chakri in 1782 looks auspicious in retrospect: the French Enlightenment was climaxing in Europe and the United States had recently declared its independence. These were historical coincidences, but Western rationalism and expansionist policies would influence the Chakri kings.

King Bhuddha Yod Fa Chulalok (or Rama I, as he later became known) quickly proved to be as intelligent as a monarch as he had been as the top general, forging a new order that sought to recreate the glory of Ayudhya but on decidedly new terms. First, he situated his palace across the river from Thon Buri in Bangkok. *Krung Thep,* as it was known in Thai (City of Angels), was crisscrossed with canals, a city on water reminiscent of Ayudhya. Using Cambodian and Lao conscripted labour, new temples and the Grand Palace were built according to ancient Buddhist cosmological principles, and included some bricks from the ruins of Ayudhya. The king installed the sacred Emerald Buddha in the new Chapel Royal. This small Buddha image, which had been brought back from a military campaign in Vientiane and presented to King Taksin in 1778, became the palladium of his reign. The second of Rama I's two coronations, organised over five years, was painstakingly designed to impress his greatness on his subjects.

Most significantly, the king set about re-establishing a sense of law and order that had been absent since the sacking of Ayudhya. He focused on the Buddhist clergy, which had become a haven for profligacy. He created the position of supreme patriarch, who was charged with maintaining discipline within the monkhood. He issued 10 edicts regulating the behaviour of monks. In one symbolic move, he rounded up,

Left *Rama I founded the Royal House of Chakri in 1782.*

29

disrobed and conscripted 128 monks to hard labour for "all kinds of low behaviour such as drinking intoxicants … wandering out at night to see entertainments, rubbing shoulders with women, engaging in loose talk …[and] boarding Chinese junks in order to obtain fanciful objects …"

The king initiated a revision of the *Tipitaka* and sponsored a new rendering of the *Trai Phum*. In his legal reformation, the *Three Seals Code*, he included the early Buddhist charter, the *Dhammasat*, creating an explicit link between the Buddhist code and practical law that is said to have been unique for the time. He adapted the great Indian tale the *Ramayana* to Thai verse, giving his kingdom its own epic, the *Ramakien*. Rama I's successful reformation was also fuelled by other factors. After subduing the Burmese early in his reign, a period of relative peace followed and burgeoning trade filled the monarchy's coffers. The new capital was a favoured trading centre of China. Rama I's mother was of wealthy Chinese ancestry. Immigrants from China resettled in the capital, so many in fact that foreign visitors to Bangkok dubiously claimed they outnumbered the Siamese. Rama I cleverly delegated power and wealth to emerging merchant families and provincial states, and before long Bangkok was the centre of a kingdom whose territory stretched beyond anything Ayudhya had ever claimed.

By the end of his reign in 1809, Rama I had combined military strength with an emphasis on the monarchy as the protector of Buddhism to create a unified and stable kingdom under his unchallenged leadership. Summing up his reign in a speech, anthropologist Stanley Tambiah argued that Rama I followed the ideology of a Buddhist king: "He appears to have been deeply infused with it and at the same time knew how to manipulate it. His rule was an orthodox expression of the concept of *dhammaraja*. At the same time, he was aware that in doing so he was able to stabilise his rule and the dynasty of which he was founder. In such an instance it is futile to separate the living of an ideology from its manipulation. As the founder of a new dynasty he legitimated his own accession to the throne, and he proved his worthiness to occupy it by performing the deed characteristic of classical righteous kingship."

Siam and the West

While Rama I skilfully established the foundations of this new kingdom, his successors would navigate it through a period of unprecedented change. The 19th century was an age of incredible invention and ideas: scientific and technological breakthroughs, advanced medicine, travel and increased trade. Western liberalism and rationalism elevated the rights of the common man and put an end to slavery in many parts of the world. By the end of the century, Western powers had slowly but surely taken control of the Southeast Asian region. All of modern-day Siam's neighbours were colonised: the British ruled Burma and Malaya, and the French ruled Laos, Cambodia and Vietnam beyond. Their peoples were subjugated and their monarchies disbanded or treated as anachronisms. How did the Siamese monarchy survive this period?

During the first half of the 19th century, under the reigns of Rama II and Rama III, the challenges had yet to fully materialise. These two kings continued to consolidate the kingdom's territory and improve its internal affairs. Taxation was reformed and opium gangs were wiped out—the opium trade became a government monopoly in the 1850s. The commercial economy prospered, enriching the throne. Several brutal campaigns were waged against neighbours, including the successful sacking of Vientiane (1827–28).

During these decades, Prince Mongkut, a future king, was coming of age. He would be admired for deftly handling the tensions between East and West. Although Prince Mongkut was the eldest celestial son of Rama II, his elder and more experienced half-brother Rama III assumed the throne in 1824. Prince Mongkut had entered the monkhood shortly before the succession, and did not contest Rama III's accession. For the next 27 years, he wore the robes of a monk, received alms at dawn and made pilgrimages throughout the country. He learned English and Latin, and studied science. As a monk, he concluded that while the social ethics of Buddhism stood

Above *After 27 years in the monkhood, King Mongkut reigned for 17 years from 1851 and was father to 38 sons and 44 daughters.*

up to emerging Western rationalist thought, its explanations of natural processes and its superstitious, cosmological aspects did not. He founded a new sect called Dhammayut, which preached a stricter adherence to the Buddhist precepts.

On a visit to the ancient capital of Sukhothai, Prince Mongkut is said to have discovered the famous Inscription One, which mentions a stone seat known as the Seat of Justice. According to the writer and former Thai prime minister, Mom Rajawongse Kukrit Pramoj, after leading the prince to the seat, villagers told him it was haunted. The prince replied, "Justice has never been known to harm anyone. If this be truly the seat of justice, it will cause me no harm." Then he declared: "Seat of stone, harm me not," and to the wonder and cheers of the superstitious villagers, stood on it. The seat and stone inscription were then brought to Bangkok and presented to Rama III.

When Prince Mongkut became king upon the death of Rama III in 1851, he continued to encourage progress while maintaining tradition. Rama III had been correct when he warned that the next threat from the outside would come from the West rather than from historic rivals such as Burma. As the British sphere of influence expanded, King Mongkut signed the Bowring Treaty with the British in 1855. This move forestalled any designs the British had on Siam and allowed the emerging class of influential merchant families increased access to trade.

King Mongkut's power during his reign was counter-balanced by powerful noble families such as the Bunnag clan. To maintain the authority and traditions of the throne, he issued no less than 5,000 new laws and strengthened the rules and hierarchy of the palace. At the same time, he admired the West's advances in medicine and new technology—printing presses, paddle-steamers and cameras arrived via the Chao Phraya river. He also invited Western experts to help develop key government services. Historian Chris Baker describes his reign as "a time of transition, suspended between different eras and different worlds".

King Mongkut was fascinated by astronomy. In 1868, accompanied by the palace entourage and a group of French astronomers, he travelled upcountry to view the moon pass in front of the sun. At the moment predicted by the king, the clouds parted and the eclipse began. For his foreign audience, this was the triumph of a progressive monarch disproving the superstitious beliefs of his subjects. For his subjects, however, it was confirmation of the special talents and wisdom of a monarch who could forecast the movement of the universe.

Revolution from Above

During this excursion, King Mongkut caught malaria and soon after passed away. His successor was the 15-year-old King Chulalongkorn, who began his reign under the regency of the patriarch of the powerful Bunnag family. After travels to Malaya, Java

Above A fresco by Italian Galileo Chini at the Ananta Samakhom Throne Hall in Bangkok depicts King Chulalongkorn abolishing slavery in Thailand. The fifth king in the Royal House of Chakri introduced many significant reforms over the course of his reign, and created a centralised system of government that consolidated the power of the crown.

and India to learn the workings of neighbouring states and bureaucracies, the king came of age in 1873. Inspired by these colonial administrations, the king immediately set out on an ambitious programme of reform and centralisation of power that threatened the income of nobles, tax collectors and various commercial fiefdoms. A crisis soon erupted. It was spurred by the supporters of the Prince of the Front Palace, or *uparat*, who has been sometimes wrongly referred to as the "second king" by Westerners. King Chulalongkorn prevailed, and later abolished the *uparat* position.

King Chulalongkorn's four-decade reign saw a complete overhaul of the administration of the kingdom. Many capable family members, nobles and Western experts supported the king's plan and helped enact his reforms. The king created the Privy Council to advise him and the Privy Purse Bureau to manage the crown's finances. He established a standing army and salaried police force, initiated new educational, health and judicial systems, reordered the Buddhist clergy and reformed labour by gradually abolishing corvée service and slavery.

Most significantly, the king established a finance ministry which centralised control over tax collection and public spending, giving the crown new clout to direct

Top left King Chulalongkorn in full regalia in the mid 1870s. **Top right** King Chulalongkorn with his son Crown Prince Vajiravudh who succeeded him in 1910. **Above** Prince Damrong and Prince Mahisara, seated fourth and fifth from left respectively, with other key officials in King Chulalongkorn's reform movement in 1896.

national development. He also replaced retiring officials from the old guard with allies who supported his new measures. In parallel, key architects of this great reform, such as Prince Damrong, began to instil in the people, through his writings and addresses, a self-conscious sense of nationhood. Thai was promoted through the new education system as the national language. The sweeping platform has sometimes been described as a "revolution from above".

This undertaking was fuelled, in part, by the threat presented by Western nations. Galvanised by the fall of neighbours to colonialism and the increasing hostility of the French, King Chulalongkorn set about consolidating territory throughout the kingdom. In provincial areas, power had previously been delegated to the local leaders of what were essentially self-governing states. These areas were, through force and persuasion, integrated into the new mechanisms of the emerging nation-state. A new postal service, telegraph and telephone system were established with the help of Western experts. By the end of his reign, modern national boundaries had been set.

The tension with the West climaxed in 1893 when two French gunboats and a steamer travelled up the Chao Phraya river. The Siamese fired from the banks. The steamer was sunk and its French crew killed. The French responded by blockading the mouth of the river and threatening further military action that might have spelled the end of Siam's sovereignty altogether. Through diplomacy, Siam retained its autonomy but at a steep cost: nearly one-third of its land in the region east of the Mekong, long coveted by France, was ceded to the French. In 1896, the colonial pressures and designs on Siamese territory eased when both Britain and France agreed to guarantee the country's independence.

What followed was a golden period for the monarchy. King Chulalongkorn travelled to Europe twice. The king himself embraced Western fashions. He sponsored motor shows, wore tailored suits and smoked fine cigars. Coins, photography, art and stamps featuring his image formed a new iconography. The king himself was genuinely adored by his subjects and the prestige of the crown among the people reached great heights. During his 40th year on the throne in 1908, a celebration feted the king as the longest-reigning monarch in the history of Siam.

King Chulalongkorn's status as a modern and progressive leader—and the many new institutions and trappings of a modern nation-state he introduced—demonstrated that Siam belonged to the community of civilised nations. A new role had emerged for the monarch. The Siamese king was now the bearer of both an ancient tradition and the agent of progress. As Maurizio Peleggi writes in *Lords of Things*: "While the main purpose of royal ceremonies under the *ancien régime* was to manifest the purportedly divine nature of kingship, the newly invented rituals of the last quarter of the nineteenth century emphasised the bond between the citizens of the modern nation-states and royal figures, whose decreasing power was to be balanced by their new public roles as embodiments of the nation and even exemplars of moral and civic virtues."

Doubts about Democracy

The reign of King Chulalongkorn also marked the beginning of a dialogue on the future of absolute monarchy. In 1887, a group of eleven princes and officials who were residing in Europe, which included three of the king's own brothers, proposed a parliamentary system under a written constitution. The group, encouraged by the king himself to engage new ideas and report to the monarch, believed that unless Siam became a constitutional monarchy foreign powers would use its supposed backwardness as a pretext for colonising the country.

King Chulalongkorn rejected the idea. The king replied that the Thai bureaucracy was still too inefficient for such a system and that there were insufficient numbers of educated people to make it a success. He believed that such a move could spark a crisis led by those, such as the current ministers, who would lose power. He stated that: "Siamese kings have led the people so that both they and the country might be prosperous and happy … They have more faith in the king than in any members of parliament, because they believe that the king more than anybody else practises justice and loves the people." King Chulalongkorn concluded that reform in Siam must be gradual, a view that would frame the discussion of democracy in Siam for the next four-and-half decades.

The kings of the Royal House of Chakri were well aware that absolute monarchy would be increasingly difficult to sustain. There were few absolute monarchies left in the world. King Mongkut had taken small and symbolic steps to create a closer relationship with the people, reviving the practice of receiving petitions and allowing the general public to view their monarch during royal processions. To demonstrate that Siam was not out of step with Western values, in 1873, King Chulalongkorn abolished the practice of public prostration. Addressing the prostrated throng from his throne, he stated: "His Majesty has noticed that the great countries and powers in Asia where oppression existed, compelling inferiors to prostrate and worship their masters, have ceased these customs … They have done so to make manifest there shall be no more oppression … His Majesty therefore proposes to substitute, in place of crouching and crawling on all-fours, standing upright with a graceful bow of the head …" The assembly stood.

After succeeding King Chulalongkorn in 1910, King Vajiravudh recognised the tall task ahead of him in maintaining his father's legacy. Writing to a foreign friend of the family six weeks after his father's death, he said: "It will be very hard to follow in his footsteps, but I will do my best for the people now committed to my charge. Although in name I am their king, I hope they will soon learn that they have in me a faithful friend and a willing servant, who is ready to do all for their happiness and welfare." The reign of King Vajiravudh (r. 1910–25), however, was unstable from the start. The king's support of the Wild Tiger Corps, a special paramilitary force the king created in 1911 to act as a front line of defence and prepare young people to fight for Siam, alienated elements within the armed forces. A group of disenchanted young navy and army officials were arrested for plotting the overthrow of the Chakri dynasty, the first such threat in its history.

Concerned about the growing number of resident Chinese, King Vajiravudh, a talented writer and dramatist, revived the Sukhothai ideal of kingship and the martial spirit of Ayudhya to forge a sense of nationalism based on shared history, culture and identity as well as attachment to the king. However, financial crises and a free press, which scorned the nepotism and extravagance of his court, guaranteed a turbulent reign. Through the model city he called Dusit Thani, he created an experiment in democracy. Built in 1918 and located on a plot of land at Phayathai Palace, Dusit Thani was a miniature town in which palace and Ministry of Interior officials were trained in the concepts and practice of democracy. Roles were acted out, and the king himself played a commoner who was a lawyer. The experiment did not assuage King Vajiravudh's critics. Increasing budget deficits made his spending on such projects and the arts seem lavish. Palace and government finances were in disarray.

When King Prajadhipok rather unexpectedly became king in 1925—King Vajiravudh had died at the age of only 44—support for absolutism was crumbling. His first significant move was to create the Supreme Council of State, populated with

Above *King Vajiravudh in uniform at the annual manoeuvres of the Wild Tigers Corps, April 1923.*

a clean slate of advisers. Privately, King Prajadhipok began a sincere dialogue about more drastic reforms such as creating the position of prime minister. In letters to elder statesman Prince Damrong and Francis Bowes Sayre, who was a foreign affairs adviser to King Vajiravudh and the son-in-law of President Woodrow Wilson in the US, King Prajadhipok fretted openly about the state of affairs.

Referring to the accusations of embezzlement and nepotism that had constantly been launched against the court of King Vajiravudh, he wrote to Sayre: "The birth of the free press aggravated matters still more. The position of the king has become one of great difficulty. The movements of opinion in this country give a sure sign that the days of Autocratic Rulership [sic] are numbered. The position of the king must be made more secure if this dynasty is going to last. Some sort of guarantee must be made against an unwise king."

In the same letter he wrote: "As you well know, the king has absolute power in everything. This principle is very good and very suitable for the country, as long as we have a good king. If the king is really an "elected king", it is probable that he would be a fairly good king. But this idea of election is really a theoretical one …"

Both Sayre and Prince Damrong advised King Prajadhipok against any serious reforms of the monarchy. Like King Chulalongkorn they did not think the country was ready for a constitutional system. Replied Prince Damrong, "Rome was not built in a day." In *The Atlantic Monthly* in 1926, Sayre wrote: "A parliament uncontrolled by an intelligent electorate may constitute an infinitely more dangerous and corrupt engine of tyranny than the most absolute of kings." The king moved to create a system of municipalities, but patience with the pace of reform had already worn thin. Parallel to this dialogue, a group of Western-educated Thais were already hatching a plan that would take the decision about the future of the country's government firmly out of the monarch's hands.

End of Absolute Monarchy

On the morning of 24 June 1932, in the space of just a few hours, a small group of men ended 150 years of absolute monarchy under the Royal House of Chakri. The coup had been planned in Paris five years earlier by seven Western-educated military and civilian officials who were disillusioned with the pace of progress in Siam. On the day of the coup, the People's Party (as they called themselves) commandeered military vehicles and tanks in the capital and detained key members of the military and royal family. They then distributed a deliberately provocative leaflet at the Royal Plaza, attacking King Prajadhipok and his government. Echoing the very same language and concepts of the Buddhist ideal of kingship which Siamese monarchs employed to legitimise their rule, the People's Party turned the tables:

"When the present king succeeded his brother to the throne, some people at first

ทัพเจ้ามีความเต็มใจที่จะสละอำนาจอันเป็นของ
ทัพเจ้าอยู่แต่เดิมให้แก่ราษฎรโดยทั่วไป แต่ทัพเจ้าไม่
ยินยอมยกอำนาจทั้งหลายของทัพเจ้าให้แก่ผู้ใด คณะใด
โดยฉะเพาะ เพื่อใช้อำนาจนั้นโดยสิทธิขาด และโดยไม่ฟัง
เสียงอันแท้จริงของประชาชน

ประชาธิปก ปร.

วันที่ ๒ มีนาคม พ.ศ. ๒๔๗๗

เวลา ๑๓ นาฬิกา ๔๕ นาที

Top *The first constitution of the Kingdom of Siam was displayed to the public in 1932 in a temporary pavilion erected in the grounds of the Ananta Samakhom Throne Hall.* Above *Part of King Prajadhipok's abdication statement of 2 March 1935 which states: "I am willing to surrender the powers I formerly exercised to the people as a whole, but I am not willing to turn them over to any specific individual or any group to use in an autocratic manner without heeding the voice of the people."*

Above *King Ananda is escorted by officials at the Constitutional Fair during his first visit to Siam as its monarch in late 1938. Aged just 13, he returned to Switzerland shortly after to continue his schooling. The eighth king in the Royal House of Chakri, he was never crowned and was represented for most of his reign by a regency council.*

expected him to rule with justice for the good of his subjects. Their hopes did not materialise. The king was above the law as before ... He rules without any guiding principle. As a result the destiny of the nation was left at random, as evidenced by economic depression and the misery and hardship of the people, which is generally known. The absolute monarch was unable to remedy these wrongs ... The king's government rules dishonestly with deception. It has made the people believe it would promote their economic wellbeing. But the people have waited in vain."

In the seaside town of Hua Hin, south of the capital, King Prajadhipok received a gentler message. Written in the royal language of *rajasap*, the hand–delivered letter from the conspirators informed the king that he could remain on the throne under a constitution. The king returned to the capital and, within a few days, Siam had a preliminary constitution—one the king read and marked "draft" to allow for further changes. Among the common people, still in the grips of the global depression, there was little dissent against this dramatic change.

The system of constitutional monarchy that took shape over the ensuing years fell far short of giving birth to true democracy in Siam. King Prajadhipok became frustrated with the People's Party's hostility towards him and proposed policies. In 1935, while residing in England, he abdicated, stating, in part: "I feel that the government and its party employ methods of administration incompatible with individual freedoms and the principles of justice. I am willing to surrender the powers I formerly exercised to the people as a whole, but I am not willing to turn them over to any individual or any group to use in an autocratic manner without heeding the voice of the people." The nine-year-old Prince Ananda Mahidol, who was studying in Switzerland, acceded to the throne. The Siamese people still had a king—a republic was unthinkable—but the status of the monarchy had reached its nadir.

A New Kingship

For virtually 16 years, there was no resident king and the monarch's affairs were administered by a regency council. A new military elite governed the kingdom and thoroughly reshaped the state. A short visit by a teenage King Ananda in 1938 had been widely welcomed by the people, but the Second World War would soon stop everyone in their tracks.

On King Ananda's second visit just after the end of the Second World War, Thailand's infrastructure and economy were in shambles. But this was also an opportunity to look toward the future. In March 1946, speaking at Bangkok's Siam Society, Prince Dhani Nivat offered a fascinating account of Thai history and monarchy. In a paper entitled *The Old Siamese Conception of the Monarchy*, he discussed Sukhothai's paternalistic style of kingship and the 10 virtues of kingship. In the audience was 18-year-old Prince Bhumibol, whose reign was to begin three months later after the mysterious death of his older brother. Citing a passage from anthropologist Bronislaw Malinowski's *Science, Religion and Reality,* Prince Dhani remarked: "A society which makes its tradition sacred has gained by inestimable advantage of power and permanence. Such beliefs and practices therefore which put a halo of sanctity round tradition will have a 'survival value' for the type of civilisation in which they have been evolved … they were bought at an extravagant price and are to be maintained at any cost."

Under the guidance of those who knew this tradition intimately—Prince Rangsit, Prince Dhani and other elder figures of the court—King Bhumibol would lead the most remarkable revival of the crown. In King Bhumibol, this revival had a most brilliant exponent. Extremely disciplined, meticulous and imbued with a great sense of duty following the death of his brother, he assiduously fulfilled his obligations as monarch and maintained the visual language, customs and trappings of the crown, for which the Thais had an inherent and deeply ingrained understanding and respect.

Like his great–great–great grandfather Rama I, he recognised the importance of maintaining and restoring tradition. Potent ritual symbolism—such as an annual ploughing ceremony linking the monarch to the farmers—was resurrected during his reign. By applying the royal code of conduct emphasising the 10 virtues of kingship and conscientiously performing royal rituals, his public image was beyond tarnish.

King Bhumibol also energetically enacted the paternalistic and righteous Buddhist concept of kingship of the Sukhothai ideal. Travelling the country and meeting his subjects, listening to their problems and creating solutions, the king initiated projects on behalf of the most needy. Possessing a passion for science like his great grandfather King Mongkut, this modern-day Lord of the Land has spent many days and nights seeking answers to the nitty-gritty problems faced by the majority of his subjects: drought and deforestation, nutrition and disease, and later even traffic. His abiding passion became sustainable development. Personal visits to villages and farms across the country led directly to thousands of small-scale irrigation, soil and natural resource projects. Through his many, mostly Western hobbies—jazz, radio, sailing, photography and oil painting—he even fulfilled his kingly duty to delight and impress his subjects with his contemporary skills and talents.

Although the palace still maintained Hindu and Brahman rituals, mainly in the form of public ceremonies and iconography, such traditions were eclipsed by the personally inspired activities of King Bhumibol. The people once again came to revere their king as a modern-day *dhammaraja*, trusting him to preside over the security and welfare of the nation—and monarchy once again came to occupy the heart of Thai life. Daily television broadcasts followed the king's travels through the country and cinemas paid tribute to him before every film. Both the wealth of the crown and the country soared. With his reign proving so auspicious, the king could do no wrong in the eyes of an adoring public.

The reverence he earned and the influence he gained were all the more impressive given they were realised under the new, constitutional form of monarchy for which he has been the key shaper. In this role, the monarch functions as the head of state and armed forces. He exercises the power of royal assent, signing new legislation into law. He also holds various royal prerogatives such as naming his heir and members of his Privy Council, and granting pardons. Through private audiences with the prime minister and cabinet ministers, he has the royal prerogative to be consulted, to warn and to encourage. In addition, his public statements and addresses have undertones of warning and encouragement, but in general his powers are limited. Yet King Bhumibol, using tradition, discipline and ingenuity, has played a decisive role in the nation's modern development and history. At the peak of his reign, the longest in Siamese history, the unexpected monarch was seen by almost all his subjects as the "father" of the people, a Sukhothai-style *pho khun* of a country of over 60 million. Seven-hundred-fifty years later, the Siamese conception of kingship has endured.

Left King Bhumibol and Queen Sirikit at the Grand Palace in 1960.

Part I: The Life

The life story of King Bhumibol Adulyadej, which encompasses some of the greatest changes in Thailand's history, began almost obscurely in the United States in 1927—not long before the Great Depression fell upon a hapless world. The son of two remarkable, hard-working people, he was raised in Switzerland. In 1946, at the age of 18, his life took a dramatic turn. His beloved brother, King Ananda Mahidol, died unexpectedly, and the young prince acceded to the throne as the ninth king in the Royal House of Chakri. The long reign that followed straddles two centuries. King Bhumibol Adulyadej broke all records for longevity for monarchs in Siamese history, and has become the longest-serving head of state in the world today. In 2011, King Bhumibol completes his seventh 12-year cycle—a lifetime milestone to which Buddhists attach great significance. Here is the remarkable story of the king's seven cycles.

A LOVE STORY, NOT A FAIRY TALE

Baby Songkla's arrival betrayed nothing of what would transpire over the course of the ensuing 12-year cycles Buddhists use to mark their lifetime milestones.

The birth took place in Cambridge, just across the Charles River from the city of Boston, at 8.45 on the morning of Monday, 5 December 1927. As the United States slouched unknowingly towards the Great Depression, the news of the day was unremarkable. According to the *Boston Daily Globe*, singer Al Jolson had a bad throat; the Chicago Bears had defeated the Frankford Yellow Jackets, the 1926 National Football League champions; and astronomers at an observatory in faraway Melbourne, Australia, had sighted a new comet in the night sky.

The baby, weighing in at a respectable six pounds, was a brother to four-year-old sister Galyani Vadhana and two-year-old brother Ananda Mahidol. The infant was swaddled safely in the nursery at the Fiske Building of Cambridge Hospital, as Mount Auburn Hospital was then known. Built in 1912, the building's exceptionally large glass window panes imbued it with a modern look well ahead of its time. Outside in the medical school of Harvard University, one of the world's great seats of learning, students hurried to their lectures. After a common touch of neonatal jaundice, baby

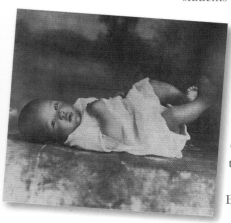

and mother spent three weeks at the hospital gaining strength before joining their family just after Christmas.

Home was a comfortable six-room apartment in Brookline rented by Mr and Mrs Songkla Mahidol, located on the first floor of 63 Longwood Avenue. This was a brooding three-storey tenement building with a half-submerged basement that lay within striking distance of the Harvard campus. Father was a courteous and unassuming Siamese medical student whom classmates addressed simply as Songkla. His young wife, Mom Sangwan, was taking courses in nursing and nutrition at nearby Simmons College.

Within hours, news of the birth was telegraphed across the world to balmy Bangkok where a grandmother rejoiced at the news of a third grandchild

Opposite *A studio photograph of Prince Bhumibol in the US, at the age of six months.*

Left *Prince Mahidol and Mom Sangwan in Bangkok in 1928, soon after concluding their studies in the US.*

and an uncle set about selecting a suitable name. Nine days later, the name reached Boston. "Baby Songkla", as the American birth certificate read, was to be called Bhumibala Aduladeja, a name spelling Westerners would struggle to reconcile with its pronunciation as "Poomipon Aduldet". It meant "Strength of the Land, Incomparable Power" and was portentous for good reason. The baby was a new Siamese prince of the third rank, and the uncle in Bangkok was King Prajadhipok, ruler of Siam.

The unassuming Mr Songkla Mahidol was in fact Prince Mahidol Aduldej, Prince of Songkla, a half-brother to the king, and the 69th of 77 children of King Chulalongkorn. The happy grandmother in Bangkok was King Chulalongkorn's second queen, Queen Savang Vadhana. What nobody would have imagined at the time was that this baby prince would through some extraordinary twists of fate one day become king as well.

At the time of her second son's birth, Mom Sangwan was still a commoner with no inkling of the sad times and triumphs that lay ahead—or that very early in their lives both her boys would accede to the throne. The honorific *mom* was a simple but respectful term of address for a commoner wife of a prince, but not a title. Her son, Baby Songkla, would become King Bhumibol Adulyadej, the ninth king in the Royal House of Chakri founded in Bangkok in 1782. King Bhumibol would accede to the throne in June 1946 after the tragic death by gunshot of his beloved older brother and closest companion, King Ananda Mahidol.

Since 1946, King Bhumibol's reign has notched up some singular firsts. He is the only monarch in the world to have been born in the US, one of the world's proudest republics. King Bhumibol has lived longer than any Chakri king, and the duration of his reign has greatly exceeded all others in Siamese history. Unlike virtually all of his predecessors, King Bhumibol has reigned not as an absolute monarch but as a constitutional monarch. With the death at age 83 in November 1989 of Franz Josef II, hereditary prince of Liechtenstein since 1938, King Bhumibol became the longest reigning monarch in the world. By the middle of 2011, King Bhumibol's reign had spanned 65 years, exceeding the reigns of Queen Victoria of Great Britain (63 years) in the 19th century and Emperor Hirohito of Japan (62 years) in the 20th century. King Bhumibol's reign straddles two centuries and represents one of the longest tenures by any head of state in recorded history. The Royal House of Chakri has stood through nine reigns and 229 years since 1782; nearly three out of every ten of these years have been with the ninth king of the Chakri dynasty, King Bhumibol, as monarch.

And this could all so easily have never happened.

The Unassuming Prince

King Bhumibol's parents were remarkable people who came from opposite walks of life in the highly stratified Siamese society of the early 20th century. Prince Mahidol was born on 1 January 1891, the seventh of eight children King Chulalongkorn had

with Queen Savang Vadhana. Their family was plagued by ill health in a time before proper healthcare systems had been developed. The children's health was not helped by the ancient Siamese tradition of marriage between royal relatives; female members of the royal family could not marry beneath their rank without forfeiting their titles. Royalty married royalty in Europe as well, but in Siam the pool was much smaller. Proscriptions against marrying foreigners were strong, and historic regional enmities fierce, so royal marriages across regional borders were rare.

Queen Savang Vadhana lived an exceptionally long life, dying in 1955 at the age of 93—fully 16 years after her last remaining child, Princess Valaya Alongkorn, had died. Apart from Prince Mahidol, three of her other five children died in their first year, and two others died at age 17. The oldest of these was King Chulalongkorn's heir apparent, Crown Prince Maha Vajirunhis, who died in 1895. Prince Mahidol suffered poor health throughout his life. Indeed, more than four years before the birth of Prince Bhumibol, he received a terrible prognosis. "Before returning to Siam in 1923, he had been told by a physician in [England] that he had not more than two years to live (a most unwise statement for a physician to make and for a patient a dark cloud under which to continue)," recalled Dr Aller G. Ellis, who established the pathology department at Siriraj Hospital in the 1920s. Undeterred, Prince Mahidol became father to two sons in the years left to him as he studied to be a physician at Harvard. Prince Mahidol's constitution was so delicate in 1928 that he underwent surgery for appendicitis under local anaesthetic because his doctors feared a general anaesthetic would kill him.

With his excellent grades but failing health, the university offered to award Prince Mahidol his degree in medicine as an aegrotat—a pass without classification given to students too unwell to sit for their final examinations. He nevertheless graduated in June 1928, *cum laude*, having insisted on taking the exams, but the strain left him ill for three weeks. At his lowest point, in April 1928, Prince Mahidol summoned an old friend, Francis Bowes Sayre, to his hospital bed to bear witness to his last wishes. Sayre was a Harvard-trained lawyer who had served in the early 1920s during the reign of King Vajiravudh as an adviser to the Siamese Ministry of Foreign Affairs. He was also a great admirer of the forward-looking prince.

"Fearing the illness might prove fatal, he asked me to come and take down a dying statement touching upon the possibility of one of his children coming to the throne of Siam," recalled Sayre in his 1957 memoirs. "In this he asked the king not to make either of [his sons] heir to the throne." When the time came to choose a successor after the abdication in 1935 of King Prajadhipok (who had been Siam's absolute monarch until the revolution of 1932), the eldest of Prince Mahidol's sons was indeed in line to the throne. Although King Chulalongkorn had fathered 77 children—32 sons and 45 daughters—by 36 different queens or consorts by the time he reached 40, the pool of princes eligible to succeed continued to drain during and after his reign, particularly in the 1920s. Neither King Vajiravudh nor his full brother and successor King Prajadhipok

Opposite *Prince Mahidol, King Bhumibol's father, in 1903 at the time of his tonsure ceremony when he became Prince of Songkla.*

Above *A postcard of a warship sent from England in 1906 by Prince Mahidol to his older half-brother Crown Prince Vajiravudh saying how much he misses him.*

had sons. The latter was childless and the former's only offspring was a daughter, Princess Bejraratana Rajasuda, born two days before his death in 1925.

Two of King Vajiravudh's full brothers, Prince Asdang Dejavudh and Prince Chudadhuj Dharadilok died in 1923 and 1925 respectively. Another son and favourite of King Chulalongkorn, Prince Chakrabongse, died in 1920 not long after divorcing his wife, Katya (Ekaterina Ivanovna Desnitsky), who was Russian. Their son, Prince Chula Chakrabongse, who later chronicled the dynasty, was excluded from the succession because his mother was a foreigner. The fact that Mom Sangwan was still a commoner in 1935 was not, however, considered an impediment to the accession of her elder son, Prince Ananda.

King Chulalongkorn sent his sons abroad for their education, mainly to England, with clear instructions that the more junior members of the family were not to present themselves as princes in English society. King Vajiravudh was a Cambridge graduate, and King Prajadhipok received his military training at the Royal Military Academy at Woolwich. England was planned for Prince Mahidol as well. After his topknot was cut in 1903 in a traditional rite of passage, Prince Mahidol was given the title Prince of Songkla. The following year, he spent four months at Wat Bovornives where his grandfather, Prince Mongkut, had been cloistered as a monk for 27 years before acceding to the throne of Siam over half a century earlier. In 1905, at the age of 13, Prince Mahidol was sent to England with Princes Asdang and Chudhadhuj, the two half-brothers who would predecease him in the 1920s.

Before entering Harrow School for a year in May 1906, the three young princes spent time in Westbury in the English Cotswolds learning the language and acclimatising. The prince's artistic inclinations were reported back to Bangkok: "With Prince Mahidol, the talent amounts, I really believe to genius," observed his tutor. "So much so that it is more than probable that he may one day become a brilliant artist."

According to Princess Galyani, who compiled biographies of both her parents, Prince Mahidol's interest in art only lasted until 1914. The paintings which survive, some signed simply with the nickname Daeng (Red), are the work of an accomplished water colourist with a keen eye for detail and proportion in his freehand drawing.

Prince Mahidol sent artworks from his travels in Europe home to his father. The last time the two were to meet was in Berlin in 1907, during King Chulalongkorn's second European tour—the king's final excursion abroad before his death in October 1910. Instead of returning to England, Prince Mahidol was placed under the supervision of a German officer, Captain Eck, by Kaiser Wilhelm II, the last German emperor. The teenaged Siamese prince attended the Prussian Military Preparatory School at Potsdam to train for an army career. During this period, German doctors applied therapies to his spine that today sound pointless and gruesome. He was also schooled in the arts and humanities, and this was to leave a much more positive and lasting impression.

According to Princess Galyani, "At that time, he had written to his father that if he were not in military studies, he would have preferred to study medicine." When he

Opposite *King Chulalongkorn makes his farewells on board Maha Chakri in 1905 as it was about to sail for Singapore with three of his sons on board. The young princes were bound for school in England. Prince Mahidol is kneeling on the left with Prince Asdang on his father's other side and Prince Chudhadhuj standing behind. The two half-brothers predeceased Prince Mahidol in the 1920s, bringing his young family closer to succession to the throne of Siam.*

Above *Queen Savang Vadhana, left, in mourning dress at Srapatum Palace in 1910, the year of King Chulalongkorn's death, with the only two of their eight children to reach adulthood, Prince Mahidol and Princess Valaya Alongkorn.*

finally returned to Bangkok after his father's death, Prince Mahidol let it be known that he would also not have minded pursuing a life in the arts.

He had spent the summer of 1908 cruising the frigid waters to Iceland and Norway, and this may have sparked his interest in matters nautical. For the time being, however, Prince Mahidol's career path was to remain within the army. That same year, he progressed to the Imperial Military Academy at Gross Lichterfelde, Berlin, passing out aged 20 in 1912. Only then—and with the personal permission of Kaiser Wilhelm II—was Prince Mahidol allowed to transfer to the Imperial German Navy as part of "Crew 1912", that year's cadet intake. From May 1912 to March 1913, he was one of 52 cadets aboard SMS *Victoria Luise* in the Baltic Sea and North Sea and cruised to the Azores, Canada, the US, Central America, the Canary Islands and Spain. He earned his sea legs but found that hammocks were "no fun at all". The ship had been modernised in 1905 and was one of five cruisers from the late 19th century used mainly for training. At the voyage's end, the ship's lifeboats were lowered and rigged for sailing races.

"Prince Mahidol's writings give the impression that he enjoyed sailing very much," wrote Princess Galyani of a sport that would later become a passion in the Mahidol family. After his time at sea, Prince Mahidol attended the Imperial German Naval Academy at Flensburg-Mürwik. In 1914, with the outbreak of the First World War, Prince Mahidol returned to Siam to serve in the Royal Thai Navy as a second lieutenant. He lectured at the Royal Naval Academy and worked on a detailed submarine project.

He also visited Siriraj Hospital where he saw nothing but misery and suffering. Feeling unfulfilled in naval life, he sought the permission of his half-brother, King

Vajiravudh, to study medicine abroad. This time it was granted, and in 1916 he moved to the US to study public health at both Harvard University and the Massachusetts Institute of Technology (MIT). *The New York Times* immediately took an interest in this altruistic humanitarian of a prince from the East.

"The prince has a vision of a New Siam, when the public health will be the serious concern of the government, the care of the body taught in the schools, sanitary living made compulsory, and the state will control marriages to make impossible the union of those not physically fit," the newspaper reported.

"I am not likely to reach the throne, but that does not worry me," Prince Mahidol told the newspaper. "My ambition is to lead a life of usefulness. I could live comfortably and [be] honoured as His Majesty's brother, but I think it is very silly that I should be honoured simply because I happen to be whom I am. If I am to be honoured, I wish it to be because I have earned my honours."

Prince Mahidol went on to describe the situation at home: "In recent years, the plague has been brought into Siam by Chinese, while cholera, beri beri, and other tropical and communicable diseases are altogether too common. The infant mortality is distressingly great. I hope to fit myself to cope with these problems or, at least, to lay the foundation for the work. Perhaps in fifty years there will be a healthy Siam."

Although only 24, Prince Mahidol had little expectation of seeing that day himself. While in the German navy, a streptococcal infection had weakened his kidneys—but not his resolve to accomplish as much as possible in whatever time he had left to him. Dr G. Stewart Whittemore, the physician who was to deliver Prince Bhumibol 11 years later, first treated Prince Mahidol in October 1916.

"He was one of those characters one never forgets, so modest and unassuming," Dr Whittemore later recalled. "Tall, husky, studious, smart, very nice fellow," recalled a classmate, Roy James Campbell, who always regretted not taking up the prince's invitation to visit Siam. Like many, Campbell was unaware of Prince Mahidol's rank until it was time for the prince to return east.

The Orphan

The life of Sangwan, the mother of two kings, could not have been more different. Born on 21 October 1900 in Nonthaburi, north of Bangkok, Sangwan was the daughter of a goldsmith named Chu and his wife, Kham. Sangwan was the third of the couple's four children. In later life, she had barely any recollection of her father or two older siblings, a brother and a sister. Sangwan's younger brother, Thomya, died in his twenties. In the early 20th century, common people in Siam were beginning to acquire surnames, and a surname requirement was eventually made law in 1913. Thomya registered the name Chukramon when he came of age. "Although mother never actually used the family name Chukramon, she should be considered as having been born a member of

Opposite A watercolour painted by Prince Mahidol of a warship after he became a cadet officer in the Germany navy in 1912.

Below Prince Mahidol, seated, in 1908 with one of his half-brothers, the future king Prince Prajadhipok.

this family," noted Princess Galyani in 1980. However, when Sangwan travelled to the US for the first time in 1917, the surname on her passport, Talapat, had been borrowed from a courtier for the purpose.

Princess Galyani's spelling of the name in English was Talabadh. She believed that the families of Sangwan's parents were not on particularly close or cordial terms. Visits between the two were rare and the strained affairs bored the young girl. "Some of her relatives claimed that the family came from Vientiane," wrote Princess Galyani. "Mother said that this was plausible, because the family liked to eat glutinous rice." Sangwan did not know her maternal grandfather's name, however. Her grandmother was Pha, and Sangwan's mother, Kham, was the fifth of Pha's six children.

Kham's great gift to her daughter was teaching her to read and write. For Sangwan, literacy would be the key to an unimaginable world far removed from the humble wooden home in Thon Buri, across the river from Bangkok, where her artisan father had moved his family. Chu used a household stove for his furnace. The family bathed from jars on the veranda of their small home, sanitation was basic, but there was food enough and books to borrow from a kindly old neighbour.

Sangwan and her best friend Phuen frolicked in the canals and dared each other to enter the haunted lots around the nearby temples. It was not a carefree childhood, however, and both her parents had died before she was nine. Sangwan then became the responsibility of her mother's sister, Aunt Suay, who made ends meet rolling cigarettes and occasionally selling sweetmeats.

Life took a dramatic change in 1909, the year before King Chulalongkorn died. Through Aunt Rod, a distant relative on her father's side, Sangwan was accepted into the household of Princess Valaya Alongkorn, the older sister of her future husband, at the Four Seasons Garden Villa in the Dusit Palace. "Not being a nobleman's daughter, mother could only become a second-grade retainer," noted Princess Galyani. The little girl ran home to Aunt Suay for a few days on at least one occasion, but was fetched back. She was cared for and enrolled at Satri Witthaya School.

After accidentally stabbing her hand with a sewing needle, Sangwan was taken to the home of Phraya Damrong Baedayagun (Huad Viravaidya), and his wife, Khunying Sa-nguan. The kindly couple had two daughters younger than Sangwan at the same school, and took to the bright little orphan who had so feared medical treatment. Sangwan was invited to stay. She turned out to be a not particularly diligent student, and even played truant some afternoons. After failing to pass into secondary school, she had to repeat her third year in primary school. Sensing she might do better with a more vocational education, Phraya Damrong suggested Sangwan consider nursing. She enrolled at Siriraj Hospital's School of Midwifery and Nursing at the age of 13, boarding there with a stipend of 15 baht a month. Occasional holidays were spent at Phraya Damrong's home prior to her graduation in 1916.

Sangwan was one of two students selected by Prince Rangsit of Jainad, a son of King Chulalongkorn and the director-general of public health at the Ministry of the Interior, to travel to the US. The two young women would pursue their studies there on scholarships provided by Queen Savang Vadhana. The destination of choice at this time would normally have been England, but the First World War was in full flight and tearing Europe apart. The other student nurse was Ubol Palakawongse na Ayudhya. The pair left in August 1917, the only young women in a group of 22 students. The sea journey via Singapore, Hong Kong, Japan and Hawaii to San Francisco took six weeks, and after their arrival the two were lodged in Berkeley, California, with the family of a doctor. They had small wardrobes dominated by sailor dresses, and always wore hats, but gone were the traditional *choongkraben* (silken pantaloons knotted at the waist) worn at home. Sangwan's first significant purchase was a box camera—the start of a hobby she would pass on to her children.

After a year, the girls travelled to the East Coast, arriving at Boston railroad station on the night of 21 September 1918. As was his custom, Prince Mahidol was standing on the platform waiting to greet arriving students. By all accounts, he was immediately smitten by the pretty 18-year-old who alighted before him. The two girls travelled to Hartford, Connecticut, where they lodged in the home of an elderly couple and enrolled at North Western School. Prince Mahidol became a regular visitor, taking the pair out on excursions with other Siamese students. It was during the time at Hartford that love blossomed and Prince Mahidol and Sangwan became unofficially engaged. By following his heart, Prince Mahidol had shattered yet another royal convention. Though already a qualified nurse, photographs from the time depict Sangwan's transformation from an apparent schoolgirl in billowy sailor suits to a young woman dressed and coiffed fashionably, and modestly aware of her charms.

Opposite Sangwan, fourth from left, with classmates in the US.

Below Sangwan, right, the student nurse at Siriraj Hospital with a friend.

Even after Sangwan had captured his heart, Prince Mahidol continued to take a paternalistic interest in all the Siamese students studying in the US. On his visits to Bangkok, he would give audiences to the parents of Siamese students in the US, some of whom were sponsored through donations from the Siam Society, which had been founded in 1904 to promote knowledge of Thailand and regional cultural awareness. The prince had close links to the Siamese Office of Educational Affairs, which from 1917 to 1927 was housed at 44 Langdon Street, Cambridge. From 1921, this building also housed the pioneering Siamese Alliance, which Prince Mahidol established as an umbrella organisation for Siamese students in the US. Thirty-five of them gathered at the Gradford Club for its inauguration on 23 July that year.

Prince Mahidol funded scholarships and regularly dipped into his own pocket, even taking out temporary loans on occasions. He personally always lived within his means. One student staying with him on his way to college left his shoes out for the staff to polish. Since the prince kept no servants, preferring to save the money for his philanthropy, the house guest was stunned to realise that his newly shined footwear had received some truly royal attention overnight.

Sangwan moved to Boston and lodged with the Kents, a university lecturer's family who took her on scenic outings. She moved again in 1919 and lodged with the Williston sisters, Emily and Constance, until her departure the following year for Siam and married life. She attended church and Sunday school, and studied algebra, Latin, French and English. Prince Mahidol also arranged visits to museums and art galleries.

The prince returned to Bangkok in October 1919 for the cremation of his aunt, Queen Saovabha Phongsri, the first queen of King Chulalongkorn. Sangwan followed in April 1920, travelling via Hawaii and Shanghai, reaching home for the first time in four years in July. In the meantime, Prince Mahidol busied himself with laboratory work at Siriraj Hospital, experimenting on amoebas and malarial protozoans. He also donated money for wards and medical facilities, and for medical scholarships.

Prince Mahidol was an unconventional and considerate man. He was determined to chart his own course, but he was not an overt rebel—though he could be impatient at times. As a youngster, he followed the normal course and sought his father's approval in all matters, and later the permissions of Kaiser Wilhelm and King Vajiravudh when necessary. His half-brother King Vajiravudh was initially sceptical about his wish to flout convention by marrying a commoner, but eventually relented.

Having fallen in love, Prince Mahidol sent his mother a letter to explain the situation and gain her blessing. "Sangwan is an orphan," he wrote. "Upon our marriage she will use my family name. In looking for a wife, my criteria by no means involved the family origin. I never thought she would have to be of royal or noble birth. No one can choose his birth. I have chosen a good person."

Queen Savang Vadhana was content to let her sole remaining son follow his heart. The happy couple were duly married with King Vajiravudh presiding on 10 September 1920 at Srapatum Palace. His bride became Mom Sangwan. Nearly 30 years later

Opposite top Sangwan, left, in Hartford, Connecticut, with Prince Mahidol and her friend Ubol Palakawongse na Ayudhya.

Opposite below Prince Mahidol was a frequent visitor to the home of Mrs Strong where the two young nurses from Siam lodged, and in 1918 he became unofficially engaged to Sangwan.

Above Sangwan in her late teens in the US.

in the same palace, Queen Savang Vadhana would preside over the marriage of her only remaining grandson, King Bhumibol, to his young bride, 17-year-old Mom Rajawongse Sirikit Kitiyakara.

Happy Newlyweds

Before leaving Bangkok, Prince Mahidol bought the land in Thon Buri on which had stood the Chukramon family's rented home, and had it rebuilt. Aunt Suay was able to live there until her death in 1930. Later, Prince Mahidol would pay for Mom Sangwan's younger brother, Thomya Chukramon, to study in Lausanne, Switzerland, where he died from meningitis in 1925. After marrying, the newlyweds returned to the US. The journey back to Boston was both leisurely and westward on this occasion, by ship from Malaya's Penang to Genoa in Italy. The couple then travelled by train to Lausanne, where as a special treat Prince Mahidol selected a luxurious hotel, the Beau-Rivage Palace. Lausanne is capital of the canton of Vaud in Romandy, Switzerland's French-speaking region, and overlooks Lac Léman (Lake Geneva).

Finally returning to Boston from Europe, Mr and Mrs Mahidol Songkla set up their first marital home at 329 Longwood Avenue in Prince Mahidol's old apartment. The

prince resumed his studies in public health, and Mom Sangwan enrolled in a pre-nursing course at nearby Simmons College. Prince Mahidol received his certificate in public health in June 1921, and the couple left Boston in September, travelling home once more through Europe, with visits to London, Paris and Berne. The journey included vital meetings with the president and directors of the international health board of the Rockefeller Foundation concerning the development of medical education in Siam. They also met with Siamese students studying in the cities they visited.

The couple returned to Europe in 1922. They were accompanying the prince's sister and sole surviving sibling, Princess Valaya Alongkorn, to England for kidney surgery. As the princess convalesced, Prince Mahidol fell sick in Paris. Sufficiently recovered, and leaving Mom Sangwan in London, he went north to Edinburgh University for further medical studies, but could not cope with the extreme cold. The couple's first child, Princess Galyani Vadhana, was born in London in May 1923.

"He also realised that he had little time left," wrote Princess Galyani of her father's faltering health at the time of her birth. Doctors offered little hope, and the family went to Southbourne and Bournemouth for seaside convalescence, then to France and back to Bangkok in late 1923. Despite his frailty, Prince Mahidol threw himself into an exhausting round of work that might have challenged a man in normal health. He took charge of university affairs at the Ministry of Education, working to modernise the teaching of science in particular. He chaired the faculty board at Siriraj College of Medicine and Nursing, served on the council of the Thai Red Cross, and also chaired the organising committee for Vajira Hospital. Even with all this, Prince Mahidol somehow made time to lecture in arts and science at Chulalongkorn University, and to continue as the main point of contact in Siam for the Rockefeller Foundation.

The effort was unsustainable. In 1925 doctors advised Prince Mahidol to rest and then to quit the tropics altogether for Europe or the US. Bangkok before air-conditioning, when Francis Bowes Sayre noted that people either steamed or baked according to the time of year, had utterly exhausted him. Although he had earned his certificate in public health in 1921, he was still determined to try again what he had been unable to do in Edinburgh—qualify as a physician—by returning to his *alma mater*, Harvard. In July, he left for Heidelberg for treatment of his renal problems. It was there on 20 September that Prince Ananda Mahidol was born.

In November 1925, King Vajiravudh died. Prince Mahidol returned home for the cremation and the coronation of King Prajadhipok—King Vajiravudh's last remaining full brother who was a year younger than Prince Mahidol. Mom Sangwan remained in Europe with the two children, and on the advice of their friend Sayre enrolled Princess Galyani at L'Ecole de Champ Soleil, a nursery school in Lausanne. Prince Mahidol finally rejoined the family in the summer of 1926, and they returned to the US. Baby Songkla would make his arrival to complete the peripatetic Mahidol family at the end of the following year.

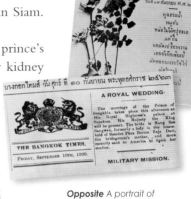

Opposite *A portrait of Prince Mahidol and his new bride, Mom Sangwan, taken in Bangkok by King Vajiravudh personally at the 1920 Winter Fair.*

Above *The menu for the wedding banquet for Prince Mahidol and Mom Sangwan held at Srapatum Palace, and the wedding notice placed in the Bangkok Times of 10 September 1920.*

CROSSING WORLDS

Prince Mahidol and his family left Boston for the last time in July 1928, returning through London and Lausanne where the two older children were briefly enrolled at Champ Soleil School once more. After recuperating in Europe, the family finally reached Bangkok at the end of the year, moving into Srapatum Palace with Queen Savang Vadhana and her large household. The residence in the palace compound had been built during Prince Mahidol's studies abroad, and it was always his wish that it should feel like "a real home, not a palace".

Nobody imagined that the small returning entourage included two future kings. Their new world was far removed from the intimate apartment in Brookline, where Prince Mahidol thought nothing of helping with the washing-up after dinner. It was a particularly frustrating time for the prince. In late February, he confided in a letter to his old friend Francis Bowes Sayre: "I am still jobless. The idea of my entering into hospital service did not appeal to anybody. They are bent on starting me into the already overcrowded career of general administration. I am of course quite prepared for this kind of disappointment."

Fully qualified as a doctor after 12 years of studies in public health and medicine with countless journeys across the globe, Prince Mahidol found himself snared by rigid protocols that included proscriptions against physical contact between royalty and commoners. Much of the elaborate ancient protocol was relaxed during the 19th century by the Chakri kings, as were punishments for infringements. King Mongkut allowed standing during his audiences. King Chulalongkorn formally abolished the eyes-averted rule and discontinued prostration. A particularly bitter personal experience informed his views on some protocols. In 1880, he tragically lost Queen Sunanda Kumariratana, the older sister of Queen Savang Vadhana and Queen Saovabha Phongsri—and aunt to Prince Mahidol. The queen and her party were travelling to the summer palace at Bang Pa-in when their vessel sank in the Chao Phraya river. Since the pages, boatmen and onlookers were forbidden to touch royalty, the young queen, who was with child at the time, drowned along with her daughter, Princess Karnabhorn Bejraratana, who was almost two.

Discouraged from practising as a physician in Bangkok, Prince Mahidol left for the northern city of Chiang Mai in late April and went to work at the McCormick Hospital, which since 1908 had been run by an American Presbyterian missionary, Dr Edwin C. Cort. The two men were kindred spirits who had met before. Cort founded the McCormick School of Nursing in 1923, and the following year it had been formally dedicated by Prince Mahidol. The prince held the work of American missionaries in unqualified esteem.

"They have done wonderful things for us," he told *The New York Times* after his arrival in the US in 1916. "They come not to make money, but to spend it. They do not quarrel over the manner in which the sacrament shall be administered. They teach, they administer to the sick, they build hospitals and schools … The work of the missionaries from America is constructive. They submit cheerfully to our laws. They do not interfere in our politics. They teach the young to be clean, honest and patriotic—not to the United States, but patriotic to Siam. We owe a great debt to the American missionaries. Their deeds are the kind that will live after them, a constant inspiration for good."

Prince Mahidol planned to stay with Cort until he could find somewhere suitable in Chiang Mai for the family. It was not to be. Within less than a month, he was taken

Opposite *Prince Bhumibol's birth certificate from the Commonwealth of Massachusetts initially recorded "Baby Songkla", which was later amended to "Bhumibal Aduldej Songkla". In Bangkok, King Prajadhipok named the baby prince. The king wrote on his personal stationery "Bhumibala Aduladeja", noting the pronunciation "Poomipon". The correct official spelling in English, Bhumibol Adulyadej, was announced in the Royal Gazette after the king's accession.*

Left *Prince Mahidol in 1928 with his third child, Prince Bhumibol.*

ill after returning briefly to Bangkok for a cremation. An English surgeon at Siriraj Hospital examined him and diagnosed an amoebic liver abscess. Dr William Perkins, an American, treated him over the next three months but it was futile. The standard treatments of the day wreaked havoc on Prince Mahidol's constitution.

Back at Srapatum Palace, Mom Sangwan nursed her husband until his death on 24 September 1929 from kidney failure. Princess Galyani was six, and remembered arriving home from school that day to be told the dreadful news by her mother who was weeping in her chambers. Of the two brothers, the baby Prince Bhumibol was not even two, and far too young to ever have any recollection of his father. Much of what King Bhumibol would learn of his father was through his stoic, devoted mother—the person who exerted the most important direct influence on his life. The stories and lessons Mom Sangwan passed on from her husband and mentor shaped vital aspects of Prince Bhumibol's thinking and actions as an adult and as king.

Prince Mahidol's early passing caused widespread grief. "I have been so very much impressed by the whole character of Songkla and all the fine feeling he left behind him here as well as wherever he went," wrote Dr David L. Edsall, the dean of Harvard Medical School. "His extraordinary combination of gentleness, sweetness, intelligence and democracy in a person who came from such high position is one of the most striking things I have ever seen."

Moving On

The remarkable love story of Prince Mahidol and Mom Sangwan had turned out to be no fairy tale. After losing virtually every member of her own family, she had also lost the husband who mentored her and gave so much. Her outwardly privileged new life was tinged with sorrow. Not yet 29, she was a widow with three young children to bring up alone in an environment that was becoming increasingly unstable politically. The days of absolute monarchy in Siam were moving to a close, and the consequences would affect Prince Mahidol's family dramatically.

Mom Sangwan persevered. She spent the next four years in Bangkok living with her mother-in-law and devoting herself to bringing up her children. She prized her time abroad for the lessons she had learned in freedom, health, nutrition and hygiene. Her exposure to Christianity had reignited her interest in Buddhism and her children were made to say bedtime prayers. She organised weekly parties at the palace, and ensured a wide variety of children were invited, including foreigners. She enrolled the children at Mater Dei School and saw to it that they followed as normal a routine as possible. Prince Ananda was an enthusiastic, bright pupil but always delicate. He arrived after the other children in his class and ate specially prepared meals. "The elder of the two brothers had never been healthy," Princess Galyani later wrote. For his final year in Bangkok, Prince Ananda moved to Debsirin School, which dated from the reign of his grandfather King Chulalongkorn. At Mater Dei, Prince Bhumibol was taught by a young Catholic nun of the Ursuline order, Sister Marie Xavier, who had been baptised Ana Pirc in her native Slovenia.

"I will never forget the exceptionally high-minded and intelligent boy prince who came to the school to start his elementary education with the other little Thais," she told a journalist from Yugoslavia not long before her death in 1987. "Even during his first days at the school, I noticed [Prince Bhumibol] had an exceptional gift for music, but he mastered other subjects with equal ease, showing a keen interest and understanding for everything around him."

Prince Bhumibol's musical awakening occurred at this time as he listened to 78 rpm records played on the family's wind-up Victrola gramophone. Much of the collection left by Prince Mahidol was Western classical music, but it also included some American jazz. Many years later, King Bhumibol told Dr Simon Wallace of the Melbourne Jazz Ensemble that the first song he could remember enjoying was a 1928 version of "Old Man River" played by Paul Whiteman and his orchestra. The accompanying vocalist was the great African-American Paul Robeson. The piece included a short trumpet solo by Bix Beiderbecke that captured the little prince's imagination.

Mom Sangwan occupied herself with various American correspondence courses, played badminton and formed a sewing circle. On one occasion, she took her lively brood for an audience with King Prajadhipok, the uncle who had named Prince Bhumibol in 1927. Everyone got more than they bargained for.

Opposite *The three children of Prince Mahidol and Mom Sangwan, from left, Princess Galyani Vadhana, Prince Ananda Mahidol and Prince Bhumibol Adulyadej.*

Below *The three children in a competition to see who can pull the ugliest face.*

Bottom *The Mahidol siblings in classical dance attire.*

"We were young royals who were rather unruly (we were then created *phra ong chao*, Their Highnesses), so they called us 'the countryside royals'," recalled Princess Galyani. In the close family circle only, Prince Bhumibol was called Phra Ong Lek. "Normally a person who had been given a name by the king would also be given a pendant bearing the king's monogram. Thus His Majesty gave our little brother his pendant. When the elder one saw the pendant, he promptly remarked 'Pretty! Got any more?' His Majesty did not get angry at all and had two more pendants brought out for us. We all ended up being given one pendant each by His Majesty."

In difficult economic times, with world rice prices depressed and debts inherited from the previous reign, King Prajadhipok was not faring well with the kingdom's restive would-be politicians, some of whom had returned from Europe bent on introducing representative democracy. They included Pibul Songgram and Pridi Banomyong, two of the students Prince Mahidol used to meet with when he passed through Paris. The rivalry between Pibul and Pridi—two clever and ambitious men educated abroad—would play out centre stage in Thai politics over the coming decades.

At the time, King Prajadhipok was staying in Hua Hin at Klai Kangwol Palace. The name of the king's seaside residence, which was completed in 1929, translates as "Far from Worries". On 24 June 1932, the king was playing at the Royal Golf Course when probably his worst worry was confirmed. News arrived that a revolution led by the so-called Promoters, who included Pibul and Pridi, had brought a swift and bloodless end to absolute monarchy by taking control of the capital. The physically diminutive king picked up his golf ball and walked off the course into a new world.

The Promoters behind the coup became the People's Party, or Ratsadon Party. They included former students in Europe, civil servants and military officers. Their initial goals were to do away with the system of absolute monarchy, put in place Siam's first constitution, and hold elections to the National Assembly—a parliament modelled on Great Britain's. The first charter confirmed King Prajadhipok's reduced role as a constitutional monarch within a fledgling democratic system. Under absolute monarchy, draft legislation was drawn up by various individuals and councils, signed into law by the king, and promulgated by announcement in the *Royal Gazette*. Henceforth, the king's role in public life would be constitutionally circumscribed and require approval from the non-royal representatives of the populace.

Any sympathies King Prajadhipok harboured for a more modern system of government were tested in a climate of mutual mistrust. A failed counter-revolution the following year resulted in some actual bloodshed, further weakened the position of royalists, and confirmed the political ascendancy of Pibul. The revolt was led by a cousin of the king, Prince Boworadet, the pre-1932 minister of war. King Prajadhipok initially withdrew to the far southern province of Songkhla. After the arrest of all his remaining brothers except Prince Rangsit, he returned to Bangkok on the royal train. Critics felt King Prajadhipok had been

too slow to condemn the coup attempt—or had even tacitly supported it. With the situation looking dismal, the king left for medical treatment in England that had been previously scheduled. He was accompanied by Queen Rambhai Barni and a nephew, Prince Jirasakdi, who the childless royal couple raised as their own son. The queen was King Prajadhipok's only wife. Although he could have had more, he was by choice the first monogamous Chakri king.

Queen Savang Vadhana was deeply attached to her late son's young family and played a major role in its daily life. She was, however, becoming increasingly concerned for the future of her grandsons should anything befall King Prajadhipok and prompt the succession question. For Mom Sangwan, the deteriorating political situation, stifling protocols which gave her headaches and the frail health of Prince Ananda all made a move abroad for the family seem wise. Prince Rangsit, the half-brother to Prince Mahidol who had picked young Sangwan for her nursing scholarship in 1916, agreed but did not regard the US, a republic, as a suitable place for raising royalty.

Mom Sangwan's memories of England were meanwhile marred by its dismal damp and cold, and the terrible time she had had there in 1923 when Prince Mahidol had been unwell. With the two most obvious choices gone, Switzerland presented an attractive alternative. Lausanne held some of the happiest memories of her married life, and the sparkling air and robust nutrition could do the children only good. Preparations for the family's departure included the engagement of a Monsieur Schweisguth to teach 10-year-old Princess Galyani some French. She proved to be a challenging pupil. "The teacher was very kind but I did not learn much. Instead of studying, I would use water colours to paint the teacher's face like a Red Indian," Princess Galyani later confessed. The long-suffering Monsieur Schweisguth probably did not discern in Princess Galyani a future professor of French at Thammasat University or the founding president of the Thai Association of Teachers of French.

Swiss Refuge

The choice of Lausanne proved exceptionally provident. It was 60 km from Geneva where the League of Nations, the precursor to the United Nations, had kept its General Assembly since 1920. In the turmoil of the coming Second World War (1939–45), there was no better refuge in all Europe than defiantly neutral and peaceful Switzerland. In April 1932, just two months before the end of absolute monarchy in Siam, Mom Sangwan and her three children departed for Europe.

In Lausanne, Mom Sangwan employed Ida, a young Swiss maid who could still be found working half days for her in 1980 aged over 70. The children were initially put back into Champ Soleil School. Prince Bhumibol then spent two years at the Miremont Elementary School in Lausanne before being enrolled, initially as a day pupil and eventually as a weekly boarder, at L'Ecole Nouvelle de la Suisse Romande at Chailly, a nearby suburb. King Ananda was already attending the school and would graduate from it in 1943. Prince Bhumibol learned French, which has always been his preferred European language, and German; English came later. His Thai was kept up

by tutors at home. As an eight-year-old, he was allowed to cycle to school and to music lessons after classes.

Prince Bhumibol's exposure to music was of course far different to anything he would have experienced in Siam. Princess Galyani recalled the three siblings falling ill with chickenpox and being confined to their beds at home. They amused themselves by singing Christmas carols learned at school. Neither she nor Prince Ananda could sing very well, she recalled, but Prince Bhumibol had "a very sweet voice".

When Princess Galyani expressed an interest in studying the piano with a teacher from Miremont School, Prince Ananda soon followed suit. Mom Sangwan rented a piano from Foetisch Frères, a local music shop. A German upright model made by Carl Hardt of Stuttgart, the piano became the musical focus of the household for all the remaining years in Switzerland. There are photographs of young King Bhumibol composing on it with a family cat looking on.

Mom Sangwan was always attentive to her children's proper nutrition and exercise. In the summer of 1934, the family went walking around the passes at Grimsel and Furka, and the source of the Rhône river, revisiting some of the places Mom Sangwan had been to a decade earlier with Prince Mahidol. In winter, the children were taken skiing on the nursery slopes at Arosa.

"She was a great teacher," King Bhumibol later recalled. "She instilled this idea of service. For instance, when we received something—money—we had to put a percentage in the box for the poor. If we did something wrong … we paid the fine not to mother but to the box for the poor people." On one occasion, Mom Sangwan discovered that Prince Bhumibol had borrowed money from a servant to buy a toy. She immediately made him return it to the shop for a refund and then repay his debt.

Apart from taxing her children 10 percent on their pocket money for good causes, Mom Sangwan inspired their interest in photography, particularly Prince Bhumibol's. His first camera, the start of a lifelong passion, was a two-franc Coronet Midget. His first film cost 25 centimes. From the six negatives, only one produced an image— and someone else took that picture. Prince Bhumibol first painted at the age of 10, which was a little younger than when his father had begun. Princess Galyani recalled their childhood years in Switzerland as warm and intimate, with conversation flowing freely. "We had a comfortable life but with discipline," she later wrote. "And I mean discipline with principles, not old-fashioned regimentation."

In 1935, however, the circumstances of that comfortable, sheltered existence changed with the abdication of King Prajadhipok on 2 March. The former king made no suggestion from his residence in England as to a possible successor. In Bangkok, a senior courtier, Chao Phraya Woraphongphiphat, had drawn up a list of candidates for Prince Narisara Nuvadtivongs, a younger half brother of King Chulalongkorn who was serving as regent during King Prajadhipok's absence.

After nearly a week of evaluating possible successors to the throne from the greatly

Opposite *Prince Bhumibol, left, King Ananda and a friend with a sun hat in the summer of 1938 at Institut Zimmerli, Adelboden.*

Above *A postcard from Prince Bhumibol in Switzerland to his grandmother, Queen Savang Vadhana saying he misses her.*

diminished pool of potential heirs left by King Chulalongkorn, the senior princes of the day settled upon nine-year-old Prince Ananda, the first son of King Prajadhipok's slightly older half-brother, Prince Mahidol. The kind of scenario Prince Mahidol had feared for his sons in 1928, when he made his sickbed deposition to Francis Bowes Sayre, had arrived. Three senior emissaries were dispatched to Lausanne to meet with Mom Sangwan and Prince Ananda. King Prajadhipok's abdication could have meant the end of the Royal House of Chakri, which had passed its 150th anniversary so inauspiciously three years earlier in 1932. An old prophesy that it would fall at that time had been only narrowly disproven. Whatever pressures came to bear upon Mom Sangwan, and whatever reservations she might have harboured privately, she consented to her oldest son becoming king of Siam.

Mom Sangwan did not, however, consent to young King Ananda being taken out of school, as the emissaries had suggested. "I promptly said that I thought otherwise," Mom Sangwan recalled in a letter to her mother-in-law, Queen Savang Vadhana. "In private tuition at home without friends and peer competition, the king would suffer from a lack of enthusiasm and feel isolated. Having to shoulder the mantle of kingship, the king would be unhappy if deprived of his childhood … It is quite necessary for a king to mix and mingle with ordinary people to learn about their habits. By doing so, it would benefit the country which is under a democratic system."

The queen had every faith in her daughter-in-law's judgment and instincts. "It's my good karma to have you as a daughter-in-law," she once wrote. "It's my grandchildren's good karma to have you as their mother for you are such an excellent mother."

After the unexpected accession of King Ananda Mahidol, the postponement of any immediate return to Siam suited all parties, including the ambitious Pibul, who would rise to become the country's third prime minister by 1938. For the time being, King Ananda would continue life as a Swiss schoolboy, postponing indefinitely his actual coronation. A council of three regents would administer his duties in his absence. Since arriving in Lausanne in 1933, the family had lived in an apartment at 16 Avenue Tissot. Following King Ananda's accession, they moved to Pully and into a substantial house later described by a correspondent for *The New York Times* as "a modest, almost obscure villa in an unfashionable suburb of Lausanne". As the home of a king, it was nevertheless *de facto* a palace—although this would not have been immediately evident to the neighbours. The "palace" was renamed Villa Vadhana after his grandmother Queen Savang Vadhana.

The 12-room, two-storey property had a red-tiled roof with an attic and cellars that offered the children all sorts of new possibilities for work and play. The boys tinkered with electric engines and radios, and built models and gliders. Prince Bhumibol was particularly adept at mechanical work, even repairing his nanny Naen's sewing machine and constructing a simple radio. Villa Vadhana's plot at that time covered 32,000 sq metres, and included a pine tree border and an orchard at the bottom of the sloping garden with a view of Lake Geneva in the distance. The orchard produced temperate

Opposite top left *Prince Bhumibol at Davos, one of the Swiss mountain resorts visited by the royal family.*

Opposite top right *King Ananda, right, and Prince Bhumibol visit a Nestlé factory with Mom Sangwan.*

Opposite bottom *King Ananda, right, playing ice hockey with his brother, Prince Bhumibol.*

fruits: apples, cherries, pears, peaches and plums. A vegetable plot was added soon enough by Mom Sangwan, who cultivated it herself during the wartime years. The two brothers kept pet mice, guinea pigs and snakes.

After King Ananda's accession, Prince Mahidol's title was raised posthumously to honour his position as father of the king. The young king's two siblings were also elevated. "Little brother and I changed our titles from *phra ong chao* to *chao fa*, or celestial prince and princess, while mother remained a commoner at first," recalled Princess Galyani. The new household at Pully was an altogether more elaborate affair than the old apartment, with extra staff and tutors. They included Anek, a Thai gentleman confined to Switzerland by tuberculosis, who served as a private secretary. The two boys often shared a room, and even after his accession Mom Sangwan saw to it that King Ananda made his own bed.

The family's first visit home in over six years lasted less than two months, and began on 15 November 1938 following a voyage from Europe on SS *Meonia*, a Danish liner. The royal party transferred to HTMS *Sri Ayudhya*, the Royal Thai Navy's flagship, amid a 21-gun salute and overhead flypast. After a spectacular reception on the Chao Phraya river at the Grand Palace's landing, King Ananda proceeded for the first time beneath a seven-tiered umbrella—which was his entitlement as an uncrowned king— to the Chapel Royal, the Temple of the Emerald Buddha. Later, his grandmother, Queen Savang Vadhana, prostrated herself in an inner sanctum of the palace before the shy and gentle teenaged schoolboy from Switzerland.

During King Ananda's first brief stay, the government of Phraya Phahon Pholphayuhasena resigned under the weight of a scandal that had been bubbling since 1937 concerning the disposition of various crown properties. On 26 December, Pibul

Opposite top One baht notes issued in 1934 carried King Prajadhipok's picture. Those issued in 1936 bore images of his nephew, King Ananda.

Opposite below On a visit to the Siamese Red Cross, of which Queen Savang Vadhana was president, from left, Prince Bhumibol, Queen Savang Vadhana, King Ananda, Princess Galyani, and Prince Rangsit.

Left Mom Sangwan flanked by King Ananda, standing, and Prince Bhumibol, sitting, at a tea party at Srapatum Palace.

assumed the premiership for the first time, and would retain it until August 1944 when the tide of war had turned decisively against the Japanese occupying forces to which he had allied himself.

One of King Ananda's formal duties during his first visit home as king was elevating Mom Sangwan to a rank befitting the mother of a king. Since Mom Sangwan had never been a queen, she became Somdet Phra Rajajonani Srisangwan—Her Royal Highness Princess Srisangwan the Princess Mother.

"To make her name rhyme with 'jonani' it was changed from Sangwan to Srisangwan, as in 'Phra Rajajonani Srisangwan', a name that mother disliked," wrote Princess Galyani, whose published writings about her mother's life concluded on the eve of the Second World War.

The young royal family returned to Switzerland for another six years while the world was transformed by the greatest conflict mankind has ever experienced. The three children would grow happily into adulthood far from home and unaware of the great trials which lay ahead.

Second Cycle: 1940–1951

A TIME OF TRANSFORMATION

Mom Sangwan's decision in early 1932 to move her young family to Lausanne had been vindicated with every passing day. The gathering storm of war broke right across the globe in the 1940s. Lausanne was only 400 km southwest of Dachau, the German concentration camp near Munich—far closer than Bangkok is to the northern Thai capital of Chiang Mai. The Swiss city became a little more austere and parochial than before; there was rationing and the borders beyond were closed to cross-national travel. Life was otherwise uncommonly normal by the standards of wartime Europe.

Just before the war began, the princess mother employed a new tutor for King Ananda and Prince Bhumibol, initially to help with their homework. In his early 30s, Cleon O. Seraidaris was of Greek origin and had lived in Switzerland since the First World War. He resided nearby with his wife and their two sons who were much younger than his royal charges. His working hours were spent at Villa Vadhana or on excursions with the boys. Princess Galyani was away during the week, boarding at the International School of Geneva.

Seraidaris took King Ananda and Prince Bhumibol cycling and rowing, and for swims. They set up an electric train set in the attic and converted an old packing case at the bottom of the garden into "Club Patapoum"—a den in which the only drinks served were soft. The trio pored over magazines and invented board games, and Seraidaris lent his scientific knowledge to modelling ships and aircraft, mechanics and tinkering with electrical gadgets and radios.

Cars were already a passion, and the family travelled around in a large Mercedes-Benz. King Ananda and Prince Bhumibol were inseparable. The gentle, more serious older brother was always indulgent and protective of the younger one—his closest companion. "They were like twins— buddies, who are fond of one another more than they are of other friends," Princess Galyani later recalled. "They would prefer to play together more than [with] anyone else."

A first-rate carpenter, Seraidaris fired a passion in both King Ananda and Prince

Bhumibol for woodworking. The princess mother encouraged the broadest possible education for her children. She led the way in her own pursuits, collecting stamps, reading widely and toiling in her orchard and vegetable plot, often dressed in shorts. Her life revolved entirely around Villa Vadhana, and she played no part in any social life Lausanne offered. Occasional visitors would be received on Saturdays when all the children were home from school. When the Japanese ambassador arrived one day with a gift of rice (for which Princess Galyani had a particular dislike), it was quietly given to charity. Seraidaris consulted with the princess mother and Anek, the private secretary, on all aspects of the boys' upbringing. A Swiss teacher visited regularly for music lessons and an English teacher as well. An older *ajarn* (teacher) coached Thai and provided instruction in *dhamma*—the Buddhist canon.

Musical Awakening

On a visit to the ski resort of Arosa in 1942, the royal family stayed at the Kulm Hotel where a jazz band entertained the guests each night. Inspired by the sound of the instrument he had first heard as an infant on the wind-up Victrola gramophone at Srapatum Palace in Bangkok, Prince Bhumibol expressed an interest in trumpet lessons. The princess mother was concerned that playing the trumpet might be too stressful on her son's young physique and consulted a doctor back in Lausanne. Whether he was

Above *Situated in an unassuming suburb of Lausanne, Villa Vadhana became home to the royal family after King Ananda's accession in 1935.*

Opposite *King Ananda, middle, and Prince Bhumibol with their tutor Cleon O. Seraidaris outside a Swiss photography shop.*

just conceding to her concerns, or because he actually believed the trumpet could be injurious to the mouth and neck of the adolescent, the doctor advised Prince Bhumibol to consider learning the saxophone instead.

A Swiss neighbour happened to be a saxophonist and offered to sell the family a second-hand Strasser Marigaux & Lemaire alto saxophone for 300 Swiss francs. King Ananda and Prince Bhumibol paid 150 francs out of their allowance, and the princess mother contributed the rest. An instructor, J. Weybrecht, who worked at Foetisch Frères and played both the alto saxophone and clarinet, was hired to come to Villa Vadhana to teach the two aspiring musicians for three francs per 30-minute lesson.

Wednesday, 17 March 1943 was a great day in the musical history of the Mahidol family. The two brothers presented themselves to Weybrecht, a diminutive gentleman from Alsace, at the study door of Villa Vadhana. King Ananda persuaded Prince Bhumibol to go first and the lesson passed quickly. Weybrecht patiently taught the younger brother how to hold the instrument and create a basic sound by blowing correctly into the mouthpiece. Prince Bhumibol emerged from the study to find King Ananda gone. Evidently, the king had changed his mind about taking saxophone lessons. Not to be outdone, the young king presented himself again after 10 days bearing a new Martin clarinet for which he had paid 150 francs.

Over the coming months, Weybrecht and his pupils met every Wednesday and Sunday, progressing slowly from single notes to scales and arpeggios. As Weybrecht taught the brothers the different instruments, they also learned to read music properly. The music teacher composed some simple arrangements for clarinet and two saxophones for the three to perform together. Besides being more fun than simply running through practice drills, this provided an introduction to the rudiments of both musical composition and ensemble playing.

That year, King Ananda entered the University of Lausanne to study law and Prince Bhumibol concluded his schooling as a weekly boarder at l'Ecole Nouvelle de la Suisse-Romande. The lessons with Weybrecht carried on at weekends. One of Prince Bhumibol's schoolmasters, Eduard Herzog, invited him to play at the annual year-end concert, joining a classical ensemble consisting of a violinist, a cellist and Herzog himself on the piano. Despite having only nine months' formal musical instruction at that time, Prince Bhumibol agreed. In front of an audience of teachers, students and their families, the ensemble played the overture to *Die Fledermaus* by Johann Strauss. Aged 16, Prince Bhumibol's first public performance included an alto saxophone solo.

During the 1943 Christmas holidays, the family returned to the Kulm Hotel where the nightly entertainment this time was provided by a twelve-piece American jazz band led by pianist Fred Bohaler. The group of musicians included an accomplished alto saxophonist from Chicago called Glyn Paque, who had played with Jelly Roll Morton, King Oliver and Benny Carter, among other American jazz greats. Paque's Chicago-style interpretation of traditional New Orleans jazz must have made a deep impression on Prince Bhumibol. When the prince much later formed the Aw Saw

Band in Bangkok, this was clearly one of his musical influences that was followed.

Prince Bhumibol's growing fascination with jazz soon took him back to Foetisch Frères where he bought a second-hand Le Blanc clarinet—an instrument the king maintains in good working order to this day. Not to be outdone, King Ananda came home with a Conn alto saxophone, which meant that both brothers could swap between clarinet and saxophone at will.

Princess Galyani was also keen on jazz and the trio devoted much of their leisure time to acquiring new recordings. The princess, who would later become a prominent patron of the performing arts in Thailand, developed a particular taste for Benny Goodman, Artie Shaw and Glen Miller. King Ananda was more taken with Louis Armstrong and the sounds of New Orleans.

The first record Prince Bhumibol bought was Louis Armstrong's "Coal Cart Blues" with "Down in Honky Tonk Town" on the reverse side. "Coal Cart Blues" featured Sidney Bechet on soprano saxophone and provided important early inspiration. Prince Bhumibol also collected Count Basie and Duke Ellington recordings. When he wasn't jamming with his brother and sister, he devoted hours to solo practice and listening to the signature styles of the great players of the day. Apart from Bechet, he was influenced by alto saxophonist Johnny Hodges, pianist Duke Ellington and trombonist Kid Ory. This was also the time Prince Bhumibol first picked up the guitar and flute.

Prince Bhumibol finished high school with a *baccalauréat* majoring in French literature, Latin and Greek awarded by Lausanne's Gymnase Classique Cantonal. By 1944, all three siblings were attending the University of Lausanne. King Ananda was studying law, and Prince Bhumibol science. The princess mother also enrolled for some courses. While in Switzerland, her studies included philosophy, French literature, Pali and Sanskrit. All the while, it was the youngest member of the family, Prince Bhumibol, who was the most carefree and light-hearted, always ready with pranks and jokes. The family was completed by two plump Siamese cats, Tito and Tita.

At the end of 1944, Herzog invited Prince Bhumibol back for the annual school concert for some alto saxophone and piano duets. The pieces included a classic 18th-century French love song, "Plaisir d'Amour", and the popular Italian aria "Caro Mio Ben". With only the two of them playing, Prince Bhumibol admitted to being so nervous that his mouth trembled slightly. A visiting music professor nevertheless congratulated him afterwards on producing a fine natural vibrato.

Switzerland's safeness and the presence of the young royal family had a magnetic effect on other Thai students from prominent families. Villa Vadhana naturally became the social hub for these young people, who arrived for dinner parties and informal music gatherings around the piano. With King Ananda and Prince Bhumibol switching back and forth between piano, clarinet and saxophone, the events attracted a growing following. The loose-knit Wong Krapong (Tin Can) Band emerged with an open-stage policy: anyone who could play anything was welcome to join in.

Prince Bhumibol finally bought himself an old trumpet only to discover that the

Swiss doctor's advice earlier had been on the mark. He managed to strain some neck muscles, and while convalescing was forbidden to play any wind instruments. Prince Chakraband Pensiri Chakrabandhu was a frequent visitor to Villa Vadhana at this time, and an amateur composer. While nursing his neck muscles, Prince Bhumibol trained Prince Chakraband to blow through the saxophone while he played the keys. Impressed by his young cousin's musical resourcefulness and determination, Prince Chakraband urged Prince Bhumibol to work on some compositions. King Ananda and Princess Galyani thought their younger brother should try his hand at the blues first because of the relatively fixed chord structure.

End of Days

The pleasures of growing up in a Swiss suburb during the Second World War were very far removed from the historic developments uprooting much of the rest of the world. During the early war years, royalty in Bangkok faced major problems. Early in 1939, Prince Rangsit of Jainad, King Chulalongkorn's 52nd child and the longest living of his sons, had been the most prominent of several princes imprisoned. He spent time in jail after being convicted of "conspiracy". Like Prince Mahidol, he had been educated in Germany, studying jurisprudence and philosophy at the University of Heidelberg. He was incarcerated for nearly five years, and impeded from offering further counsel to the princess mother in Lausanne.

The situation in England—where Mom Sangwan had fortunately opted not to take her family in 1932—was also far from happy. On 30 May 1941, King Ananda's predecessor King Prajadhipok died of heart failure. He had spent most of his years in exile near London at Compton House, Virginia Water, in the quintessentially English county of Surrey. The kind uncle who had given Prince Bhumibol his name in 1927, and bejewelled pendant four years later, was only 48.

Without official representation from either the Thai or British governments, King Prajadhipok was cremated in a simple service that was austere by Thai standards. The ceremony was conducted at Golders Green Crematorium in North London to the strains of Mendelssohn's violin concerto in E minor. For Londoners, this was among the worst of times as they endured the so-called Blitz raining down from the heavy bombers of Germany's Luftwaffe.

The fighting in Europe was spreading across the world and a brazen attack at the end of the year finally dragged the reluctant US—Siam's great ally against predatory European colonial power—into the Second World War. On 7 December 1941, the day President Franklin D. Roosevelt predicted would "live in infamy", Japanese Imperial Navy bombers attacked the US Pacific Fleet lying at anchor at Pearl Harbor in Hawaii. Another brazen act of war even further from Japan occurred almost simultaneously in Thailand and is much less well remembered. Japanese ground forces reached the

Opposite top left The prime minister, Field Marshal Pibul Songgram, in uniform.

Opposite top right An allied bomb attack on lock gates of Bangkok's Phasi Charoen canal, 18 April 1945.

Opposite bottom King Ananda takes the salute as allied forces march along Ratchadamnoen Avenue on 19 January 1946. Supreme Allied Commander, Southeast Asia Command, Lord Louis Mountbatten is standing to the left of the flagpole in a white uniform.

outskirts of Bangkok after coming ashore in Chon Buri province, just to the east of the capital. They also landed at various points along the Isthmus of Kra in southern Thailand and northern Malaya. Unlike Pearl Harbor, the invasion of Thailand was not unexpected. On 6 December, the Japanese ambassador in Bangkok had finally dashed any hopes that Thailand might be able to remain uninvolved in the widening conflagration by requesting through passage to invade Burma to the west—a British colony like Malaya and Singapore to the south.

Prime Minister Winston Churchill advised Pibul by telegram that the British were in no position to offer any protection to Thailand. Even in the face of an insuperable and seasoned military force, the Thais did not initially acquiesce. The Thai Citizens Duty in Wartime Act, only passed in September, called for the defence of national sovereignty. Actual fighting flared for three days from 8 December around the southern provinces of Prachuap Khiri Khan, Chumphon, Surat Thani, Songkhla and Nakhon Si Thammarat. The Thais were unable to muster a concentrated force to deter the dispersed invasion that was under way, but offered resistance where they could.

Prime Minister Pibul Songgram was out of Bangkok on the day of the invasion but ordered a ceasefire on 9 December. On 21 December, Thailand's relationship with Japan became an alliance. Whatever the motives ascribed to Pibul at this time, the move undoubtedly spared countless Thai lives in a conflict caused by others.

On 25 January, a declaration of war was issued by Thailand as an ally of Japan against the US and Great Britain. At a time of seriously reversing fortunes the British took this very badly—to the extent that war reparations were demanded from Thailand in 1945. Thais living in London suddenly found themselves designated "enemy aliens" in the country many of them regarded as a second spiritual home. Mom Rajawongse

Footnote 1: All this placed Lord Louis Mountbatten, the Supreme Allied Commander in Southeast Asia based in Kandy, Ceylon, in an unusual position. "For the last two years Mountbatten had been presiding over a joint headquarters of which the British section was at war with Siam while the American was not," recorded his official biographer. "Hostilities, however, had never been conducted with noticeable energy and early in 1945 the regent [Pridi] offered to bring over his army to the allied side and asked for arms. 'It was sufficiently unusual to be offered command of the enemy army in war,' commented Mountbatten, 'but to be asked to equip it as well seemed a shade over the odds.'" He nevertheless recommended the Free Thai Movement be armed.

Seni Pramoj, a brilliant British-educated lawyer, was serving as the Thai ambassador in Washington at the time and the Thai declaration of war on the US was never delivered. Instead, Mom Rajawongse Seni made a historic broadcast from San Francisco to announce the formation of the Khabuan Kan Seri Thai, or Free Thai Movement, as a resistance movement against the Japanese occupation.

The absence of King Ananda from Thailand ensured his safety and removed him as any kind of bargaining chip. Prince Bhumibol was also safe at his side. The government in Bangkok was divided. Pibul carried on as the pro-Japanese premier while his finance minister, Pridi Banomyong, secretly became the head of the Free Thai Movement in Thailand, going by the code name Ruth. Much to the annoyance of the Japanese, from 1943 onwards British and American intelligence agents started operating in Bangkok.

By 1945, Britain's Force 136 and the Free Thai Movement were undermining the Japanese occupiers with strong support from the US Office of Strategic Services (OSS), the forerunner of the Central Intelligence Agency (CIA). The Americans did not wish to see their vast expenditure of men and treasure in the Asian theatre used to re-establish European colonial interests, particularly in Burma and French Indochina— Cambodia, Laos and Vietnam. They also did not support any British move to punish Thailand for wartime collaboration with Japan.[1]

The war in Europe ended on May 1945 when Admiral Dönitz announced Germany's capitulation, bringing an end to the Third Reich. The historic announcement was made from the German Naval Academy at Flensburg-Mürwik where Prince Mahidol had been a naval cadet more than 30 years earlier. The surrender finally freed his widow and three children from their wartime haven in Switzerland. The war in Asia, however, continued until the dropping of the atomic bombs on the Japanese ports of Hiroshima and Nagasaki, and the final surrender by Japan on 2 September to the supreme commander of the Allied Powers in Japan, General Douglas MacArthur, aboard the battleship USS *Missouri* lying at anchor in Tokyo Bay.

Pridi finished the war with the upper hand over Pibul in their constant political tussle. A few days after the ceremony in Tokyo Bay—the first moment Pridi could see the opportunity for the royal family's safe return—he sent a cable to Lausanne. As the regent newly appointed by parliament he humbly beseeched King Ananda's return. Pridi pointed out that the king would come of age on 20 September and his regency should technically lapse at that time. The carefree days in Switzerland were over and the time had nearly come for young King Ananda to assume his role as Thailand's constitutional head of state.

Back in the Thai capital, some Japanese dignitaries were given a farewell tea party. Amid the global celebrations in late 1945, Bangkok became a serious party town. There were balls and dances every night as the shackles of occupation fell away. A major charm offensive was meanwhile under way to make the arriving British feel less disgruntled.

Homecoming

The British Royal Air Force Douglas DC-3 arrived at Don Muang International Airport on 5 December 1945, Prince Bhumibol's 18th birthday. When the royal party descended on to the apron, King Ananda looked deeply serious. His younger brother, bespectacled with his tie askew and trademark camera around his neck, was taken care of by the youngest of four *mom chao* present, Prince Bhisatej Rajani, who would later help with King Bhumibol's development work in northern Thailand.[2] The royal party adjourned for lunch in the Don Muang Airport buildings and started to take stock of the vast changes that had taken place since King Ananda and Prince Bhumibol departed in January 1939 just ahead of the outbreak of war in Europe. "I had been away from Thailand for seven full years," King Bhumibol later recalled. "I was almost completely unaware of what had been going on with my country and my people."

King Ananda was by now 20 and legally an adult. Pridi's regency was coming to a close. Equipped with a Swiss law education and fresh from the sheltered and domesticated existence the princess mother had created in Lausanne, King Ananda had much to learn in a land that was in many respects baffling. He was intent on doing the job well in the treacherous seas of Thai politics, and a correspondent for *The Times* of London gave him high marks for gravitas and sincerity in this new environment.

Others noticed a certain awkwardness. "Ananda, [the] Siamese remember, was a strange young king," John Stanton reported in *Time*. "Full of Western ideas, he refused to talk to visitors who sat on the floor below him Siamese-fashion, insisting that they sit on chairs level with himself. Since shyness is a Siamese characteristic, the visitors often found themselves unable to talk in such a presumptuous position; king and subject would sit in silence, both blushing."

Soon after King Ananda's return, Lord Mountbatten arrived in Bangkok for a march past by allied forces. He took an interest in the young king's challenging situation. To European eyes, notorious for being unable to gauge the age of Asians, the king looked five years younger than he actually was. Mountbatten beheld a lonesome boy, "his sloping shoulders and thin chest hung with gorgeous diamond-studded decorations …" An aide described Mountbatten's view of King Ananda as "the perfect mixture of respect to the king and a fatherly attitude to the small boy at his side". On one occasion Mountbatten accompanied the king in a car travelling across Bangkok. "The king sat immobile, looking nervously straight ahead," wrote Mountbatten's official biographer Philip Ziegler. "Mountbatten leant across and suggested he acknowledge the cheers of the crowd by saluting or bowing. The king was much struck by this advice and at once acted on it thereby no doubt breaching the rules of a millennium of royal etiquette but noticeably increasing the enthusiasm of the people."[3]

The royal brothers were constant companions and when they visited Sampheng Lane in the Yaowarat Road area, Bangkok's Chinese business centre, Prince Bhumibol was King Ananda's shadow and official photographer. Indeed, Princess Galyani later

Below *King Ananda, the princess mother and Lord Mountbatten in Bangkok in early 1946 as the royal family adapted to the much more formal demands of public life in Bangkok.*

Opposite *King Ananda, accompanied by the princess mother and Prince Bhumibol, is greeted by the regent, Pridi Banomyong, upon his return from Switzerland in late 1945.*

Footnote 2: Eight years Prince Bhumibol's senior, Prince Bhisatej had interrupted his university studies at Cambridge to join the British Army as one of Winston's Irregulars, training in the high mountains of Nepal. As a member of Force 136, he was infiltrated by flying boat back into southern Thailand, and from Surat Thani kept the allies informed of Japanese shipping movements.

Footnote 3: Mountbatten was an influential but flawed witness to this period. "The truth, in his hands, was swiftly converted from what it was to what it should have been. He sought to rewrite history with cavalier indifference to the facts to magnify his own achievements," noted his biographer Philip Ziegler. Indeed, Ziegler kept a sign on his desk that read: "Remember, in spite of everything, he was a great man."

Footnote 4: MacDonald had been a journalist in civilian life. On the eve of his departure, it was suggested that he stay on in Bangkok and open an English-language newspaper. MacDonald cancelled his departure plans, found himself six local partners and on 1 August 1946 launched the *Bangkok Post* as an afternoon daily from a shophouse on Krung Kasem Road.

commented that Prince Bhumibol's first experience of kingly duties came from observing his brother through the lens of a camera. He was paid a monthly stipend of 100 baht as a contributing photographer to *Standard Magazine*, which was owned by Prince Prem Purachatra. The royal visit to Sampheng was considered courageous, given the prevailing ethnic tensions and recent riots. Many Chinese were strongly anti-Japanese and still hostile to Thais who they felt had collaborated during the war years.

Over the next six months, the royal brothers acquired a surplus US army jeep for their less formal outings and formed a gun collection, which they stored at their residence in Borombiman Mansion inside the castellated white stucco walls of the Grand Palace. In the afternoons they would conduct target practice on a lawn there and became familiar with the handling and care of firearms. During this time a trophy US army issue Colt 45 was given to them by Alexander MacDonald, who had been made station chief of the OSS in Bangkok immediately after the war.[4]

The return to Thailand in 1946 occasioned Prince Bhumibol's first serious jazz compositions. It all started with some musical fragments he showed Prince Chakraband, who had been so much a part of the brothers' musical evenings at Villa Vadhana. The older prince encouraged Prince Bhumibol to complete them and offered to write lyrics. Prince Bhumibol's first finished piece was "Saeng Tien" (Candlelight), a New Orleans-style blues arrangement completed in April.

Prince Bhumibol initially resisted publishing the piece because he found Prince Chakraband's lyrics melancholy. Although African-American blues were intrinsically mournful, he thought something more uplifting and hopeful at the end would be better. The creative process eased and Prince Bhumibol was able to turn out more works in

a relatively short time. His second and third compositions were "Yarm Yen" (Love at Sundown) and "Sai Fon" (Falling Rain), also with lyrics by Prince Chakraband.

"HM Blues" followed soon and like "Love at Sundown" would become a perennial favourite. Although people often assumed that "HM" referred to "His Majesty" it was composed by Prince Bhumibol before his accession. "HM" stood for "hungry men" and was an insider's joke from the evenings in Lausanne: while the guests ate their meal and enjoyed the music, the band members played hard and went hungry.

Prince Chakraband's lyrics consisted of a single verse and chorus:

We've got the hungry men's blues.
You'll be hungry too, if you're in this band.
Don't you think that our music is grand?
We've got the hungry men's blues.
You've eaten now all of you.
We'd like to eat with you too.
That's why we've got the HM blues.

Prince Bhumibol later asked Prince Chakraband to write "Never Mind the Hungry Men's Blues" to a swing melody from another composition, "Duang Jai Kap Kwam Ruk" (Hearts and Love).

We used to be so hungry,	*But now we know that you all*
We used to be so blue;	*Enjoy the song we play along*

Above *Prince Bhumibol follows his brother the king with his trademark camera in hand.*

Right *A photograph taken by Prince Bhumibol through the car window while accompanying King Ananda to visit the troubled Sampheng Lane area on 3 June 1946.*

Opposite *King Ananda, right, with Prince Bhumibol during their last outing together to an agricultural fair in Bang Khen on 5 June 1946.*

The whole night through.
We used to be so unhappy,
We used to be so blue;
But then you gave us supper,
We love to play all night and day
For all of you.
Les croissants au jambon,
Et sandwiches sont tres bon;

The punch's fine, the good wine
Have all been wonderful
To band of mine.
We used to be so hungry,
We used to be so blue;
But then you gave us supper,
You've been so kind, so
Never mind the HM blues

Tragedy Strikes

Musical pursuits, however, took a back seat after a tragic turn of events. On 5 June 1946, Prince Bhumibol accompanied King Ananda to an agricultural fair in Bang Khen in Bangkok a few days before the brothers were due to leave for the US on their way back to Switzerland. The departure was postponed because some constitutional adjustments requiring King Ananda's signature were not ready. The king also developed a stomach problem that was inconsequential. Early on the morning of 9 June, he was in his chambers in the Borombiman Mansion. He had been seen there in bed by his mother and a page, and out of bed by another page.

Prince Bhumibol last saw King Ananda briefly the night before, and the brothers said very little. The prince was on his way out to a ceremony near the Ministry of Commerce for Raksa Dindan military reservists, where he was standing in for the indisposed king. Upon returning home Prince Bhumibol went directly to bed. The next morning, learning from a page that his brother was still in his room, Prince Bhumibol took breakfast alone on the landing outside King Ananda's chambers. He did not disturb the king and returned to his own room on the same floor at the other end of Borombiman Mansion.

The event that followed thereafter has never been clearly explained. At 9.20 am, about 20 minutes after Prince Bhumibol had left the breakfast table, a shot rang out. A bullet had entered King Ananda's forehead over his right eye and exited as a more minor wound into the bed's mattress. The king was evidently lying on his back at the time of the shot, which apparently came from the Colt given to the brothers by MacDonald. The pistol had a special safety catch system involving a squeeze grip designed to guard against accidental discharge. The alarm was raised by a page, Chit Singhaseni, who ran to the princess mother's chamber, calling out, "The king has shot himself."

The household was plunged into confusion. The princess mother and a royal nanny arrived. The king's mother beheld her dead son and sobbed, *"Nand ja, Nand ja!"* ["My dear Nand, my dear Nand!"]. Prince Bhumibol was one of the next to reach his brother's chambers. "When I arrived, he was dead," he told correspondent David Lomax in *Soul of a Nation*, a 1979 BBC television documentary.

There was no isolation of the death scene, so within minutes it was contaminated. The presumed weapon, the Colt lying beside the right-handed King Ananda's left hand, was handled by a page, a nanny and later the chief of police. Utterly distraught, the princess mother bathed King Ananda, assisted by Prince Bhumibol, the nanny and the two pages. Ice blocks were laid beside the body and a fan brought in.

One of the first reports issued by the Associated Press quoted the palace as saying the death had been an accident and a radio broadcast said the same. The size and design of the weapon made it unlikely that the accident could have been self-inflicted, and King Ananda was not wearing the spectacles he would have needed with his poor eyesight to be inspecting the weapon properly. With King Ananda lying on his back, either dozing or asleep, a struggle with someone else over the weapon seemed unlikely.

Pathologists reported that there were no powder burns, inward bullet trajectory, or normal site selection for a deliberately self-inflicted wound—factors that would appear to work against suicide as an explanation. There has been speculation about a girlfriend in Switzerland, fellow student Marylene Ferrari with whom King Ananda had communicated by postcard during his time away from Switzerland. If it was serious, such a relationship would have drawn unfavourable comment in royal circles and have been ill-starred as King Ananda moved towards his coronation and permanent residence in Thailand. But in the meantime, King Ananda was due to return to Switzerland to complete his law studies and had much to look forward to. The king was to fly home via Washington, where President Harry S. Truman had invited him to the White House, and then on to London, where King George VI had asked him to tea at Buckingham Palace. He was said to be excited about the impending visits and had made an enthusiastic farewell visit to the supreme patriarch.

A panel of 15 physicians was convened to conduct a post-mortem, 12 of whom concluded murder to be the most likely explanation. Dr Edwin Cort, the missionary physician from Chiang Mai with whom Prince Mahidol had briefly resided in 1929, was among them. He was quoted as saying that the position of the wound and the track of the bullet seemed to show that the death was the result of assassination rather than suicide. An accident was also deemed improbable, the panel concluded. A censorship board was set up to vet further publicity on the matter. In October 1946, after King Bhumibol's return to Lausanne, a commission of inquiry concluded that King Ananda's death could not have been accidental. The alternatives were suicide or murder, but no conclusion was drawn either way.

In 1948 and 1949, Dr Keith Simpson, pathologist to the British Home Office and founding chairman of the Department of Forensic Medicine at Guy's Hospital London, was consulted first by a senior Thai police officer and then by Dr Songkran Niyomsen, Thailand's first forensic pathologist. The scene in Borombiman Mansion had not been photographed but from the detailed written evidence given to him and extensive discussions, Dr Simpson endorsed the panel of doctors in Bangkok, ruling out suicide or self-inflicted accidental death.

"This is not a case of suicidal discharge nor of accident, but one of deliberate killing by firearm," Dr Simpson concluded in his report. The British pathologist was prepared to come to Bangkok in 1950 to give evidence in the trial of three royal members of staff hauled up in 1947 for conspiracy in regicide, but it did not come to pass.

"Owing to some crisis in politics in this country, it is not sure that this trial will continue," Dr Songkran, the pathologist in Bangkok, wrote in apology—inferring the kind of political interference King Bhumibol would mention 30 years later in his interview with the BBC. "If a new government is formed, the aspect of the trial may be changed; and we doctors who confirmed regicide do not know our fate yet. We are expecting a *coup d'état* any morning on waking up; besides, communist invasion may come any time."

A protracted trial failed to establish the identity of the killer. The proceedings involved acquittals that were later rescinded and failed appeals. Two royal pages and a secretary were executed in 1955 after being convicted of complicity in regicide. The executions did not bring closure to one of the most tragic and mysterious moments in modern Thai history.

In the late 1990s, a theory based on unidentified sources was advanced that King Ananda's death was the work of Colonel Tsuji Masanobu, a Japanese "spy" who had supposedly avoided prosecution for war crimes by making himself useful to the Americans, and was allegedly hiding out in Bangkok. The theory fails to provide a motive or to explain why somebody in hiding would risk attracting attention by murdering the most prominent person in the kingdom. Japanese accounts place Tsuji

Opposite *A photograph of King Ananda taken by Prince Bhumibol during an address at Paknam, near Bangkok, on 5 May 1946.*

Left *Borombiman Mansion in the Grand Palace, where King Ananda died from a gunshot wound in unexplained circumstances on 9 June 1946.*

in Thailand at the end of the war and in contact with nationalist Chinese, but not at the time of King Ananda's death the following year. In November 1945, Tsuji left Thailand for Vietnam, travelling to Kunming, China, in February 1946 and from there to Chunking. He was in Nanjing in July 1946 and did not return to Japan until May 1948. Tsuji disappeared in Laos in April 1961 and was legally declared dead in 1968.

In his interview with the BBC in 1979, King Bhumibol said: "Many people wanted to advance not theories but facts to clear up the affair. They were suppressed—and they were suppressed by influential people in this country or in international politics." King Bhumibol told the BBC that the investigation "proved that it was not an accident, or not a suicide. One doesn't know."

Ninth Reign

Although there has never been any consensus on the truth behind King Ananda's violent and premature death, there was no question as to his heir: his sole brother, Prince Bhumibol, who acceded to the throne the very same day. In early September 1946, King Bhumibol left Thailand to resume his studies in Switzerland. "I have to leave this capital and leave you because it is essential that I re-create myself," he told his subjects in a radio broadcast.

King Bhumibol later recalled his departure: "While travelling down Ratchadamnoen Avenue, I saw so many people trying to approach the car … I was very much afraid that the car was going to run over someone's foot. The car moved at the slowest speed possible, and did not get going until it reached Wat Benchamabophit. While on the road, I heard someone shout, 'Please do not abandon the people.' I felt like shouting back, 'If the people do not abandon me, then how can I ever abandon the people?' But the car was by then moving fast and I was already too far away. "After boarding the plane, I could still see people shouting their best wishes. However, when the plane started, all the people's voices were drowned out by the noise of the engines … The plane circled the city three times … I could still see people around the city looking up."

True to his farewell radio broadcast, King Bhumibol returned to the University of Lausanne and changed his course of study from science to law and political and social sciences—taking on his late brother's studies in disciplines that would serve him better in his unanticipated role as king.

In early November 1947, Field Marshal Phin Choonhavan staged a coup. Pibul backed it and assumed the premiership the following April. For Pridi Banomyong, the coup and accusations against him after King Ananda's death were the final blows to his political career. As the wartime regent and incumbent prime minister he had at the very least failed to keep King Ananda safe. Security forces were closing in to arrest him. With the help of a British diplomat, Pridi escaped to Singapore in late November aboard a small oil tanker. He went into self-exile in China for 20 years—which placed him beyond extradition—and subsequently resided in France. He died in Paris in 1984. By his own account, Pridi returned to Thailand briefly in 1949, rallying elements of the Free Thai Movement, the navy and marines in a disastrous coup attempt against Pibul. Some have questioned whether Pridi was actually in the country. Whatever the case, his supporters did briefly win control of the area around the Grand Palace, Sanam Luang and Thammasat University. Troops commanded by Field Marshal Sarit Thanarat put the rebellion down and Pridi's remaining people were purged from the government and the military. Many did not believe Pridi had played any role in King Ananda's death, but after the 1949 failed coup he never came home and offered no explanation himself beyond saying he did not know who was responsible.

"It was better for Pridi to stay quiet and not be accused of being anti-monarchy," observes Professor Suchit Bunbongkarn, director of Chulalongkorn University's Institute of Security and International Studies. "Pridi had nothing to do with the Communist Party of Thailand, which is revealing."

Pridi himself once observed enigmatically, "History keeps rolling on into the future without an end. I will leave it to you and members of future generations who wish to see the truth to find the answer." Looking back with hindsight on another occasion, Pridi said: "In 1932, I was 32 years old. We had a revolution but I was inexperienced. When I had more power, I had no experience and when I had more experience, I had no power."

Opposite *The front page of Sri Krung newspaper, 11 June 1946, with the headline: "Prince Bhumibol accedes to the throne" and sub-headline "The sudden death of King Ananda causes nationwide mourning."*

Left *King Bhumibol in mourning dress after his brother's death.*

Engagement in Europe

Postwar Europe, blighted by austerity and the ashes of war, did at least offer much greater freedom of movement. King Bhumibol took advantage of this to travel about and indulge his passions for jazz and motoring, occasionally driving the 400 km to Paris to listen to favourite musicians. He was generally quiet and introspective. "If he drove to Geneva for Chinese food, he would just eat and leave," recalled Thanpuying Maneerat Bunnag in a 1976 interview. "He did not stay on and go to other places. When there was a party, he usually played music while other people were dancing."

At the end of 1947, King Bhumibol came of age. During his continued absence abroad, the five-man regency council in Bangkok remained in place with his uncle, Prince Rangsit, at its head. The king marked the occasion of his coming of age quietly and said he would not be returning to Thailand until King Ananda's cremation, which was planned for 1948.

Nothing would run to plan that year, however. Love came knocking at his door in the shape of a cousin, the pretty and vivacious Mom Rajawongse Sirikit Kitiyakara, the oldest daughter of the leading Thai diplomat in Europe, Prince Nakkhatra Mangala Kitiyakara. An aspiring pianist, she was studying in Europe when the pair first met at Fontainebleau outside Paris. By Queen Sirikit's subsequent account, King Bhumibol was late and it was not love at first sight on her part. That would all change soon enough, but not before disaster struck Prince Mahidol's family yet again.

On Monday 4 October 1948, King Bhumibol was driving a Fiat Topolino, a small

car named after the Italian counterpart of Mickey Mouse. King Bhumibol's brother-in-law, Princess Galyani's first husband, Aram Rattanakul, was in the passenger seat. The young men were at Morges, 10 km outside Lausanne on the road to Geneva, when a lorry braked hard to avoid a pair of cyclists. The 600cc car ploughed into its tailgate. Both occupants suffered head injuries. King Bhumibol sustained serious damage to his right eye—which he subsequently lost—concussion and back injuries. Aram was also left with some cracked ribs.

After his release from hospital in Lausanne, King Bhumibol returned home to Villa Vadhana to convalesce. This turned out to be more enjoyable than anticipated since it provided an opportunity to see the lovely girl who had first caught his interest at Fontainebleau. After the accident—and with the approval of the princess mother—Mom Luang Bua Kitiyakara enrolled her daughters, Mom Rajawongse Sirikit and Mom Rajawongse Busba, at a nearby boarding school, the Pensionnat Riante Rive. The two girls were allowed out each afternoon for tea at Villa Vadhana. As King Bhumibol recovered, the romance blossomed. The couple became engaged, and announced this formally on Mom Rajawongse Sirikit's 17th birthday, 12 August 1949, at the Royal Thai Embassy in London where her father was ambassador. The engagement ring was the one Prince Mahidol had given Sangwan nearly 30 years earlier.

"This is very precious," said King Bhumibol. "It is my gift to you."

"I'm still too young and have never been in love before," replied Mom Rajawongse Sirikit. "It also excites me …"

Opposite A portrait of Mom Rajawongse Sirikit at the age of 16 in 1949 taken by King Bhumibol in a field near Lausanne.

Above King Bhumibol and Mom Rajawongse Sirikit in Lausanne on 13 September 1949, a month after their official engagement.

New Life

In May that year, King Bhumibol travelled to Paris to attend the 1949 Paris International Jazz Festival, which included Tadd Dameron and the Miles Davis Quintet among the headliners. On this personal outing, the king was particularly impressed with the performance of composer, saxophonist and clarinettist John Dankworth. The British musician represented a welcome challenge to American exclusivity in jazz. Dankworth played alongside American bebop pioneer Charlie Parker, considered one of the most innovative artists in jazz at the time, and went on to tour Europe with King Bhumibol's early musical hero, saxophonist Sidney Bechet.

In February 1950, it was reported that a white elephant had been found to present to King Bhumibol for his coronation—a propitious Oriental regal accoutrement King Ananda had never acquired. That same month, the happy young couple boarded a train in Lausanne for Villafranche and sailed from a modern world to an ancient one—across the Mediterranean, through the Suez Canal, across the Indian Ocean past Singapore and up into the Gulf of Thailand where they were met at the mouth of the great Chao Phraya river, the fabled River of Kings, by HTMS *Sri Ayudhya*, the Royal Thai Navy's flagship. The couple transferred to a naval launch for the long-awaited royal homecoming, travelling upriver to the Grand Palace with its gilded roofs glistening in the hot afternoon sunshine of 25 March. Three planes overhead sprinkled popped rice over the straining throngs of happy spectators below. When a jetty near Memorial Bridge gave way under the strain of it all, it was a moment of cooling hilarity rather than calamity. Next morning, the king gave alms to the monks at the Chapel Royal, the Temple of the Emerald Buddha, while the women present watched from behind a wooden screen. Not far away stood the magnificent golden urn that for nearly four years had contained the mortal remains of King Ananda awaiting cremation.

On 29 March, in an awesome spectacle meticulously orchestrated by Prince Rangsit before an estimated crowd of a half million, 200 brightly-clad soldiers hauled the massive ancient chariot-hearse from Wat Phra Chetuphon (Wat Pho) beside the Grand Palace on to the Pramane Ground, the old name for Sanam Luang restored for the duration of royal cremations. There, a great golden Phra Merumas—a towering representation of Mount Meru—had been erected for the royal funerary rites conducted by Brahman priests to the haunting wail of blown conch shells. King Bhumibol, who had visited his brother's urn alone for hours at a time whenever possible, followed King Ananda on foot in his final journey—as he always had in life.

The urn was transferred to a palanquin, and in the tradition of Buddhist cremations, walked anti-clockwise around the magnificent gilded crematorium three times, and then raised aloft between the earth and the heavens for the final rites. At the appointed hour, King Bhumibol placed the first flame to ignite the funeral pyre.

"Women in their requisite black mourning dress squatted on the ground, sobbing bitterly," reported Swiss correspondent Walter Bosshard. "Men stood together in solemn silence, not taking their eyes from the fire which was transforming to ashes a king whom the people had barely known."

Mom Rajawongse Sirikit stayed in Deves Palace, her father's home, in the weeks before the royal wedding on 28 April at Srapatum Palace—Lotus Pond Palace—where Prince Mahidol had been married and passed away. The ceremony was presided over at 10.24 am by the king's grandmother, Queen Savang Vadhana, and could not have been simpler. The dowager queen anointed their foreheads and poured lustral water from a sacred shank. Having paid the 10-baht marriage fee, the couple signed a palace marriage register without listing their occupations. There were erroneous reports, however, that King Bhumibol listed his as "ruler of the country". The honeymoon couple departed for Hua Hin. Six of King Bhumibol's songs were playing in Thailand that month and they included some topical lyrics:

> *In the kingdom of my dreams,*
> *You are my queen.*
> *Please don't let me just dream,*
> *Please make my dreams come true —*
> *In wonderland.*

A week later, the royal couple were back in Bangkok in a wonderland of their own. The Baisal Daksin Hall at the Grand Palace was the setting for King Bhumibol's long-awaited coronation. The king was presented with 26 items of royal regalia, the most important of which, the Great Crown of Victory, he placed upon his own head. Seated upon a throne made of gilded wood, this was the only day in his entire reign that King Bhumibol would wear the 7.3-kg stupa-shaped crown. Fully attired for the first time as king, he swore an oath to his subjects: "We shall reign with righteousness, for the benefit and happiness of the Siamese people."

In the afternoon, King Bhumibol gave a royal audience to members of the royal family, dignitaries and the diplomatic corps. In a magnificent ceremony closed to the press, King Bhumibol was revealed from behind a gold curtain, enthroned as a living deity surrounded by the full regalia of his kingship. In a ceremony that followed, Queen Sirikit was raised by the king to the rank of full queen—Somdet Phra Nang Chao (Sirikit) Phra Barom Rajini—and presented with accoutrements befitting her newly elevated position. King Bhumibol finally went in a procession to the Chapel Royal, the Temple of the Emerald Buddha, borne upon a palanquin in a golden royal cloak and a large broad-rimmed hat turned up on one side. Inside the temple, the supreme patriarch recited Buddhist precepts, followed by 80 monks chanting to bless him as defender of the Buddhist faith and all other religions in the kingdom. Two days later, King Bhumibol addressed diplomats, foreigners and members of the public from a balcony at Sutthaisawan Prasat Hall.

Far removed from the wonderfully arcane coronation in Bangkok, Michael Todd's *Peepshow* opened to a packed house at the Forrest Theatre in Philadelphia. It was slightly controversial for some of the revealing female costumes. One of King Bhumibol's

Opposite *Bangkok residents crowd the banks of the Chao Phraya for a glimpse of King Bhumibol travelling upriver by launch on his return with his future wife and queen, Mom Rajawongse Sirikit.*

Above *King Ananda's cremation on 29 March 1950 was held at the Pramane Ground (Sanam Luang), nearly four years after his death. The ceremony was meticulously orchestrated by his uncle, Prince Rangsit, at a specially erected Phra Merumas—a towering golden representation of the great Mount Meru.*

Opposite top left King Bhumibol during the ablution rites, conducted early in his coronation ceremony.

Opposite top right King Bhumibol sits on his throne after ritually placing the Great Crown of Victory upon his own head during his coronation on 5 May 1950, the only day he has ever worn the 7.3 kg-headpiece of the Royal House of Chakri.

Opposite bottom King Bhumibol in ancient attire progresses on a palanquin to the Chapel Royal, the Temple of the Emerald Buddha, after his coronation.

Top Mom Rajawongse Sirikit Kitiyakara signs a marriage certificate at Srapatum Palace on 28 April 1950.

Above King Bhumibol and Queen Sirikit on their wedding day.

Left King Bhumibol appears in public for the first time after marrying the newly elevated Queen Sirikit.

compositions was listed in the programme as "Blue Night", and was described by one reviewer as "a haunting beguine". Todd's lavish set paid tribute to the kingdom with a facsimile temple and Thai-inspired costumes and dance.

"My music was called 'Blue Day' but Todd changed the tune and the name: he called it 'Blue Night'," King Bhumibol told a foreign correspondent many years later, shaking his head in mock regret. "Maybe it was because of the 12-hour time difference between here and New York."

A critical and commercial success, *Peepshow* soon moved to the Winter Garden Theatre on New York's Broadway, racking up 278 performances there over the next eight months. *Billboard* highlighted "Blue Night" in its review: "[Dancers] Myrtill and Pacaud interpolate a stunning Siamese adagio in the first act's sock finale to a tune by Bhumibol (in private life HRH the King of Thai) [sic]," the magazine reported.

"Blue Day" went on to become one of King Bhumibol's most recorded compositions outside Thailand, with versions by the Count Basie Orchestra and Larry Carlton among others. The latter recorded it as the opening track on his album "The Jazz King". The song remains popular in Thailand where vocalists customarily sing the Thai verses followed by their English counterparts.

After their spectacular, life-changing sojourn in Thailand, the young newlyweds returned to Switzerland for the conclusion of King Bhumibol's treatment with a specialist. They started a family with the birth of their first daughter, Princess Ubol Ratana Rajakanya in Lausanne on 5 April 1951. The new royal family returned to Thailand by sea aboard the SS *Meonia* once again, just in time for King Bhumibol's 24th birthday on 5 December. They were met by Prime Minister Pibul in full uniform with a bright sash as warplanes dropped rose petals from above.

There had been much political intrigue during the king's absence in Switzerland. Pibul had numerous enemies, including a treacherous valet. At various times, there were unsuccessful attempts to shoot, stab and poison him. Some believed these narrow escapes were proof of his charmed existence. That proposition was seriously tested in June 1951 when Pibul was taken hostage by a group of naval officers during the commissioning into the Royal Thai Navy of the *Manhattan*, an old US dredger supplied to help lower the sand bar in the Chao Phraya river. In front of a group of astonished American officials, the prime minister was marched off at gunpoint to HTMS *Sri Ayudhya*, the navy's old flagship.

The ship was bombarded by loyal troops and aircraft—and duly sank. In the melee, Pibul confirmed his indestructibility by climbing overboard and swimming to shore. There was serious bloodshed in the following days and further purges of the navy in store. Indeed, its operational base was permanently moved to Sattahip, 130 km from Bangkok on the Gulf of Thailand's eastern seaboard.

The political jockeying continued throughout 1951. The Democrat Party of Mom Rajawongse Seni Pramoj, who was briefly prime minister after the war, proposed constitutional reforms that would have enhanced King Bhumibol's powers in relation to

the armed forces, the Senate, ministerial appointments and constitutional adjustments. On 26 November, with King Bhumibol finally steaming home aboard the Danish liner SS *Meonia* to permanent residence in Thailand, the army staged a bloodless putsch. It was dubbed the Silent Coup, or Radio Coup, since its progress was announced over Radio Bangkok and anybody not listening had little idea of what was unfolding. The overnight dissolution sidelined the Democrats. Pibul was promptly reinstalled as prime minister and a modified version of the 1932 constitution tabled. "Subsequent elections and appointments created a military-dominated parliament," noted historians Chris Baker and Pasuk Phongpaichit. "The royalists had been demoted to junior partners in the ruling alliance. The military was in command for the next two decades."

With such palpable tension in the air, it was small wonder King Bhumibol looked so grim when he came ashore on 2 December and beheld his ministers. "Clad in naval uniform, the bespectacled king was not seen to smile once during the arrival ceremonies at the royal landing, the requisite visit to the temples, and a two-and-one-half mile drive past more than 100,000 adoring subjects," reported the Associated Press. Such mixed signals would set the tone for the years to come.

Third Cycle: 1952–1963

MOVING CENTRE STAGE

At 24, King Bhumibol's formal education and life in Switzerland were behind him. His future career as the king of Thailand was not one he had chosen or expected. As the king began to make sense of his new place in the world, and to gauge what would be required to stay above the quicksand of Thai politics, Prime Minister Pibul Songgram had problems of his own. Pibul had been Thailand's principal wartime prime minister, serving from late 1938 until August 1944, when his pro-Japanese government found its position on the losing side untenable. His second term in office ran from April 1948 to September 1957, when he went into permanent self-exile.

In the early 1950s, with his main political rival, Pridi Banomyong, in self-exile in the newly established People's Republic of China, Pibul was finally in the presence of an adult monarch—not a minor represented from afar by a regency council. King Bhumibol had long since come of age, and was already beginning a family that would soon present the prospect of a secure succession.

Academic accounts of this period focus on the inevitable tension between King Bhumibol, who had sworn at his coronation to reign for the benefit and happiness of his people, and the first prime minister in Thailand to test the workings of a constitutional monarchy with the reigning king firmly in place. It was never a close working relationship, and they remained distant for the next six years.

"The way Pibul viewed the king was hardly surprising," comments Professor Suchit Bunbongkarn. "From his point of view, he was one of the people who launched the 1932 revolution and the king was very young." Suchit argues that there were inevitable points of friction in the relationship rather than outright antagonism.

Pibul could not "play the substitute king as easily as he once had," observes American historian Joseph J. Wright. "The Lord of Life, the manly, young King Bhumibol, had come home. He had brought with him a radiant young bride, Queen Sirikit, and together they began to warm the cold emptiness left in the nation's heart by Ananda's tragic death. Pibul's new campaign for public adoration was perceived as a competition with the king for the public's loyalty."

Having studied law in Switzerland, King Bhumibol was asked soon after his return to sit as a judge and hand down some minor civil and criminal rulings—as King Ananda had before him. He was then presented with a Bar Association gown by an official from the Ministry of Justice.

When the 1952 constitution was due for the royal signature in March, King Bhumibol was away in Hua Hin. The absence reminded all that his presence could not be taken for granted, and this was the first time the question of King Bhumibol's constitutional right to be consulted in such matters arose. The amended version of the 1932 charter nevertheless went through after the king's return to the capital. Pibul was reconfirmed as prime minister on 24 March, but with less than half the Cabinet in attendance. In April, seven members of King Bhumibol's Privy Council were appointed, with Prince Dhani Nivat as president and a number of other senior princes as members. One was King Bhumibol's father in law, Prince Nakkhatra Mangala Kitiyakara.

"The king now speaks with some bitterness about the early years of his reign, though without mentioning names," Barbara Crossette of *The New York Times* reported in a lengthy profile in 1989. "When I'd open my mouth and suggest something, they'd say: 'Your Majesty, you don't know anything,'" the king recalls. "So I shut my mouth. I know things, but I shut my mouth. They don't want me to speak, so I don't speak."

Francis Bowes Sayre was Prince Mahidol's good friend and confidant. He was a foreign affairs adviser to Siam in the 1920s during the reign of King Vajiravudh, and had also been on close terms with King Prajadhipok and the Mahidol family. In 1950, he wrote some prophetic words of encouragement to King Bhumibol:

"Do not let yourself become discouraged. The Thai people themselves have great qualities … They yearn to have back in their midst their king and leader. They will be loyal and true to you … [Economic] problems which menace so many countries do not beset Siam. The country's greatest dangers lie in other directions than these.

"To meet such problems, your own course will be clear," Sayre went on. "You will follow the pathway which your father always followed, the pathway of selfless service for his country and its people. Your ideals, like his, must be kept untarnished and shining; and your constant compass if you would avoid shipwreck must be utter goodness and integrity of character. Nothing else will so surely win your people's hearts and strengthen your reign."

"I shall try not to get discouraged," King Bhumibol wrote back. "I know I must hold on [to] what I think is the right thing to do, and I can assure you I shall try my best." In 1953, King Bhumibol invited Sayre to Bangkok to bestow upon him a Royal Cypher Medal engraved with his royal initials in diamonds. "It was a rare mark of distinction, given to but a few," noted Sayre with satisfaction. He had already been honoured with a Grand Cross of the Order of the White Elephant and given the title *phraya kalayanamaitri* (Lord of Sincere Amity) by King Prajadhipok. The earlier accolades rewarded Sayre's dogged lobbying on Siam's behalf against the economically

Opposite *Francis Bowes Sayre sits at his desk in the US State Department in 1943. The Harvard-trained lawyer served as an adviser on foreign affairs to King Vajiravudh in the 1920s and was on close terms with Prince Mahidol.*

Above *Prince Dhani Nivat, president of the Privy Council and valued adviser early in King Bhumibol's reign.*

hobbling unequal treaties of eight colonial-era powers. The task had taken him all over Europe and culminated in a memorable encounter with an Italian leader who proved quite well disposed to the Siamese: Benito Mussolini. "He gave us a reassuring smile," recalled Sayre. "Our hearts leaped; his words spelt victory for Siam."

Cold War Years

By 1953, the predatory European powers of the 19th century were spent forces. Trade-based colonial competition had been supplanted by ideological confrontation and the Cold War was chilling East-West dialogues. The new challenges facing Thailand included the spread of communism, and anything giving rise to the discontent it fed upon: poverty, disease, ignorance and injustice.

One of the main political players of the day, General Phao Sriyanond, was cracking down on an alleged communist plot to subvert the monarchy. He claimed there were 2,000 Thai and 10,000 Chinese communists on the loose. The penalty for membership of the shadowy Communist Party of Thailand (CPT) was 10 years to life. When Pridi's wife, Thanpuying Poonsuk, surfaced in late 1952, she was arrested and kept in custody for 84 days. Alleged Chinese communists and other undesirables were deported to China in the early 1950s.

Communist broadcasts attacked "US imperialists and the Thai reactionary

Right Children outside the Ananta Samakhom Throne Hall with signs in English and Thai welcoming delegates to the first SEATO conference in Bangkok in February 1955.

Opposite Prince Wan Waithayakon at the United Nation General Assembly in New York in 1956

government", but it was all much more than a war of words. In September 1954, the Southeast Asia Treaty Organization (SEATO) was formed as an East-West anti-communist alliance. Signatories to the defence pact in Manila were Australia, France, New Zealand, Pakistan, the Philippines, Thailand, the UK and the US. SEATO was headquartered in Bangkok and its first meeting in February 1955 was chaired by Thailand's foreign minister, Prince Wan Waithayakon.[1]

The Bandung Conference in Indonesia in April that year was an important precursor to the Non-Aligned Movement of the 1960s. It was attended by 29 African and Asian countries and dedicated to ending racism and all manifestations of colonialism. Prince Wan was approached by China's courtly premier, Zhou Enlai, who wanted Thailand to recognise the young People's Republic of China. Prince Wan was unwilling to compromise Thailand's warming relations with the US and declined. Some years later, Thai playwright Suwat Woradilok and his wife were jailed upon their return from a tour of China with a cultural troupe of 48. Suwat had met with Pridi and coached Zhou in the *ramwong*, the great dance of friendship in Thailand and much of the region.

"The United States feels that no matter what happens, Thailand's King Bhumibol Adulyadej can unify the country," *The New York Times* reported at about this time as the US continued to bolster relations in sometimes creative ways. "The United States has helped distribute hundreds of thousand of coloured pictures of the king throughout the country. Rumours race across Bangkok, where the king and queen live, like brush fire. At times, it appears that an open battle is about to break out between police and the army. Then the crisis passes."

In 1958, the US pushed the 140-km Friendship Highway into Isan, the kingdom's neglected and undeveloped Northeast. Thailand was no mere passive aid recipient, however. The first of 10,000 Thai troops were deployed to the Korean peninsular against communist forces in 1947, and 91 were killed in battle. King Bhumibol presided at many of the cremations for the fallen. In his public addresses, the king increasingly mentioned the overarching concern for national security—and the need for vigilance against the communist threat at home and abroad.

In March 1962, Thai foreign minister Thanat Khoman issued a joint statement with Dean Rusk, his counterpart in Washington, committing the US to support Thailand in the event of communist attack, both direct and indirect, on the basis of the SEATO Southeast Asia Collective Defence Treaty and bilateral arrangements.

"The Secretary of State reaffirmed that the United States regards the preservation of the independence and integrity of Thailand as vital to the national interest of the United States and to world peace," read the joint statement. "[Secretary Rusk] expressed the firm intention of the United States to aid Thailand, its ally and historic friend, in resisting communist aggression and subversion."

Soon afterwards, the US request to station troops in Thailand was granted.

Footnote 1: The Southeast Asia Collective Defence Treaty, or the Manila Pact, is still in effect even though the Southeast Asia Treaty Organization (SEATO) no longer exists. Thailand therefore remains a treaty ally with the US. In recognition of the closeness of Thai-US security cooperation, the US designated Thailand a Major Non-NATO Ally (MNNA) in 2003.

Young Family

In the early 1950s, the population of Bangkok was approaching a million and average life expectancy was only a little over 50. Per capita income was less than US$100 per annum. *The New Yorker* described Bangkok's international airport as the most up to date in Southeast Asia, but its temples, canals, snake farm and neglected royal barges were only just giving first succour to a potentially promising tourism industry.

"The unique part of our visit was the chance it gave us to come to know His Majesty, to talk with him alone and feel his utter sincerity and determination to surmount his towering problems," recalled Sayre of his visit in 1953. Faced with so many contradictions, and rather than be distracted by devious and obstructive politicians, King Bhumibol looked around for things to do that were "within my rights" and benefited his people directly. His efforts to combat the great scourges of the day, particularly leprosy and tuberculosis, date from this period, as do many of the foundations he created as operating bases for his philanthropy and development work.

Effectively confined to Bangkok and Hua Hin, the king reached out to his people in different ways. People were astonished one day to find their young king mingling with the crowd around the equestrian statue of King Chulalongkorn at the Royal Plaza. In 1952, he built a road with help from the Border Patrol Police and the Highways

Department to Huai Mongkol Village in Prachuap Khiri Khan province. In September, he started broadcasting jazz and classical music for an hour late each morning on Radio Aw Saw—the initials in Thai for Ambara Mansion. The initials would also provide the name for King Bhumibol's Aw Saw Band, which succeeded his first jazz ensemble band in Thailand, the Lay Kram Band. In English, this was the Antiquity Band—an allusion to those of its musicians already well advanced in age.

King Bhumibol supported erection of another statue in Thon Buri honouring an earlier monarch, King Taksin, who ruled for 14 years before the founding of the Royal House of Chakri in 1782. King Taksin was the first to rally Siamese forces against the invading Burmese after the sacking of the old capital at Ayudhya.

"Let this be a memorial for the present and the future, to give us the heart and the strength to defend and maintain the liberty regained for us by King Taksin," King Bhumibol declared at its opening in 1954, touching as always on the themes of national security, inclusiveness, cohesion and sovereignty.

One of the king's first forays into development work was fish breeding. Later, King Bhumibol's home at the Chitralada Villa of Dusit Palace would have an arboretum planted by forestry experts from Kasetsart University. The palace also hosted a rice cultivation project and a pioneering dairy farm. In 1961, the king was pictured in the palace's extensive grounds experimenting with a small "iron buffalo" tractor.

If there was any upside to King Bhumibol being denied a more clearly defined role as head of state during his early years back in Thailand, it was being able to devote himself to his young family while he adjusted to a country that was in many ways quite foreign to him.

On 28 July 1952, Prince Vajiralongkorn was born. A brother for Princess Ubol Ratana, born a year earlier on 5 April, this was the most significant male birth to a ruling king in the Royal House of Chakri since the birth of Prince Prajadhipok in 1893. Escorted by Princess Galyani, the princess mother flew back from Switzerland in time for the birth. She received a big welcome at the airport for her first visit since her departure after the tragic event of June 1946. In an ancient ceremony, King Bhumibol trimmed a lock of his three-month-old son's hair. Prince Vajiralongkorn's full name runs to almost 70 words, and took over a month to compose.

The family would be completed with the birth of two more daughters: Princess Sirindhorn Debaratanasuda on 2 April 1955, and Princess Chulabhorn Valayalaksana on 4 July 1957. In late October that year, the royal family took up permanent residence at the Chitralada Villa of Dusit Palace. In 1958, the Chitralada School was opened, primarily for the four young children. Princess Ubol Ratana was already seven and would complete her education in the US. Her brother, Prince Vajiralongkorn, was six and would go on to school in England and Australia. The two younger princesses were only three and one at the time, and when their turn came would be educated entirely in Thailand. The Chitralada School accepted children from all walks of life, including some foreigners.

Opposite *King Bhumibol and Queen Sirikit with their four young children in the late 1950s. The oldest, Princess Ubol Ratana, is sitting next to her father with her hand resting on his knee. Prince Vajiralongkorn is sitting in front with Princess Sirindhorn alongside him. The youngest sibling, Princess Chulabhorn, is standing with her mother.*

Above *King Bhumibol trims a lock of hair from Prince Vajiralongkorn, his son of three months, in 1953.*

Rites of Passage

Queen Savang Vadhana, the king's grandmother, died at the end of 1955 at the remarkable age of 93 and was cremated the following year. In October 1956, having pardoned 3,000 prisoners, King Bhumibol performed an important rite of passage for Thai men by entering the Buddhist monkhood for 15 days. During this time, Queen Sirikit was appointed regent, which permanently elevated her title.

"I have always entertained the idea of being ordained as a monk under the great religion and in accordance with royal custom," the king said at the time of his ordination. "Buddhism comprises teachings to lead men to good conduct and is rich in precepts which are logical, highly impressive and inspiring."

King Bhumibol was ordained Bhumibalo Bhikku in the Chapel Royal, the Temple of the Emerald Buddha, donning saffron robes presented by the princess mother. He moved to Wat Bovornives and occupied the same quarters his great-grandfather Prince Mongkut had lived in for 27 years before he became king. During this time, Bhumibalo Bhikku made morning alms rounds, walking the streets barefoot and receiving offerings from ordinary people. He was just one among many thousands of monks performing the same simple, age-old ritual in the capital.

As King Bhumibol once more—Strength of the Land, Incomparable Power—the former Bhumibalo Bhikku continued to practise meditation and listen regularly to recorded sermons by the most respected monks of the day. He regularly met with Phra Yanasangvara, the abbot who guided him at Wat Bovornives and later became supreme patriarch, for *dhamma* studies.

The venerable monk introduced the king to *vipassana,* a form of meditation which brings the practitioner to a clearer understanding of reality and liberation from attachment and thus from suffering. The practice requires disciplined focus on physical sensations, such as breathing, walking or speaking a particular phrase, to explore the connection between mind and body. By carefully observing the connection, the practitioner gains deeper awareness of physical and mental processes, greater self-control, insights into the nature of reality and a feeling of peace.

Just weeks after King Bhumibol's time in the monkhood, Benny Goodman, the "king of jazz", and his band arrived in town and "played the palace" three times with King Bhumibol always sitting in. It was a dramatic change of roles, and a remarkable shift from an ancient world to a contemporary one. "He is simply the coolest king in the land," jazz great Lionel Hampton once observed.

"His Majesty had apparently been waiting for this trip with saxophone at the ready," the *Saturday Review* reported of Goodman's visit. "Some of the most beautiful women in the world danced with generals, admirals, and other high court officials. The queen herself, who could rival Her Serene Highness Princess Grace, happily danced to kingly sax choruses, weaving in and out of warm blowing by the Goodman band."

Goodman presented King Bhumibol with a clarinet but the king of jazz failed to

Opposite top *Prince Vajiralongkorn venerates Bhumibalo Bhikku, as his father King Bhumibol was known during the 15 days he spent in the Buddhist monkhood in 1956.*

Opposite bottom *King Bhumibol made daily alms rounds in the early mornings just like any other monk in Thailand during his time at Wat Bovornives.*

Above *Queen Savang Vadhana, the second queen of King Chulalongkorn, died in 1955 at the age of 93.*

respond to a last royal command for an encore. In good humour, the king of Thailand played "Memories of You" on the new clarinet. "Diplomats present commented that there could be no better way of cementing friendly relations with King Bhumibol Adulyadej than for Benny to stay indefinitely," reported the *Saturday Review*.

Beyond Bangkok

In the early 1950s, Pibul had paid a 10-day visit to Isan, the neglected Northeast, and made various promises about development to the impoverished region that lacked power, piped water and other infrastructure. It was ripe for communist infiltration with the Pathet Lao just across the mighty Mekong river in Laos supported by the North Vietnamese. For his part, King Bhumibol was by now able to spread his wings a little beyond Bangkok and Hua Hin and made visits in the Central Plains to Suphan Buri, Ang Thong and Sing Buri provinces.

As *phra chao phaen din*, Lord of the Land, it was not until late 1955 that he visited Isan—becoming the first Chakri king to do so. The king and queen made a 19-day tour of the region, visiting 14 provinces and travelling over 2,000 km by road and rail. After that initial warm welcome, King Bhumibol made a return visit in 1958, the first of many. He visited southern Thailand for the first time in 1959. In the years to come, the king would spend more time upcountry than in Bangkok, visiting all of the kingdom's 70 plus provinces and residing in specially constructed upcountry residences.

To nobody's great surprise, investigation of a vaguely rumoured plot to assassinate King Bhumibol in Nong Khai province during his first visit to the Northeast turned up nothing. The welcome rolled out for the king by the local people was warm and heartfelt. This gave Pibul serious pause for thought as he continued to lose the unspoken popularity tug of war with the young monarch. Earlier that year, Pibul returned from a nine-week, 22-capital world tour that had taken him through Asia, the US, Europe and Africa. The Thai prime minister had been personally received by President Dwight D. Eisenhower for dinner and golf, and addressed the US Congress.

The trip planted ideas in Pibul's head that would contribute to public discontent and his downfall. In July, Pibul pledged to stamp out the lucrative opium trade, which oiled the palms of some powerful political figures at the time. The following month, he promulgated the Political Parties Bill to open the way to multiparty elections. Part of Sanam Luang was designated as a Hyde Park Corner area for people to come and air their views and grievances—an invitation to disaster as it turned out. Thailand's Hyde Park was closed in February 1956 after protests against the 51-percent appointed National Assembly got out of hand. There were arrests and protests scrawled in blood outside the prime minister's home.

The 51-percent rule meant that Pibul's position should have been secure, but the general election in February 1957 did not go well for him. It returned a weak coalition

Below Pote Sarasin briefly served as prime minister following an election in the wake of the 1957 coup that forced Pibul and some of his key supporters to choose to move abroad permanently.

Opposite A Bangkok traffic jam in the 1950s.

led by the Seri Manangkasila Party of General Phao Sriyanond. Free elections were promised for 1962—once people were "better educated" in the ways of democracy. There was uproar. Protesters, including students from Chulalongkorn University, cited widespread fraud and demanded a fresh ballot. By March when King Bhumibol opened parliament, a state of emergency was in force. General Sarit Thanarat had already resigned from the government to put some open water between himself and Pibul's sinking ship. The prime minister's legendary charmed existence was deserting him.

In May, the 2,500th anniversary of Buddhism was marked with major celebrations organised by the government, including a ceremony at Sanam Luang. King Bhumibol, who had pardoned 10,000 prisoners for this very special occasion, presided instead over another ceremony at Phutthamonthon, casting images of the Buddha. The king also did not appear for the first royal barge procession since the 1932 revolution as he was unwell. In addition, the grand spectacle, staged along the Chao Phraya river, did not include the traditional presentation of *kathin* robes to monks. Therefore, the monarch's presence was not required.

By September, 60 MPs had defected and Phao had resigned. Pibul was unable to present any way forward when summoned for an audience with King Bhumibol. Sarit stepped in bloodlessly on 17 September. Two days after his effortless coup, a royal decree was issued dissolving parliament and setting elections for three months later.

"The coup had nothing to do with the king but with the deep rivalry between Phao and Sarit," says Suchit. "It was a rivalry in terms of almost everything—politically, economically, even the opium trade." A broken man, Pibul headed off in his Ford Thunderbird for the Cambodian border, while Phao, his wife and some key aides climbed aboard a plane to Switzerland. Both once immensely powerful men would

die in exile, Phao in 1960 from a heart attack at the age of only 52. After Cambodia, Pibul went to the US and India, where he became a monk at Bodhgaya in northeastern India. He died in Japan on 11 June 1964 at 67, having sent a cryptic message to Pridi, his erstwhile nemesis living in China, asking for forgiveness.

Sarit's party won the election and Pote Sarasin briefly served as prime minister, followed three months later by Field Marshal Thanom Kittikachorn for the first time. In October the following year, Sarit finally became prime minister himself in the face of what he said was a mounting communist threat. His Revolutionary Party was quite unlike the revolutionary Promoters of 1932 who had been educated overseas. The key political players surrounding Sarit were military officers who undoubtedly coveted power—but were not in any way anti-monarchists.

"The fact that Sarit, Thanom and [Field Marshal Praphas Charusathien] came from a different generation from Pibul, and that they were educated and trained entirely in Thailand, made it easier for them to make accommodations with the throne," noted political scientist Thak Chaloemtiarana in 1974. "These leaders were not identified as anti-royalists, and had not participated in the overthrow of the monarchy. They were not directly influenced by Western liberalism and their political experience was very parochial. The king still had an aura of sacredness and purity to this elite and its relationship with the throne reflected this."

Indeed, Sarit openly proclaimed deep respect for King Bhumibol on numerous occasions: "The love and enthusiasm for you does not merely exist within the country," the field marshal declared. "Foreigners also praise your impeccable personality. Diplomats and foreign dignitaries who have had the opportunity to meet you have spread your fame. It has become internationally well known that Thailand is lucky to have a king worthy of worship."

The monarchy's prestige and trappings enjoyed a genuine renaissance on Sarit's watch. The Royal Ploughing Ceremony, which harked back to the Ayudhya era, was permanently restored in May 1960. It had been discontinued in 1936 but was briefly revived by Pibul in 1947 as part of his cultural revitalisation programme. Since 1962, the rice grains used in the ceremony at Sanam Luang have always been supplied from the experimental plots around Chitralada Villa. The Royal Kathin Ceremony was revived having been also discontinued in the 1930s, and the royal barges were repaired. Celebration of 24 June, the day of the 1932 revolution, as National Day was stopped. The trooping of the colours at the Royal Plaza, when troops swear their renewed allegiance to the throne, was instituted as a major display of military pomp on the eve of King Bhumibol's birthday in 1959. In a sign of the changing times and new official sensitivities, a local newspaper, *Siang Angthong,* was closed for a week for inappropriate positioning of a picture of Queen Sirikit. It augured much tighter control of the media in royal coverage and this has endured through the intervening decades.

After the 1957 coup which dispatched Pibul, *The New York Times* took stock of Thailand's new strongman: "Sarit Thanarat certainly lacks the supple temperament and easy manners that usually characterize political leaders. He is brusque, sparing of speech and sometimes crotchety. He says he is not comfortable in the social situations that accompany official positions."

Although Pibul and Phao had been allowed to go into self-exile, Sarit could be ruthless. Public executions of suspected arsonists and communists won plaudits from those who believed a strongman was needed for good social order. Even in the 21st century there remains nostalgia in parts of Thai society for Sarit-style direct action, particularly when it comes to tackling societal woes such as drugs. Sarit had strong views on most things. He regarded the twist, the latest Western dance craze, as decadent, but he had some lifestyle issues of his own. A heavy drinker in his day, Sarit was in poor health throughout his premiership. In early 1958, he underwent surgery in the US for liver problems that would eventually cause his death from cirrhosis in 1963. His diet in his latter years was reported to be rich in orange juice and nuts. After his death, more than a hundred self-professed mistresses and minor wives emerged from the woodwork to lay claim to various parts of his estate. Most of this wealth, however, turned out to have been funded from the public purse and had to be recovered. King Bhumibol and Queen Sirikit visited Sarit on his deathbed, and Sarit clasped the king's hand to his head. He was the only Thai prime minister to die in office and a state of national mourning was declared after his passing. As befitted his status, Sarit's elaborate funeral rites were royally sponsored.

Diplomatic Triumphs

Sarit always wanted international recognition for Thailand, and more specifically US support for counter insurgency and development. He personally lobbied President Eisenhower in mid-1958 when John Foster Dulles, a leading Cold War warrior, was secretary of state. The US gave US$20 million in aid for defence and development that year alone. US-built airbases opened in Korat, Ubon Ratchathani and Udon Thani provinces in early 1960.

Sarit travelled widely in Thailand but lacked the time, interest and cosmopolitan experience for international diplomacy. On the other hand, Thailand's young multilingual, polymath monarch could perform this role better than anyone in the kingdom. During one of his first state visits—to South Vietnam in late 1959—King Bhumibol spoke French when the occasion permitted. Later, he would speak English to Australians, Americans and Britons, and German to Austrians and Germans.

Visits to South Vietnam, Burma and Indonesia in 1959 and 1960 enjoyed such success that more ambitious tours were planned further afield. During Sarit's five-year tenure, King Bhumibol and Queen Sirikit visited 23 countries, 10 of which belonged to the exclusive club of monarchies. In 1960, when they visited the US and 15 other countries, the royal couple were abroad for more than six months. Their travels were strenuous and time consuming, and often separated the king and queen from their young children for extended periods.

"Sometimes we had to leave our residence by eight o'clock in the morning by plane or car," Queen Sirikit later recalled. "The whole month through [in the US], we were nearly never back at our residence before midnight or one o'clock in the morning." As they travelled, King Bhumibol was constantly polishing his speeches and preparing to meet people ranging from fellow heads of state to Thai students studying abroad. He travelled as the personification of the Thai nation, representing his people even on occasions when he felt unwell.

"I learnt another important lesson for visiting other places with the king: that I could not become sick when I went on an official visit to another country," Queen Sirikit wrote. The hard work that went into the itineraries overseas had its rewards. The royal journeys sparked enormous international interest and raised Thailand's profile as never before. King Bhumibol, for his part, seemed perfectly at home abroad—wherever he happened to be. "I was born here in this country, so I can say that the United States is half my motherland," King Bhumibol informed President Eisenhower when he arrived at Washington Airport in 1960. "This visit is somewhat of a sentimental journey."

In the days that followed, the young king of Thailand and the elderly president of the US got on well and exchanged recipes for ice cream and noodles. Much more serious ideas which shone a light on King Bhumibol's and the government's concerns and thinking were also raised on occasions when vacuous pleasantries could so easily have been the order of the day.

"American assistance is to enable the Thai to achieve their objectives *through their own efforts*," King Bhumibol said in his address to the US Congress on 29 June. "I need hardly say that this concept has our complete endorsement. Indeed, there is a precept of the Lord Buddha which says: 'Thou art thy own refuge.' We are grateful for American aid; but we intend one day to do without it."

As his father Prince Mahidol had done with *The New York Times* 44 years earlier, King Bhumibol sang the praises of selfless American missionaries "who shared with our people the benefits of modern medicine and the knowledge of modern science".

"In giving generously to foreign countries, the United States is, in my Thai eyes, applying the old concept of family obligations upon the largest scale," King Bhumibol told a special joint session of Congress. "When a country feels reasonably confident of its own security, it can devote more attention to economic development. As you are all aware, my country is classified as under-developed. The average income of a Thai is only about $100 a year. You will understand what great urgent need there is to increase the income and raise the living standard of my people."

In July 1960, King Bhumibol gently alluded to his father once more—and also to the great importance of education—in his address at a banquet given in his honour in London by Queen Elizabeth. "In my country, the British character has been very much admired," he said. "The sense of fair play, the sporting instinct and the unwavering fortitude—these are the qualities that attract and inspire. For this reason, my grandfather, King Chulalongkorn chose England as the first country to send the first group of Thai

Opposite *King Bhumibol and Queen Sirikit with President Sukarno during their visit to Indonesia in 1960.*

Above *King Bhumibol makes his historic address to a special joint session of the US Congress during his state visit.*

Opposite page clockwise from top *King Bhumibol and Queen Sirikit appear on a talk show during their state visit to the US in 1960; the king in Norway, 1960; heavy press interest in the royal couple coverage in the US, 1960; the king and queen during their visit to the Vatican, 1960.*

Top *King Bhumibol visits La Garde Républicaine in Paris to review a French honour guard.*

Above *The Thai royal couple in the Philippines, 1960.*

Left *Queen Sirikit performs a traditional Thai dance in Burma, 1963.*

Above A portrait of Queen Sirikit taken by King Bhumibol as she looks out from an aircraft window during a lengthy series of state visits to Europe and the US in 1960.

Opposite top A crowd in Japan strains politely for a view of the Thai royal couple during their visit in 1963.

Opposite bottom In 1962, King Bhumibol and Queen Sirikit resumed their foreign travels with a tour of Asia, Australia and New Zealand—where a particularly friendly sign depicting a kiwi and an elephant greeted their arrival.

students for study abroad. His choice was fully justified. These students distinguished themselves in their various fields of study. They made valuable contributions to the modernization, progress and advancement of their country."

There were much lighter moments during the royal travels. In the US, there were visits to Hollywood, and encounters with Walt Disney and Elvis Presley and a ticker tape welcome in New York. King Bhumibol also returned to Greater Boston, his place of birth and first home. He honoured the doctor who delivered him, his "first friend", and the four American nurses who cared for him. "He was a very good baby indeed," recalled Dr W. Stewart Whittemore. "His mother was a wonderful patient. She never complained." The *Boston Globe* reported: "The king noted that he had been termed 'a nice baby,' and 'I hope I have grown into something nice'."

"[King Bhumibol] had his audience laughing when he ended a sentence with 'etc., etc., etc.,' as did his ancestor—the king in *The King and I*," reported *The Washington Post* after a remarkably informal meeting with American reporters. "It was totally unexpected because King Bhumibol has refused to let *The King and I* be shown in his country. It is not a true picture of his ancestor, he says." The American reporter had got it wrong. The frivolous Hollywood musical had indeed been banned in Thailand in 1956—but not by King Bhumibol. The ban was announced by Prime Minister Pibul, who sometimes also served as minister of culture. The king spoke of the historically flawed musical in an address to the Motion Picture Association of America, noting that it "might have brought about a serious incident between our two countries".

"The Thai people have always shown a great reverence to their kings and take it badly if one of their kings is depicted in a comedy," King Bhumibol explained. "Having seen the film myself, I personally regard it as very entertaining and magnificent, and might have recommended it, had I not known the true historical facts and the sentiments of my people. The film, however, has done considerable service to my country. It has been a great piece of public relations for us."

King Bhumibol won plaudits for his wisdom and wit. He delivered more than 60 formal speeches during his first visit to the US in 1960, and numerous impromptu talks. On his visits to the US and Canada in 1967, he gave 38 speeches in a one-month period in Thai, English and French. The royal journeys in the 1960s were far removed from pleasure trips, and involved long journeys to distant places with sometimes inhospitable climates. They nevertheless raised Thailand's international profile immeasurably—and literally turned heads. Queen Sirikit quickly became a fashion icon, and was regularly ranked among the world's best dressed women.

"Women in the crowd cried out at the sight of the queen's ankle-length, slim fitting gown of orchid pink Thai silk shot with gold thread, caught at the waist by a wide gold and diamond studded belt finished with a huge diamond clip," reported an Australian journalist in early 1962. The ravishing mother of four was a constant presence at her busy husband's side, and the world was in awe of her beauty, poise and remarkable fashion sense. Queen Sirikit was a dazzling magnet to the world's media,

whether dressed in Western *haute couture* by Pierre Balmain and other leading designers of the day, or breathing fresh life into traditional attire made from sumptuous Thai silks in tropical shades. Newspaper columnists bled ink on one of the world's most beautiful women and magazines with her radiant smile on the cover sold out.

The royal diplomatic successes included a visit in 1963 by General Ne Win. The new Burmese leader, who had taken power in Rangoon in 1962, lamented past tensions between the two countries. "Our forefathers had warred against one another for no other purpose than to enhance their prestige through military conquest," said the general ruefully. He later thanked his host for lavish hospitality "such as could be expected only from one's closest relative". It was extraordinary praise from the leader of a country that had been one of Siam's greatest historical foes.

In a wider context, Thailand's foreign minister at the time, Thanat Khoman, believed King Bhumibol's diplomatic initiatives in the early 1960s—particularly his first return visit to the US—were vital to the national wellbeing. "The underlying objective of His Majesty's state visit was to make Thailand known internationally and to seek Western support in countering the spread of communism that was a threat to our national security," Thanat later recalled. "More than any other period in the past, His Majesty's state visits have earned our Thailand overwhelming international recognition and acknowledgement. His were not sightseeing excursions, but working trips as crucial to the country's survival as was countering the colonial threat that Thailand faced during the reign of King [Chulalongkorn] ... As a result of His Majesty's diplomatic efforts, Thailand was able to embark on significant initiatives in the arena of foreign affairs which included its role in helping to establish ASEAN [the Association of Southeast Asian Nations]."

THE PEOPLE'S KING

In his mid 30s, Thailand's monarch was in his prime—a picture of vigour and health who brought a confident and optimistic touch to his many interests. With his young family growing up, the 1960s were a time of hard work—and also of personal fulfilment. King Bhumibol's national development initiatives continued to gain momentum, and a number of foundations were established at this time. In 1966, the Bureau of the Royal Household was reorganised into 10 divisions in response to its growing and more diverse needs. The king's sporting and cultural accomplishments meanwhile won genuine admiration at home and abroad.

All this took place against the backdrop of the Cold War and its ideological clashes. As the Vietnam War escalated, the American military presence in Thailand grew dramatically to support the kingdom as a bulwark against the spread of communism—the very antithesis of monarchy. One of the more striking photographs from this time shows Queen Sirikit at a practice range behind sandbags, casually dressed with her hair tied up, firing a rifle. Next to her is King Bhumibol in military attire.

During frequent visits upcountry, the king generally wore military fatigues with a soft cap. The rugged garb, with slotted canvas belt and numerous pockets, was eminently practical for his war on underdevelopment. A foreign correspondent observed at the time: "He often appears solemn and melancholic in public. But outside Bangkok he appears relaxed and at ease, and those who know him say that, while of a serious nature, he is in fact far from sad." Wherever he went, the king projected order and purpose. On his carefully planned forays into the Thai hinterland, he carried detailed maps that he taped together himself in advance and carefully annotated.

"When he made a personal trip in casual wear, a small row of sharpened pencils were usually tucked inside his shirt pocket," wrote Police General Vasit Dejkunjorn, a former chief of the royal court police, in his personal memoir, *In His Majesty's Footsteps.* "He preferred to do things himself. Sharpening pencils was one of them." In private, members of his Aw Saw Friday Band saw him clean and care for his own instruments.

He also handled his own communications. "Another indispensable item for the king and a candidate for additional royal regalia was a radio receiver," noted Vasit.

Although Queen Sirikit would continue to make regular trips abroad in the coming decades, the couple's state and official visits with large retinues were coming to an end. The king and queen made their last state visit in Asia to the Philippines in July 1963. The following year they went to Austria, which they revisited in 1966 along with West Germany. In 1967, they toured Iran, the US and finally Canada for a three-day state visit. Since then, King Bhumibol has spent only one night outside Thailand, and that was during a brief state visit to neighbouring Laos in 1994.

Not long before his final visit to the US, King Bhumibol reminded his people of the threat posed by communism. "The opposite side has revealed its intention that Thailand is to be the next target of aggression," he said in a New Year's address. "A very great danger might reach us any day. None of you must be put off your guard." At the Metropolitan Museum of Modern Art, the king addressed the cream of New York society at a reception held in his honour: "The Thai people are a fighting people. We have kept our liberty and independence for hundreds of years. We are not militant. We just have to fight to keep the most essential thing for a man. And that is freedom."

King Bhumibol was received at the White House by Lyndon Baines Johnson, the president who escalated US involvement in the Vietnam War at great cost to his political career. Johnson himself had visited Thailand the previous year as Thai–US relations intensified. Guests at the banquet in Washington included actor John Wayne

Opposite King Bhumibol talks to a hill tribesman on Doi Pui, Chiang Mai province, in 1969.

Above King Bhumibol and Queen Sirikit found themselves the centre of attention wherever they ventured around the kingdom.

and jazz greats Duke Ellington and Stan Getz. The backdrop to the visit, however, was far removed from show business. Addressing increasing domestic discontent with the US-led war in Vietnam, King Bhumibol criticised the US anti-war lobby as "a kind of war of brainwashing". He called for proper moral support for the forces deployed, which included Thai personnel. "A soldier fighting wants support from the home front," he told reporters. "This is sapping his efforts and it is not very nice for him."

King Bhumibol could be forthright in his anti-communist views. "Communism is impractical," he said in an interview with *Look* magazine. "Life is not each to his needs. The one who works today should get the money and the goods, not the one who doesn't work. Communism can be worse than the Nazis or the Fascists. In practice, it is more terrible than a dictatorship. If, however, a dictator is a good man, he can do many good things for the people. For a short while, Mussolini did many good things for the Italian people. But once he was bitten by the 'bug of empire', he was finished."

Staying Home

King Bhumibol and Queen Sirikit were changing the face of royal diplomacy, and in the process putting Thailand firmly on the VIP world map. Among the first guests they received were the Danish royal couple, King Frederik IX and Queen Ingrid, at the newly built Bhubing Palace in Chiang Mai. The visit reflected the warm historic ties between the Thai and Danish royal families. In early 1968, Mohammad Reza Shah Pahlavi and Empress Farah, who the year before had received King Bhumibol and Queen Sirikit at Tehran's Golestan Palace, paid a state visit. At the end of the year, Japan's Crown Prince Akihito arrived for the first time with Princess Michiko. President Richard Nixon visited in 1969, as did the crew of Apollo 11, and Vice President Spiro Agnew the following year. The king continued to host at least two state visits a year until the late 1990s, and to receive the broadening stream of royalty and notables who made their way to Thailand for both public and private visits.

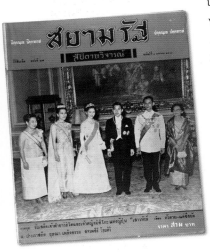

The curtailment of his foreign travel did not result in King Bhumibol spending more time in Bangkok. "If the country is faced with difficulties and people in the remote areas are suffering, we cannot simply stay put in this paradise of a capital," he remarked not long after returning home permanently—alluding to at least one reason he no longer considered lengthy foreign absences appropriate. Instead, King Bhumibol travelled more widely in his kingdom than any other Thai king—not just in the Chakri dynasty but in all of Siamese history. His great-grandfather, King Mongkut, had made pilgrimages to various parts of Siam during his 27 years as a monk, but his journeys did not compare to what was possible in the modern age of road, rail and air travel. King Bhumibol's extensive and intimate knowledge of the entire country, and his focus on the development of some of its most neglected areas, are hallmarks of the reign.

The royal family was spending at least eight months of the year outside the capital in one of a growing number of provincial residences that supplemented Klai Kangwol, in Hua Hin. The royal villas are technically palaces, but were designed as practical working bases. Bhubing Palace in Chiang Mai province in the North was built in 1959. Thaksin Ratchaniwet Palace in Narathiwat province in the South was first used in 1973, and Bhuban Palace in Sakon Nakhon province in the Northeast the following year.

The southern palace in Narathiwat is at the foot of Khao Tanyong overlooking the sea, and is unusual for its location beside a Muslim graveyard. Locals have special access rights through the palace grounds. The locations of the other provincial palaces were also elevated, and not in especially prosperous or secure areas. They served as departure points for trips to often remote and underdeveloped tracts, where government officials seldom ventured.

The intrepid nature of some of these journeys fostered close relationships between the palace and the military and Border Patrol Police (BPP). In 1972, a time of heightened communist insurgency, King Bhumibol established with military support the Romklao schools in areas where teachers were fearful to work due to communist insurgents, particularly in the Northeast. Later, government teachers were able to take up positions in frontier areas where most students were from migrant hill tribes. This project was regularly expanded with the involvement of the princess mother, and later Princess Sirindhorn. While children in remote areas gained an education, the initiative improved relations between security forces and villagers. The king also set up special schools for poor students and the children of soldiers wounded in clashes with insurgents.

A key objective of such projects was equipping people to help themselves. Formal classroom education was often not an option for the disadvantaged. Not long after the Romklao schools were launched, the king established the Phra Dabos schools to provide vocational training to those denied proper schooling by circumstance. "He wants every Thai to have the chance to study," Princess Sirindhorn later explained. "His Majesty said that the concept of the Phra Dabos project is like that of hermits, or Phra Dabos, in folk stories. In the old days, anybody seeking knowledge would go into the woods to stay with the Phra Dabos, serve them and learn from them."

With King Bhumibol's development efforts taking him to remote parts of the country, it was never possible to guarantee complete security. "In certain areas, the [communist] insurgents had so well infiltrated the populations that it was hard to separate friends from enemies. So, every travel to the red or even the "pink"—semi-infiltrated—areas gave me and other security officers huge worries," recalled Vasit Dejkunjorn, who joined the royal security detail in the late 1960s.

The police general sometimes found himself at loggerheads with Prince Bhisatej Rajani, who was in charge of hill tribe development projects in the remote North. On one occasion, Vasit was irritated by the prince taking the king miles on foot to see

Opposite *This early January 1965 issue of Siam Rath Weekly features on its cover the visit by Crown Prince Akihito and Princess Michiko of Japan, centre. They are hosted by King Bhumibol and Queen Sirikit, who are joined by Dowager Queen Rambhai Barni, left, and the princess mother, right.*

Above *Provincial royal residences are technically palaces but they served as working bases. They included, from top, Bhubing Palace in Chiang Mai province; Klai Klangwol Palace in Hua Hin, Prachuab Khiri Khan province; and Thaksin Ratchaniwet Palace in Narathiwat province.*

a single coffee tree planted in a field previously used for opium cultivation. But King Bhumibol was satisfied with direct proof that coffee could be grown in the area. "I was reminded again [that] His Majesty's policy is not one of 'rushing development' but letting people learn by themselves at their own speed," wrote Vasit.

Journeys could be unpredictable and eventful. A crowd once enveloped the royal motorcade in Nakhon Sawan, a major town in the Central Plains. The convoy was brought to a standstill, creating a security nightmare. Unfazed, King Bhumibol and Queen Sirikit climbed out and mingled with a benign but curious crowd. Later in the far South, King Bhumibol, Queen Sirikit and Princess Sirindhorn were extracted by armoured car from a sensitive area near Ban To Mo after their vehicle became stuck in mud along a road construction project. At the time, officials were reporting regular bombings nearby by ethnic Chinese guerrillas from the Communist Party of Malaya.

Personal Pursuits

While there was plenty to be concerned about with the spreading war in Indochina and domestic communist insurgency, King Bhumibol still made time for his personal pursuits. In 1959, he had taken up painting once more, producing mainly small- to medium-sized oil on canvas paintings until 1967 when—just as his father Prince Mahidol had done in 1914—he stopped permanently. His output included 104 paintings in both realist and abstract styles, and featured a number of portraits of his favourite artistic muse, Queen Sirikit. King Bhumibol consulted with many of the leading Thai artists of the day, including Fua Hariphitak and Uab Sanasen, and held occasional painting salons at the palace. Some saw his abstracts as inspired by Edward Munch and Oskar Kokoschka. Seven of the king's paintings were displayed at the 15th National Art Exhibition in 1964, with regular showings thereafter. In an interview published in *Geo* magazine, the king, looking at some of his canvases said, "This is called 'Subversion'—there is greed, anger and evil … I painted it with a knitting needle. And this is called 'Red Hand'. I did it once when I had a fever from pneumonia … Every artist has a feeling of being crammed in, and every artist wants to explode."

It is music, however, that has been King Bhumibol's abiding passion.

"His personality has so many different aspects, his work is so rigorous, and his responsibilities so arduous, that music is the time when he can put these cares away and relax with people who respect him—and whom he respects—as creative artists," commented one of his band members.

Professional musicians were also invited to play with the royal band. "It can be intimidating when you're about to start playing with the king," recalled Ading Dila, a saxophonist and well-known figure in Bangkok music circles who was a guest on occasions. "But once the music gets going, you forget about it."

Throughout the 1960s, King Bhumibol continued to make his own music, releasing 17 compositions before the end of the decade. The most ambitious work from this period—and arguably from his entire musical career—was the "Kinnaree Suite". It was written in four movements ("A Love Story", "Nature Waltz", "The Hunter" and "Kinnaree Waltz") for a balletic interpretation of "Manohra", a traditional dance-drama from southern Thailand. Fusing traditional Thai music and dance with Stravinsky-like impressionism, blues, ballet and modern dance, the production premiered at Bangkok's Red Cross Fair in 1962. Two years later, when the king and queen were visiting Austria, the Niederösterreich Tonkünstler Orchestra performed the suite along with other royal compositions including "Falling Rain" and "Love at Sundown". Two days later, King Bhumibol became the first honorary member from Asia to be inducted into Vienna's Academy for Music and Performing Arts. He was the 23rd musician to be included in the academy, joining some of the most renowned artists of the day, including Yehudi Menuhin and Pablo Casals.

On his 40th birthday, the king completed the English lyrics for his 41st song, "Echo". The four previous songs in the king's catalogue also included lyrics penned in English: "Still on My Mind", "Old Fashioned Melody", "No Moon" and "Dream Island". As with "Dream Island", the lyrics are romantic idylls that beckon softly:

> In a dream,
> I'm on a desert island,
> Waiting for you,
> Hoping you've not forgotten.

> How happy
> I would be to see you near.
> And how sorry
> If you don't appear.

Opposite King Bhumibol and his family dining informally at a camp in Chiang Mai province in 1964.

Below King Bhumibol playing piano at Chulalongkorn University.

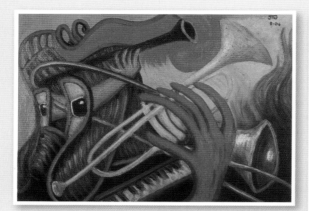

> *Like old times,*
> *We'd listen to the sea*
> *Which is like music*
> *Leading to ecstasy.*

> *Though knowing*
> *It is no use to be blue,*
> *I keep dreaming*
> *It may well come true.*

King Bhumibol's Aw Saw Friday Band was named after its end-of-week evening broadcasts. Pathorn Srikaranonda, the son of King Bhumibol's longtime musical collaborator Manrat Srikaranonda, first played with the band at the age of only 14. Pathorn recalls how the king compared the musical group to society. "He says everyone in the band has his own duty. The singer is not more important than the bass player or drummer … everyone is equally important in producing the music. Likewise, this applies to society at large. If everyone in society knows and performs their own duties, society will progress and be peaceful. There is no inferior or superior, whether in class or musicianship—music itself is king and nothing else matters."

"He is so humble about his playing that he doesn't want to be recorded or filmed," says Pathorn, explaining why recordings of King Bhumibol performing are quite rare. "Playing music with the band is something personal for him. We cooperate, and try to keep ourselves low profile as well."

In the 1970s, King Bhumibol produced only four compositions before essentially retiring for the next few decades. Three compositions reflected the instability of the

Opposite King Bhumibol produced over a hundred oil-on-canvas paintings before stopping altogether in 1967. They included, clockwise from top left, an untitled musical semi-abstract (1963); a portrait of Queen Sirikit (1963); an untitled and undated semi-abstract figure study; "Going to Market" (1961); and a portrait of the king's father, Prince Mahidol (1961).

Above King Bhumibol at his easel enjoying one of his favourite recreational activities in the 1960s.

period, and were composed to boost the morale of the military and other security forces: "Kwamfan An Sungsud" (The Noblest Dream), in 1971; "Rao Su" (We Fight) in 1973; and "We-Infantry 21" in 1976. The fourth piece mourned the passing of a member of the Aw Saw Friday Band.

Setting Sail

King Bhumibol's enthusiasm for sailing was ignited in his late 30s and early 40s, spurred at first by his construction of a half dozen dinghies with the assistance of Prince Bhisatej. "His Majesty learned how to build sailing boats before he really learned how to sail," recalls Prince Bhisatej. "He said he knew about carpentry because at school in Switzerland he went to classes, but he didn't know how to build boats," the prince recalls. "He was a very diligent woodworker and headed for the Chitralada Villa workshop whenever he had free time."

Prince Bhisatej remembers the king returning from official functions in regal attire and immediately changing into his carpentry clothes. The prince had constructed his own first dinghy in the car porch of his palace in Bangkok. Special glue was procured for local sawmills to turn out marine-grade plywood. The first boat the pair built at Chitralada Villa was based on a two-man Enterprise design and took five months to finish. Upon its completion the day after King Bhumibol's birthday in 1964, it was named *Rajpatan* (Royal Design). After manhandling the boat through the doorway, the craft was tested on a large pond near the Chitralada Villa where the royal elephants usually take afternoon bathes.

The king's first opportunity to participate in a sailing race presented itself a few months later during a visit by Britain's Prince Philip, the Duke of Edinburgh. Since the duke was a keen sailor, a race from the Royal Varuna Yacht Club in Pattaya to nearby Koh Lan was organised. Twenty-eight Enterprises and three smaller OK dinghies participated. Prince Philip helmed the *Tane Tai,* a boat belonging to a club member, while the king sailed *Rajpatan* with Prince Bhisatej crewing. "One or two of the other boats closed on us, but His Majesty kept them in our wind shadow, giving us some excitement. *Rajpatan* took line honours to the excitement of the queen and her guests waiting on the beach," Prince Bhisatej later wrote. Gracious in defeat, Prince Philip presented a catamaran to King Bhumibol, who named it *Pla Duk.* This means "catfish" in Thai—a clever play on words that refers to both the catamaran and the duke.

King Bhumibol's second self-built boat was an OK-class dinghy which he named *Vega*. The single-handed, 13-foot craft has a big sail area and a relatively sharp v-shaped ("hard chine") hull. With good wind, an OK dinghy demands plenty of strenuous "hiking out" by the helm to keep the boat moving forward without capsizing. Hiking out involves the sailor hanging out over the side with feet hooked beneath restraining straps. Strong winds and long distances make this tough on the legs and abdomen.

In April 1966, *Vega* was subjected to a formidable sea trial when King Bhumibol sailed it west to east across the Gulf of Thailand from Hua Hin in Prachuap Khiri Khan province to Sattahip in Chon Buri, the home port of the Royal Thai Navy. The weak breeze for much of the day was blamed on the good folk of Hua Hin petitioning the weather gods for the king's safe delivery from stormy weather. Early in the morning, the king set off from the beach in front of Klai Kangwol Palace accompanied by Prince Bhisatej and Prince Birabongse Bhanudej in separate dinghies.

With Queen Sirikit and Princess Ubol Ratana aboard HTMS *Chandra* shadowing their progress, the dinghies took 16 gruelling hours to reach Sattahip—a voyage of some 64 nautical miles. Many of the hours at sea were spent out of sight of land. Some years later, the Trans-Gulf Race was established along the course the king pioneered, but sailing east to west. The original wooden rudder from *Vega* became the race trophy for the renamed annual competition, the Vega Rudder Trophy Race.

Recalling one race in the early years, British sailor Jocelyn Waller said: "It was very windy that day, probably 20 to 25 knots of breeze. I sailed a two-man dinghy, and at one point in the middle of the gulf we were on the trapeze for five hours straight. We won by half an hour because the fleet had become completely dispersed in the conditions. Some sailors ended up almost in Prachuap [Khiri Khan], others way up the coast, well after dark, and the naval escort ships had trouble keeping all of them in sight. Luckily no one came to any harm but everyone realised it was a bit dangerous, the king himself most of all. At his request the course was changed so that it ran along

Opposite top King Bhumibol jams with the Aw Saw Band.

Opposite bottom The score from "Echo" for which the king also penned the English lyrics.

Below King Bhumibol at work at Chitralada Villa on one of a half dozen sailing dinghies he made personally.

the coast within sight of land." Added Waller: "The king loved going to Hua Hin, I think, not only because it was very private but because he could indulge in the two things he enjoyed doing most: playing music and going sailing."

Another British sailor, Peter Cummins, reminisced: "A day sailing with the king starts when he appears in the doorway of the palace adjoining the dinghy club's social room, dressed in shorts, shirt, barefoot, cap in hand, ready to go sailing. He would go sailing during the day and play music at night, and was happy to have others join in. There were always around 20 or 30 dinghies in the water, manned by friends, court people and naval protectors. The king loved to go what he called 'fox hunting'. We would launch off the beach, and whoever was appointed the fox would sail off with a head start. Everyone else would chase him, try to catch him, and you'd usually end up on some island somewhere. A picnic would be enjoyed, and it would be someone else's turn to be the fox."

King Bhumibol formed his Royal Chitralada Yacht Squadron to facilitate competitive sailing. Prince Bhisatej was one of his main racing rivals. Another, Prince Birabongse, was better known in the West as Prince Bira of Siam, or B. Bira, from his time as a world-class racing car driver in the 1930s and 1950s. Prince Bira sailed in the Melbourne, Rome, Tokyo and Munich Olympics. Dr Rachot Kanjanavanit, an engineer, was another Olympic-class sailor in the squadron.

The atmosphere in Hua Hin was always fun but sporting and keenly competitive. The king often lost his early races. "I became champion three times and after that the king took over," recalls Prince Bhisatej. "At the beginning, he didn't have much experience in sailing and racing. After the third year, the king began to win."

On one occasion, King Bhumibol was forced back to shore after colliding with Prince Bhisatej. To show there were no hard feelings, the king added Prince Bhisatej's name to the list of those due to receive the Order of Chula Chom Klao. "It was a week before the ceremony," recalls Prince Bhisatej. "Prince Dhani came to the king with the list of people who should receive the award. He said the reason my name came into his mind was that I rammed him. He should have given way, but he was too slow. I rammed him and he had to retire." Prince Dhani advised King Bhumibol that he felt the feisty sailor who had nearly sunk him was too young for such an elevated honour.

One of the highlights of King Bhumibol's sailing years was winning a joint gold medal with Princess Ubol Ratana in the OK dinghy class at the Fourth Southeast Asian Peninsular (SEAP) Games in 1967, just a few days after celebrating his 40th birthday. The royal family's interest in sailing undoubtedly spurred the Thai team to a clean sweep of golds in the sailing events in the waters off Pattaya.

"The Fourth SEAP Games were exceptional in three respects at least," noted one chronicle of what became the SEA Games. "Firstly the patron of the games, His Majesty the King, participated. Secondly, the president of the organising committee, Air Chief Marshal Dawee Chullasapya, also competed. Thirdly, they both won gold medals."

"His Majesty, sailing boat TH27, found his main rival in Princess Ubol Ratana in

TH18," the chronicle continued. "Both won three and came second in two of the six races scheduled for the OK class. His Majesty withdrew from the fifth race after apparently missing the second buoy marking the course. The error might have cost him a gold to himself, but not much grief for he ended up sharing the winner's rostrum with his daughter." The medals were presented in the National Stadium by Queen Sirikit on 16 December, which has since been celebrated as National Sports Day.

Open Gates

On 9 June 1971, King Bhumibol marked the 25th anniversary of his accession to the throne. He drove through the capital in an open-top limousine, inspected troops and received a 21-gun salute before making a national address. It was the first silver jubilee celebration in the Royal House of Chakri since King Chulalongkorn's in 1893.

The following year, on 28 December, the designation of an heir apparent was given ritual confirmation. In a magnificent and arcane ceremony in the Ananta Samakhom Throne Hall, the old parliament building overlooking the Royal Plaza, King Bhumibol poured lustral water over the head of his only son, Prince Vajiralongkorn, and invested him as crown prince at the auspicious moment of 23 minutes past midday. The heir apparent had come of age earlier in the year, and now had *Maha* (Great) added to his title. The anointing of a crown prince had not occurred for 77 years since the elevation

Opposite King Bhumibol, Prince Bhisatej and Princess Ubol Ratana on the beach with a clutch of sailing trophies.

Above left King Bhumibol sailing in Dong Tan bay, Satthahip, Chon Buri province, in November 1969.

Above right King Bhumibol with his oldest daughter, Princess Ubol Ratana, at the Fourth SEAP Games in 1967 when both won gold medals for sailing.

of the future King Vajiravudh. A glittering garden party was held that night.

There was much to talk about at the celebration. At nearly the same time as the investiture, the Israeli Embassy had been taken over by four terrorists belonging to the Black September group, who declared it Palestinian territory. In a remarkable piece of negotiation, Air Chief Marshal Dawee and Chatichai Choonhavan, the deputy foreign minister, offered themselves in place of the trapped Israeli diplomats and, after a 19-hour siege, flew with the Palestinians to Cairo.

Before being allowed to leave the country, the terrorists apologised for inadvertently choosing such an auspicious day for their terrorist action. They spoke by telephone from the embassy to a *Bangkok Post* journalist, who found them remarkably garrulous and apologetic. "We have told the government and the generals from the army that we are sorry," their contrite spokesman told the journalist. "We are most sorry we did not know this day. We love your king, he is very good and beautiful … I hope some of the Thai people will become Palestinian commandos like us." Israel's prime minister, Golda Meir, meanwhile praised the Thais for their exemplary diplomacy. "I want to thank the Thai government for its help, devotion and ability," she said.

For some time after his investiture, Crown Prince Maha Vajiralongkorn, remained the sole possible heir from King Bhumibol's immediate family. The crown prince was still single and had opted for a military career, attending Australia's Royal Military Academy at Duntroon in the mid-1970s. Back home in Thailand, he was a serving officer during a period of internal conflict. The situation of the crown prince being the sole male heir was partly addressed with a constitutional amendment in 1974 that allowed a princess to be eligible to accede to the throne.

The weight of King Bhumibol's official duties since his return from Switzerland in 1951 had steadily increased, and the trend steepened markedly as the 1960s progressed. A court circular kept from the mid 1950s to early 1970s divides the king's duties into about a dozen categories: government, military and private functions; audiences for the cabinet, bureaucrats, citizens, foreign dignitaries and royalty; traditional and private ceremonies; meetings with students and subjects; and visits abroad. During the 1950s, these activities totalled less than 200 each year. They nearly doubled in 1961, and by 1971 had almost tripled. Indeed, four years after the king's complete discontinuation of travel abroad, there were 596 royal events that had to be attended to in addition to his work in national development.

The greatest increases in the king's activities were recorded in his private sector functions—including weddings and funerals—which more than doubled to over 120; and in his audiences with ordinary citizens. These averaged about 50 per year in the first half of the 1960s, and surged to over 140 a year during the second half of the decade. At this time, the king's formal encounters with government officials remained fairly constant, but he also had at least two or three meetings each month with students and other non-official subjects he had not met with previously.

King Bhumibol was quite clearly keeping himself apart from the process of government, and making efforts to meet people from all levels of society in order to gain a diversity of perspectives. This sometimes left him critical of official policies. The land rights of the poor have always been a sensitive issue and he was concerned that new legislation criminalised people who had done nothing fundamentally wrong. In 1973, the king spoke out for people living in newly designated forest reserves:

"The law enforcers are more to blame than the people," King Bhumibol said. "The government earmarked the forests despite the fact that there are already people living in them. We employ the forest reserve law on the people who live in the originally unreserved forests. We just mark the maps and suddenly the forests become reserved areas. That's rather odd. Legally speaking, these villagers are violating the law which was legitimately made. But realistically speaking, who are the violators of the law? It's those who marked the maps—because the forest-dwelling people were there before the designation. They have human rights. It's a case of the government violating the people, not the people violating the law."

Many viewed King Bhumibol as sensitive and nimble in addressing such complex social problems at a local level. During the 1960s, there was a surge in donations to the king to disburse for religious, educational and medical purposes, disaster relief and anti-communist programmes. The monetary figures involved increased almost six-fold between 1963 and 1970, and were supplemented by considerable material donations. "Because of the increasing popularity and prestige of the throne, private citizens and organisations [made] sizeable contributions to charity and educational foundations established by the monarchy," noted political scientist Thak Chaloemtiarana.

Opposite top King Bhumibol and Queen Sirikit inspect an area in Chiang Mai following a serious blaze in early 1968.

Opposite bottom Emblem for the silver jubilee of King Bhumibol's accession in 1971.

Above King Bhumibol and Queen Sirikit take the salute during a special military parade along Ratchadamnoen Avenue for the silver jubilee of his accession to the throne.

King Bhumibol's efforts continued to earn him public affection. He was seen by many as more compassionate and engaged than the government. The political backdrop at this time was also darkening. The public was becoming discontented with the government of Field Marshal Thanom Kittikachorn and his deputy prime minister, Field Marshal Praphas Charusathien. The pair held power for almost a decade, and their government was widely considered moribund. As early as 1966, Thanom promised a new constitution for the following year, but it did not materialise. Good turnouts in local elections in 1967 suggested a popular thirst for greater political involvement. A boycott of Japanese goods in 1972 was meanwhile evidence of heightened student activism and growing political awareness.

By early 1973, one of the great watershed years in modern Thai politics, there was particular public frustration with the slow drafting of a new constitution by a committee headed by Praphas. Outrage against the government reached a turning point after a helicopter crash near Nakhon Pathom exposed the flagrant violation of Thungyai Naresuan Wildlife Sanctuary near the Burmese border in Kanchanaburi and Uthai Thani provinces. The crash revealed that some senior government officials and their friends had been shooting wildlife from the helicopter. The government's clumsy attempt at a cover-up only added fuel to the fire.

Students at Ramkhamhaeng University who produced a satirical magazine about the event and the government were expelled. More than 10,000 students demonstrated for their reinstatement, the removal of the university rector Sakdi Phasuknirand, and, for good measure, a new constitution within six months. Sakdi reluctantly stood down, but the tension continued in the ensuing months. The National Student Centre of Thailand (NSCT) announced it was independently drafting a new charter.

By early October, such student activism had spread well beyond Ramkhamhaeng and Thammasat universities to other campuses—and the youngsters were not alone. Even Thanom's own brother, Sa-nga Kittikachorn, a police major general, was openly critical. "If the demanding of the constitution is to be interpreted as treason, then there are probably 38 million traitors in Thailand at present," he declared, referring to the kingdom's population at the time.

After 13 students involved in drafting the alternative charter were arrested, and one charged with treason, ever increasing numbers of students and demonstrators massed at Thammasat University in Bangkok. On 13 October, an estimated 400,000 protesters took to the streets around Democracy Monument in what was one of the largest political rallies in Thai history. The air was thick with heady idealism, and many students marched with portraits of King Bhumibol and Queen Sirikit held high above their heads. The symbolism was powerful and emotive, proving loyalty to the monarchy and nation while invoking a higher authority they felt was on their side.

In an attempt to mediate, King Bhumibol gave separate audiences to both the prime minister and student leaders, talking at more length in the early morning hours to nine representatives from the NSCT. He urged a peaceful outcome to the crisis, and

Opposite To show they are supportive of the monarchy, students hold up portraits of King Bhumibol and Queen Sirikit during the anti-government disturbances they initiated in October 1973 to bring down a dictatorial military regime.

Above *King Bhumibol's television address to the nation on the night of 14 October 1973 turned the tide of violence at a time of constitutional collapse.*

Opposite *King Bhumibol accompanied by Queen Sirikit, Princess Sirindhorn and Princess Chulabhorn meet with demonstrators who had taken refuge in the grounds of the Chitralada Villa after King Bhumibol had ordered the gates be opened.*

there was, briefly, some hope of a resolution. On the morning of Sunday 14 October, however, the situation unravelled as security forces opened fire on the crowds, with shots audible at the palace. An official count put the dead at 77 with 857 injured. Clusters of students were sprayed with machine gun fire from helicopters. The crowd moved from the Royal Plaza towards the Chitralada Villa at the Dusit Palace, which is surrounded by sturdy railings and a moat.

"The king was keenly aware of the seriousness and severity of the situation," recalled General Vasit, who was supervising palace security. "[He] ordered the royal guards and police officers inside and around Chitralada Villa to remove live rounds from all firearms to ensure that military and police officers in the service of the king were also in the service of his people and would not harm them."

The palace gates were then thrown open to provide refuge to the demonstrators, who were met by King Bhumibol walking around the palace grounds in a white short-sleeved shirt. He was accompanied by the rest of the royal family, including the princess mother. That evening, looking tired but resolute, King Bhumibol appeared on national television dressed in a light business suit.

"Today is a day of great sorrow, the most grievous in the history of our Thai nation," said King Bhumibol in an address that would long be remembered as one of the defining moments of his reign. "Through democracy, we elect members of parliament who, in turn, elect members of the government responsible to them," the king explained. "At this juncture, however, the council of ministers is not elected by the people. I nominate them, as befitting the present situation."

At this moment of grave crisis, King Bhumibol announced the appointment of Sanya Dharmasakti as the new prime minister. Through a bold and decisive move, he had literally pulled the kingdom back from an abyss, but there were still some tense days ahead. For the first time in his reign, the king had been drawn openly into the political fray, compelled by the political vacuum to exercise his moral authority and bring closure to a severe national crisis.

Although Thanom had resigned as prime minister, he technically retained control of the armed forces, and it was not until 16 October that Thanom, his son Colonel Narong Kittikachorn and Praphas—the "Three Tyrants" as they were dubbed—finally flew off into exile. It emerged that as the crisis had deepened, army chief General Kris Sivara had played a critical role in denying the government reinforcements that could have caused greater bloodshed. In one heated confrontation, Kris reportedly told the trio: "These young people—they are our children."

Commenting on the extraordinary turn of events, *The New York Times* wrote: "To say the mobs of mostly unarmed students had defeated the armed forces of the largest and most powerful nation on the Southeast Asian mainland would be an over-simplification. But, in effect, that was what had come to pass."

Sanya, the new prime minister, was a privy councillor and the rector of Thammasat University. When he learned of his appointment, he realised he had been set an extremely hard task by King Bhumibol. "I knew that I had to be prime minister when I heard His Majesty's speech broadcast," he later recalled. "At the time, I was already in Chitralada Villa. I was there once on the 13th and again on the 14th morning. It is a protocol in the time of unrest that privy councillors have to be on hand to serve His Majesty. It is the honest truth that I only knew I would become prime minister on the night of the 14th through His Majesty's broadcast."

After his address to the nation, King Bhumibol spoke to Sanya directly. "He told me that my duty was to put an end to the gun smoke and smell of blood as fast as I could," Sanya recalled. Thanom's legislature resigned en masse, to be replaced a few months later by a National Convention of 2,436 members that was charged with electing a representative 299-member National Legislative Assembly which, in King Bhumibol's words, would "truly represent interests, occupations, professions as well the spectrum of views and opinions in our country". The selection of these new political horses took place at the Royal Turf Club's horse racing stadium adjacent to the Dusit Palace. The stadium was spacious and had tote machines normally used for betting that could be used to count votes.

Sanya's government lasted only 16 months and was bedevilled by numerous problems including high energy prices. It nevertheless managed to put a new constitution in place within 12 months.

Health Scare

After the health-conscious upbringing given him by the princess mother, King Bhumibol and his family kept in shape by eating well and exercising regularly: sailing, playing badminton, taking regular runs and long walks. The Chitralada Villa at Dusit Palace in Bangkok has a three-kilometre jogging track. There is another at Klai Kangwol Palace in Hua Hin, where Queen Sirikit also enjoyed lengthy swims in the sea. In Chiang Mai, the royal family often jogged from Bhubing Palace down the road towards Doi Suthep. Out in the field, courtiers, attendants and the odd journalist found difficulty keeping up with the king. Indeed, Vasit finally left the court police after concluding that he was no longer physically up to a job so demanding both physically and mentally. "I learned soon after joining the court security force that officers of both higher and lower ranks in the force did not drink at all and that many meditated," he recalled.

On a morning in early 1975, King Bhumibol cancelled his programme for the day and remained in bed at Bhubing Palace with a raging fever that would continue for a week. "One evening, I saw a female doctor walking down from the palace, crying," recalled Vasit. "I knew then that the king was not merely ill but was in serious condition."

It was initially believed that the king had contracted scrub typhus during an outing to the hill tribes in Chiang Mai province. Laboratory tests revealed that he was in fact suffering from pneumonia caused by mycoplasma bacteria which, like scrub typhus, induces a rash. The illness was almost certainly contracted during a visit to a hill tribe village. At such times, the king was invariably in close contact with impoverished people, some of whom were chronically sick.

During this grave illness, King Bhumibol's nurses included the princess mother. On arrival, she threw open all the bedroom windows to let in fresh air. As he finally recovered, the king saw no reason why his illness should be an excuse for others not to get on with their daily business. "I have said before: routine work must be carried out," he wrote sternly to Vasit. "Even though you are not told to do the work, you nevertheless must do it. There is no need to repeat an order for routine work. Whether or not I am ill, the work needs to be done according to the set policy."

Indeed, continuity and the wellbeing of Thailand's monarchy were particularly sensitive topics that year as Indochina fell to communist forces. On 17 April 1975, Phnom Penh, the Cambodian capital, was taken by the Khmer Rouge and the former kingdom consigned to more than three years of genocidal misrule under the Democratic Kampuchea regime of Pol Pot. A fortnight later, Saigon, the capital of South Vietnam, fell to the forces of North Vietnam. It was renamed Ho Chi Minh City as part of the country's unification under the communist rule of Hanoi. Laos came under the full control of the Pathet Lao not long afterwards, bringing an end to its ancient monarchy.

In July 1975, Prime Minister Kukrit Pramoj made an official visit to the People's

Opposite *Professor Sanya Dhammasakti, the rector of Thammsat University and president of the Privy Council, only learned that he was to become prime minister from King Bhumibol's televised national address on the evening of 14 October 1973.*

Left *Thai Prime Minister Kukrit Pramoj, sitting left, signs a communiqué with Chinese Premier Zhou Enlai, sitting right, to normalise relations between the two countries.*

Republic of China and met with Chairman Mao Zedong. During the visit, Kukrit signed a historic communiqué with his Chinese counterpart, Premier Zhou Enlai, restoring diplomatic relations between Thailand and the Chinese mainland, which had broken down during the Cold War following the communist takeover in China in 1949, and as a result of Thailand's close relationship with the US.

When the time came to give his birthday speech in December, King Bhumibol showed himself unperturbed by the falling dominos of Indochina. He said Thailand would prevail because of its accumulated merit from the righteous efforts of its Siamese forebears. "Our ancestors have accumulated good deeds for many long years, hundreds of years," he observed.

"They have persevered in their efforts with integrity," he continued. "As we have learned from history, Thai warriors fought for the security of our nation. Thai rulers have laid foundations for the country, and have preserved its independence with such tenacity that enables us to enjoy the benefits of an invaluable inheritance."

In the same speech, King Bhumibol chided those who had already fled or predicted national collapse. "Some people predicted that, by the end of this year, Thailand will not appear on the world map any more," he said. "And later on, when the existence of Thailand is still evident, I heard another story: next year 'Thailand' would become 'Dieland'. It was some time ago that I heard about this. I understand that it is a deliberate plan to obliterate our country from the world map. We will not allow that to happen. I think that it is a kind of intimidation plan. But if we all remain united and help each other, we will not die. And the proof is that everyone who is standing here is not yet dead. This is not yet 'Dieland'."

GOOD NIGHT AND GOOD MORNING

The years immediately following King Bhumibol's resolute words about 'Dieland' were challenging. After the communist victory in Cambodia and Vietnam in April 1975, and the abolition of the Laotian monarchy by the Pathet Lao government not long after, there was great suspicion and fear in Thailand of leftists, both actual and alleged. Various rightist groups fed on this and often lashed out violently. They included thugs like the Red Gaurs, militant Buddhists such as the Nawaphon, and the Village Scouts—a rural militia organised by the Border Patrol Police in 1971 to counter the Communist Party of Thailand (CPT). Vocational students were another volatile group, easily roused to gratuitous violence. There was a constant underlay of student and worker unrest and general civil disorder at this time, and King Bhumibol openly reprimanded vocational students for wanton acts of violence. More and more, the country was both ungovernable and seemingly under threat.

"It is easy to understand how [King Bhumibol], in 1975 and 1976, could have become increasingly convinced the political conflict in the system of open politics was threatening the very foundations of the monarchy," wrote political scientists David Morell and Chai-anan Samudavanija. "The palace began to see student, labour and farm leaders as communist agitators, or at least as deeply influenced by such elements. Frightened people began for the first time to consider the demise of the Chakri dynasty as a distinct possibility."

The many problems facing the government of Prime Minister Mom Rajawongse Seni Pramoj were aggravated in August 1976 by the unwelcome return from Taiwan of Field Marshal Praphas Charusathien, the disgraced former deputy prime minister who had been forced into exile in October 1973. Soon after his return, two people were killed and 60 injured in clashes at Sanam Luang between leftist students from Thammasat and Ramkhamhaeng universities and rightist vocational students and Red Gaurs, a militia that had been formed to support the security forces. An initially defiant Praphas said he would fight any charges related to the October 1973 events. After an audience with King Bhumibol, however, he returned to Taiwan. "I came here as a sick, old man hoping to die in the land of my birth," the chastened former military strongman said as he left.

Praphas's visit in August was a prelude to the terrible events of 6 October 1976—one of the darkest days in modern Thai history. In mid-September, former prime minister Field Marshal Thanom Kittikachorn arrived at Don Muang International Airport in the saffron robes of a novice, and proceeded to Wat Bovornives to be ordained. Thanom had made an unsuccessful attempt to return in 1974, and was as unwelcome to Prime Minister Seni this second time as Praphas had been in August.

On 23 September, King Bhumibol and Queen Sirikit visited the temple where Thanom was staying but, according to the abbot, did not meet with him. The situation intensified as Red Gaurs kept watch on the temple with its deeply controversial new monk cloistered within. Thanom's ordination placed any government respectful of the sanctity of the Buddhist clergy in a very difficult position. Thousands of students and leftists demonstrated at Sanam Luang against the former military strongman's presence. Within a week, two activists had been garrotted and strung up in Nakhon Pathom province. Police involvement was strongly suspected. On 4 October, a mock hanging, intended as a re-enactment of the Nakhon Pathom incident, was staged by students at Thammasat University, and questionable photographs of it appeared in the *Bangkok Post* and *Dao Siam* newspapers. One of the students pictured in the mock hanging bore a striking resemblance to Crown Prince Maha Vajiralongkorn, and this whipped up anti-leftist sentiment even more.

Whether this agitation was deliberately instigated, or was the outcome of a terrible series of ill-considered escalating acts of violence, is still hotly debated. What is not

Opposite *The government of Prime Minister Mom Rajawongse Seni Pramoj found itself in a very difficult position after the controversial former prime minister, Field Marshal Thanom Kittikachorn, returned from self-exile in the robes of a Buddhist monk.*

Left *Former military strongman Thanom Kittikachorn makes a morning alms round during the five months he spent as a monk in 1976.*

in dispute is that early on the morning of 6 October, a brutal assault was mounted on Thammasat University campus by police, soldiers, Village Scouts, Red Gaurs, Nawaphon and vocational students. Although a few students were armed and were reported to have fired back, the overwhelming force was irresistible. A terrible maelstrom of pent-up rage and anti-communist hysteria was unleashed. Students on the campus and Sanam Luang were beaten, stripped, humiliated, shot, lynched and burned alive. The lucky ones were arrested without serious misadventure.

"Getting rid of Praphas, Thanom and Narong [Kittikachorn in 1973] had been a positive act in nearly everyone's view, but the social disorder that followed their departure was viewed as negative," argued Morell and Chai-anan. "The rightist leaders and their new organisations were committed to destroying the students and their leftist allies; and by October 1976 most Thais were ready to tolerate such a move." After the October bloodbath at Thammasat, at least 5,000 students fled to the forests and CPT sanctuaries, mostly in the North and Northeast. The communists generally maintained a policy of not criticising the king or the Buddhist clergy, both of which were counterproductive to their cause. Thanom remained in the monkhood for five months and lived out his long life in Thailand.

Many were appalled and traumatised by the violence. Dr Puey Ungpakorn, a veteran of the Free Thai Movement, progressive economist and a widely respected governor of the Bank of Thailand from 1959 to 1971, resigned as rector of Thammasat University and left the country, living the rest of his life abroad in the UK. Puey had been receiving death threats long before the bloodbath in which, officially, 46 people died. It is widely believed the true figure was higher.

At six in the evening of 6 October, Seni's floundering government was toppled in a coup by the National Administration Reform Council, the junta of Admiral Sa-ngad Chaloryoo. Two hours later, Sa-ngad and army chief General Kriangsak Chomanand were received at Chitralada Villa for an audience they had requested with King Bhumibol. The mood in the palace was sombre. Princess Alix Napoleon, a royal guest from Belgium, was entertained alone by Queen Sirikit until 11 pm when King Bhumibol joined them for dinner. Next day, some donors to royal projects were also granted an audience. In the evening the king went for a run, alone with his thoughts.

Two days after the Thammasat debacle, Thanin Kraivixien, a conservative supreme court judge, was appointed prime minister. He promised to bring Thailand to full democracy in 12 years. Thanin's government proved more assertive than anything seen in the previous three years, but alienated much of the public and the military. Within a year, Thanin was toppled by General Kriangsak Chomanand, a much more convivial figure noted for his good cooking and common touch. Kriangsak exercised a moderating influence over the next two-and-a-half years as he grappled with high imported energy costs and the influx of refugees fleeing communist rule in Indochina.

Back to Work

King Bhumibol appointed Thanin a privy councillor, but kept himself well apart from the perilous entanglements of politics. Apart from his development work, the king's public engagements—which ranged from taking the salute at military parades and presenting degrees to donating *kathin* robes and presiding at major funerals and weddings—continued to consume an enormous amount of time. These duties were invariably carried out with great seriousness, and sometimes required meticulous attention to wonderfully arcane detail. At such times, he betrayed no hint of emotion—even when people close to him passed on.

In early 1977, Princess Vibhavadi Rangsit was killed in Surat Thani province in the South while delivering supplies from the royal family to Border Patrol Police. She was mortally wounded when ground fire penetrated the police helicopter she was in as it landed at Wiang Sa, a communist-infiltrated district. The princess's untimely death was widely mourned, and a new highway leading north from Bangkok was subsequently named in her honour. A relative and devoted aide to King Bhumibol, Princess Viphavadi's life had been spent in royal service at home and abroad. The king and queen presided over her funeral rites. Whatever the setbacks, there was still much to be done in these restive times.

Danger sometimes arose from more unexpected quarters. In September that year, King Bhumibol was driving himself back to Thaksin Ratchaniwet Palace in Narathiwat province when his car was struck by a speeding motorcycle carrying three men. The driver, who lost a foot in the accident, turned out to be an off-duty policeman on his

Opposite *Students were forced to lie down before security officials after the bloody storming of Thammasat University early on 6 October 1976.*

Above top *Protesters gather before a backdrop declaring, "Resist dictatorship, banish tyrants".*

Above bottom *A policeman fires off another round into the Thammasat campus.*

way home from drinking. King Bhumibol sat in his car while the unconscious men were taken off to hospital, and then continued his drive home. He instructed that nobody be punished excessively for the incident, and paid the hospital bills personally.

The very next day, King Bhumibol and Queen Sirikit were making presentations to Village Scouts at a community hall in Sateng, Yala province. Muslim representatives from the region and the provincial governor were in attendance when two small explosions rocked a tent full of local people about 50 metres from the royal party. Normal procedure would be to evacuate dignitaries as quickly as possible, but this did not happen and nobody dared tell the royal party to leave. The king and queen remained impassively in place as about 40 people who had been injured were removed to hospital. The king then addressed the crowd on the importance of remaining calm and collected when danger strikes. Queen Sirikit later described in an interview how officials wanted to downplay the seriousness of the incident and get the royal family back to the palace. "The king told them to drive back to the hospital," she recalled. "When we arrived, we were shocked because there was lots of blood. There was one girl of 17 or 18 whose lung had collapsed. Another girl was about to go blind. There were many people hurt and blood everywhere." The palace paid the hospital bills.

At this time, moves were made to secure the succession in the Royal House of Chakri. On the morning of King Bhumibol's birthday in 1977, at the Amarindra Throne Hall at the Grand Palace, Princess Sirindhorn was blessed with lustral water by her father and given symbolic bael leafs to place over her left ear. She was 22 at the time, and her full title became Somdet Phra Theprat Ratsuda Chao Fa Maha Chakri Sirindhorn Ratthasima Khunakon Piyachat Sayam Borommaratchakumari—Maha Chakri being the significant new inclusion. She could accede to the throne should circumstances require it, but this did not place her in any kind of competition with her older brother, Crown Prince Maha Vajiralongkorn, who married the same year. Their older sister, Thunkramom Ying Ubol Ratana, was at the time living overseas in the US with her husband Peter Jensen, and had relinquished her royal title at the time of her marriage to him in 1972. The couple met while she was studying nuclear physics at the Massachusetts Institute of Technology. In 1980, Thunkramom Ying Ubol Ratana returned for a four-day visit to the delight of her parents.

"She stepped from her car and fell to her knees before the king," reported the Associated Press from local newspaper coverage. "His Majesty hugged the princess," as court retainers looked on. Both Princess Sirindhorn and her younger sister Princess Chulabhorn completed their studies in Thailand. Princess Sirindhorn has never married, while Princess Chulabhorn wed in 1982.

Although the king continued to play music and host sailing parties on weekends at Klai Kangwol in the 1980s and 1990s, he could find much less time for his personal pursuits than before. The serious illness in early 1975 had caused a particular hiatus in his sailing. One of the highlights of the year remained a regatta that was sailed off the palace beach at Hua Hin when members of the Royal Thai Navy were invited to fill out the fleet. Among some 130 royal dinghies, nearly 60 were kept at Klai Kangwol for the Royal Chitralada Yacht Squadron, and another 30 at Chitralada Villa. The boats included Mod- ("ant") class dinghies, which were a scaled-down hybrid of International Moth- and OK-class dinghies that had been specially designed by King Bhumibol to suit the smaller physiques of many Asian sailors. At one stage, Mod-class dinghies were included in the SEA Games, the premier regional sports event held every four years. The annual royal regatta in Hua Hin was carried on until 1985, after which King Bhumibol ventured out only occasionally for private, non-competitive sails.

After Uthit Tinakorn Na Ayudhya, a member of the Aw Saw Friday Band, passed away in 1979, the king composed a melancholy instrumental, "Blues for Uthit", which was broadcast on Aw Saw Radio. It was a rare personal indulgence at the time, and a long way from the much more carefree periods of musical creativity in earlier decades. King Bhumibol fondly remembered composing "Falling Rain", one of his most popular compositions. "I became inspired while I was listening to music on the radio," the king recalled in 1981. "I felt the music in my head sounded better, so I turned off the radio and scribbled it down on a piece of paper. I remember that it was in May. People liked that song. They said it was beautiful. I felt overjoyed."

Above Politics

Because the actions on 6 October were taken against the students in the name of protecting the monarchy, and because the palace was not perceived as being as sympathetic to the students as it had been in 1973, the events that day opened up

Right King Bhumibol talks
candidly with BBC reporter
David Lomax for the
documentary Soul of a
Nation, screened in 1979.

Opposite King Bhumibol
talking with Prime Minister
General Prem Tinsulanonda
during a visit to an irrigation
project in the North,
16 February 1981.

the monarchy to criticism it had rarely received before in the reign. None of these comments were particularly public. Thailand's *lèse-majesté* law had become stricter since the late 1950s, and punishments for offenders were increased after the 1976 events.

For his part, King Bhumibol has always been quite circumspect in his contact with the press, more so in the past 20 years, and avoids overtly political comments. Although he sometimes reprimanded negligent or corrupt officials on visits upcountry, he did not criticise individuals personally in his public addresses. He has always considered comparisons to other royal families inappropriate since they exist and function in quite different environments to Thailand's.

On the occasions when he has given interviews, however, he has been remarkably open—even when the questions were obviously not particularly welcome. In 1979, a BBC crew was allowed unprecedented access to the royal family and produced *Soul of a Nation*, a finely filmed documentary narrated by Sir John Gielgud. The over two-hour programme aired only once in the UK and has never been publicly aired in Thailand—although there has never been any attempt to prevent private showings.

"I made four trips to Thailand and found that the royals could not have been more welcoming or friendly," recalls David Lomax, who was the reporter. During one of their interviews, he asked King Bhumibol how he kept himself above the political swirl and away from people seeking influence. "We keep in the middle, neutral, and in peaceful co-existence with everybody," replied the king. "That is the way of doing it. We are in the middle. We could be crushed by both sides, but we are impartial. One day it would be very handy to have somebody impartial, because if you have in a country only groups or political parties which will have their own interest at heart, what about those who don't have the power ... who are just ordinary people who cannot make their view known? They must look up to somebody who is impartial. And if one wants to destroy somebody who is impartial, well, one destroys one's self. That is why one must keep this impartiality."

Lomax also asked King Bhumibol about stepping in at times of national crisis: "It seems to be a very bad thing to defuse a crisis because one touches politics," commented the king. "But if we try to speak and to put some reason into the heads of people, I don't think that is so bad. And even the word 'defusing' the situation—I don't think that is very bad. If you don't defuse a bomb, it will blow up. And if it blows up, it will be very good fireworks—but for the one who looks from afar."

King Bhumibol dismissed speculation about the royal family being involved in politics: "The royal family is in the limelight so that if we think something, we do something, they will look at it," said the king. "If they look at it, it doesn't mean that we are playing politics ... Even when I am going out to look at the site of a small dam or asking the people if they have had enough to eat this morning, I am beginning 'to play politics'—I am accused of playing politics."

Political scientists Morell and Chai-anan reflected: "The king's fundamental political interests are aligned with stability rather than change, with law and order rather than the political noise of representative processes. Although he has demonstrated his interest in social and economic reforms, his model of change is that of very gradual, incremental modifications." A few years earlier, King Bhumibol had alluded to the importance of conservatism, noting that there was no guarantee innovations would be an improvement on older ways of doing things. "Having given this some thought, I believe creative changes should be made in a gentle manner, putting into consideration knowledge, thoughtfulness and reason. All parties should be allowed to cooperate—correct what should be corrected, promote what should be promoted, and create new things that fulfil aspirations," he said.

Focus on Development

In 1980, a vehicle for the kind of incremental national development favoured by King Bhumibol arrived in the shape of the new prime minister, outgoing army chief General Prem Tinsulanonda. General Kriangsak had chosen to resign when it became clear he had lost the support of the military. Prem became prime minister for what would turn out to be more than eight years in office—a period of marked stability and prosperity that contrasted dramatically with the rollercoaster political dramas of the 1970s.

Prem, the bachelor general who described himself as being "married to the army", was born in Songkhla in the South in 1920, and was noted for his restrained but effective counter-insurgency strategies in the mid 1970s, which got him accelerated promotion

to the top army position during Kriangsak's premiership. In 1980, as prime minister, he issued order 60/23 which gave amnesty to Communist Party of Thailand remnants, a fading threat whose support at home and from abroad was already disappearing.

Prem shuffled his coalition partners regularly, and had been through five cabinets by the time he decided to withdraw in mid 1988. This was a period of gradual democratisation. Prem never stood for election as a member of parliament, but was elected prime minister constitutionally by parliament—and always won confidence motions. The steely, retired general with his disarming smile was not universally popular, and was on occasion targeted for assassination. In one incident, a rocket-propelled grenade aimed at his convoy was deflected by a tree.

One of Prem's more serious challenges came in 1981 when his former deputy, General Sant Chitpatima, led the so-called April Fool's Day Coup. The power grab was foiled when it emerged that Prem had escaped from Bangkok to Nakhon Ratchasima (Korat), the gateway to the Northeast—to join King Bhumibol and Queen Sirikit. Sant was able to leave the country and spent some time exiled in Rangoon, the Burmese capital. No one openly gave voice to concerns that King Bhumibol had been drawn into politics by the incident. The endorsement of Prem and his legitimate government was, however, a clear rebuke to rogue elements within the military—but not one that would keep them at bay permanently. Prem for his part gave an emotional speech at a cabinet meeting on 8 April about the invaluable counsel given to him by King Bhumibol during the coup attempt.

Everybody was again reminded of the vital stabilising role King Bhumibol played in national life the following year. In July, he was struck down by the same mycoplasma-induced pneumonia that had nearly killed him in early 1975. The raging 40-degree fever and other complications returned. Mycoplasma bacteria are very resistant to antibiotics and it is extremely unusual for anybody to contract the illness twice. The royal family cancelled its annual residence at the southern Thaksin Ratchaniwet Palace.

King Bhumibol was shown walking around early the following month, and attending ceremonies for Queen Sirikit's birthday on 12 August. Unusually, the queen opened up to reporters about her concerns that her husband always worked too hard. The king often stayed up long into the night working on projects, poring over maps and reports, and surfing the airwaves. He suffered a temporary relapse on 19 August and continued to experience heart palpitations. At his birthday speech at year's end, he said the illness had been so severe that at one point he felt he had entered the "twilight zone".

King Bhumibol's working practices and long hours were well known. A key collaborator on royal development work, Dr Sumet Tantivejkul remembers often working by torch and car headlights at project sites late into the night, surrounded by swarms of insects flying into everyone's mouths and ears. "Sometimes we were so tired we would get home at 1 am and not bother to shower," he recalls. This was selfless work that continued until everybody was flagging. On one trip the king ignored the voracious mosquitoes as he engrossed himself in his map and notes. When he returned home, his arms and legs were swollen from hundreds of tiny bites. On another occasion, Sumet had finally got to bed after a long day when he was woken by the telephone at 3.30 am. On the verge of swearing, he answered only to find King Bhumibol on the line. They proceeded to discuss in detail the particular project they had been working on for the next 90 minutes. At the end, the king asked: "Should I say good night or good morning?"

King Bhumibol had urged Sumet to join the National Economic and Social Development Board instead of pursuing a diplomatic career after his return from France in 1969 with a doctorate in political science. When the king eventually asked Sumet to work with him on his royal development projects, he was frank about what was on offer: "I have nothing to give for working with me, besides the happiness you will gain from helping others."

King Bhumibol was constantly seen on television and in the print media at work in the countryside. By the time of his second illness, there were well over 1,000 Royal Development Projects peppered across the length and breadth of the kingdom, comprising water source development and protection, agricultural development, environmental protection, livelihood development, transportation, public health and welfare, and training and awareness programmes. In 1979, the first "living museum" opened. The Khao Hin Sorn Royal Development Centre in Chachoengsao province was the first of several research stations where officials studied how the problems faced by the provincial areas could be solved. Five more "living museums" were opened over the next two years, each based in a different part of the country.

Left King Bhumibol in August 1982 accompanied by Crown Prince Maha Vajiralongkorn, Princess Sirindhorn and others during a walking exercise prescribed by his doctors. Prime Minister Prem was invited to join in after arriving to wish the king well and present flowers.

Simply keeping track of all these initiatives and activities was a major challenge. The king had thousands of maps and files at his Bangkok residence, and separate offices and people in charge at the project sites. The various government ministries and departments also contributed separately on the projects. A lack of overall streamlining often impeded progress. In 1981, there was a major overhaul of these arrangements with the establishment of the Coordinating Committee for Royal Development Projects—later renamed the Office of the Royal Development Projects Board. Sumet, who had been secretary-general of the National Economic and Social Development Board, was put in charge. The board consolidated project management, and eradicated any duplication of work already being done by government agencies. The new arrangements also expedited fast track implementation of some projects that might have become bogged down in a more political or bureaucratic process.

The Prem government's support for royal development projects enabled them to dovetail better with overall national development plans. Issues that might fail to show on the national radar sometimes had a better chance of being addressed with the more micro royal approach—which prided itself on being attuned to regional differences.

"By the local sociological environment, we mean certain characteristics and ways of thinking which we cannot force people to change," the king once observed. His approach was never to go in and blindly dispense instructions. "We can only suggest. We cannot go in to help people by trying to make them the same as us. However, if we go in and find out what the people really want and then fully explain how they can best achieve their aims, the principles of development can be fully applied."

Princess Sirindhorn, King Bhumibol's second daughter, acted as a personal secretary on many of these visits. "First, he must know all the geographical conditions of the area; the height, the depth, everything," explained the princess. "It seems he knows the entire country very well. That is because he has had first-hand experience, which he believes is very important. And that is why he always drives the car himself during field trips and doesn't mind walking. He said it gives him insight into the place."

While travelling by helicopter, the king worked on his papers. "He would be very angry if we fell asleep," recalled Princess Sirindhorn. "He said that to ride in a helicopter, using petrol paid by the public, is a privilege. And therefore we must make the most of it, for the people. We can't just listen to the whirr of the engine and go to sleep." The king was concerned that government funding for royal projects should not be wasted or in any way tainted. Anybody found accepting kickbacks, or buying up land around project areas for profit, could expect dismissal.

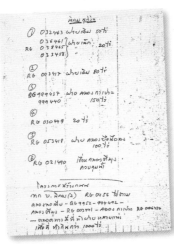

While King Bhumibol had gone out of his way to restore ritual and mystique to the monarchy during his reign, he was often openly disdainful of unwarranted protocol and formality upcountry. His style of interaction with local people was direct and informal, vastly removed from the overbearing condescension that characterised the approach of many public officials. On one occasion, a special seat that had been prepared for him was ignored. Instead, he sat on the floor with neatly folded legs and

Opposite *King Bhumibol's handwritten notes on plans for an irrigation project he had initiated.*

Left *King Bhumibol visits the Bangkok Metropolitan Administration's Flood Control Centre in 1983 when perennial flooding in the capital was already a major problem.*

spread his maps out among those present. A touch of humility, he said, was important for those who really wanted to help.

"Villagers are your teachers," the king explained. "You must learn from them first, about their way of life and culture, and then use your knowledge to complement the work, and in advising them." Sumet remarked on the king's aversion to "yes men" and excessive deference. "Dialogue is a constant process. Argument occurs all the time," Sumet said. "If you are close to him, you will see how charming he is. He constantly asks for opinions until he is satisfied with the answer."

Unparalleled Respect

In return for his national development efforts, and his interactions with ordinary people, King Bhumibol began to be accorded the type of esteem not seen since the reign of his grandfather King Chulalongkorn. "With his image of devotion to the peasantry, constant ceremonial presence, promotion as the centrepiece of national identity, and increasing longevity, the king's *baramee* (accumulated merit) steadily increased," historians Chris Baker and Pasuk Phongpaichit wrote in reference to the 1980s. "The new generation of courtiers and royal supporters celebrated the monarch as a modern *dhammaraja* and a moral counterweight to the excesses of military and business."

In 1982, King Bhumibol discussed kingship in a long interview with *Leaders* magazine. "The king," he said, "is, perhaps, above the law but, in fact, he is under the law—under the law which is the Tenfold Practice or Duties of Kingship … One could call it the Ten Commandments of Kingship. It is very old; it dates from the time of the Buddha. Among others, one must be truthful, diligent and do things with care."

King Bhumibol went on to discuss how this traditional view of kingship blends with modern constitutional monarchy: "A leader is like a symbol, whether he happens to have power or not. So a constitutional monarch is first a symbol of the country, and if that constitutional monarch is successful, he must become a living symbol of the country. He must change with the country but, at the same time, he must keep the spirit of the country. It's like being a representative … or the soul of the country. That means that all the people who compose a country have different characters, but the common character of a people must be embodied by the king."

King Bhumibol also discussed less ethereal matters like appointing prime ministers: "In the constitution, it is written that the king appoints the prime minister. This is a system in which perhaps the experience of the king can be of use in looking for people who would be suitable for prime minister. The president of parliament will come and have a consultation, but the king may have more power because the people have faith in their king." King Bhumibol said that as "chief of state" his opinion only counted if he had earned the respect of his subjects. "If the chief of state is no good, they will make him into a rubber stamp. But if the chief of state is better, they will perhaps ask for his opinion because the opinion is respected." King Bhumibol also said he believed he had a role to play in situations not covered by the constitution. "If there is a rule, I go by the rule. But if there is no rule then my opinion would be heard."

In a long article scrutinising Thailand's constitutional monarchy, the *Far Eastern Economic Review* sounded a note of caution: "King Bhumibol has won as well as inherited the respect of his people for his character, hard work and good judgment. Those qualities have led the nation to look to him to provide some force to keep in check the conflicts of unprincipled politicians, ambitious officers and assorted self-interest power groups, and to maintain a focus of unity and stability during a period of rapid social change. But the king's qualities may have led the people to expect too much of the monarchy, a standard of wisdom that will prove unsustainable."

In 1982, however, celebrations of the Rattanakosin Bicentennial, the 200th anniversary of the establishment of Bangkok as the capital of Siam and of the founding of the Royal House of Chakri by Rama I, were met with joy on the streets of Bangkok. Among many projects undertaken to mark the anniversary, the Fine Arts Department oversaw the restoration of the Chapel Royal, the Temple of the Emerald Buddha. A major exhibition of the king's paintings was also held. The nationwide celebrations at this time set a new standard for marking milestones relating to the dynasty and King Bhumibol's reign, and attracted international interest.

Writing in *Asiaweek*, Robert Woodrow took the occasion of the bicentennial to reflect on the special place the monarchy occupies in the collective Thai psyche: "Kingship is fundamental to the Thai perception of themselves as a proud and free people; without it, they would lose that identity; their cohesion and self-esteem would

be shattered. While the Thais have pride, their monarchy will endure."

In 1985, a full–bore royal cremation was held for Queen Rambhai Barni, the widow of King Prajadhipok who had been cremated in 1941 at Golders Green Crematorium in north London with barely anyone present. For many who recalled the sadness of King Prajadhipok's lonely passing, there were elements of catharsis and atonement to be found in the magnificent farewell given to his beloved queen four decades later.

King Bhumibol himself was more philosophical than maudlin when he talked about the passing of time. On his birthday in 1986, he commented: "Fifty–nine is still young, but 60 is old even though there is not much difference. It depends on our way of thinking. If we think we are old, then we are old ... We work until our retirement, then those who replace us continue our work and maintain continuity ... So we need replacement the same as the water that flows down the river."

These birthday speeches were closely followed and becoming more philosophical. "They constantly returned to the theme of unity and the need for good men to rule the country," noted Baker and Pasuk. "At times he showed displeasure at the institutionalised disunity in representative democracy and political party competition: 'between these two sides there is only talk, talk, talk, talk and they argue, argue, argue.'"

As King Bhumibol completed his fifth cycle in 1987 and reached the age of 60, there was much celebration at a time of stability and prosperity. A grand parade in homage to the king was staged at Sanam Luang beside the Grand Palace. It was a triumphant end to a year that had seen parades of elephants and a royal barge procession, and been declared "Visit Thailand Year" as part of a very successful tourism promotion campaign. Indeed, it was a remarkably happy end to a cycle that began under some of the darkest political storm clouds of the reign.

MORAL AUTHORITY

On 2 July 1988, King Bhumibol had been on the throne more than 42 years, passing his grandfather King Chulalongkorn's record to become the longest reigning king in the 206-year-old Royal House of Chakri—and indeed the longest reigning monarch in seven centuries of recorded Siamese history.

King Bhumibol acceded to the throne in 1946. On 13 November 1989, with the passing at 83 of Franz Josef II, hereditary prince of Liechtenstein, he became the longest reigning monarch alive, well ahead of a number of European sovereigns, including Prince Rainier III of Monaco, King Baudouin of Belgium and Queen Elizabeth II of Great Britain, who acceded in 1949, 1951 and 1952 respectively. Franz Josef had acceded in 1938, and reigned 51 years. He was the longest reigning monarch for only 10 months following the death of Japan's Emperor Hirohito after a 62-year reign.

King Bhumibol's longevity and enduring popularity were cause for national celebration and attracted considerable international interest. The following year, King Bhumibol's youngest daughter, Princess Chulabhorn, presided at a ceremony in Cambridge, Massachusetts, his place of birth, naming a city square in his honour. The site was rededicated a few years later by Princess Sirindhorn. A poll of 40 million people by the Ministry of Interior honoured the king on his 60th birthday in 1987 with the title "Maharaj", making him King Bhumibol Adulyadej "the Great". In palace circles, the title is considered both incorrect and improper, and is not used because it is only appropriate as a posthumous honour.

Return to Bangkok

In an extended profile in 1989, *The New York Times* reported on how the king effected change through his work. It noted that he had "devised his own blend of majesty and popular accessibility" which enabled him to avoid two extremes: "complete

subservience to politicians and royal wilfulness". Particularly in his development work, King Bhumibol argued that waiting for green lights from politicians would ensure nothing ever got done. "The other way is to do too much," he warned. "That doesn't work either. We must be in the middle, and working in every field."

King Bhumibol generally applied this strategy to his work in rural areas. Since the early 1950s, most of his development efforts focused on remoter, more inhospitable parts of the kingdom neglected by the government and provincial authorities. Some in Bangkok grumbled quietly about being neglected by their king. "There are some who say that the king speaks a provincial Thai," the king commented in 1992 in a detached allusion to the issue. "This perhaps happened because the king has been talking with the provincial people rather a lot. Thus, it ensued that his accent changed a little."

The king also mused on the changes in Thai spoken in the sophisticated capital far from the Thai heartlands: "I considered this and opined that, in fact, the Bangkok Thai language is not the correct Thai language. It is rather a composite language. The original Thai language is, in reality, the language that is called provincial. In the North, in the Northeast, in the South, the people in the villages speak the same or a very similar language. It means that the real original language is not that of Bangkok."

This did not amount to a language barrier, however. In the late 1980s and early 1990s, King Bhumibol's attention was drawn increasingly to the problems facing

Opposite The crest of the Chaipattana Foundation, established in 1988 to expedite King Bhumibol's development work.

Above King Bhumibol lectures on how Thailand's major river and canal network affects seasonal flooding in Bangkok.

Bangkok, particularly perennial flooding, air pollution, waste water and gridlock traffic. A city which had only reached a million people in 1954 had become Greater Bangkok by 1990 with nearly 11 million inhabitants when those unregistered officially were included—almost a fifth of the national population. People in the capital had become richer than ever before, but could they honestly claim their quality of life had improved? Were they happier or healthier?

To try and address some of these problems, in 1988 King Bhumibol established the Chaipattana Foundation with Princess Sirindhorn as president. The foundation's name means "Victory through Development". In Bangkok, its main remit was to look at flooding and waste water issues. Some of the solutions offered were simple and organic—the use of water hyacinth for example, a ubiquitous, fibrous waterborne weed, to absorb pollutants.

King Bhumibol donated millions of baht in the early 1990s to road building projects for traffic alleviation and personally mapped an extra westbound route to take advantage of the unused land beneath the Rama IX section of the city's second stage expressway. In 1994, he donated over US$500,000 to purchase equipment for the city's traffic police. The king was one of the first people to advocate building underpasses in the city, something traditionally considered risky given heavy seasonal flooding. He advocated greater use of the Chao Phraya river—a cost-efficient, ancient economic artery—for transporting heavy goods, particularly grain and construction materials.

The king was also one of the strongest proponents of developing the southern stretches of the capital's ring road. Only completed in recent years, the toll road enables traffic between the Gulf of Thailand's eastern and western seaboards to bypass congested Bangkok. Some engineers had doubts about the piling work needed so close to the mouth of the Chao Phraya river, but these difficulties were overcome.

The capital's low-lying, flat terrain only allows floodwater to drain slowly. Most of the canals have very shallow gradients, and easily silt up or clog with weeds. During the wet season, massive volumes of water flow down the Chao Phraya and its tributaries heading for the Gulf of Thailand. High tides coming the other way considerably aggravate the slow run-off.

Annual flooding was a crisis that left city officials grasping for solutions. The most vulnerable areas were north and east of the capital. Every year, these parts were knee-deep or worse in storm water, bringing transport to a grinding halt, and flooding homes and businesses. The king's frustration with the lack of progress prompted him to become more personally involved in 1996. In his 1995 birthday speech, he had offered a long and detailed analysis of water management in the capital and addressed the need for improved upstream flood barriers.

A childhood memory inspired a possible solution to the flood surges. When King Bhumibol was very young, his family had kept monkeys. "A monkey can keep almost an entire bunch of bananas inside its cheeks," he recalled. "Only later will the monkey take the bananas out, chew and swallow them." King Bhumibol had first mooted his *kaem ling*, or monkey cheek, theory in 1980. A budget of 375 million baht was approved in 1983 for dredging 19 canals along nearly 175 km, and building 43 pumping stations. Over the years, the monkey cheek projects helped regulate flooding by augmenting the capacity of existing public canals and reservoirs. In conjunction with the Bangkok Metropolitan Authority and the Royal Irrigation Department, the king oversaw efforts to store up water from heavy downfalls that could later be released gradually and less destructively. Projects on both banks of the Chao Phraya included construction of new dikes, retention basins and canals, the creation of a green belt and the dredging and enlargement of existing canals and waterways.

The city's pumps, run-offs, storm drains and water gates were also being steadily upgraded, complementing the strategy. Although parts of Bangkok still sufffer occasional flooding, the duration and severity have been significantly reduced. Much of Bangkok's river, canal and standing water was also extremely polluted—a poisonous, bubbling soup of washed-off pesticides, industrial effluent, sewage and floating garbage.

"Now water in the Chao Phraya river is completely black, and not only in places," the king said. "The waste matter entering the sea causes the sea to be polluted, and the fish to die. When these fish die, they then constitute waste matter while decomposing. A cycle cannot be created to turn this waste matter into something good like fertilisers. Neither can this waste matter be disintegrated. This is the cause of water pollution."

The king offered some innovative solutions. One was water hyacinth, the ubiquitous floating weed, to filter water from biological and chemical waste. King Bhumibol was particularly taken with what he called the "poor man's project"—a sustained effort to clean up a swampy, heavily polluted lake in the Makkasan area of north-central

Opposite *The Chaipattana Aerator patented by King Bhumibol was designed to restore life to stagnant and fetid water.*

Left *Heavy floods inundate Sanam Luang and the Grand Palace in late 1995.*

Bangkok. Water hyacinths and aerators were put to work. It was a cheap and simple solution with no adverse impact on people living in the area.

"Public parks are regarded as lungs while Makkasan lake is comparable to kidneys, cleansing the city's blood," remarked the king. "If they work poorly, we die." Clean water was used to flush out and dilute polluted water in a complementary process in which "good water chases bad". King Bhumibol had designed and patented the Chaipattana Aerator, a mechanical device that churns foul water for oxygenation. There was also an economic spin-off. The harvested hyacinth could be turned into compost, livestock feed, fuel briquettes or biogas. Nothing need go to waste in this environmentally virtuous cycle.

Blast from the Past

In the early 1990s, Thailand's political environment was less virtuous. In February 1991, a plane carrying Prime Minister Chatichai Choonhavan and part of his cabinet to an audience with King Bhumibol in Chiang Mai was diverted on a Bangkok taxiway during the bloodless coup which installed the National Peacekeeping Council (NPKC) under the chairmanship of the armed forces supreme commander, General Sunthorn Kongsompong. The junta's four other members headed the army, air force, navy and police. Of these, army chief General Suchinda Kraprayoon was the most powerful.

An early decision made by the NPKC—and one the junta possibly came to regret—was asking former diplomat and businessman Anand Panyarachun to serve as prime minister. His appointed government was in place for just over a year leading up to fresh elections, and pushed through a significant raft of overdue deregulation and reform. This included comprehensive environmental legislation, tax restructuring, value added tax, liberalising international education, and the introduction of lead-free petrol, compulsory crash helmets for motorcyclists and meters for taxis. There were some lingering constitutional issues, however, including whether the prime minister should have to be an elected member of parliament and how senators should be appointed.

After elections in March, protests and hunger strikes over the constitution were staged outside parliament. These dragged on for weeks. The poll had produced a new coalition but not a prime minister. At the coalition's request, Suchinda finally stepped into the premiership—having earlier promised never to do so. The result was uproar in Bangkok. Tens of thousands rallied at Sanam Luang to protest what they regarded as a brazen power grab by a self-interested military. At the head of the demonstrations was a retired soldier, Major General Chamlong Srimuang, a former governor of Bangkok and devout Buddhist—albeit one with a remarkable capacity for political confrontation.

On a hot Sunday night in May 1992, without any warning, Chamlong moved an overwhelmingly peaceful crowd from Sanam Luang. The destination, Government House, was close to Chitralada Villa, King Bhumibol's main residence. Along the route

Opposite *Former diplomat and businessman Anand Panyarachun was twice appointed prime minister in the early 1990s during times of political crisis.*

Left *Soldiers advance along Ratchadamnoen Avenue towards Democracy Monument during major political disturbances in May 1992.*

was a barricaded choke point, Paan Faa (Heaven's Gate) Bridge, where police had been stationed. Ill-equipped and poorly trained, they attempted to hold back violent elements that had infiltrated the crowd. Many were hurt on both sides during an eruption of water cannons, Molotov cocktails, bullets, rocks and batons.

During the night and into the early hours of Monday morning, police stations and vehicles were torched as the city descended into anarchy. The next day, troops attempted to disperse demonstrators by firing into the air but to little effect. Chamlong was arrested and with darkness descending it was clear a night of violence lay ahead. Along Ratchadamnoen Avenue troops fired volleys into the air while demonstrators sat and drummed the ground with plastic water bottles, peacefully but adamantly refusing to back off. The crowd was no youthful rabble. Many were educated professionals with careers, expensive cars, new mobile phones—and genuine democratic aspirations. Buses and lorries were hijacked and driven into the army lines. The foyer of the old Royal Hotel became a casualty ward as the dead and wounded were brought in—often to spirited applause—for attention from selfless young doctors and nurses.

As the night wore on, the crowd on the street dissipated, many taking refuge in the hotel. Well-trained arsonists with a more sinister agenda then set about burning down the Public Relations Department and other government buildings nearby, including a tax office. The distinctive thump of heavy machine guns could be heard around Sanam Luang in the pre-dawn hours. Just before first light, a whistle sounded, and the hotel was stormed by veteran infantrymen who arrested everybody on the premises without firing a single shot. Hundreds of men were stripped of their shirts and had their hands bound behind their backs. It was eerily reminiscent of scenes just across the open expanse of Sanam Luang at Thammasat University in October 1976.

There was violence again on the night of Tuesday 19 May, but it was more dispersed throughout the city with evidence of outright criminality and opportunistic score settling. The security forces and demonstrators were both exhausted with no way forward. The government had lost any credibility it may have had and offered no solution. Both Crown Prince Maha Vajiralongkorn and Princess Sirindhorn were overseas on official trips following developments. They both broadcast pleas for calm.

"People recognised for their kindness and gentleness should use reason and turn to each other and talk," said the crown prince from Seoul. "Everything can be negotiated," echoed the princess from Paris. "The problems can be solved in a peaceful way."

Meanwhile, in Bangkok observers were asking about King Bhumibol's whereabouts. There was considerable speculation over his silence, and people wondered how much he knew about the complete collapse of law and order in the capital. "Rumours have spread in the capital that he is being held under virtual house arrest and that anti–Suchinda troops in the north are planning to free him," reported Agence France-Presse. "A government spokesman, in an unscheduled television and radio broadcast Wednesday, was obliged to deny that the king was a prisoner."

Television footage of the political violence, much of it shot by Thai crews but not broadcasted, was spreading throughout the capital as fast as VHS cassettes could be copied in a city notorious for video piracy. But it was another recorded piece broadcast on national television on Wednesday night that was to really grab world attention.

Dressed in a light suit, King Bhumibol appeared sitting on a sofa with the controversial prime minister, Suchinda, and the prime minister's main opponent, Chamlong, on the carpet in front of him. Also on the carpet was the president of the Privy Council, Sanya Dharmasakti, who had been appointed prime minister after the king's previous major intercession in October 1973. Privy Councillor Prem Tinsulanonda, a more recent former prime minister, sat alongside Sanya. "It may not be a surprise as to why I asked you to come to this meeting," intoned King Bhumibol in a distinctive, measured and slightly rasping voice that was barely audible. "Everyone knows how confused the situation is and that it may well lead the country to complete ruin."

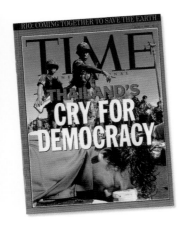

"I would request especially of the two of you, General Suchinda and Major General Chamlong, to sit down and consider together in a conciliatory manner and not in a confrontational manner, a way to solve the problem, because our country does not belong to any one or two persons, but belongs to everyone. Therefore, we must cooperate with one another and not confront one another, because the danger is that when people get in a state of blind fury and act in uncontrolled violence, they will not even know what they are fighting about or how to solve the problem. They will only know that they must win.

"But can there ever be a winner? Of course not. It is so very dangerous. There will only be losers—that is, every one is a loser, each side in the confrontation is a loser ... If a great destruction occurs in Bangkok, then the country as a whole is also

destroyed. In such a case, what is the point of anyone feeling proud to be the winner, when standing on a pile of ruins and rubble?"

The effect of the king's call for reason from the middle ground by apportioning blame evenly produced a national, collective release of breath. The remaining groups of protesters began to disperse as word spread. By the following morning, the last troops were picking up spent shell casings before withdrawing from Sanam Luang in convoys back to their barracks.

Eschewing politics for many years, Chamlong headed off to his forest retreat in a remote part of Kanchanaburi province, saying nothing to reporters. The following Sunday, Suchinda made a brief television appearance to announce his resignation to allow "the situation to return to normal". He admitted responsibility for his mistakes and requested all parties to "discard their doubts and seek reconciliation and cooperation to correct the situation and further develop the nation to the best of their respective abilities for the benefit of the country and the happiness of the people".

Suchinda said very little else publicly for many years to come. His departure after barely six weeks in office did not solve the underlying problem of finding a new premier, however. The six-party, pro-military coalition controlling parliament was widely expected to put forward another nominee: Air Chief Marshal Somboon Rahong. The following Wednesday evening, Somboon was at home dressed in a white uniform waiting to receive proclamation papers from the palace confirming him as the new prime minister. News suddenly came through that the name of Anand Panyarachun had already been placed before King Bhumibol by the speaker of the house, Arthit Ourairat, and the proclamation papers signed. Reporters waiting outside Somboon's home cast objectivity to the winds and burst into applause.

"Anand is a very capable man and I am very happy he has been appointed," Somboon said on live television in a remarkable display of grace under pressure. Anand's mission was to restore order and return power to the people. Elections were held after only four months and the Democrat-led coalition of Prime Minister Chuan Leekpai took office for three years. For the next 14 years, all parliaments were freely elected by popular vote, and prime ministers and governments were nominated through democratic parliamentary procedures. In 1997, Anand led the drafting of the most comprehensive and progressive constitution Thailand has seen to date.

There is still speculation about what would have happened to the flickering flame of Thai democracy without King Bhumibol's dramatic, eleventh-hour intercession in 1992, but Anand disputes the notion of "royal intervention". He contends: "The term has been used indiscriminately about one or two prime ministers who have been royally appointed." Speaking of 1973, when the king appointed President of the Privy Council Sanya Dharmasakti prime minister, Anand says: "At the time, there was a complete political vacuum. The normal political process for appointing a prime minister could not function—there was complete chaos."

"Even in my case after the 1992 May events, I think the king's position was quite clear. He did nothing to contravene the constitution," says Anand. As in 1973, King Bhumibol used his reserve power, prestige and moral authority to pull the nation back from the brink of calamity and set it once more on a constitutional course.

"The past situation has proved that nothing good can emerge from violence," King Bhumibol commented in his birthday speech at the end of that year. "Violence and fire can only scorch and burn. But too much cold creates inactivity, and nothing can be done. Excessive cold can also kill. Therefore, one must act sensibly."

Lao Interlude

In April 1994, King Bhumibol travelled abroad for the first time in 27 years to a destination much closer than the north Americas in 1967: the People's Democratic Republic of Laos right next door—a country that had ceased to be a kingdom in 1975, and which the king had never before visited. The closest King Bhumibol had come was on 16 December 1968 during the Vietnam War period when security was a much greater concern. He met King Sisavang Vatthana aboard a floating pontoon moored in the Mekong river, which forms much of the Thai-Lao border, for the inauguration of a cable from the landlocked-kingdom to the north delivering hydropower from the Nam Ngum Dam. On that occasion, King Bhumibol had rebuked his M16-toting bodyguards for looking unduly fearsome. They were told that the king and queen wished for "a welcoming and respectful meeting with the neighbouring Laotian monarch". The reason for King Bhumibol's visit in 1994 was the inauguration of the Friendship Bridge, which connected Thailand and Laos across the mighty Mekong

Below Chuan Leekpai became prime minister for the first time in 1992.

Opposite left Over 30,000 Lao and Thai people competed in a 45-km marathon to mark the opening of the Friendship Bridge in April 1994.

Opposite right Prime Minister Chatichai Choonhavan, left, proposes a toast in January 1990 after signing a memorandum of understanding with Laos and Australia to construct the US$30.5 million Friendship Bridge across the Mekong river.

for the first time. The bridge's elegant spans stretch over a kilometre. It was built with Australian funding and engineering after the Thai prime minister, Chatichai Choonhavan, summoned the Australian ambassador in Bangkok, Richard Butler, to Government House. Butler immediately relayed Chatichai's request to his prime minister, Bob Hawke.

"Canberra had it costed in about 24 hours, advised Hawke, who approved it, and then instructed me to tell the Thai PM, yes, we would do it—provided an Australian company could build it," recalls Butler. The deal was further sealed in a peremptory face-to-face exchange between the two prime ministers.

"We need a bridge," said Chatichai Choonhavan, who was never a details man.

"We'll build it," replied Bob Hawke, as they moved on to the next agenda item.

"It was fantastic for Chatichai Choonhavan and Bob Hawke," recalls Chatichai's son Kraisak, who was one of his father's key advisers at the time. "Thailand and Australia must be remembered as the first partners to stop conflict in the region. Everybody else had to follow—how could they oppose peace?"

At the Friendship Bridge's opening, King Bhumibol was the guest of President Nouhak Phoumsavanh. That night at the presidential palace in Vientiane, the king heard his own music played by a Lao orchestra to an audience familiar with it drifting across the Thai airwaves over many decades. In the course of the previous five decades, the king had produced 78 compositions in different musical genres. Princess Sirindhorn had been a regular visitor to Laos since 1990, serving as a royal emissary and lending support to orphanages and temple restorations. The next morning, the king and queen visited Wat That Luang Neua, the national shrine, to make offerings. Afterwards, another reception was held in their honour at the presidential palace.

"The seating arrangements only partially conformed to Thai protocol," noted Australian anthropologist Dr Grant Evans. "The Lao president and prime minister and their wives sat on chairs at the same level as the royal visitors underlining their equality, while before them seated on the floor … were the Lao high officials and their wives, acknowledging their own ritual inferiority. What is striking about this occasion is the ease with which the Lao officials and their wives conformed to royal protocol and the obvious delight they took in moving within the charmed circle of the Thai king."

The following year, King Bhumibol sent *kathin* robes with a donation to Wat That Luang Neua, with the Lao president personally attending the ceremony. "The offerings were made again in 1996, and it was as if the Thai king had become a proxy for Lao royalty," observed Evans. King Bhumibol's visit and the concomitant warming of relations were a major diplomatic step forward for the two neighbours after a bloody border spat at Ban Rom Klao in 1987 when a logging dispute got out of hand. In 1997, Laos finally joined the Association of Southeast Asian Nations (Asean), which Thailand had co-founded in the late 1960s during the anti-communist "secret war" in Laos being waged by the US with Thai support.

Royal Writing

Over the years, King Bhumibol has translated an eclectic selection of work into Thai—foreign writing and ideas that he clearly felt his compatriots should read. Much of this work was published in the 1990s, including a celebrated chapter on Buddhist economics from E.F. Schumacher's book, *Small is Beautiful,* which many regard as one of the most influential economic tracts of the 20th century. A protégé of John Maynard Keynes, Schumacher was a British economist who made a visit to Burma in 1955.

"From the point of view of Buddhist economics," Schumacher later wrote, "production from local resources for local needs is the most rational way of economic life, while dependence on imports from afar and the consequent need to produce for export to unknown and distant peoples is highly uneconomic and justifiable only in exceptional cases and on a small scale."

Buddhist economics, according to Schumacher, encourages full employment and fosters an economy combining a high degree of human satisfaction with moderate consumption. This allows "people to live without great pressure and strain". Schumacher argued that with limited physical resources, modest consumption would reduce conflict. People living in self-sufficient communities would be less likely to engage in large-scale violence, he reasoned.

"While the materialist is mainly interested in goods, the Buddhist is mainly

interested in liberation," wrote Schumacher. He observed that Buddhism seeks the middle path rather than extremes, and is therefore not antithetical to physical well-being. "It is not wealth that stands in the way of liberation, but the attachment to wealth; not the enjoyment of pleasurable things, but the craving for them," he wrote.

Schumacher also struck another powerfully resonant chord with King Bhumibol when it came to forest preservation and regeneration. He observed that followers of the Lord Buddha were taught to plant and care for trees. "Much of the economic decay of Southeast Asia (as of many other parts of the world) is undoubtedly due to a heedless and shameful neglect of trees," Schumacher contended.

It is not difficult to see why Schumacher was a muse for King Bhumibol's thinking on economics. The king's political translation work took him in a much less expected direction, however. In Lausanne in the 1940s, King Bhumibol's unassuming "palace" in the Swiss suburbs, Villa Vadhana, was home to two Siamese cats, Tito and Tita. At that time, Josip Broz Tito and his partisans were successfully fending off German forces in the Balkans. As the founder of the Yugoslav Federation after the war, President Tito continued to struggle against the Soviet Union, communism and later the economic embrace of the Comecon countries of Eastern Europe.

King Bhumibol never visited Yugoslavia but translated *Tito: A Biography* written by Phyllis Auty a few years after its publication in 1970. The book gives an account of Tito's struggle to preserve Yugoslavia's independence and right to self-determination. The king began work on the translation at a time when Thailand was deeply involved in its struggle against communist insurgency.

Auty's book reveals Tito as more of a nationalist than a leftist ideologue, and describes how as a leader he was able to overcome ethnic tensions, unifying diverse people to achieve greater common objectives. Tito's example in uniting fractious elements was relevant not just to Thailand but to the wider region. For example, Burma (which became Myanmar in 1989) has long endured ethnic insurgencies and was viewed by some as a potential Balkans in Southeast Asia. King Bhumibol's translation was completed in 1976 at the height of the communist threat in Thailand but not published until 1994, well after the Communist Party of Thailand had faded into oblivion—but at the time Yugoslavia was bloodily falling apart. Tito died in 1980, and had visited Burma in 1955 and 1959, but never came to Thailand.

King Bhumibol also expended considerable effort translating *A Man Called Intrepid* by William Stevenson. This was a biography of Sir William Stephenson (no relation to the author), the Canadian spymaster for the allies in the Second World War who went by the codename Intrepid. The king described the work as "an exciting secret war book", in which Stephenson ferrets out critical information on the enemy with assassinations, espionage, guerrilla armies, resistance movements and suicide missions.

Although the accuracy of some of the material in the book has been questioned, King Bhumibol had reason to be grateful to Stephenson. The spymaster defended Thailand against British demands for war reparations and was supportive of the king in his early years. King Bhumibol's translation is titled *Nai In Phu Pid Tong Laang Phra* ("Mr In, Who Puts Gold on the Back of the Buddha Image"). The idiom refers to the practice of earning merit by putting gold leaf on Buddha images: those who apply gold to the back of an image do good without seeking attention or credit.

King Bhumibol's interest in allegories and fables was evident in his more creative writing. He saw valuable lessons in the *Mahajanaka*, an ancient, allegorical tale of an incarnation of the Lord Buddha. He spent nearly 20 years researching the story written

in Pali as part of the *Khuddaka Nikaya Jataka* in the massive Buddhist canon, the *Tipitaka*. He adapted the story in Thai and then translated it into English. Local artists were commissioned to illustrate the story to make it accessible to children. The king's retelling was intended to make the story more relevant to the challenges facing Thailand. It highlights the perseverance King Mahajanaka showed in overcoming dangers and treachery. The ancient king's unstinting efforts were shown to bring peace and prosperity to his kingdom.

In one episode, Prince Mahajanaka survives a storm that sinks his ship. While his crew helplessly bewail their fate, the young prince wraps himself in oilskins. All the other seamen drown, but the prince survives the waves for seven days and seven nights without succumbing to fatigue or despair—even though there seems no hope of rescue. Mani Mekhala, the goddess of clouds and rain, impressed by the prince's spirit, eventually brings him safely ashore. In the introduction, King Bhumibol writes that the book is "meant to show that one has to persevere to achieve an aim". Commentators have offered explanations of the lessons in the *Mahajanaka*. Dr Prawase Wasi, one of Thailand's foremost medical figures and social thinkers, explained that the prince's action in wrapping himself in oiled skins showed "self-reliance".

Opposite *Illustrations of episodes from the king's allegorical book in which Prince Mahajanaka survives shipwreck through presence of mind and fortitude.*

Above *Mahajanaka was first published in 1997.*

"Most people, when they don't see the shore, will give up and stop trying," Prawase observed. "The problems of society are so immense, they sink into hopelessness."

One of the book's most memorable allegories describes a healthy mango tree that had been uprooted and stripped bare while another tree nearby is left untouched because it bears no fruit. Prawase sees this as an analogy for improvident development. "The uprooted mango tree represents development driven by greed," he observed.

King Mahajanaka tries to defeat ignorance and build mutual understanding. He creates a place of higher learning. "We are sure that time has come to establish that institute," he says. "[The people] lack not only technical knowledge but also common knowledge ... common sense: They do not even know what is good for them. They like mangoes, but they destroy a good mango tree." One journalist viewed the *Mahajanaka* as morally prescriptive: "The gods will only help those who help themselves first, or those who have the wisdom and the courage to persevere." The book's depiction of a City of Ignorance, a dark place afflicted by drunkenness, gambling, sloth and ignorance, meanwhile reflected the ills in contemporary Thai society.

"Thaitanic" Economy

After so many years of research and writing, the *Mahajanaka*'s publication in 1997 was remarkably timely. The book appeared as Thailand plunged into an unprecedented economic crisis, a victim of the so-called Asian economic flu. Great efforts were made to promote the work, and over 600,000 copies in various editions were printed.

Thailand's spectacular economic growth in the early 1990s at times went double digit and placed it at the top of global economic league tables. Inflation was low and foreign investment poured in for automobile manufacture, electronics, textiles and other light industries, property development and service industries. Tourism boomed. Shopping malls, hospitals, international schools and golf courses mushroomed. Thailand looked set to become another Asian tiger economy. The kingdom was enjoying some of the best credit ratings in its history. With more relaxed financial regulation, more competitive offshore borrowing was available. And with the Thai baht securely pegged to the solid US dollar, what could possibly go wrong? Hedges were for gardeners.

By early 1997, Thai companies and private individuals were seriously exposed should the unthinkable happen and the currency be floated—a notion many regarded as close to a national affront. But the baht was overvalued and a plump target for currency speculators. Other signs did not augur well. Yields on investments were disappointing, bureaucracy still onerous and exports down. The stock market had slumped and foreign capital was finding more attractive perches elsewhere in the region.

As 1997 ground forward, a financial meltdown gathered pace. High performing financial institutions suddenly became insolvent. In a two-month period, 58 local finance companies had their operations suspended by the financial authorities—and virtually all of them never reopened. After the Bank of Thailand depleted 90 percent of the kingdom's foreign reserves defending the baht in early July, the government of General Chavalit Yongchaiyudh was finally out of options and had to float the currency. It plummeted from 25 to the US dollar to 57 at its lowest point. Much of Thailand's economy had been reduced to smouldering ruins. The skeletons of half-constructed high rises dotted the Bangkok skyline for the next decade. In August, the International Monetary Fund stepped in with a US$17-billion bailout and mandatory economic remedies that were unpopular and hotly debated. Many wondered if the bitter medicine—imposed austerity and financial regulation—was worse than the actual economic contagion in Asia.

As the extent of the damage became apparent, there was national consensus that nothing similar should ever happen again. Even Crown Property Bureau-invested companies had taken multi-billion dollar hits from unhedged foreign loans. In November, Chavalit stepped aside and was replaced by Chuan Leekpai in his second term as prime minister at the head of a coalition led by his Democrat Party. The real work of rebuilding the economy then began.

For King Bhumibol, the crisis only confirmed many of his long-held concerns about greed, overextension, imprudence and failure to plan ahead properly. As early as 1993, he had been gloomy and pessimistic—preoccupied with many concerns, including drought and bad traffic. "This is a period of decline, it seems," said the king. "People complain a lot; they complain that the traffic is extremely congested."

"The standard of living, the law and order, the livelihood of the people, and even the security of the country are not as good as they should be," the king observed. "Everyone knows that in each one's life, there are moments of happiness as well as of

Opposite Parts of old Bangkok were dwarfed by towering concrete edifices. Some leapt skyward at the rate of one floor a week in the run-up to the construction bubble of the 1990s.

Left For some in the boom years, the Stock Exchange of Thailand was the best legal casino in town.

sorrow. This also applies to the life a nation; sometimes there is happiness, sometimes there is sorrow; let it not, however, be to excess. Even too much happiness can have negative effects on one's well being." King Bhumibol had always been concerned about heedless, runaway growth that neglected the basics. So when the economy finally imploded in 1997, public interest in his views on business and economics ignited. His prescriptions and reservations had been much easier to ignore in the headlong gold rush of the boom years leading up to the financial disaster. In his 1997 birthday speech, King Bhumibol reminded his people of some forgotten basics:

"I have often said to such an audience as this that to be a tiger is not important. The important thing for us is to have a self-supporting economy. A self-supporting economy means to have enough to survive ... I have often said that a self-sufficient economy does not mean that each family must produce its own food, weave and sew its own clothes. This is going too far, but I mean that each village or each district must have relative self-sufficiency. Things that are produced in surplus can be sold, but should be sold in the same region ... so that the transportation cost is minimised."

"Doing so might prompt some distinguished economists to criticise that [this] is out of date," the king continued. "Some other people say that we must have an economy that involves exchange of goods that is called 'trade economy' not 'self-sufficient economy' which is thought to be unsophisticated. However, Thailand is a country that is blessed with self-sufficient productivity."

Although King Bhumibol always made it clear that he never advocated total self-sufficiency and economic isolation—the models of autarky so disastrously pursued by countries such as Burma and North Korea—his ideas were subsequently crystallized into the Sufficiency Economy theory to make the distinction clearer.

As he has grown older, King Bhumibol's birthday speeches have become more sermonly, yet their discursiveness and lack of formal drafting meant they never lost their fireside-chat quality. Listeners became intimates—and each year really found out what was on the king's mind.

"I used to criticise those who speak a lot," the king confessed in 1996. "'Oh, that person speaks so much.' Now, I have become the same … Sometimes, while I am speaking—Oh! I notice a few people here and there dozing off *[laughter]*. Again, I am tongue-tied because it means that what I say induces somnolence. This is curious *[laughter]*. But it could also be an honour *[laughter]*, meaning that my words are soothing *[laughter]*, and get them spellbound."

Having chided himself, the king warned his subjects to be wary of demagogues who speak too well—possibly sensing the coming economic catastrophe. "Perhaps I do not speak well," he said. "If I speak well, you will be spellbound. But if the words mesmerize the audience, that is not so good. It seems that the speaker who hypnotizes the listeners is subject to criticism, because when the listeners are mesmerized, they may be induced to follow ideas that may be wrong; this is not right and can be dangerous."

Irrespective of whether they were sleep-inducing or mesmerising, the king's words continued to have impact. Thai media, both public and private, have always extended wide coverage to anything he says. School children are told to memorize parts of his speeches as class assignments. The government's public relations organs have published numerous books, and his Sufficiency Economy thinking has entered the national curriculum. Many of King Bhumibol's speeches appear on government websites, and the television evening news still begins with royal coverage. But this is not to say that everything he says or writes is well understood.

"The king himself is so complicated," comments Khunying Ambhorn Meesook, a former senior official at the Ministry of Education, president of the Lifelong Learning Foundation and trustee of the king's Rajaprajanugroh Foundation. "It is difficult for people to understand him." She believes people expect to be told clearly what to do, but the king prefers they think for themselves. "He has ideals and a vision that the people could not follow … He is a real educator because he is a good learner," she says. "The king has the ability to get information from people and then synthesize it."

Passing Years

"I have to ask her to repeat certain things to me," King Bhumibol told a French journalist in 1992, speaking of his mother. "I want to make sure I won't forget anything. She has taught me everything." In 1995, the king lost the most important teacher in his life. Earlier in the year, the king had endured another bout of ill health, experiencing high blood pressure and faintness. He was hospitalised at Siriraj Hospital where the ailing princess mother was also being treated. "At first, I did not really go to see her—I

Opposite *King Bhumibol with his greatest teacher, his mother Princess Srinagarindra.*

was practically knocked out," the king later admitted. Doctors decided an operation was needed and arrived with a document for him to sign authorising an angioplasty—a relatively straightforward and non-invasive surgical procedure.

"As I had not signed it, they could not proceed," recalled the king. "So they went to my mother who was herself not well, but she signed the document consenting … When it was over, and I woke up from the anaesthesia, oh what a relief—I felt so much better! I could breathe—everything was bright and clear! At that moment, my mother ordered her personal physician to push her wheelchair into my room and she smiled when she saw me. She said, 'Oh, I am glad, so glad that you are strong now.'" The princess mother's own health continued to decline, however.

"I went to visit her nearly every day at the hospital," the king recalled. "Her condition did not improve, until in the end the doctors could not find any way to save her, although they had tried their best to the end." The princess mother's last moments were spent with King Bhumibol, Princess Galyani and her oldest grandchild, Thanphuying Tasna Valaya Sorasongkram (the only child of Princess Galyani).

"It was a consolation for us that her own two children were at her bedside to hold her hand together with her favourite grandchild whom she had reared and who had taken care of her," the king recalled. "The three of us held her hand till she passed away peacefully … When she passed away, we did what she had told us. 'Mother is already old; I may die any time. When I die, don't cry; I forbid it. I don't want you to cry because death is a natural thing. Everyone has to die.' But at this juncture, seeing that she was getting weaker and weaker, we eventually realised that she could not live any longer but we still did not want her to die. Anyway, once she died, it is natural that we should miss her."

The princess mother was 94 when she passed away on 19 July 1995 at Siriraj Hospital where she had trained as a nurse 80 years earlier. There followed 100 days of mourning at court, and 15 days for government employees and state enterprise workers. The nation honoured the remarkable life of the little orphan Sangwan who became the mother of two kings and lived 66 years of her life as a widow.

THE 50th ANNIVERSARY CELEBRATIONS OF HIS MAJESTY'S ACCESSION TO THE THRONE

Although the princess mother had continued to spend time in Switzerland after King Bhumibol's permanent return to Thailand in 1951, her humanitarian work among the people won her widespread love and respect. Indeed, many chose to remain in black for longer than the national mourning period. Her magnificent cremation at the Pramane Ground (Sanam Luang) was staged in March the following year. Some 1.4 million people presented sandalwood flowers at the crematorium and nearly 40 temples elsewhere in the capital.

Three months later, King Bhumibol and Queen Sirikit were back at Sanam Luang leading ceremonies to mark the 50th anniversary of King Bhumibol's accession. The spectacular celebrations included a candlelit vigil in front of the glittering Golden Jubilee Pavilion, and a massive military parade along Ratchadamnoen Avenue. In October, Queen Elizabeth arrived at her own request for her second state visit to Thailand—a

Opposite top *The emblem commemorating the 50th anniversary of King Bhumibol's accession to the throne.*

Opposite bottom *During the 1996 golden jubilee celebrations, massive decorations were erected along the length of Ratchadamnoen Avenue.*

Left *Queen Elizabeth inspects the honour guard upon her arrival in Bangkok in 1996. It was a rare second visit to a non-Commonwealth country for the British monarch.*

very rare event for a non-Commonwealth country—to honour King Bhumibol. A highlight of the visit was a spectacular royal barge procession. At a state banquet, she addressed King Bhumibol as "Sir, My Brother"—just as Queen Victoria had done in her communications with King Mongkut more than 130 years earlier. "I repeat it tonight with heartfelt sincerity," said the queen.

British officials were bowled over by the scale and lavishness of the arrangements made by their Thai hosts. These included a 50-car motorcade from the airport where almost the entire Thai royal family had been on hand to welcome the British royals. "Royalty is revered here to an almost medieval extent," reported one British correspondent. "When the queen stood up to speak the 100 assembled Thai dignitaries rose with her, prompting sedentary Buckingham Palace officials to leap to their feet."

Amid the celebrations, there remained concern for the king's health. He ended up undergoing another angioplasty procedure in the mid-1990s to deal with narrowing arteries, and found himself tiring easily. His travels upcountry were further reduced, and in 1998 he hosted only one state visit—instead of the normal two—when he welcomed President Tran Duc Luong of Vietnam. As modern Bangkok finally celebrated the official opening of its 60-billion baht, 23.5-km SkyTrain on 5 December 1999, the international media once again took note of the 20th century's most enduring head of state. Retirement, however, was not an option for Thailand's monarch—even at 72.

QUESTIONS AND ANSWERS

A king writing about dogs might brush against certain sensitivities in Thailand, but none that deterred King Bhumibol. In 2002, he produced a slim, photo-filled book about his favourite canine, Tongdaeng ("Copper"), in both Thai and English. The Thai ridgeback was brought to the palace in 1998 as a homeless pup, and went on to produce numerous litters. On the surface, the book is a simple homage to a beloved pet. It tells the unusual story of a stray adopted by a king, and the devotion its master receives in return. Writing in the third person, King Bhumibol reveals his enormous affection for the loyal pet. If her master is away, Tongdaeng loses weight from the stress. The king praises his dog's "respect toward the elders and her good manners" as well as her gratefulness to those who care for her. "Apart from being grateful to her benefactors, Tongdaeng teaches discipline to her children." He describes incidents in which Tongdaeng snarls at her puppies when they misbehave:

"Those who don't understand, thinking that Tongdaeng is really going to bite her children, would interfere and chide Tongdaeng, but His Majesty knows that is the way that Tongdaeng uses to teach her children, and he forbids those who would interfere by saying, 'Tongdaeng is teaching her children.' His Majesty understands that Tongdaeng might feel hurt if she is reprimanded when she is doing her duty." In a revealing passage alluding to Thailand's stratified society, the king writes that Tongdaeng does not treat dogs of lower status with contempt:

"The fact that Tongdaeng is the king's favourite dog has not made her haughty or puffed up. On the contrary, she is respectful of everybody ... Tongdaeng shows gratitude and respect—as opposed to people who, after becoming important, might treat with contempt someone of lower status to whom they should be thankful."

On the day a new illustrated edition was released in November 2004, more than 200,000 copies were bought, easily outstripping records set by the Harry Potter series in Thailand. This edition was unusual for the way it depicted the king—or rather did not depict the king. His image was left as a glowing white figure on the page.

"It wouldn't be proper to draw the king in a cartoon," explained Chai Rachawat, the lead illustrator who had also worked on *Mahajanaka* in the 1990s.

One reviewer commented on the book: "Readers discover messages on morality and manners on almost every page—a much appreciated counterbalance to the endless stories of corruption that surround Thailand's political elite. When chasing other dogs around trees [Tongdaeng] insists that the group always goes clockwise. For many readers this is interpreted as a call for national unity in the face of a parliament rent by arguments among MPs that often reduce the debating chamber to chaos."

Political Fissures

The Thai parliament at the time the book about Tongdaeng first appeared was, in fact, more ordered than usual. The constitution drafted in 1997 took full effect in early 2001 after the second government of Chuan Leekpai completed its term and polls were held. One of the new charter's effects was to reduce the number of small parties which in the past had so often cobbled together wobbly, self-serving coalitions. This

Opposite *The unusual non-depiction of King Bhumibol in the popular illustrated book he penned in homage to his favourite dog, Tongdaeng.*

Above top *Tongdaeng sits with King Bhumibol at Khao Tao reservoir during traditional boat races in October 2008.*

Above right *The Tongdaeng stamp collection issued in September 2006.*

adjustment worked to the advantage of telecoms billionaire Thaksin Shinawatra, who had moved into the political arena in the mid 1990s with the Phalang Dharma party of former Bangkok governor Chamlong Srimuang. In 1999, Thaksin forged new political alliances when he set up his own party, Thai Rak Thai (Thais Love Thais). Thaksin was a new force in Thai politics, with good political branding, clear platforms and, most importantly after his election in 2001, an unassailable parliamentary majority.

Although the economy had made a strong recovery from the financial crisis of 1997, the kingdom soon faced other problems. These included gathering restiveness in the South and a widening problem of methamphetamine abuse. The handling of both would prove extremely controversial for Thaksin's government. In his 2002 birthday speech, King Bhumibol had expressed his concern about the mounting drug problem. In early 2003, Thaksin declared a war on drugs that led to the deaths of 2,275 people in a three-month period. Many of the deaths appeared to be extrajudicial killings. On the eve of the king's next birthday speech, Thaksin declared victory in the war on drugs.

"Yesterday the prime minister declared a victory over drugs. That is good but I hope that the victory will be sustainable," said the king. "The prime minister must assign the national police chief to look into the deaths of the 2,500 people and investigate how they died and announce this to the public."

Discontent in three Muslim-dominated provinces of Yala, Narathiwat and Pattani had tailed off in the 1980s and 1990s, but saw a resurgence during Thaksin's first term for reasons apparently unrelated to issues elsewhere in the Islamic world. In January 2004, a state of emergency was declared after a raid on a military arsenal and the torching

of three police stations and 17 schools. The situation worsened in April 2004 when security forces stormed Krue Se, an especially revered mosque in Pattani. Thirty-two people hiding there were among the 107 people killed that day, including five soldiers. In October, 1,300 protesters were piled into army trucks at Tak Bai in Narathiwat, causing 78 to suffocate among 87 who died in a single confrontation. Over 400 people had already died in the troubles that year—among the more than 4,600 killed overall in the southern unrest between 2004 and 2011.

During Queen Sirikit's annual visit to Thaksin Ratchaniwet Palace in Narathiwat in 2004, she was so disturbed by the deteriorating security situation that she spoke openly of arming people for personal defence. During an audience in late 2004, King Bhumibol called on all sides to show restraint and seek a peaceful solution to the problems in the south. "He expressed his concern over the situation in the South and he asked the government to consider being more lenient in dealing with the problem and to allow locals to participate in problem-solving," Thaksin said afterwards.

The grave issues in the South fell suddenly out of focus after one of the largest recorded shifts in the earth's surface precipitated a tsunami just after Christmas in 2004. The devastating wave struck Thailand's Andaman coast and the island of Phuket. The 8,000 killed in Thailand included 21-year-old Bhumi Jensen, the son of King Bhumibol's eldest daughter, Thunkramom Ying Ubol Ratana. Bhumi, who was named after his grandfather, had been jet skiing and was walking along the shore at the popular beach resort of Khao Lak in Phang Nga province. Crown Prince Maha Vajiralongkorn identified the body after it was recovered the following day, and personally flew it to Bangkok for funeral rites attended by the entire royal family at the Grand Palace.

A couple of months after the tsunami, with the country still reeling from the scale of the tragedy, Thaksin was elected to a second term with an unprecedented absolute majority of 350 seats for his Thai Rak Thai out of the 500 in the House of Representatives. Unlike any Thai politician before him, Thaksin courted ordinary voters, particularly upcountry, with promises of healthcare, local grants and other incentives—which he generally delivered promptly. His critics claimed his policies were populist and self-serving, and that he was throwing money at problems which needed more nuanced, long-term solutions. Thaksin's commanding CEO-style of governing was almost presidential in comparison to prime ministers before.

His hold on power, however, was not as ironclad as it seemed. Thaksin became embroiled in a very public dispute with a former ally, media magnate Sondhi Limthongkul, who responded by launching the People's Alliance for Democracy (PAD) as an anti-government force. Thaksin said the dispute with Sondhi stemmed from a television venture that failed to pass regulatory hurdles—for which Sondhi blamed Thaksin.

In September, Sondhi's popular talk show on government-run Channel 9 was axed by Thaksin's government. Whatever the original cause of their conflict, it became conflated with the issue of loyalty to the monarchy. Sondhi's followers wore yellow

Opposite *Trouble in the South: an armed militiaman accompanies a Buddhist monk on his morning alms round in Pattani province.*

Above *King Bhumibol's US-born grandson, Bhumi Jensen, was one of some 8,000 people killed in Thailand by the tsunami that struck in 2004.*

shirts—some emblazoned with "We Fight for the King"—at their weekly anti-Thaksin rallies. Thaksin sued Sondhi for defamation.

In his birthday address, King Bhumibol asked the warring parties to stop squabbling. "The public has had enough—they don't want it any more," he said. The king also expressed his discomfort with Thailand's law of *lèse-majesté* and its increasing abuse for political reasons. When criticism is prohibited, and people are jailed for *lèse-majesté*, "the damage is done to the king", said King Bhumibol, noting that monarchs are criticised in other constitutional democracies. "Saying that the king can do no wrong is an insult to the king, as it shows the speaker does not regard the king as a human being. Actually I want criticism. I have to know if people agree or disagree with me when I'm doing things." King Bhumibol's words did not hold back the rising tide of *lèse-majesté* complaints lodged by people with no connection to the palace to "protect" him. Rising from virtually zero in preceding years, there were 30 cases in the year after his 2005 birthday speech and 164 in 2009.

Constitutional Crisis

Political forces would increasingly try to draw King Bhumibol into the turmoil and ultimately set off a protracted constitutional crisis. The turning point came in January of 2006 when family proxies for Prime Minister Thaksin sold the remaining half of Shin Corp, the huge telecoms company he had founded in the 1980s, for US$1.9 billion to Singapore's Temasek Holdings. The deal ruffled some national security sensitivities, and raised eyebrows all around for being tax free. It was as unwise politically as it was financially shrewd. Independent media, academics and even Thaksin's political mentor Chamlong Srimuang, decried the sale. Before eventually turning against Thaksin, Chamlong suggested the prime minister consider making a major charitable donation to perfume the deal.

Out of sorts and facing daily protests of up to 100,000 people, Thaksin called a snap election in early April 2006—fully three years ahead of schedule. The premature poll was effectively a national referendum on Thaksin's popularity and legitimacy, since his parliamentary majority was never in question. The Democrats and other key parliamentary parties opted to register their discontent with the prime minister through an outright election boycott. Thaksin won 16 million votes, and nearly 60 percent of the ballot. His third consecutive landslide victory in a general election was another first in Thai politics, but something of a pyrrhic victory. Notionally, the new parliament could pass any law it wanted—without even a token debate. Naturally, its democratic credentials were open to dispute.

Even before the election, Sondhi had been at the forefront of calls for King Bhumibol to appoint a new prime minister, a power that Sondhi and some academics argued the king could exercise under article seven of the constitution. The opposition Democrat

Opposite *Prime Minister Thaksin Shinawatra was a powerful new force in Thai politics. He won three general elections decisively—the last of which was nullified by the courts because of electoral irregularities.*

Left *People's Alliance for Democracy demonstrators in yellow shirts. The movement developed from a business dispute which conflated an anti-Thaksin political agenda with loyalty to the monarchy. In November 2008, yellow shirt protesters brought Thailand's multi-billion dollar tourism industry to a standstill by causing the closure of Bangkok's two international airports.*

Party endorsed this view, but the king emphatically did not. He considered such action unwarranted by the circumstances. Even though the election called by Thaksin had been flawed, and a full-blown constitutional crisis appeared to be developing, there was still a caretaker government in place, a functioning court system and security forces operating within a proper command structure. This fell well short of the complete political and constitutional breakdowns seen in 1973 and 1992 when King Bhumibol had little alternative but to step in as a last resort to refloat the ship of state.

Most of King Bhumibol's reported comments on the mounting constitutional crisis during this period were made to judges and reflected his exasperation with the general willingness to bend or ignore the law. "It is, pardon me, a mess. It is irrational," King Bhumibol said of demands for him to appoint a new prime minister. "The article [seven] refers to the full effect of the constitutional monarchy," he argued. "It doesn't permit the king to do whatever he wishes. If he did, it would be overstepping his mark, doing something beyond his authority. That's not democracy."

In late April, King Bhumibol said that constitutional responsibility for addressing the crisis rested with the Supreme Administrative Court and the Constitutional Court, which had powers to issue rulings under the new constitution. "I have ruled under many constitutions and worked many decades, and now people ask me to act according to my own discretion," he told a group of new senior judges. "I cannot do it." The swearing-in ceremony was later broadcast nationwide and clarified King Bhumibol's opinion of the election and its implications. "Having only a single candidate from one party running in an election is not internationally accepted," he said, referring to the opposition boycott. "It's not correct and it's not democracy ... You cannot ask the king to be the decision maker," the king continued. "I have always done everything in line with the constitution. So there can be no royally-appointed prime minister."

"When a crisis happens, you cannot shift the responsibility to the king. The king does not have that duty." There was some dramatic irony in King Bhumibol feeling impelled to remind his subjects of the limits of his constitutional powers from Klai Kangwol Palace in Hua Hin—the very place where his uncle, King Prajadhipok, was residing when he discovered he had lost his absolute powers in the 1932 revolution.

"Another point is whether it was right to dissolve the house and call for snap elections within 30 days," the king told the judges. "If it was not the right decision, it must be corrected. Should the election be nullified? You [judges] have the right to say what is appropriate or not. If it is not appropriate, it is not that the government is not good but, as far as I am concerned, a one-party election is not normal. The one-candidate situation is undemocratic."

"We still adhere to our original demands that the election was unjust and undemocratic," said Sondhi. He called on Thaksin and his government to resign and "pave the way for a neutral prime minister, appointed by the king, to supervise new elections".

In early May, the Constitutional Court ruled the results of the 2 April election as null, but by then the constitutional crisis was going on ice. After the April election, Thaksin had decided to take time off from the premiership, ostensibly in deference to a major national celebration: the 60th anniversary of King Bhumibol's accession to the throne on 9 June. The king's birthday and other royal occasions had provided useful breathing spaces during periods of national stress.

"My reason for not accepting the post of prime minister is because this year is an auspicious year for the king, whose 60th anniversary on the throne is just 60 days away," said Thaksin. Less than a month later, however, he returned to what was still a caretaker premiership in time for the lavish celebrations. These had been minutely planned long in advance by the government and palace, and involved an unprecedented set of invitations to 27 royal families around the world, of which 25 attended.[1]

On 9 June 2006, 60 years after acceding to the throne under tragic circumstances, King Bhumibol appeared on a balcony of the Ananta Samakhom Throne Hall, the old parliament building, to behold one of the more remarkable scenes in his long life. Stretching before him across the Royal Plaza and down Ratchadamnoen Avenue, well over half a million people had gathered for an emotional display of respect, loyalty, affection and gratitude. It was the first public outdoor mass audience since 1999—and only the sixth in the entire reign. Very few in the crowd could recall a time King Bhumibol had not been on the throne. Many were in tears, and almost all wore yellow, the royal colour—and also the traditional Siamese colour for a Monday, the day of King Bhumibol's birth in 1927. During a time of political crisis, this awe-inspiring show of loyalty was bigger than any protest that preceded it or would follow. Indeed,

Opposite *Emblem commemorating the 60th anniversary of King Bhumibol's accession to the throne in 1946.*

Left *King Bhumibol waves from the balcony of Ananta Samakom Throne Hall with Queen Sirikit at his side.*

the occasion was remarkably apolitical and the nation celebrated collectively.

"The fact that so many people showed up today is a testament to the loyalty and gratitude that all Thais have for the king," commented Thaksin, who as caretaker prime minister participated prominently in the ceremonies and eulogies. Photographs of the occasion continue to sell widely, including one of a light moment when Princess Sirindhorn darted out from behind her father to snap a picture of the huge yellow-hued throng before him. Over the five-day celebrations, there were group shots of King Bhumibol and Queen Sirikit with their family and foreign royal guests, a royal barge procession and a sumptuous banquet. Afterwards, special itineraries were organised for the royal guests, many of whom headed off to inspect various royal projects.

As Thailand struggled to get a handle on functioning constitutional democracy, the whole world was unexpectedly reminded of the kingdom's undoubted virtues: its rich and ancient heritage, its tradition of warm hospitality—and its normally remarkable capacity for compromise and pragmatism. Indeed, the bitter political wrangling had up to this point been relatively peaceful.

Footnote 1: Bahrain, Belgium, Bhutan, Brunei, Cambodia, Denmark, Japan, Jordan, Kuwait, Lesotho, Liechtenstein, Luxembourg, Malaysia, Monaco, Morocco, the Netherlands, Norway, Oman, Qatar, Spain, Swaziland, Sweden, Tonga, the United Arab Emirates and the UK.

Top left King Bhumibol and Queen Sirikit sit at the centre of a remarkable royal group portrait taken in the Ananta Samakom Throne Hall on 12 June 2006.

Top right King Bhumibol and Queen Sirikit greet Emperor Akihito and Empress Michiko of Japan as they arrive for an exceptionally fine banquet at the Grand Palace on 13 June.

Opposite bottom A huge crowd of well-wishers dressed mostly in yellow fills Royal Plaza, straining for a view of King Bhumibol on the 60th anniversary of his accession as the ninth king in the Royal House of Chakri.

Left As the second longest-reigning monarch present, the Sultan of Brunei proposes the toast at the grand banquet. The third longest-reigning monarch present, King Carl XVI Gustav of Sweden, is standing on King Bhumibol's left.

Bottom The royal barge procession progresses along the Chao Phraya river past the Grand Palace in June 2006.

Bottom left Navy personnel in ancient attire man the heavily gilded barges.

Never Say Never

The political stalemate endured, however, and the tensions resumed soon after the nationwide celebrations ended. Citing concerns about a possible outbreak of violence in the capital—and contending that Thai society was too divided by politics and debased by government corruption—army chief General Sonthi Boonyaratkalin staged a bloodless coup in September 2006, an action that had been rumoured for months. It came just ahead of the annual military promotions in October when rivals in the military routinely jostle for rank and influence. Thaksin was in New York with some key cabinet members for the UN General Assembly when the tanks rolled. The generals suspended the ambitious 1997 "people's constitution", which had lasted longer than any of the 15 that preceded it since 1932, and dusted off a time-tested manual for military intervention from 16 successful earlier putsches.

"We have no intention to rule, but intend to return power to the people as soon as possible, to preserve peace, and honour the king, who is the most revered of all Thais," Sonthi said in a broadcast to the nation.

"I would say the king did not have anything to do with the coup," says Professor Suchit Bunbongkarn. "It turned out to be a disaster for the palace." Ten days after the coup, General Surayud Chulanond, a former army chief and supreme commander and member of the king's Privy Council, agreed to step down from the council to serve

as prime minister for a little over a year. He would rejoin the Privy Council after completing his term. The only other serving privy councillor to have become prime minister was Sanya Dharmasakdi in October 1973—a time of considerably graver national crisis and much greater violence.

General Surayud was highly regarded from his time in the military for his integrity and professionalism but brought little fresh political momentum to his appointment. His government was also much less successful in following up paper trails to prove actual malfeasance by Thaksin than many would have expected—given that the ousted prime minister's alleged corruption was a leading justification cited for the coup. Thaksin's assets in Thailand were frozen.

The main case pursued by the authorities related to a large property purchase in Bangkok from a state agency that was made by his wife, Khunying Potjaman. It was not until September 2008 that this was finally ruled to be a conflict of interest given Thaksin's position as prime minister. Khunying Potjaman had by then been convicted of tax evasion (she was acquitted on appeal in August 2011), and Surayud's government was already gone.

Above *Bangkok's 2006 coup made headlines at home and abroad.*

Left *The appearance of tanks and troops on Bangkok's streets in late 2006 marked a return to old-style politics.*

In its short term, it had pushed a raft of legislation through the unelected parliament, including the controversial Computer Crimes Act. The legislation was designed, in part, to tackle a variety of anti-monarchy material being posted on the Internet in the aftermath of the 2006 coup. Although many of the Internet postings were juvenile and malicious, using crass language and doctored images, there was at the same time an unprecedented upturn in serious discussion about the role of the monarchy and the Privy Council in political life.

The King Never Smiles, written by an American journalist, Paul Handley, and published by Yale University Press in 2006, was a harbinger of this more intense journalistic and academic scrutiny of the crown. The only critical biography of King Bhumibol ever printed, many in Thailand dismissed it for its gossipy content, inaccuracies and mean spiritedness. It was nevertheless a new departure in commentaries on Thai society and its workings. The book, which has not been distributed in Thailand, offers a stark counterpoint to any treatment of the monarchy hitherto seen.

A Fine Line

The king, like monarchs around the world, is constrained from engaging in public debate or criticism by the proscriptions of his constitutional role. While King Bhumibol has the right to be consulted, the right to encourage and the right to warn—prerogatives he pursues through audiences and occasional official speeches—he does not defend himself publicly or engage in open debates.

His annual birthday addresses, however, are unscripted and quite intimate, akin in many ways to national fireside chats. By the millions, people tune in to hear what the king has to say each year, and what is on his mind. "It's the only time he can say things in a certain way—not defending himself but clarifying certain things," explains former Prime Minister Anand Panyarachun.

In the past decade, the birthday speeches were followed with particularly close interest. There was therefore disquiet in 2008 when King Bhumibol did not appear at the Sala Dusit Dalai to speak on the eve of his birthday, as he had done for almost four decades. Sit-ins at the capital's two international airports by yellow shirt protesters had led to their closure by airport authorities. His words were keenly anticipated. The king's empty chair was televised surrounded by other members of the royal family, including Crown Prince Maha Vajiralongkorn and Princess Sirindhorn. The king was suffering from a sore throat and running a fever. In the following two years, the king was in poor health and residing at Siriraj Hospital, and also did not speak.

During the course of 2008, the polarised politics which preceded the coup had resurfaced. The country was divided over Thaksin, who was living abroad but hoping to return. When the party endorsed by Thaksin came to power in the first election after the coup, yellow-shirted PAD protestors occupied the grounds of Government House for much of the year, and finally brought Thailand's multi-billion dollar tourism industry to a standstill with the airport takeovers for more than a week in November. After two consecutive prime ministers allied with Thaksin were removed from office by court rulings, a new coalition led by the opposition Democrat Party took office.

The legal rulings and change of leadership may have temporarily appeased the PAD but unrest resumed as Thaksin's supporters clad in red shirts took to the streets. A particular target of their wrath was Prem Tinsulanonda, the former army chief and prime minister, and current president of the Privy Council, who they claimed supported the 2006 coup. Some members of the royal family had also attracted criticism for attending the funeral of a young yellow shirt demonstrator killed in a security crackdown. Speculation and gossip about the sympathies of various royal family members in the political turmoil became rampant.

The king himself showed no sign of playing favourites, however. As Anand, who has often spoken candidly about the king's relationship to politics, commented: "The king always has to be on the side of the people. Whenever the country is in trouble, they look to the king. It is very difficult when they still have that mindset. On the other hand, he can't be oblivious. He knows the pulse of the country. He takes note of people's sentiments. He doesn't have to act on them, but he must not appear to be rejecting them. It's a fine line."

"After 1973 and 1992, people always expect him to do something," says Professor Suchit Bunbongkarn. "Different situations have different explanations, but the role of the monarchy has always been carried out within the constitution. The king's ability has been to understand the changing political landscapes—and power landscapes— from the Cold War to the period of globalisation. He has been able to help stabilise political situations and make the country move forward."

"His constitutional powers are nominal," says Anand. "When you talk about 'the king can do no wrong', it's nominal. He has moral authority, he is the font of justice, he is the repository of trust, faith and whatever—but these have nothing to do with constitutional power." As a constitutional monarch, the king signs laws, proclamations and appointments of ministers, civil servants, judges and generals. He does not personally draft the documents or promote individuals. Yet that does not mean he does not influence the government. As Anand once said in a speech to Chulalongkorn University: "His Majesty alone possesses continuous political experience and has always kept to constitutional proprieties. His remarks, whether made privately or publicly, have always been listened to with great attention and circumspection. His indirect influence on government policies and measures cannot, therefore, be underestimated."

The king has many sources of information, including friends, to keep his finger on the country's pulse. For more specialist counsel on specific technical or legal issues, he can call upon members of the Privy Council—who serve at his pleasure and whom he almost never meets as a group. "They only advise me when I ask them," King Bhumibol once commented.

The political turmoil continued through 2009. Red shirts forced the abandonment of an Asean summit in the main seaside resort of Pattaya. In 2010, they occupied the main shopping district of central Bangkok for two months, bringing business almost entirely to a halt. After the police proved incapable of taking the situation in hand, and negotiations between all parties had broken down, the military acted on 19 May to disperse the demonstrators. By official count, 91 people including soldiers died in the 2010 March to May protests, and a number of buildings were attacked by arsonists during the red shirt retreat.

Left Members of the pro-Thaksin United Front for Democracy Against Dictatorship rally in red.

Above *King Bhumibol in a pink blazer takes a photograph of the many people waiting to greet him after his confinement at Siriraj Hospital in late 2007.*

Opposite top *Princess Galyani, King Bhumibol's older sister and closest surviving relative, passed away in early 2008.*

Opposite bottom *King Bhumibol, Queen Sirikit and Crown Prince Maha Vajiralongkorn appeared on the balcony of the Chakri Throne Hall at the Grand Palace for the occasion of King Bhumibol's 80th birthday on 5 December 2007.*

Bangkok governor Mom Rajawongse Sukhumbhand Paribatra described the period from mid-March as "perhaps the most tragic period in the 227-year history of Bangkok". It had left people in the capital traumatised and society divided at all levels. "I would call this the greatest crisis in the history of Bangkok," Sukhumbhand said in an address to the Foreign Correspondents' Club of Thailand. "Divisions in our society were never this deep," he maintained.

"Two-hundred-and-forty-three years ago, when one of our former capital cities, Ayudhya, was burned down, we had the luxury of blaming it on foreign invaders," said Sukhumbhand. "This time we don't have any excuse." The governor described reconciliation as a necessity, not a luxury:

"All the people who love Bangkok must now forget what their favourite shirt colours are. We have to come together, look ahead, move ahead, join hands in reconstructing, restoring, rehabilitating the city that we love. There is no other way. If the people of Bangkok do not do this, who will do it for us?"

King Bhumibol's youngest daughter, Princess Chulabhorn, said in a television interview the following year that the violent debacle in May 2010, and the torching of buildings in the capital, had profoundly depressed her father. Over a year after order was finally restored to the capital, Prime Minister Abhisit Vejjajiva called a general election for early August 2011. His Democrat party, which had headed the governing coalition, lost to the Pheu Thai party supported by Thaksin. Pheu Thai secured 265 of 500 seats in the House of Representatives, and this was only the second time a political party had won an outright majority in a Thai general election. History was also made by Pheu Thai's new leader, Yingluck Shinawatra, the youngest sister of Thaksin Shinawatra. At 44, she became Thailand's first female prime minister having only left the world of business for politics in May of that year.

A Family Affair

Over the years, rumours have swept through the kingdom that the king might abdicate or even retreat into a monastery. As with virtually all rumours relating to the royal family, they are ignored by the palace lest by denying one, another is inadvertently given false credibility. Most are simply groundless. The courtiers closest to the royal family and most knowledgeable are also the most circumspect and averse to outside discussion. Undue praise or any suggestion of over-familiarity with the royal family are equally frowned upon. Rumours therefore spring from sources well removed from the intimate innermost circles, and are dubious from the outset.

King Bhumibol has spent most of his "retirement" years at Klai Kangwol, the seaside palace in Hua Hin built by his uncle King Prajadhipok in the late 1920s as a gift for Queen Rambhai Barni. The king returned to Bangkok in 2006 during a bout of ill health. Although the king's mobility had not improved as much as was hoped for after back surgery in late 2006, he made a good recovery otherwise. In mid-October 2007, there was genuine national apprehension when he was suddenly hospitalised for treatment of a clot and what was described as an insufficient blood flow to the brain. When he reappeared in good time for his 80th birthday, his choices of bright blue, green and pink blazers provided light relief and lifted the public mood.

By April 2008, he was granting occasional audiences back at the Chitralada Villa which proved him to be in excellent mental shape. Visitors were asked not to wear yellow or black. At one, he informed his foreign guests in effortless English that he planned to be around for a good many years to come. Late in 2009, however, a serious bout of pneumonia—and further back problems that continue to confine him to a wheelchair—raised inevitable concern.

The king has resided at Siriraj Hospital since September 2009, occupying the 16th floor of the Chalermprakiat Building. From there, he enjoys a commanding view across the Chao Phraya river that winds through Bangkok, the city founded by the Royal House of Chakri in 1782, with Thammasat University's Tha Prachan Campus in the foreground and the Grand Palace beyond. At Siriraj Hospital, the king is near Thais from all walks of life in a way that would be impossible at any of the palaces in which he could choose to reside.

"Definitely, he feels more at ease if he is near doctors, but he has no life-threatening ailments," says an occasional visitor. Over the years, more care has been taken to ensure that royal medical bulletins are not unduly intrusive but sufficiently detailed—as

were those issued by the hospital for the king's sister, Princess Galyani Vadhana, when she fell seriously ill in 2007. One of her last public engagements had been attending the magnificent final dress rehearsal for the royal barge procession marking the 60th anniversary of her brother's accession in 2006. King Bhumibol was at her bedside when she passed away from abdominal cancer at the hospital on 2 January 2008.

Although King Bhumibol suffers many of the usual infirmities of age, particularly in regard to lost mobility, he continues to take an interest in the world around him. Those closest to him have made sure he remains engaged with his favourite pastimes. A famous jazz band from New Orleans, Preservation Hall, played for him at Siriraj Hospital, and his own Aw Saw Band still jams occasionally on Saturdays with Princess Sirindhorn always joining in. On another occasion, the king was taken downriver by boat for the official opening ceremonies of two elegant new bridges in the Chao Phraya estuary, Bhumibol One and Bhumibol Two, and a new water gate.

In late 2010, as a foretaste of the celebrations for his 84th birthday on 5 December 2011, King Bhumibol inspected an F1 racing car, and was given a detailed briefing on it by Mark Webber from the Red Bull team. Red Bull, a household name around the world, owes its origins to Krating Daeng, a popular Thai energy drink. The Australian driver put the car through its paces the next day along Ratchadamnoen Avenue in front of 150,000 onlookers.

For King Bhumibol, who enjoyed nothing better than driving himself to the furthest corners of his kingdom, the interest in motor sport dates right back to 1935 and 1936 when he and his older brother King Ananda tracked the triumphs of Prince Birabongse Bhanudej on the great European racing circuits of the day. Indeed, Prince Bira's most famous race car, Romulus, still enjoys pride of place in the Sala Dusit Dalai near the Chitralada Villa, the king's main residence. In June 2011, the king gave an audience to Supoj Sublom, the permanent secretary for transport, and Yuthana Thabcharoen, governor of the State Railways of Thailand. Again showing more of his old form, the king quizzed them on traffic and flooding, and the capital's new railway links.

Siriraj Hospital of course provides some of the best medical care in the kingdom. It also has a very special emotional attachment for King Bhumibol. Chalermprakiat, the name of the king's building, means "commemorative", and much is commemorated at Thailand's oldest hospital. The grounds contain monuments to the hospital's founder, King Chulalongkorn, the king's grandfather; to his sister, Princess Galyani; to his brother, King Ananda; to his mother, Princess Srinagarindra; and to his father, Prince Mahidol. It was at Siriraj that the king's mother, young Sangwan, trained to be a nurse almost a century ago. And it was here at much the same time that his father, Prince Mahidol, first realised that a life in public health and medicine was the greatest contribution he could ever make to Siam's development. Indeed, Prince Mahidol's tangible legacy lives on at Siriraj more than anywhere else, in the buildings and systems he created—and in the remarkable life of the infant son he left behind.

Opposite top During an audience at Siriraj Hospital on 27 June 2011, officials report on traffic congestion in the capital, flood prevention measures, new rail links and other matters which had often taken the king's interest in the past.

Opposite bottom In late 2010, King Bhumibol enjoys a detailed briefing by Australian F1 racing driver Mark Webber, a member of the Red Bull team. The king's love of all forms of motoring dates back to his childhood years in Switzerland in the 1930s.

Above The Chalermprakiat Building at Siriraj Hospital in Thon Buri where King Bhumibol has resided since 2009.

Part II: The Work

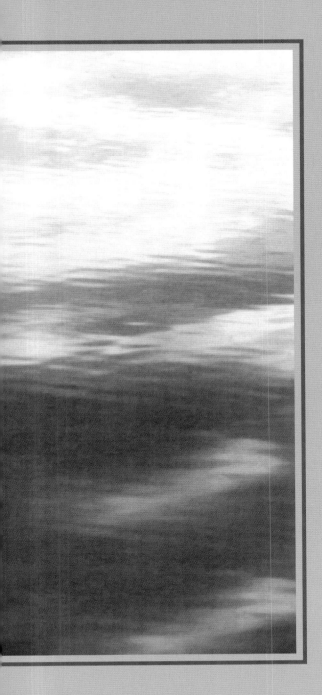

"I do whatever I think is useful," King Bhumibol once commented on his role as monarch. This unassuming definition had countless applications and real impact on the security and well-being of the kingdom. Through visits to every province of the country—travels that covered more than 48,000 kilometres in many years—the king saw for himself the challenges facing Thailand's rural population. Focusing on healthcare, education, and improved management of natural resources, the king initiated thousands of development projects far and wide, many of which were vehicles for his own ideas and innovations. By the 1990s, the king had developed his idea of "Sufficiency Economy", which sought to balance sustainable, prudent economic development with social, environmental and ethical concerns.

Above King Bhumibol, in late 1970, shows hill tribe villagers in Ae Ko village, Mae Hong Son province, how to properly administer medicine to a baby.

FUNDAMENTAL HEALTH

When the king's reign began, the state of the country's public healthcare system was poor. Outbreaks of epidemics such as cholera could be devastating and access to healthcare virtually impossible in the more remote parts of the country. The king responded by promoting the physical health of the people through a variety of measures. He established hospitals and clinics. Through his dairy and fish breeding projects, he encouraged better nutrition. On his travels, he instructed medical units to accompany him and provide on-the-spot treatment to the sick. To soldiers injured while serving the country or Thais afflicted by natural disaster, the crown offered its support. Continuing the legacy of his father, the king presented scholarships and awards to support the advanced study of medicine. These initiatives have complemented a public healthcare system that has improved dramatically over the last few decades.

In the wake of the Second World War, new leaders and newly independent nations were emerging across the developing world. The challenges they faced were daunting: shattered infrastructure, hunger, malnutrition and disease. The kingdom of Thailand had been spared the worst ravages of war, but it had not escaped unscathed. Bangkok had been bombed, and parts of Chiang Mai city burned by retreating Japanese soldiers. Food, fuel and medicines were in short supply.

Thailand was far removed from the centres of advanced medicine in Europe, where the king grew up, or the US. Travel around the kingdom in the days before paved highways was arduous. Medical care was rarely available outside Bangkok, the northern city of Chiang Mai and all but the largest towns. The maternal mortality ratio was well over 400 deaths per 100,000 live births. Infant mortality was 62 per 1,000 infants aged under one year. Epidemics and infectious diseases were common, and sanitation and hygiene miserable.

"There were no doctors. No hospitals," says Dr Prawase Wasi, a leading healthcare specialist and social commentator, recalling his childhood in Kanchanaburi province more than 60 years ago. "Anyone who had appendicitis or diphtheria died. My grandmother developed mild diarrhoea and died because there was no treatment available." Thais lived only 50 years on average. Malaria and cholera were persistent scourges. Between 1945 and 1950, smallpox infected more than 60,000 people, killing a quarter of them. The same period saw nearly 600 cases of plague. Yaws, cholera, dengue and polio were all prevalent. However, the disease that Thais dreaded the most during those difficult post-war years was tuberculosis. Once transmitted, it was often fatal. Constrained by a rudimentary public health system and limited resources, government officials were unable to contain it.

In July 1949, King Bhumibol, at that time a young law student in Switzerland, made a 300,000-baht donation to a new laboratory that was being constructed at the Pasteur Institute in Bangkok. Sanctioned by the United Nations (UN) and aided by the World Health Organisation (WHO), the institute would produce and store the vaccine that would become instrumental in curbing the spread of tuberculosis in Thailand. With this contribution, the king began a lifelong commitment to public health, carrying on the legacy of his grandparents and parents—his mother was a trained nurse and his father had been a doctor.

Improving public health would be a top priority for the monarch, especially during the first decade of his reign. The king's initiatives focused mainly on infectious diseases and providing basic necessities and infrastructure. For Thailand to become self-sufficient, its

Far left King Prajadhipok and Queen Rambhai Barni at the opening ceremony of the Asdang Building at Siriraj Hospital in 1928.

Left Queen Savang Vadhana with student members of the Thai Red Cross at Rajini School in Bangkok.

66 Yaws, cholera, dengue and polio were all prevalent. However, the disease that Thais dreaded the most during those difficult post-war years was tuberculosis. It was easily transmitted and often fatal. 99

people had to become healthy. Without access to public health services, generations would stay trapped in a cycle of poor health and poverty, crippling the nation's efforts to advance. At the macroeconomic level, the burdens of disease and disability drain national resources. At the household level, they can leave families destitute. As King Bhumibol observed, "good physical health is a factor supporting economic progress and social security of the country because it leads to good mental health. Physical and mental fitness enable the individual to effectively serve the nation while refraining from imposing burdens on the nation."

A Long Road Ahead

The beginnings of a modern public health system in Siam were initiated during the reign of King Bhumibol's grandfather, King Chulalongkorn (r. 1868–1910). Having lost a son, Prince Siriraj, to dysentery, King Chulalongkorn commissioned the building of Siam's first permanent hospital. Founded in 1888, Siriraj Hospital was mandated to deliver healthcare to all. It remains among the largest and most advanced medical institutions in the country. King Chulalongkorn also established a medical division under the Ministry of Education, a nursing department, and medical and midwifery schools at Siriraj. The first Western medical textbook was published in Thailand, and a sanitation management programme piloted in Samut Songkhram province. In another landmark development, the Thai Red Cross was founded in 1893. Queen Savang Vadhana, King Bhumibol's grandmother, became its president for many years and was herself active in public health.

King Chulalongkorn's son King Vajiravudh (r. 1910–25) funded the building of Chulalongkorn Hospital in partnership with the Thai Red Cross. The Pasteur Institute, Saovabha Institute, the Army Medical School and Vajira Hospital were also established. Medical and sanitation departments under various ministries were merged into the newly created Public Health Department, and pharmacies opened across the country. Under King Prajadhipok (r. 1925–35), the Public Health Department was reorganised, and laws defining and regulating the practices of modern and traditional medicines were passed. During the late 1930s, the country was still suffering the effects of the Great Depression. In the 1940s, it was under Japanese occupation and plagued by political strife. When King Bhumibol returned from Switzerland in 1950 for his coronation, the kingdom he inherited, despite the efforts of

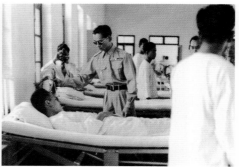

his forebears, was in generally poor health and very much in need of reconstruction.

On 6 April 1950, a month before his coronation, King Bhumibol and his fiancée, Mom Rajawongse Sirikit Kitiyakara celebrated Chakri Day and presided over the opening of the Red Cross Fair, a key fund-raising event for the organisation. The king also visited the tuberculosis treatment centre there and questioned the minister of public health, Luang Payungvejchasart, on treatments: "I want to see Thai medicine progress," he explained.

While progress was initially slow, campaigns launched by the government with international agencies were starting to make headway. Yaws, a tropical infection of the skin, bones and joints, was an initial target. An estimated 1.5 million Thais suffered from the disease. A mass campaign of inoculations with penicillin, launched with support from the WHO and UNICEF, steadily brought transmission under control. After a decade, cases of yaws were rare, and since that time doctors have gone their entire careers without encountering it.

In 1953, the king presided over the opening of the landmark facility to which he had donated in 1949 from Switzerland. Constructed to produce and store Bacillus Calmette-Guérin (BCG), the vaccine used to combat tuberculosis, the Mahidol Vongsanusorn Building was vetted by experts from the WHO's Staten Serum Institute in Denmark. The freeze-dried BCG vaccine manufactured there became the first biological product from Thailand to be registered. Experts trained Thai personnel on production of the vaccine and quality control.

The king's concern about the spread of tuberculosis continued something of a family tradition. In 1920, his father, Prince Mahidol, had produced a ground-breaking paper on combating the disease. In the late-1930s, teams of health professionals, under the young King Ananda's patronage, were charged with trying to curb its transmission. By the mid-1950s, with the new facility operational and with guidance from the WHO, production of the BCG vaccine rapidly increased. Public health officials embarked on a mass vaccination programme and in less than a decade more than five million had been vaccinated. Mobile treatment units were established in Bangkok, Thon Buri and Chiang Mai.

Reaching many Thais was still difficult. Most outlying provinces were almost impossible to access. Public health facilities and doctors were uncommon there. In December 1956, the king donated two mobile medical units to the Ministry of Public Health to aid in the campaign and provide other treatments, but the needs remained overwhelming. In the 1960s, there were few doctors serving people in the Northeast and other regions far from Bangkok. By 1966, however, tuberculosis control was integrated into general health services. As these

Far left *King Bhumibol at the unveiling ceremony for the statue of his father, Prince Mahidol of Songkla, at Siriraj hospital in 1950.*

Centre *King Bhumibol visits a patient in hospital. The king helped launch a number of new medical facilities during his reign.*

Left *King Bhumibol launching Vejapah on 19 January 1955. The king funded the floating clinic to provide medical services to people who lived along rivers and canals.*

steadily expanded throughout the country, the programme was made a fixture.

In the early stages of implementation, one million people a year were being vaccinated. In 1967, to boost the numbers of qualified personnel working on the response, the Central Chest Hospital initiated a graduate programme for nurses in tuberculosis control. By the mid-1970s, tuberculosis control was a feature of all provincial health services. While tuberculosis has defied eradication efforts, it is no longer the scourge or source of fear it once was.

The king's role in combating the disease was typical of his efforts in public health. Unlike his work in other fields, such as agriculture, where he could apply his own scientific and engineering background and aptitude in developing solutions, the king had no formal medical education and could not contribute research of his own. In fact, Dr Sumet Tantivejkul, secretary general of the Chaipattana Foundation, believes that many of the king's early initiatives and projects focused on public health precisely because they did not require the king's own fieldwork. His ability to move about the country was rather limited in the 1950s; research takes time and positive results would not have been assured. The health initiatives that emerged made use of treatments and methods that had a proven track record, even if they were new to Thailand. Although the Ministry of Public Health, and many others working in the field, was chiefly responsible for building the public health system and extending medical services to the people, the king's projects and donations addressed gaps in the system, complemented the work of public health officials, and helped garner public support.

Signature Project

Of all the health threats that Thailand faced in the 1950s, few were more conspicuous and stigmatising than a disease that had persisted for centuries. Leprosy, as the king noted in an audience granted to the director-general of the Department of Health at the time, was still afflicting many people and universally feared by the public.

The director-general, Sawat Daengsawang, believed that with appropriate funds, training and facilities, leprosy could be eradicated within a period of ten years. Sawat proposed that a new facility be built in stages at the leprosarium in Phra Pradaeng in Samut Prakan province. King Bhumibol approved the planning, donated the initial capital and adopted the work under his patronage. On 16 January 1960, accompanied by the princess mother, King Bhumibol

presided over the opening of the Rajprachasamasai Institute.

The name signifies that the king ("Raj") and the people ("pracha") assist mutually ("samasai"). The institute had taken two years to construct. It featured a centre to train medical personnel and healthcare workers in leprosy treatment and control, as well as a research laboratory to find new treatments. Additionally, a sanatorium and hospital were opened later, as well as a school for the children of lepers. The sanatorium eventually housed between 600 and 800 patients from around the country.

Dr Teera Ramasootra, who would become the head of the institute, had just graduated from medical school in 1957 when he was urged by Sawat to apply to work on the new campaign against leprosy. "When we started, there were only two doctors and 95 leprosy workers," recalls Teera. "It was impossible to treat. When the king became involved, everything changed. He lit the way for us. We had hope we could succeed."

Teera, who would eventually go on to study at Johns Hopkins University and at Temple University, became an expert in skin pathology and one of Thailand's first epidemiologists. When his wife, Pantyp, received a government scholarship to study nursing in the US, the couple could not afford the living expenses, so King Bhumibol gave her a grant for that purpose. Before leaving, Teera and Pantyp were given an audience with the king. "He said he hoped I would still work on leprosy when I returned. I gave him my promise that I would," Teera remembers.

Leprosy was not a field that attracted many people. Lepers remained feared because of misunderstanding about how the disease was transmitted, and the physical disfigurement of those suffering from it. Ninety-five percent of the population is actually immune to leprosy, which is caused by a bacterial infection similar to tuberculosis. Even for those who are not immune, it requires close and prolonged contact with an infected person to pass on the disease. Yet leprosy was still dreaded by everyone, as the king recalled in 1997: "On a tour of the provinces, [in Narathiwat, 25 March 1959] I saw sitting among the people a man who had leprosy. My personal doctor pointed him out to me, saying that the man had 'that kind of disease', not daring to say out loud that it was leprosy. Anyway, I approached the man and asked where he lived and how he was doing. My doctor was shocked and was alarmed. This meant that even a doctor did not know that the disease is not easily transmitted."

Dr Teera concurs, "The stigma then was worse than the stigma that we saw later against people suffering from AIDS." Even the healthy children of lepers were often denied an

education because others thought they would spread the disease. At the Rajprachasamasai School, in order to show such attitudes were misguided, healthy children of parents who did not have leprosy were integrated into the school.

The king served as an important agent in changing perceptions toward people suffering from leprosy. Teera recalls that when the king visited the sanatorium he would not only speak with patients, but also accept their offerings of jasmine garlands. "He touched the patients. He talked with them and he smiled. These were very important meetings. He tried to show that he never had prejudice of any kind. The public saw this. It was also important for the doctors to see, because the doctors were also afraid." Recalling the king's words to those working at the Rajprachasamasai Institute, Teera said: "To treat patients you have to be able to treat their heart, to touch their heart. Not just their pain or symptoms. You have to make them see that leprosy can be cured."

In 1997, King Bhumibol commented: "The patient's morale is essential." The benefit of encouragement is twofold, he said. "One is the willingness to get admitted to the hospital; the other is the agreement to receive the treatment. In the past they ran away when the word 'hospital' was mentioned, and once admitted, they would seize on the first opportunity to run away. They refused to be treated, and that is the most dangerous thing."

In the end, defeating leprosy took more than the ten years predicted. The breakthrough came in 1981 when the WHO recommended a triple-drug therapy of clofazimine, rifampicin and dapsone. This therapy was extremely effective, and was adopted rapidly by health professionals. By 1991, just ten years after the introduction of the triple therapy, Thailand succeeded in essentially eliminating the disease. When Thailand's leprosy control efforts began in 1957, the prevalence was 50 cases for every 10,000 Thais. By 2010, the prevalence was 0.11 cases per 10,000 Thais—a level low enough for the WHO to officially consider the disease eliminated, although monitoring and prevention measures continue.

When those involved in the response announced they had succeeded in their efforts, King Bhumibol told them to maintain surveillance, as migrants from neighbouring countries could potentially reignite the problem. The Rajprachasamasai Institute founded a migration surveillance project. The king also noted that old lepers could still be seen begging on city streets, so the institute developed a rehabilitation project for elderly and deformed lepers and established a welfare fund for them.

Observing the strong similarities between leprosy and the later HIV and AIDS pandemic,

especially the stigma and discrimination against the children of those infected, the king instructed Teera and others to help those children get an education. The institute responded by opening its school to the children of those infected with HIV.

Basic Needs

Another major public health threat of the 1950s was polio. Although Jonas Salk had developed a vaccine in 1952, it was not licensed until 1955 and not immediately available in the developing world. Well into the 21st century, polio still exists in parts of Asia and Africa despite having been eradicated long ago in the West. In the early 1950s, a wave of polio swept across Thailand. King Bhumibol raised donations to fight the epidemic. A relief fund was launched and fully equipped wards, along with equipment for long-term rehabilitation for those afflicted, were built with his help. In 1952, the king donated two iron lungs to Siriraj Hospital. In 1953, he presented more funds to the Thai Red Cross and presided over the opening of the National Blood Centre.

To increase support for other health initiatives, he submitted private films of the royal family to be shown at theatres around the country in 1954, starting with the Chalermkrung Royal Theatre in Bangkok. Money was raised from the ticket sales, but it wasn't enough for the purpose the king initially had in mind—the construction of facilities at Siriraj Hospital where children with infectious diseases could receive care. King Bhumibol dipped into the Privy Purse to add to the total. Other members of the royal family and some private individuals also contributed. The building was opened on 9 June 1957 and named after the king's late older brother, King Ananda.

In 1958, a cholera epidemic hit Thailand and took 18 months to bring under control. When cholera strikes, patients rapidly become dehydrated and many die quickly. The king, who wanted to ensure that public health officials would have the resources needed to confront future outbreaks, instructed officials to look into domestic production of saline solution. "The project proved successful, and the saline solution produced was of good quality, costing only a fraction of the foreign product," says Sumet. "Thus the foundation of a saline solution industry was laid for the country."

Continuing a tradition established by the king's grandmother, Queen Savang Vadhana,

Far left *Thai public health workers and an American volunteer doctor inoculate a baby in 1955.*

Left *An iron lung as pictured in 1952. The king donated two iron lungs to Siriraj Hospital.*

❝ The Anandamahidol Foundation helped foster the development of a corps of medical professionals who would help drive the advance of the public health system. ❞

and carried on by his father, the king also promoted medical training. In 1955, he honoured his brother's memory by establishing the Anandamahidol Fund, which grants scholarships for advanced study abroad in medicine. The fund would eventually sponsor students for degrees in many branches of science and technology and occasionally other disciplines. On 3 April 1959, the king elevated its status to the Anandamahidol Foundation.

According to Dr Suwit Wibulpolprasert of the Ministry of Public Health, scholarship recipients, after completing advanced studies abroad, return to pass on their newfound knowledge. "Several research institutes have been established for returnees to undertake research studies in the country," he said. Between 1959 and 2011, a total of 293 students received advanced degrees abroad on scholarships from the foundation. Some early recipients of scholarships became leaders in establishing their branch of healthcare in Thailand, such as Dr Charas Suwanwela, a specialist in neurosurgery, and Dr Prawase Wasi, a specialist in haematology. The Anandamahidol Foundation helped foster the development of a corps of medical professionals who would help drive the advance of the public health system.

New Sources of Nutrition

From the beginning of his reign, King Bhumibol observed that many of the health problems of the people were rooted in malnutrition. In this area, the king became famous for two projects in particular, both inspired, in part, by the work of international experts working in Thailand. The first was initiated in 1951 in Bangkok's Ambara Mansion. The king had received a gift of several *pla moh tet* (or *Tilapia mossambica*) fish from Dr S.W. Ling, a regional fishery biologist working with the Food and Agriculture Organisation (FAO). Hoping the fish might provide a more reliable source of protein for the people, the king invited officials from the Department of Fisheries to turn his palace swimming pool into a breeding ground.

Farmers in Thailand typically caught fish in rivers and ponds but were not accustomed to breeding them. Stocks were in decline. Two years later, in 1953, he distributed the resulting fish fry through the fisheries department to village headmen and district officials around the country. From this initial venture, fish culture expanded. In fresh water ponds, farmers bred the fish and found a new source of sustenance for their families—and extra income as well.

In 1965, the king once again used his palace grounds for fish breeding after Crown Prince

Akihito (the current emperor of Japan) presented the king with 50 *Tilapia nilotica* fish fry. This time a pond on the grounds of Chitralada Villa was used and the results were even better. The fish, which was native to the Nile River, were not only easier to breed than *pla moh tet* but tasted better as well. The fish, given the Thai name *pla nil* by the king, remains one of the most popular in the country to this day.

The second nutrition project the king is well known for relates to dairy, which was not widely consumed in Thailand before the 1960s. The king's project was inspired, in part, by a series of exchanges with the Danish royal family and a Danish FAO expert working in Thailand. On his state visits abroad, the king was always interested in exploring projects that he might be able to implement in Thailand, and on his visit to Denmark in 1960 he toured a milk plant. Meanwhile, in Thailand, Danish agronomist Gunnar Søndergaard, who worked for the FAO in Bangkok during the late 1950s, had noted that the only milk available at that time was sweetened condensed milk made from powder. With the support of the Danish Agricultural Promotion Board and the Thai Ministry of Agriculture, Søndergaard began dairy farming on a piece of land 140 km north of Bangkok.

In January 1962, Søndergaard received King Frederik and Queen Ingrid of Denmark, who were visiting Thailand, and their host King Bhumibol. Duly impressed, King Bhumibol decided to launch his own small milk cow dairy project on the grounds of Chitralada Villa. Known as the Suan Chitralada Dairy Farm Project, it originally featured five cows and a bull donated by the Danes. Initially, the project was not conducted for commercial purposes but as a demonstration project from which farmers could learn how to raise milk-producing cows and sell the milk. Hundreds of farmers followed the king's lead. A milk collection centre was set up for the farmers and pasteurized milk was offered to the public at a low price. Soon, delivery men on bicycles and later on motorcycles were carrying milk around Bangkok. In time the project led to the launch of a semi-commercial Thai-Danish milk venture.

The dairy farmers' response was so enthusiastic and successful, in fact, that by 1966 a crisis had ensued: there were not enough processing factories or market demand to meet the supply. As one dairy family member recalls, the farmers began in desperation to feed the surplus milk to their pigs but even then excess milk was still discarded. The farmers petitioned the king for help, claiming they were on the verge of bankruptcy.

The king stepped in to help process some of the excess supply, setting up the Suan Dusit Milk Powder Plant on the grounds of Chitralada Villa. "Consider the plant as a model

Far left *King Bhumibol pays a visit to the milking stalls in the royal dairy farm.*

Centre *King Bhumibol inspects a machine for powdering milk produced by his dairy herd in the grounds of Chitralada Villa.*

Left *King Bhumibol releases pla nil into a pond near Chitralada Villa.*

plant," the king said at the opening in 1969. "Whoever wishes to acquire knowledge or to make a dairy business successful and beneficial for the people and for the national economy as a whole may come and observe the activities of the plant at any time," he said. In time, processing plants in Chitralada Villa were producing milk tablets, cheese, ice cream, butter, condensed milk and even distilled water, making sure that nothing went to waste. Also in response to the crisis, the king had launched the Nong Pho Powder Milk Plant in Ratchaburi province from where the initial petition for help had been sent. Over time, it developed into the Nong Pho Dairy Co-operative which paid special attention to the workers' welfare. Schooling was offered to their children, who would often follow in their parents' footsteps and join the co-operative themselves later in life.

The dairy initiative revealed the king's preference for taking a holistic approach to business. He would look in depth at all the processes and factors involved in his model venture, from the experimentation, and the development of products to the welfare of the workers. From cow to consumer, efficient, cost-effective ways to manage dairy farming were worked out, stressing not profits but the socio-economic benefits gained.

The publicity surrounding the king's experimental and pilot projects on the palace grounds also did much to raise awareness among the Thai public of the health and nutrition benefits of dairy. Milk cows can still be seen by motorists passing by the palace on Si Ayutthaya Road in Bangkok. If the Thai people associate cow's milk with King Bhumibol and his projects, King Bhumibol gave credit where credit was due. In 2010, on behalf of the king, Princess Sirindhorn bestowed upon dairy farmer Gunnar Søndergaard the rank of Commander of the Most Admirable Order of Direkgunabhorn.

Direct Contact

In the mid-1960s, after having visited numerous foreign countries with Queen Sirikit, King Bhumibol expanded his journeys around rural Thailand, spending several months each year inspecting villages and planning development projects. These trips would have an enormous impact on both the king and the Thai people, as he could gauge for himself the extent of the people's problems, consult with villagers and begin formulating ideas for possible assistance. On these travels, it was obvious that many people were in poor health.

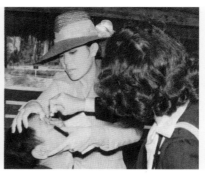

The king established clinics at his palaces in Sakon Nakhon, Prachuap Khiri Khan, Narathiwat and Chiang Mai provinces where anyone could come for free healthcare. More famously, in 1965, he instructed his personal physician to treat villagers during his upcountry trips. This idea followed a tradition established by his grandmother Queen Savang Vadhana, who, according to Dr Sanjai Sangvichien of Siriraj Hospital, would bring court physicians with her on her provincial travels and have them treat local people. Aside from his personal physician, King Bhumibol enlisted the help of the Royal Medical Team from the Royal Medical Division of the Bureau of the Royal Household. Other medical professionals also offered their help. The king's entourage expanded to include royally sponsored volunteer medical teams. These consisted of surgical teams from Siriraj Hospital and Phra Mongkut Klao Hospital, and ear, eye, nose, throat and allergy teams along with the mobile dental unit from the Royal Thai Army.

In a 1969 speech to the doctors participating in the mobile treatment programme, the king praised their work: "To go to train in rural areas has been considered backward. Actually this idea is quite out of date. The most modern idea is when the doctors who study medicine go out and practise. The main objective of being a doctor is to cure people of sickness."

The medical teams sometimes preceded the king's arrival to take stock of the health problems of the villagers. Often, King Bhumibol would lead the way to the hamlets and conduct an informal, rapid health assessment of his own. Prevention was always a component of the king's approach, and his team would distribute mosquito nets to protect against malaria, salt for those lacking iodine in their diets and warm clothing for those living in mountainous areas, not to mention lollipops to the kids.

When the entourage came across people with illnesses too serious to be treated in their homes, the patient would be transported to a provincial hospital and the medical unit would assist in treatment. Officials followed up, ensuring that the patient received proper care and the family also received assistance if needed. Many of the villagers treated during these visits had never seen a doctor in their lives. "At that time, what we call community hospitals were still very small. Some hospitals had only one doctor, and many had no doctor at all," the king's personal physician, Dr Songkram Supcharoen, says.

Describing the upcountry visits, Sumet Tantivejkul of the Chaipattana Foundation says, "People would come to him with their sufferings, and one of those was health problems. They would bring their babies to him." It was not uncommon to see King Bhumibol kneeling

Far left *King Bhumibol looks through a microscope during a visit to a medical facility. The king has helped advance medical research through his foundations and scholarships.*

Centre *Queen Sirikit helps an eye doctor tend to a patient.*

Left *King Bhumibol observes doctors from a mobile medical unit treating children in a remote area.*

on the ground, asking questions of villagers, explaining nutrition and healthcare, writing detailed notes on medicine bottles or packets to ensure that villagers clearly understood the instructions, and even administering medicine. "He joked with us afterwards that he was taking care of people like a quack doctor," remembers Prawase Wasi. Songkram recalls a time when the king had the medical unit bring a hospital bed for an ill subject in the South, and assisted in hauling it up to the villager's house on stilts.

King Bhumibol's physicians weren't always happy about the close contact he had with his subjects. "When he goes to villages he gets close to people. Sometimes with children, he gave them medicine himself. When the children coughed, it was easy for him to get ill," Songkram says. At times King Bhumibol did fall ill from these encounters, contracting dysentery on one occasion and, more seriously, mycoplasma pneumonia in 1975. He was the first person in Thailand diagnosed with that type of pneumonia, said Songkram, who was summoned to treat the king in Chiang Mai.

Prawase believes the king's hands-on approach prompted a crucial change in thinking among the Thai medical establishment. Doctors and healthcare officials began to realise that medical treatment and public healthcare had to be distributed. They realised volunteers, health workers and nurses should play a role in this. "This was the groundwork for what is now called 'basic healthcare work'. I think that the king played a great role here in changing attitudes," says Prawase. "And he did it without giving orders but by setting an example."

Helping Veterans

By the late 1960s, a communist insurgency was smouldering in many rural swathes of the country and Thailand had sent troops to fight alongside the Americans in the Vietnam War, bringing new attention to the casualties suffered by soldiers, police and other security personnel and civilians as a result of armed conflict. In 1968, the king established a vocational training centre for military veterans disabled by the war. The centre was established at Phra Mongkut Klao Hospital in Bangkok, which had been a locus of support and rehabilitation for disabled veterans since the 1950s. It was there that Major General Pratum Sutachuta had established a rehabilitation unit offering artificial limbs and physical therapy. To this day, staff, who mostly have only primary school education, craft artificial limbs under the supervision of doctors.

The prosthetics, some of which are now of comparable quality to those produced in more developed countries and produced at a fraction of the cost, even attract foreign buyers.

As the war in Indochina as well as the insurgency in Thailand peaked, King Bhumibol created a programme to assist the wounded. Launched on 2 April 1975, the Sai Jai Thai Foundation raised public donations to help those maimed or wounded in the fighting, as well as the families of those killed in action. The king appointed his daughter Princess Sirindhorn as the foundation's chairperson. The funds are first used as a safety net, mainly for emergency assistance, until state agencies can properly respond. But they are also used for monthly lifetime allowances for those crippled in the conflicts, with lump sum payments to the families of the deceased.

Although by the early 1980s the insurgency had been almost completely quashed, soldiers and security personnel continue to be wounded in border and other conflicts. Casualties have risen sharply since 2004, when a near-dormant insurgency reawakened in Thailand's deep south. About 4,000 security personnel and their families were still receiving assistance from the Sai Jai Thai Foundation in 2011.

Village Doctors

In the early 1980s, the number of doctors in rural areas remained insufficient, with one doctor per every 14,742 people in the South, one per every 12,419 people in the North and one per every 28,424 in the Northeast. To help villagers help themselves, in 1982, the king launched the "village doctors" programme, in which some villagers would receive basic healthcare training. This idea was in many ways similar to the community health worker (CHW) idea that had gained currency in 1978 at the International Conference on Primary Health Care held at Alma-Ata in what is today Kazakhstan. For decades, some developing countries had been instructing and using grassroots-level workers, called extension workers, in agricultural and community development programmes. They in turn trained people in their communities, spreading knowledge and development.

The Ministry of Public Health had experimented on a very small scale with community health workers, but the security situation in the late 1970s and some opposition from medical professionals inhibited its development. King Bhumibol's project was launched with

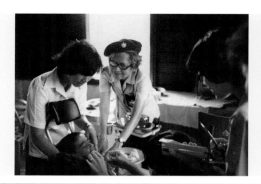

volunteers in Chiang Mai province. Selected villagers were taught prevention techniques, how to administer first aid and about nutrition—especially in relation to pregnant mothers and young children. The use of traditional herbal medicines for simple ailments was encouraged, but the "village doctor" would also learn when and how to refer patients to district or provincial hospitals for more serious treatment. The training was later expanded to Sakon Nakhon and Narathiwat, both provinces where the king maintains a residence. Thousands of village doctors from 22 provinces were eventually trained.

At first, as with the Ministry of Public Health's attempts at a similar initiative, there was resistance. "A group of doctors was against it. Their reaction was that these people are not qualified to be delivering healthcare. But what they are delivering is very basic," says Sumet of the Chaipattana Foundation. Resistance soon gave way to support, especially as the government of Prime Minister Prem Tinsulanonda launched its own rural development programme. Prem, who had earlier been the regional army commander for the Northeast, was supportive of the king's belief that development could defeat insurgency, and his successive administrations promoted King Bhumibol's strategies and goals. Around the same time the Ministry of Public Health chose to scale up its own community health worker programme. In the ministry's version, village doctors were community health volunteers, and by the turn of the millennium more than 650,000 of them had been trained nationwide.

A Team Effort

In general, after the 1960s, King Bhumibol devoted more attention to other development issues besides public health, in part because other members of the royal family, especially the princess mother, carried the torch for him. A nurse by training, the princess mother continued her late husband's practice of granting scholarships to promising medical students, brought samples of anti-tuberculosis drugs with her when she returned to Thailand in 1945, established a 500,000 baht revolving fund for the Faculty of Medicine at Siriraj Hospital to send students overseas for study, founded the Thailand Nursing Association, donated money for several hospitals and nursing schools, and was the patron of the Disabled Assistance Foundation and the Foundation for Lepers in Lampang province. She is also known for her "flying doctors"—a service she helped establish in the early 1970s whereby volunteer doctors

Far left *The princess mother, a qualified nurse herself, assists volunteer dentists in the field.*

Centre *Princess Chulabhorn, the youngest of the three daughters in the royal family, shines a torch while a doctor from the Royal Medical Unit treats a boy with an injury.*

Left *King Bhumibol, accompanied by Princess Sirindhorn, talks to a child during one of his visits to a village upcountry.*

provided consultations to those in remote villages by radio, and in serious cases travelled to isolated hamlets by small aircraft to deliver care. In 1990, she was awarded the Health-For-All Gold Medal by the WHO for her work.

In addition, the government was doing more to improve public health. In fact, despite Thailand's economic difficulties during the early part of the 1980s, the period from 1978 to 1987 is regarded by the Ministry of Public Health as something of a golden era—and considered more equitable than the period that followed. It was a decade of expansion in which nearly all districts had community hospitals and nearly every *tambon*, or subdistrict, had a health centre and midwifery services. The positive effects were easy to measure. The difference in the doctor/population ratios between the Northeast and Bangkok, which had been as high as 21-fold in 1979, dropped to less than nine-fold by 1987.

Development experts often look to certain key statistics, such as life expectancy, maternal and child mortality rates and immunisation rates to measure the progress and status of health and healthcare in a country. In Thailand, maternal mortality fell from 130 per 100,000 live births in 1977 to 27 in 1988. Coverage of basic immunisations, which contribute to reducing child mortality, rose from 20 to 50 percent in 1977 to 80 to 90 percent by 1987. Mortality rates for under fives fell from above 4 per 1,000 in the late 1970s to 2.3 in 1987. Infant mortality dropped from 51 per 1,000 lives births in 1977 to under 32 by 1987. Meanwhile, life expectancy rose from 58.0 years for males and 63.8 for females in 1976 to 63.8 and 68.9 respectively by 1986. Healthcare was also becoming more equitably distributed: by 1990 there was one doctor for every 11,314 people in the Northeast. While that still indicated a great need for more medical personnel in regions outside of Bangkok, it was a marked improvement compared to a decade earlier when there was just one doctor for every 28,424 people in the Northeast. Other regions also saw similar improvements in doctor-to-population ratios.

Nonetheless, gaps in coverage still existed and some health issues had yet to be dealt with or were overlooked. For example, high numbers of villagers suffered from goitre, a swelling of the thyroid gland to the point of deformity. The condition was caused by iodine deficiency, which also seriously compromised children's general development and was the most common preventable cause of brain damage. In the early 1990s, King Bhumibol launched a pilot initiative on iodine deficiency control known informally as the "Salt Roads" project. The goal was to trace back from the user to the source and iodize the salt free of charge at the site of production. The survey, first launched in Samoeng district of Chiang

Mai province in 1993, revealed that most of non–iodized salt was granulated and came from the Northeast. Once again, King Bhumibol had served as a catalyst. Public health officials then worked with the private sector and local salt producers to iodize the salt at its source. Although by the turn of the 21st century iodine deficiency was no longer a serious public health threat, the last decade has seen a resurgence of the problem.

The early 1990s also marked the proliferation of a new dangerous threat to public health: the HIV and AIDS epidemic. The first recorded case of HIV in Thailand was in 1984, but it wasn't until near the end of that decade that the seriousness and the extent of the problem became apparent. Thailand was fortunate to have Mechai Viravaidya from the Prime Minister's Office in the government of Anand Panyarachun from 1991–92, who confronted the problem and began instituting public health measures to attempt to control and even reverse the spread of the epidemic. At about the same time, King Bhumibol made donations to Wat Prabat Namphu, a Buddhist temple in Lop Buri province that serves as a hospice for people living with HIV and AIDS, and as an education centre to teach the public about the disease. While still among the hardest-hit countries in Asia by the epidemic, Thailand has been praised by several UN agencies for its comprehensive response.

Growing Pains

The 1990s saw further expansion of the public and private health systems. However, a number of factors contributed to declines in terms of equitable access to healthcare. The growth of private hospitals resulted in more doctors, nurses and others leaving public hospitals for better compensation. Imports of expensive equipment and pharmaceuticals rose considerably. Procedures that often may not have been necessary, such as caesarean sections, were encouraged and led to more beds being filled in private hospitals. That kind of potential conflict of interest went hand-in-hand with reports of corruption—and malpractices involving procurement of medical equipment and pharmaceuticals were exposed in the health sector.

Challenges would continue even with the introduction of the 30-baht health care scheme by the government in 2001. Under this programme, visits to a doctor at public hospitals were limited to a cost of 30 baht per consultation for most Thais. In 2007, the cost was waived entirely. The result is that access to basic healthcare is now almost universal, although some

Far left *An example of the devastation caused by tropical storm Harriet in 1962 at Laem Talumphuk in Nakhon Si Thammarat province.*

Centre *Relief supplies for victims of Tropical Storm Harriet were initially stockpiled at the Chitralada Villa after they had been raised through appeals broadcast on the king's Aw Saw Radio station.*

Left *King Bhumibol personally presents cooking utensils to storm victims.*

expensive medical procedures are not covered. Funding the system is a challenge, with some hospitals finding that their costs are not all being covered by the government. Nonetheless, the programme has proven generally effective and popular.

As the decades passed, the need for new royal projects devoted to health became less necessary. Instead, the king's assistance focused mostly on responding to emergencies. Tropical Thailand has always been vulnerable to typhoons and cyclones, and the crown has responded during times of hardship through the Rajaprajanugroh Foundation, which has its origins in a devastating 1962 typhoon. When tropical storm Harriet slammed into the Isthmus of Kra in October of that year, devastating 12 coastal provinces, the storm surges swept away homes and destroyed crops. At least 600 people were killed and more than 10,000 people were left homeless. After the king appealed for donations to help those in need, money from the public flowed into Chitralada Villa—a total of 10.8 million baht in all. It was used to buy blankets and medical supplies which were given to doctors, nurses and relief workers heading to the South. The rebuilding effort would take years. The king also contributed to that effort, donating funds for reconstructing a dozen schools levelled by the storm.

As the emergency response wound down, it became apparent there was money left over. King Bhumibol decided to invest these funds in establishing the Rajaprajanugroh Foundation. The foundation is dedicated to providing relief to victims of disasters, both natural and man made. It relies on over 1,500 volunteers around the country who have been trained in first aid, childcare, accident prevention, disaster relief and planning. In its first 20 years alone, it responded to 2,390 incidents, providing aid to over 3.9 million people. The foundation did more than distribute food, water and medical supplies. It also rebuilt homes destroyed by fire and flood. Among the major disasters in which it played a role in the national response were Typhoon Gay, which struck Thailand in 1989 and killed 458 people, and the Indian Ocean tsunami in 2004 that claimed more than 8,000 lives in Thailand.

Awards

By the early 1990s, King Bhumibol's work in public health was well recognised, not just by Thais, but by the international community. On 24 November 1992, the WHO conferred upon him its Health-for-All Gold Medal. In presenting the medal, the WHO Director-

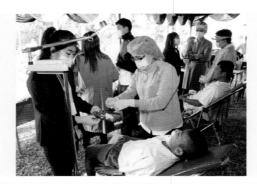

Right *The Mobile Dental Unit in action.*

Centre *Relief supplies collected by the Rajapra-janugroh Foundation are loaded ahead of being delivered to victims of Cyclone Nargis, which devastated lower Myanmar in April 2008.*

Far right *The Vejapah floating clinic travels between remote riverside villages. The clinic remains in service for the benefit of people living in isolated waterside locations.*

General Dr Hiroshi Nakajima said: "Through site visits, [King Bhumibol] has striven to acquire a personal understanding of health problems in remote areas of the country. His Majesty has shown a deep awareness of the health needs and priorities of the rural population, and other under-served groups within Thailand."

As the decade continued, the king also received awards from the International Council for the Control of Iodine Deficiency Disorders, the American College of Chest Physicians (for his work on tuberculosis), the Lions Club, and the International Union Against Tuberculosis and Lung Disease, among others.

King Bhumibol in turn began giving awards himself. In 1992, to mark the centenary of his father's birth, the king inaugurated the annual Prince Mahidol Awards. They were created to honour the memory and contributions of the king's father, and also to recognise and foster achievements in medicine and public health—the two fields studied by Prince Mahidol. Awards are given in each category.

According to Dr Supat Vanichakarn, the secretary-general of the Prince Mahidol Award Foundation, the foundation is the only entity that gives an award in the field of public health in addition to medicine. "Awards are not given solely for making a new discovery. It has to be used for the benefit of mankind," Dr Supat said. Recipients are chosen after careful screening and selection by a committee of advisers at the Prince Mahidol Award Foundation. At a ceremony in Bangkok, a medal bearing the likeness of Prince Mahidol and a prize of US$50,000 is presented to each winner. In 2012, the 20th anniversary of the awards, the prizes will be increased to US$100,000 each.

Although several Thais have received the Prince Mahidol Award, including Mechai Viravaidya and Dr Wiwat Rojanapithayakorn for their work in responding to the HIV pandemic in Thailand, the vast majority of the 59 winners have been foreigners. These recipients represent an impressive sampling of eminent medical and public health professionals from around the world. Two of the winners have gone on to receive the highest honour of all, a Nobel Prize. These were Dr Barry Marshall of Australia for his work in proving that the H. pylori virus was the actual cause of most peptic ulcers, and Professor Harald zur Hausen of Germany for his findings on the causes of cervical cancer. Another Prince Mahidol Award winner of note, Dr Margaret Chan, received an award for public health in 1998 for her leadership in controlling the spread of avian influenza in Hong Kong. Chan was later appointed director-general of the WHO.

Healthy Future?

Thailand has made great strides in delivering healthcare. In areas commonly used to measure development, the numbers tell the story. Maternal mortality—mothers who die during pregnancy or childbirth—has fallen from over 400 per 100,000 in 1950 to just 12 for every 100,000 in 2009. Infant mortality has fallen from 62 deaths for every 1,000 live births to just eight, while under-five mortality is 14 per 1,000 live births. Life expectancy has increased from an average of 50 years in 1950 to 69 years. Advances always come at a cost, and the economics of healthcare is one of the challenges facing Thailand's public health system as it enters the second decade of the 21st century. Thailand is, however, on track to achieve most of the UN's Millennium Development Goals by 2015, including those aimed at health: reducing child mortality, improving maternal health and combating HIV, malaria and other diseases.

The greatest challenge for Thailand, as for many countries in East Asia, is reducing disparity. The proportion of doctors in rural areas compared to Bangkok has markedly improved. Today, there is one doctor for every 2,870 people in the Northeast, a dramatic improvement from the one for every 28,424 in 1980. Similarly, there is one doctor for every 2,250 people in the South, and one for every 2,002 people in the North. But with one doctor for every 565 people in Bangkok, imbalances clearly remain. Drawn to higher-paying positions with more resources in Bangkok and other big cities, full-service quality healthcare is harder to find in rural areas and barriers to access still remain.

Thailand has been praised for successfully curbing the spread of HIV. Effective programmes are in place and having positive impacts on other communicable diseases. The ability of the public health system to respond to outbreaks and emergencies was demonstrated in the aftermath of the tsunami, and the SARS and avian influenza epidemics. As Thailand has progressed, however, new and different health problems have emerged. Pollution in cities and near industrial areas is blamed for respiratory and other illnesses. Changing diets have led to alarming rates of obesity and diabetes. The stresses of modern life have contributed to over-consumption of alcohol, drugs and their attendant health problems. Thailand's love affair with the automobile hasn't been matched by concern for safety: nearly 40 people each day die on the road, one of the highest rates in the world. The country's public health system, however, thanks in part to the initiatives and attention of King Bhumibol, is well positioned to meet these challenges.

Above *Students of Klai Kangwol School in Hua Hin listen as King Bhumibol briefs them during a visit to the Khao Tao reservoir in Prachuap Khiri Khan province. The reservoir is a royal project intended to improve water resource management.*

LEARNING FOR LIFE

A devout Buddhist who is deeply interested in science, King Bhumibol has applied his own background to his vision of education and learning. Knowledge, he argues, is useless if not applied ethically and for the practical benefit of others. Heeding his own advice, King Bhumibol tried to fill the gaps in an educational system that would occasionally leave the nation's poor or disadvantaged behind. He initiated a distance-learning programme and encyclopaedia project, opened new schools in border areas and promoted vocational workshops. In speeches and by serving as an example, he promoted ideas that countered the traditional rote learning approach in Thailand, emphasising the importance of creativity, logical thinking, analysis and the life-long pursuit of knowledge.

"Our educational system was in disarray as never before," former education minister Mom Luang Pin Malakul once wrote, recalling the situation at the end of the Second World War. "Schooling was interrupted as people fled the war to seek refuge somewhere else. A large number of school buildings were devastated by the bombs … Destroyed with them was much of the country's educational equipment and teaching materials. Worse yet, teachers were forced to find other jobs in order to survive." Academic standards had plunged; many students were unable to complete four years of mandatory schooling and it was difficult to induce teachers to return to their previous work.

When King Bhumibol returned home from his liberal, European-style education in Switzerland in 1951, the country was still struggling to get back on its feet. Observing the generally poor state of the country's educational system, the king helped launch and support initiatives similar in tenor to his healthcare work—establishing basic infrastructure, for example, such as setting up schools in remote areas. In general, his goal was to create educational opportunities for those who had none. As with much of his work, the king's initiatives typically targeted provincial areas and the most disadvantaged.

"The reason I would like everyone to pursue knowledge and establish themselves is so that they can have a prosperous life, with happiness and self-reliance as the first step," the king once explained. Summing up his views on another occasion, he said, "A holistic education that covers moral etiquette, general subjects and vocational training is an important base to develop the skills of a person so that he can contribute to the prosperity and stability of the country in the future."

Over the ensuing decades, the main messages of the king's speeches on education as well as the goals of his own initiatives remained remarkably consistent. Influenced by his own scientific bent, the king emphasised that theoretical knowledge must be tested and adjusted through real-life application. He encouraged a broad-based approach toward teaching that would inspire analytical and problem-solving skills over rote learning. As a devout Buddhist, he emphasised that academic learning should always be complemented by morality and mindfulness if knowledge is to be applied in ways that genuinely benefit both the individual and society. He also said he believed learning to be a life-long process.

The king's words and actions carried added weight because he clearly took his own advice. His ethical standards, especially in comparison to some other leaders in society, meant that students keenly attuned to adult hypocrisy could not so easily dismiss his exhortations to

❝ The reason I would like everyone to pursue knowledge and establish themselves is so that they can have a prosperous life, with happiness and self-reliance as the first step, the king once explained. ❞

work for the public good. Moreover, his own work was focused on national development, and offered solutions based on observation, analysis and practical application. Finally, through field trips and research related to his projects, the king's dedication to life-long learning was readily apparent to the public. Over the course of his reign, the king's speeches helped establish him as a moral leader in times of national crisis and, in general, as a dispenser of wisdom and *dhamma* [Buddhist teachings] in the vein long conceived for Buddhist kings.

New Frontiers

At the beginning of his reign, the young king had to face the stark fact that many of his subjects had no access to education at all. Thus, most of his efforts focused on filling gaps so that all Thais could receive some degree of formal schooling or engage in a process of life-long learning. In some cases, this meant simply opening new schools. Later initiatives took advantage of new technology such as television and the Internet to disseminate better quality teaching. From rural study centres for farmers to an encyclopaedia project, his ideas were based on the simple premise of increasing access to knowledge.

The first school the king contributed to was at Klai Kangwol palace in Hua Hin. It had been founded by King Ananda to serve the children of palace personnel. The contribution of King Bhumibol's personal funds, later augmented by private and government support, enabled the school to provide free education to poor students in the local area. The school has steadily expanded and by 2011 had more than 2,000 students from pre-school to high school with 17 branches of study, including vocational education.

Moved by the plight of the disadvantaged—lepers, the poor, hill tribes, the isolated, the disabled and those affected by natural disasters—the king also funded many Chao Pho Luang Upatham schools, which were launched by the princess mother and staffed by Border Patrol Police. In addition, the king initiated the extension of Buddhist education to be provided by knowledgeable monks at four different schools attached to temples while lay teachers were responsible for secular subjects. The king also launched the Rajprachasamasai School in Phra Pradaeng for the offspring of leprosy patients. The children did not have leprosy themselves, but were treated as possible sources of contamination and often barred from regular schools. The school expanded from only 30 students to some 3,500.

King Bhumibol typically sets up foundations to carry out his educational work. Privy councillor Dr Kasem Watanachai said the king's usual approach is to first analyse the educational challenges faced by a particular group. "He then thinks how best to serve that segment of the population," he adds. Often, the king would try out solutions in small-scale pilot projects. If the results are promising, a non-profit foundation is established to attract funding and carry out activities.

In the period 1963–73, when government funding was scarce, the king raised some 121 million baht in donations. From this, education projects received 25.4 million baht, second only to the Thai Red Cross. Typically, projects begun with the king's personal funds would later attract government funding. By the 1960s, the projects had created a partnership between the monarchy and the government that has become an important feature of the king's development work.

The foundation model also allowed the king to leverage his financial resources. He could sometimes move much more quickly than the government on urgent problems. "His Majesty has often expressed negative feelings about government bureaucracy. Government projects take a year or more to get started, so we work on problems where there is a need to take action now," comments Dr Sumet Tantivejkul, secretary-general of the Chaipattana Foundation, which was established in 1988. "A foundation can work more quickly."

The king's foundations have never been intended to supplant or compete with the government, notes Sumet. Long-term, large-scale actions must always be taken by the government. "This way we have two budgets—the foundation to move quickly and the government budget for the longer term," says Sumet.

In 1963, when King Bhumibol raised funds to help children orphaned by a natural disaster in southern Thailand, there was money left over. These funds were used to establish the Rajaprajanugroh Foundation to re-build schools in areas hit by disaster. When more donations flowed in, the foundation extended its mission to help disadvantaged children throughout the country. For example, schools for hill tribe children in Mae Hong Son province were opened. When a tsunami hit Thailand's southern coast in December 2004, the Rajaprajanugroh Foundation built four new schools in Phang Nga, Phuket, Krabi and Ranong provinces. By 2010, donations from the public increased its funds to nearly four billion baht and the foundation was able to support 44 schools. [*For details of the Rajaprajanugroh Foundation, see page 207.*]

Far left *King Bhumibol visits a classroom at Rajprajasamasai School.*

Centre *King Bhumibol, accompanied by Queen Sirikit, opens the first Romklao School on 31 October 1973. It was built with the cooperation of the army and villagers of Nong Khaen in Nakhon Phanom province near the border with Laos.*

Left *A school at Wat Sri Chan Pradit in Samut Prakan province where monks help educate children following an initiative of King Bhumibol in 1977.*

In 1972, during a period of active communist insurgency in the country, the king established the Romklao schools in areas where teachers were unwilling to work. The king later arranged for trained Border Patrol Police (BPP) personnel to teach and run the schools in these frontier areas; most of the students were from hill tribes. The project was regularly expanded with the help of the princess mother and later Princess Sirindhorn, and comprised more than 200 schools by 2010. The project provided children in remote areas with an education and improved sometimes antagonistic relations between security forces and local people. The king also set up special schools for poor students and the children of soldiers wounded in clashes with insurgents.

King Bhumibol recognised that formal classroom education was not always well suited to the needs of the disadvantaged. In 1975, he established the Phra Dabos schools for those who, generally due to poverty, had dropped out of the formal education system. In place of academic studies, the Phra Dabos Foundation offers practical vocational training. Princess Sirindhorn said the foundation's concept harked back to forest hermits, the Phra Dabos of folk stories, who people joined in the woods and served in order to gain an education. "He wants every Thai to have the chance to study," Princess Sirindhorn said of her father. Many of the public donations to the king, including those made during his illness in 2009, went to the Phra Dabos Foundation. Kasem, who serves as the foundation's secretary general, organised the "One Coin, One Wish for His Majesty the King" project in which the public was encouraged to include small donations with their get-well wishes. Donations were collected at Thai commercial banks, government offices, universities and shopping centres across the country. Kasem says the funds raised provide full scholarships for about 120 people a year to attend the Phra Dabos schools.

The king has not focused exclusively on marginalised communities. He has also supported higher learning. In 1953, he began funding scholarships in memory of his late brother. This developed into the Anandamahidol Foundation in 1959. Since King Ananda had wished to promote advanced medical studies, the first Anandamahidol scholarships were granted to medical students headed overseas for high-level training. Dr Khunying Ambhorn Meesook, who has been serving the royal family for more than 60 years, says the influence on the king of his late brother has not been fully appreciated. "His brother is always in the back of his mind," she says. The foundation now has an endowment of US$77 million.

The king also revived the King's Scholarships, which were first awarded by his

Left *King Bhumibol grants an audience to recipients of the Anandamahidol scholarships, which he established and named in honour of his late brother, King Ananda Mahidol.*

grandfather King Chulalongkorn in 1897, to enable promising young Thais to study abroad. The programme had been cancelled in 1933, the year after the revolution that ended absolute monarchy. King Bhumibol has also established scholarships to support advanced studies in Pali and Buddhism. Kasem, who oversees these scholarships, says the king was "quite worried that monks could stray from the real path" if they failed to gain a correct and in-depth understanding of Buddhism.

As a child, King Bhumibol loved the Book of Knowledge, an English-language encyclopaedia purchased by his mother. Because there was nothing comparable in Thai, in 1968 the king used some of his own money, supplemented with funds raised by Lions Clubs in Thailand, to launch a comprehensive children's encyclopaedia. Written in Thai and attuned to local needs, the project brought together hundreds of technical and educational experts who wrote articles catering to three distinct intellectual levels. King Bhumibol based this approach on personal experience.

"The idea of dividing the encyclopaedia to serve three groups of youth derived from the different ages of my children," he said. "So I thought, if we can make it happen, all four of my children will benefit from it." The king recommended that the easiest level be designed for children under 10 and printed in large, easy-to-read type. The next level was for students under 15 with more detail and smaller type. The third level provided more technical information for older students and parents helping their children. "This project is a very special one, not like any other projects," King Bhumibol said on its 15th anniversary. "Because it is the Thai encyclopaedia project, it is especially Thai." All the articles are written from a Thai perspective by local experts—none are translated from other languages. Articles on music concentrate on traditional Thai instruments and forms. All the literature discussed is Thai. Technical articles, however, are written to international standards.

"This project is an instrument to transfer knowledge, culture and ethics for the next generation," the king said, describing encyclopaedias as "books that include all the knowledge that humans have gathered since ancient times, processing it for later generations."

He added: "Normally, this knowledge is learned at schools or educational institutions. But because of the lack of teachers and schools, there needs to be a source of knowledge which enables people to learn by themselves … The purpose of this encyclopaedia is to point out to readers and users that all sciences are related. In short, it is education for underprivileged children and a conjunction of all sciences."

> ❝ Some 2.4 million copies of the encyclopaedia have
> been printed and distributed to more than 30,000
> schools and libraries, or sold throughout the country.
> Since each volume is used by many children, the
> project has probably reached more people than
> any other royal venture. ❞

According to the project's director, Khunying Maenmas Chavalit, the programme expanded from contributions from 10 volunteers to hundreds of experts. The biggest challenge, she says, was to get them to write clearly at all three levels. An editorial committee reviews all the contributions for accuracy and readability. "His Majesty checks each volume and is very particular," Khunying Maenmas says. "One time he sent back a drawing of a pig saying that its ears were drawn incorrectly—tilting the wrong way. So you can see we must be very careful." The first 10,000 copies were distributed in 1973. Half were donated to schools and libraries around the country, and half sold. The project grew. The four volumes originally planned had by 2010 become 35 volumes. Some 2.4 million copies of the encyclopaedia have been printed and distributed to more than 30,000 schools and libraries, or sold throughout the country. Since each volume is used by many children, the project has probably reached more people than any other royal venture.

Today, most of the encyclopaedias are sold in bookshops at low prices. All contributors still volunteer, says Khunying Maenmas, ensuring the project remains lean and cost effective. Plans are also under way to include CD-ROM versions with the hardback editions and to release the encyclopaedia over the Internet.

By the 1980s, King Bhumibol's development projects had achieved some success, so he sought ways to disseminate the practical knowledge gained from these projects. Believing that development lessons had to be tailored to differing local conditions, he established six royal development study centres in various regions of the country. "The centres are intended to be the venues for study and research according to different areas because in each particular area there are different characteristics," he explained in 1983. King Bhumibol wanted the study centres to collect and disseminate information buried uselessly in the organisational silos of ministries and departments. The study centres provided a holistic alternative at a far more accessible local level: "Normally each agency has its own independent centre with no other agencies involved," the king explained. "However, the royal development study centres gather in one place officials and experts from every department and division in various fields; agricultural, social and related educational promotion. This means the people can obtain different fields of knowledge at the same time."

The study centres also embraced some other core beliefs of the king in relation to education, namely that learning is a life-long process and that education must be continually refreshed through research, application and study to remain relevant. Each centre serves

as "a centre for exchange of experiences among academics, development workers and the people". The king called on the study centres to use a multidisciplinary approach. Typically, people from the dozen or so villages closest to the centres are most actively involved. They help test new methodologies, plant varieties, seeds and technology in real-life conditions. Such villages provide models that farmers from more distant locales can see for themselves. Training courses are open not only to local people, but, increasingly, to visitors from other developing countries. The model has already been adopted in Laos and Lesotho. [*For details of the study centres, see page 252.*]

With his lifelong interest in communication technology, King Bhumibol became interested in the potential offered by distance education. The king initiated a project at the Mahidol University Computing Centre to digitise the *Tipitaka*, the highest scriptural canon for Buddhist teachings, beliefs, and practice. The centre put an electronic version of all the Buddhist scriptures on CD in 1994 with a comprehensive database and advanced search capabilities for easy reference. More famously, the king used satellite television for improving the quality of education at remote and under-resourced schools. The king's Distance Learning Foundation was established with 50 million baht presented by the Telephone Organization of Thailand. According to Khwankeo Vajarodaya, the foundation's president, the king personally supervised the configuration of the main classroom used for broadcasts at Klai Kangwol School. The project, which began broadcasting on the king's birthday in 1995, is particularly useful to schools without teachers for key subjects. The signal is also carried into private homes by the leading cable television provider in the country, but it was never intended to supplant classroom teaching, or to provide edutainment to home viewers.

"With a severe lack of teachers in the rural areas, our mission is to deliver basic education to the doorsteps of all remote schools," Khwankeo wrote in 2007. "Student morale at the remote schools has improved. They know they are given the same quality and standard of education, the same teacher and tutor, the same periods for study, and the same treatment as His Majesty the King's students."

The foundation's broadcasts cover both primary and secondary school curricula, as well as vocational training, community education, university education and classes in six languages. The existing classrooms at Klai Kangwol School serve as studios for the telecasts. The school, while teaching its own students in 12 grades, also produces educational programming on 15 different channels that broadcast 24/7. Chaiyut Saenamwong, the school's manager, says

Far left, centre and left King Bhumibol's Distance Learning Foundation broadcasts lessons directly to schools across the country from the classrooms of Klai Kangwol School in Hua Hin. The objective is to make quality teaching more broadly available, particularly in remote areas, where full staffing of schools is not feasible, even for some mainstream subjects. Distance learning techniques are particularly valuable in foreign language training.

two-inch thick handbooks are provided with broadcast schedules, teaching plans, handout materials and homework assignments that can be easily photocopied. "We don't think that just putting the students in front of the television is effective," says Chaiyut. "We supply good materials and excellent teaching on the screen, but our teachers cannot interact with the students at remote locations. This is the role of the onsite teacher—to answer questions, monitor student performance and help them with class activities like science experiments."

Each classroom has two cameras, an overhead projector and a digital slide system, but they are otherwise far from high-tech. Students sit at battered wooden desks that are crammed together. Programme technical directors sit in tiny glass cubicles monitoring equipment and cutting back and forth between the cameras and the visual aids.

The project produces hundreds of hours of new educational programming each month with only 60 teachers and 110 technical staff. Top teachers are attracted to the school by the honour of serving the king and the opportunity to be seen on television throughout the country. On screen, teachers are paid an extra 500 baht per hour but that hardly makes up for the extra time it takes to prepare for a televised course. Money is not a motivation.

"In some schools, I am sorry to say, teachers don't prepare very thoroughly, but here they all spend a lot of time on preparation. They often work late at night because they don't want to be embarrassed by appearing unprepared on national television," says Chaiyut. Teaching standards are of great importance. Teachers found lacking are asked to undergo further training. Those that can't do better are eventually asked to leave.

While most broadcasts cover the national curriculum and are produced by the school's regular teachers, daily programming on three channels and weekend programming on all channels focuses on non-formal learning—anything from cooking to foreign languages. The non-formal educational programmes and most foreign languages are taught by volunteer teachers or produced by specialist organisations, such as the Institute for the Promotion of Teaching Science and Technology.

Private companies pleased to be associated with the king and high-tech education provide scholarships and housing that enable poorer children to attend Klai Kangwol School. The king and an agro-industry company offer full scholarships for 10 students at each level to come from remote border areas to study at Klai Kangwol. The government assists by providing some teachers and administrators, which is cost-effective to the public purse as well.

The project, however, has not been without its problems. In 2009, the Ministry of

Education decided that it needed to be reviewed because many schools were not making good enough use of the educational broadcasts. "[The ministry] has decided to step in because we have found accumulated problems with the project over the past 13 years. More than 20,000 satellite dishes have been bought with a budget of billions of baht, but the schools rarely make use of them," commented then Education Minister Jurin Laksanavisit in the *Bangkok Post*. "In many cases," he said, "the dishes have become another school antique."

According to a survey by the Office of the Basic Education Commission, 3,964 satellite dishes and learning equipment for the project had been left unused. The process for purchasing equipment was changed, with schools given the funds to buy the equipment they need rather than funnelling purchases through the foundation. Chaiyut says the project is sensitive to the problems, and responded with extra teaching handbooks and a free telephone call-in system. It experimented with teleconferencing to remote schools, and also enlisted the National Electronics and Computer Centre to make lessons available on the Internet. "We offer the schools a choice—if they want our teaching, they can have it, but they don't have to take it," Chaiyut says.

The enduring problem of finding teachers willing to stay at remote schools means there will continue to be a need for distance learning, but technology will never offer all the answers. In 1996, soon after the start of the distance learning broadcasts, King Bhumibol commented: "Nowadays, we have high technology that offers better means of expanding the schools and disseminating knowledge, but there is nothing that can replace an education that develops knowledge and edifies the mind."

Degrees of Knowledge

While most of the king's efforts in education were focused on expanding basic infrastructure and access, he was also aware of the importance of encouraging the country's university graduates, top minds and future leaders. Among the first public duties of the young king upon his return to Thailand was to preside over the graduation ceremonies at universities and military academies, a practice initiated by his uncle, King Prajadhipok. King Ananda had also presided over a diploma ceremony at the Faculty of Medicine at Siriraj Hospital.

The degree ceremonies were very formal and protracted. The king sat in a stiff, upright

Far left *King Bhumibol with school children.*

Centre *King Bhumibol, accompanied by Queen Sirikit, awards degrees to students from Chulalongkorn University for the first time in 1950.*

Left *The king addresses graduates at Chulalongkorn University in 1981, when Princess Sirindhorn was awarded her Master of Arts.*

position for hours on end in order to personally hand the diplomas to thousands of university graduates. According to Police General Vasit Dejkunjorn, who worked in royal security for 12 years, the king drew on certain meditation techniques to maintain the same position for so many hours. "He is aware of bodily aches and discomfort, but lets those feelings go, as if detached from them," Vasit recalled in his memoirs. For the graduates, the moment was often considered a highlight of their lives—the pride of completing their studies combined with the honour of sharing a brief but significant moment with their king. Photographs of the occasion are commonplace on walls and mantles in homes throughout the country.

Although arduous, these ceremonies provided students with a chance to hear the king's views on education first hand—and they were often quite different from those commonly expressed in Thailand at the time. In general, the king challenged complacency by downplaying the importance of paper degrees and exam results. He encouraged the graduates to extend and apply their knowledge. As early as 1955, he told graduating students at Kasetsart University: "I would like to remind you that even though you have completed your studies in accordance with the syllabus, and have been conferred a degree, you should keep in mind that this is just the first step in education. You must study and train yourself further. As in all branches of science, new knowledge is always obtained through experiments and research. If you fail to keep up, you will soon become out-dated."

King Bhumibol saw learning as, in his own words, "a never-ending process. Those who wish to advance in their work must constantly seek more knowledge, or they could lag behind and become incompetent." This perspective gained more significance as the pace of change accelerated and Thailand increasingly sought to compete in the developing global "knowledge economy". The king also discouraged the notion that education was simply the accumulation of facts. "Life experiences are a well from which to draw knowledge and wisdom," he said. "You should not get stuck with text book or theoretical knowledge too much … Or else you will get confused and be unable to work when you find out that practice is not in line with theory."

The king emphasised the importance of creativity, logical thinking and analysis. "You should not think that you are studying in order to pass an entrance exam because our existence doesn't depend on whether you marked down the right multiple choice answer on your exam," the king told students at Srinakharinwirot University. "Our existence depends on working and analysing various problems."

Left *King Bhumibol prays with fellow monks at Wat Bovornives in Bangkok during his 15 days in the monkhood in 1956. He continues to practise meditation and to listen to recorded sermons delivered by the most respected monks of the day.*

The Moral Compass

In 1956, King Bhumibol spent 15 days as a monk at Wat Bovornives, the royal temple where his great grandfather, King Mongkut, had once been abbot. The experience had a lasting effect. After leaving the temple, the king continued seeing Phra Yanasangvara, the abbot who advised him in *dhamma* study and later became supreme patriarch. The venerable monk also introduced him to *vipassana*, a form of meditation that enables the practitioner to gain deeper awareness of physical and mental processes, greater self-control, insight into the nature of reality and a feeling of peace.

King Bhumibol's meditation and *dhamma* studies have continued throughout his reign and the king listens regularly to taped sermons by the most respected monks of the day. "Being at peace is to know how to make your body and mind still even amidst confusing and alarming situations," the king once said. "Attempts to control your mind and body will lead to mindfulness and clear understanding of rationale, of truth and justice. This is the start of the road to the solution of problems that has no dead end."

Naturally, Buddhism helped form the king's vision of education. This was not an unusual connection to make. The king may have attended school overseas, but Thais had traditionally been educated in temples with monks as teachers. Buddhism had long provided essential moral and ethical guidance to Thais. The king reinforced this relationship, once remarking: "Education can be divided into two kinds. One is academic education, which will be useful to the country after [you] graduate. The other is the knowledge of *dhamma*. [That] is how to think and behave in order to benefit oneself. One who has both academic and *dhamma* education will have wisdom."

In speech after speech to graduates, he reiterated the importance of social ethics. In a speech in 1969, for example, the king said: "Academic subjects that you are constantly being tested for do not alone account for your survival and will not create benefit for yourself, for others, or for the country. Those with knowledge also need other additional qualifications to bring themselves and the nation to survival and prosperity. The necessary qualifications are a tender conscience, honesty in thought and deed, loyalty to the nation and your patrons, selflessness and not taking advantage of others, generosity as befitting your status and position, and, most importantly, perseverance. Practise doing projects on your own both big and small, simple and complicated, with determination, without sloth, carelessness or vulgarity."

66 Attempts to control your mind and body will lead to mindfulness and clear understanding of rationale, of truth and justice. This is the start of the road to the solution of problems that has no dead end. 99

On another occasion, in 1967, he said: "To achieve desired results that are also beneficial and morally just, you need more than just knowledge: You need honesty, sincerity and justice. Knowledge is like an engine that propels a vehicle. Moral principles are the steering wheel or rudder that lead the vehicle safely in the right direction."

In time, through his words and deeds, the king himself became the nation's moral compass. He exerted this influence through public speeches, notably his birthday addresses, as well as in his speeches to top government officials and in private audiences. For example, in December 1997, during the financial crisis in Asia, King Bhumibol used his birthday speech to relate some sobering anecdotes about people who came to him to borrow money. The point of these stories was that those who were modest in their requests, and careful in their expenditures, were able to repay loans and prosper. Those who failed had not studied their investment, had invested too much, lost control of their expenses or took loans with onerous interest rates. The king described giving a loan to a man who needed an eye operation for his son. The man never repaid the debt, but reappeared one day asking for a loan to buy a house. "I could tolerate him no more because he should be in a position to have a house on his own. The house that he requested was a rather big one. If I gave him that house as he requested, he would later on ask for housekeeping expenses. Furthermore, as the house was big, he would probably bring relatives and friends to live in it. That would further increase the expenses, so I said no … After that I heard no more of him. I tell you these things because they are the causes of the crisis we are going through."

Former Prime Minister Anand Panyarachun consulted frequently with the king during his two spells in office. "The impact of His Majesty's teaching does not come from his power," says Anand, "but from his judgment, his deeds and his moral authority—his *baramee*, or accumulated merit, from over 60 years of work on behalf of the people. His Majesty is a very good teacher, but he never, ever lectures. He tells stories, or he brings up issues and just talks about them. He doesn't try to convince you—he tries to make you think."

Khunying Ambhorn says her audiences with the king are always a challenge. "He would tease me by saying some awful remark just to goad me into differing. So, when forced to disagree, I begin by using an old, formal address that indicates I am ready to be punished for my inappropriate act." The king, she says, sometimes provokes people to try to get a genuine reaction because he gets tired of people telling him what they think he wants to hear. "The king is willing to listen, so it's our own fault for failing to say what we mean," she says.

Khunying Ambhorn says the king has always been enthusiastic about a wide range of subjects and has learned from many people. "He is a real teacher because he is a good learner," she says. "The king has the ability to get information from people and then synthesize it." Sumet of the Chaipattana Foundation concurs, "His Majesty never says do this or do that; he wants people to think for themselves. Instead, he tells stories that allow people to draw their own conclusions. He gives examples—whether in stories or in reality through his projects that people can see and touch." This style was apparent even in the king's own brief stints acting as a classroom teacher for two video lessons produced by the Distance Learning Foundation. One concerned ways to improve soil quality and the other was about rainmaking. In the soil quality video, the king and a small group of students and officials examine core samples of soil from an early effort to reduce soil acidity. The king speaks informally without notes, commenting on the samples, sometimes asking officials to clarify technical points. He also tries, without much success, to get the smiling, but obviously overawed students to participate and ask questions.

When addressing civil servants, judges or ministers, the king typically focuses on core values such as duty, honesty and service to nation. Key themes of many of the speeches are integrity and unity or cooperation. "When you have clearly analysed the issue with a heart that is unbiased, then only will true understanding arise, leading to a just decision and action," the king once advised. "You must set your mind to be objective, not allowing any prejudice to prevail. Let your heart be led by truth and justice based on reason and morality." On another occasion, he said, "Knowledge and intelligence, and efficient equipment alone cannot help us create total prosperity and stability for the country. To do so we need one other element, that is unity, or cooperation, so that we can use that knowledge, intellect and equipment to create true prosperity as desired."

Reforming National Education

In spite of the king's work and words, Thailand's national educational system has a mixed record. On the one hand, opportunities and access have improved dramatically over recent decades and the percentage of those completing elementary or more advanced studies has greatly increased. Confirming this progress, by the 1990s, the task of presenting diplomas

Far left *A Border Patrol Policeman teaches students at a Border Patrol Police school.*

Centre *High school students in Phetchaburi province attend lessons in an open-air classroom made from split bamboo.*

Left *Students at Mattayom Wat Benjamabophit School in Bangkok at prayer during morning assembly.*

had become far beyond the capacity of the king alone. There were nine national research universities, 22 public universities, 41 provincial level universities, nine technological universities and more than 50 private colleges and universities with tens of thousands of graduates each year. For the larger universities, graduation ceremonies often extended to two or three days. Although King Bhumibol had resisted delegating the duty for many years, apparently worried he might disappoint graduates, the education system had expanded so much during his reign that he could in good conscience finally delegate some of the duties, first to members of the royal family, and later to high-ranking royal representatives.

The Thai education system meanwhile has struggled to meet the demands of a more sophisticated, globalised economy. The abilities of Thai students in maths and science, as shown in international tests, have begun falling behind other Asian countries. Employers complain that Thai students leave university without the ability to analyse, innovate, use information technology or find and organise information. Tests have shown uneven standards between schools, with small and rural schools far behind their urban counterparts.

The king's vision of education—lifelong learning, broad-based studies and application, bolstered by ethical considerations—has on occasion been actively integrated into the national curriculum. In the aftermath of the student unrest and the overthrow of the military government in October 1973, for example, key Thai educators launched an effort to reform the educational system. Some aspects of this reform movement reflected ideas raised by King Bhumibol in his speeches on education. These included more attention to rural schools, decentralisation of educational management to local organisations, greater continuity between primary and secondary education and lifelong learning.

In the early 1990s, the government worked on an education reform plan that led to a 1996 report titled "Thai Education in the Era of Globalization: Vision of a Learning Society". It called for lifelong learning, improved educational management, more educational options, a greater role for the private sector, mechanisms to improve quality, and decentralisation of school management and curricula. Both educational reform and administrative decentralisation were mandated by the 1997 constitution and the 1999 National Education Act that shifted Thailand's educational philosophy in directions long advocated by King Bhumibol. The act, reflecting the king's concern for the inclusion of the have-nots in education, called for a system providing lifelong education for all, participation of all segments of society in education, and continuous development of knowledge and learning processes.

The new policy put greater emphasis on critical thinking than on traditional rote learning, and on lifelong learning rather than paper degrees. The reforms provided for decentralisation of administration to some 300 local educational areas and allowed rural schools to adjust their curricula, at least partially, to meet local needs. There was greater emphasis on scientific knowledge, and more leeway given to local wisdom and traditional knowledge. More use was to be made of information and communication technologies to promote learning by both students and teachers. To provide more coherent policies, the Ministry of Education, the Bureau of University Affairs and the Office of the National Education Commission were merged into a single ministry. With the approval of the king, teacher training colleges throughout the country were renamed Rajabhat Institutes and given the status of universities. This provided better access to tertiary education in outlying areas.

Educational reform efforts continued under the government of Prime Minister Thaksin Shinawatra, but also ran into controversy. Kasem, appointed education minister in 2001 under Prime Minister Thaksin's first government, resigned after only four months in office due to conflicts over the reforms with ministry bureaucrats and politically powerful cabinet members. The reforms called for "student-centred learning", and appeared to encourage students to take the lead role in the classroom.

King Bhumibol expressed concern over "the government policy of new thinking, whereby the students are supposed to teach the teachers". In his 2003 birthday address, the king said that such a complete role reversal was impossible because children lack experience. At the same time, he said, "teachers must allow students to ask questions. The question 'Ah! What is this?' is how a student teaches the teachers."

"Education reform means the encouragement of questioning," he said. "One should not misconstrue questioning as casting doubt on teachers, on directors-general, on permanent secretaries, on ministers—excuse me, I of course mean vice-ministers … Children are entitled to ask questions, and they have the right to be listened to. They ask because they don't know and want to learn. Some have eccentric ideas, and they deserve to be listened to. I speak from my own childhood experience. My foreign teachers answered when I asked: 'What is this?' I was encouraged to continue asking and to learn."

King Bhumibol teased Prime Minister Thaksin by noting that although his policies encouraged student questions, when it came to his style of government the premier himself seemed to prefer the old style of top-down teaching with few questions or objections allowed.

The king said he was in a position to express concerns about the directions of educational reforms, because he had followed "government education policy since before the prime minister was born".

Subsequent educational reform efforts appear to have been more in line with King Bhumibol's thinking. In 2010, the government of Prime Minister Abhisit Vejjajiva announced another round of reforms, including a high-level organisation to manage education and improve teaching quality. Abhisit said the reorganisation would focus on implementation, including the development of learning methods and improvement of educational standards at schools, particularly smaller ones.

Kasem, however, noted that although senior bureaucrats in education often cite the king's speeches, their actual views differ. This has led to problems in implementing effective reforms. "I don't think the Ministry of Education looks at educational reform the same way as the king," he says. Khunying Ambhorn, who spent much of her career in the ministry, agrees. "Indirectly, he has influenced a lot of us," she says, "but deep down, many [in the ministry] fail to comprehend the real meaning of the king's ideas." The king, however, remains revered for his focus on helping improve the standards of education in the country, increasing access and emphasising the importance of morality. On the king's 80th birthday, an official tribute was issued: King Bhumibol and His Enlightened Approach to Teaching. The occasion of his 84th birthday in 2011 was used to honour King Bhumibol as the "Teacher of the Realm" (*Khru Haeng Paendin*)—an unofficial title that recognises the king's 60 years of continuous teaching through deeds, speeches and writings.

Above *The king talks to officials at the Pikun Thong Royal Development Study Centre located in the far south of Thailand in Narathiwat province.*

A KING FOR ALL REGIONS

King Bhumibol made the development and effective management of the country's natural resources the central focus of his work. Travelling to meet with the villagers to discuss their needs, in each part of the country he initiated projects to address local challenges. These problems included devastating drought in the Northeast, the scourge of opium in the North, poor soil in the swampland of the South and weak rice yields in the plains of central Thailand. Sometimes the project the king initiated was as straightforward as a small dam. Occasionally, they were more ambitious, such as the regeneration of a swathe of abandoned land. Against the grain of large-scale modernisation, the king typically promoted site-specific measures that were sensitive to the environment and socio-economic conditions of the people, and aimed at creating self-sufficiency. This work in the countryside, which fulfilled the Buddhist ideal of the *dhammaraja*, or righteous king, became a distinctive feature of his reign.

At the beginning of King Bhumibol's reign in 1946, Thailand was already a leading rice exporter and its farmers, long dubbed the "backbone of the country", accounted for roughly 80 percent of the country's 17 million people. Many aspects of Thai rural life, however, were troubling. Most farmers could provide only a subsistence existence for their families. Rural areas lacked roads, electricity and piped water. While farmers in North America and Europe typically worked with tractors and large mechanised combine harvesters, and could count on developed transport infrastructure, the ordinary Thai family ploughed small plots with a couple of buffaloes and struggled to get fresh produce to market. Farmers also suffered from recurring floods and drought.

Thailand has the third largest land mass in Southeast Asia after Indonesia and Myanmar (formerly Burma), and its vast countryside has long been subordinate to the capital. Whereas in several developing Asian countries, including Japan, South Korea and Taiwan, where the agricultural infrastructure was efficiently developed and used to fund industrial expansion and government bureaucracy, in Thailand, middlemen controlled the rice mills and distribution, and little government money was used to improve farmland. In addition, successive governments extracted income from the rice trade by imposing a premium—an export tax on the staple that could run as high as 30 percent. The domestic price of rice was also kept artificially low, which placated an occasionally restive population in the cities and government employees. One former Thai agriculture minister admitted later that the policy made agriculture "weaker and weaker" and the farmers "eternally poorer".

The central government was not completely blind to the plight of farmers. Irrigation and flood prevention had been on the minds of administrators since the reign of King Chulalongkorn, but the focus was typically on the Central Plains immediately to the city's north—the kingdom's richest rice-growing region. Records show that even in this bountiful region, rainfall was often insufficient and crop yields disappointing.

In 1950, the government secured World Bank loans for the development of its water resources, leading to the Chao Phraya Diversion dam, and the Bhumibol and Sirikit dams. Building infrastructure was considered an important component in the battle against communism. Successive Thai governments made serious efforts to expand communications and open up isolated areas of the country. From the 1950s, the US contributed significant aid as part of the anti-communist alliance in Southeast Asia. In addition to military funds and the stationing of US troops in the country, it supported a programme of accelerated rural

66 The chance meeting at Huai Mongkol was to have longer repercussions than anyone could have imagined that afternoon. It inspired, in part, the royal development work of the decades to follow. 99

development. New roads—notably the Friendship Highway from Saraburi to Udon Thani in the Northeast—were constructed, as were market places, health clinics and wells. These projects were intended to improve rural living conditions and opportunities, and also to bring isolated areas into the reach of security forces.

The king's interest in national development grew with his early tours of the countryside, particularly during drives to nearby villages from his seaside residence in Hua Hin, Klai Kangwol Palace. On one trip at the beginning of the monsoon in 1952, his jeep got stuck in the mud. The farmers of Huai Mongkol near Hua Hin rarely saw strangers negotiating the tortuous, rutted track through the forest and across fields to their village. To this day, Lee Sae Loe remembers the jeep getting bogged down behind her family's wooden house.

"There were jokes made as some villagers and soldiers helped push the jeep out of the mud," the 69-year-old Lee, who was 11 at the time, recalls. "It was only when the young driver got out and introduced himself that our men realised they had just helped our king." The monarch was still newly returned to Thailand and his time was largely spent in Bangkok where he performed official duties. The countryside beyond his palaces was little more than a blur of forests and paddy fields viewed from a train window. The shacks and muddy roads stood in stark contrast to the manicured Swiss suburb in which he had spent his youth.

The king chatted with the villagers. They told him that the markets in Hua Hin were over 25 km away, and the delivery of a simple load of bananas by truck or handcart was arduous. A proper road was needed. Soon after, the king donated some bulldozers to the Naresuan Border Patrol Police. Within six months, a porous, red earth road had been pushed through to the village. Travel time to the market was cut from almost a day to a matter of hours.

The chance meeting at Huai Mongkol was to have longer repercussions than anyone could have imagined that afternoon. It inspired, in part, the royal development work of the decades to follow and provided an early model for action. First, the king established direct contact with ordinary people and learned something of their problems. Second, he offered practical suggestions to help address their needs—based on his own research and knowledge. Third, in order to cut through bureaucratic red tape, he made use of his own contacts, influence and resources to implement a solution. Afterwards, he monitored results and progress.

Such a hands-on approach was unusual for any head of state—especially a Siamese or Thai monarch. Commoners could not even gaze upon the visages of ancient Siamese kings. Even in modern times, ritual and hierarchy reinforced the notion that the king was akin to

a living god. King Bhumibol was beginning to engage directly with his poorest subjects, and then act as a catalyst for development. While many of the issues he addressed were localised and obscure, they generally involved the fundamental underpinnings of Thai rural existence: land, water and security. The solutions he offered were not grandiose but aimed at providing basic needs and infrastructure so that people became more able to help themselves. Over the following decades, and through literally thousands of projects nationwide covering a broad range of issues, development work was to become the hallmark of King Bhumibol's reign.

First Forays

In 1953, the king and queen travelled in the Central Plains for the first time. The government-run development projects they saw were mostly dams and irrigation canals. More ambitiously in 1955, the royal couple took an extended trip to Isan, the neglected and undeveloped Northeast, where many spoke Lao or Khmer. Travelling 680 km by train and 1,592 km by road, they received a rapturous welcome wherever they stopped.

It was the first time a Chakri king had visited this part of the kingdom, and proved an eye-opening experience for all concerned. Arriving in each new town as bands played and costumed girls danced, the village headmen would attempt to present the king with petitions—often overwhelming him with their problems. King Bhumibol was left in no doubt about the immense problems people faced in this drought-plagued region. Rainfall could only support one annual rice crop and hunger soon followed whenever it was insufficient. As he noted, people could get by without electricity—and most people in the countryside were doing just that—but without water, "man cannot survive". According to some accounts, this trip was also the starting point for the king's idea to experiment with and apply the novel technology of rainmaking in Thailand.

Later, writing in his personal journal, the king explained: "From that time on, I have thought about this seemingly insoluble and paradoxical problem: when there is water, there is too much, it floods the area; when the water recedes, it is drought." Effective management of water resources has been an abiding national challenge that became the king's own overriding preoccupation. The lifelong search for answers had begun.

By 1958, after Field Marshal Sarit Thanarat, who was from the Northeast, became

Far left *King Bhumibol and Queen Sirikit during their groundbreaking 1955 tour of the Northeast—the first tour of the region by a king of the Royal House of Chakri.*

Centre *The king and queen on an inspection trip to Bhumibol Dam in Tak province on 4 March 1957.*

Left *King Bhumibol and a young Prince Vajiralongkorn ride an early "iron buffalo" on the grounds around Chitralada Villa.*

prime minister, King Bhumibol travelled more frequently and widely, and began to play a more active role in national affairs. During provincial visits, he initially offered help in the form of first aid, healthcare teams and small new schools. He also supplied basic necessities, including iodised salt, mosquito nets, bags of rice and blankets. By the early 1960s, the king had developed a greater understanding of the challenges facing the countryside. While he did not have the constitutional authority to take on grand schemes on the scale of a major, multipurpose dam, smaller-scale ventures and initiatives were possible.

In May 1960, the Royal Ploughing Ceremony was held for the first time since 1947. The ancient rite was performed to try and ensure sufficient rain and an abundant harvest, and to stave off pestilence and floods. The occasion symbolically brought farmers and their perennial concerns into contact with the monarchy. The king took the ceremony seriously, noting that Thailand was rare among countries in having a state ceremony to achieve a good harvest. "All farmers must have realised that auspiciousness is very important for their activities, since they have to depend on several factors for a successful harvest," he said, adding that if they combine the power of their minds, "we can generate great strength".

Two years later, the king introduced an annual ceremony honouring the Holy Rice Mother, which was held at Chitralada Villa, his main residence in Bangkok. The event was held each year directly after the ploughing ceremony, and farmers were invited and offered packets of seeds. Those responsible for outstanding yields were given awards. Farming was backbreaking work, yet farmers seldom received any praise for their efforts.

While the ceremonies helped take care of the spiritual side of securing a good rice harvest, the king's rides on a diesel-driven "iron buffalo" designed by Mom Rajawongse Debriddhi Devakul and the rice experiments he began at the palace in 1961 sought scientific answers to the troubles besetting the "rice bowl of Asia". The king taught himself disciplines related to rice cultivation, seeking out local and foreign experts to fill gaps in his knowledge or help run projects. Sometimes weeks of intensive study went into understanding subjects well enough so that he could have meaningful discussions with specialists. While hard physical labour was generally left to others, the king was not averse to getting his hands dirty by planting crops and learning about farming methods directly.

The king's experiments in the difficulties of rice cultivation were instructive. It was crucial to match the right varieties of rice with appropriate cultivation techniques and to take into account different soils and the availability of water. He suggested that after the rice

had been harvested, crop rotation, including the planting of legumes, should be practised. This loosened the soil and generated green compost that enriched the soil for the next rice crop. The creation of compost using leaves, humus, manure and even rice husks provided an organic alternative to chemical methods, according to the king. The common practice of burning off the rice stubs after harvest and the addition of chemical fertilisers and pesticides to flooded paddy fields might offer a few quick fixes to farmers, but the methods had some long-term negative environmental effects. A secondary crop offered farmers the chance of some extra income.

As a constitutional monarch, King Bhumibol did not have the power to instruct the government on rice prices and taxes, but he could offer farmers advice on productivity and stock management if they cared to listen. Outlining a plan for rice banks, he suggested that it was important to have a common stock of rice in case of shortages or lack of money. "When the villagers have more money or are able to grow their own rice, they will have to return the rice they borrowed plus interest. The common rice stock will help the people to understand the importance of saving and how to live and cooperate with one another," he explained.

In 1961, the same year the king began his rice experiments, he began growing trees. Inspired by the majestic yang na (*Dipterocarpus alatus Roxb*) trees that line part of the road to his summer palace in Hua Hin, the king sought to encourage the sustainable use of forests by serving as an example himself. After stopping his car one day to collect yang na seeds, he propagated them at his summer palace with the help of officials from the faculty of forestry at Kasetsart University. These were then planted in a demonstration forest on the grounds of Chitralada Villa. The planting ceremony was timed for the celebration of the 10th birthday of Prince Vajiralongkorn on 28 July 1962. The prince and his classmates from Chitralada School dug holes and planted the first saplings, eventually totalling 1,250 trees. In due course, the king planted many species of native trees in what developed into an arboretum.

Project Showcases

In 1962, King Bhumibol travelled south from Hua Hin to the coastal village of Khao Tao, where he talked to villagers. Their poor living conditions were due in part to soil erosion and freshwater scarcity. The local headman showed him around, pointing out how

seawater contaminated what little water supply the village had. The king arranged with the government's Royal Irrigation Department (RID) to build a 600,000 cubic-metre-capacity earth-fill dam that blocked seawater from flowing into a natural channel, and which trapped rainwater flowing in. He injected 60,000 baht of his own money to initiate the project, and returned to the site several times to check on its progress.

Khao Tao reservoir, which was built in 1963, was the king's first reservoir. It proved that there were many development challenges that could benefit from his touch. Another such challenge was the neglected scrubland of Hup Kapong in Phetchaburi province. The king had received a complaint from local farmers about the difficulties they faced raising crops in the arid conditions there. Having read how Israeli experts had brought life to the desert in the Middle East, the king called on privy councillor Mom Luang Dej Snidvongs to find suitable land in the area on which to conduct experiments.

The Hup Kapong Land Management and Development Project began in 1966 with 500 *rai* (about 200 acres) of land. Called the Thai-Israel Rural Development Project, the aim was to break up and add life to the sandy, compacted soil and then grow vegetables by applying Israeli irrigation techniques. With Israeli expertise and technology that included elaborate sprinkler systems, numerous vegetables and fruits were cultivated and evaluated—including asparagus, string beans, tomatoes and mangoes.

As part of the project, the local government gave away 25-*rai* plots of seemingly worthless land from a 10,000-*rai* tract. Loans of 10,000 baht were made to landless farmers willing to take part in the experiment. Only two families initially took up the offer. Within a year, the families were able to make a profit from the sale of the vegetables and corn they had grown— and return the start-up loan. The following year, 82 families seized the opportunity, a number that eventually increased to 128 families. They set up what was to become the king's first cooperative, developed to bottle, package and label produce for the market. Eventually, the local community built a school and temple on the site. Meanwhile, Queen Sirikit introduced a handicrafts project in which indigenous materials were used to make handbags and baskets so the women could earn extra income.

Hup Kapong farmer Rabiap Saengsila, 80, recalls King Bhumibol visiting her and her husband at their dirt-floored shack. She says he often came to check on them: "I remember one time working on my land and the king came unannounced and joined me, helping me pick asparagus." The first year was productive and her family made a good income from the

Far left *King Bhumibol, accompanied by Queen Sirikit, addresses members of the Hup Kapong cooperative in 1978.*

Centre *King Bhumibol marks the start of construction work at the Khao Tao reservoir in 1963.*

Left *An aerial view of the completed Khao Tao reservoir.*

sale of their vegetables. But it was hard work and at night Rabiap said she had nightmares about the endless lines of string beans waiting to be picked. In time, the family shack made way for a wooden house and eventually a brick house. Rabiap said the king liked to bring guests to her farm to show them around as he was proud of what had been achieved.

Rabiap recalls that when the king visited he would stress, "If you work hard, your life will become comfortable in the future." Through careful development of the soil and use of reservoirs, ponds and piped water, Hup Kapong became a showcase for sustainable farming. The project eventually attracted hundreds of visitors each year, and led to another 2,580-*rai* cooperative being set up nearby at Don Khun Huai. The king's ideas did not necessarily work for everybody who came to learn about the farming methods. "It is up to the person," says Sombut Tantisungwarakun, the Hup Kapong Land Management and Development Project director. "We don't force people to learn from the king's project, but many don't learn properly, and they fail."

Opium Scourge

Far from the lowlands of Hup Kapong, the hill tribe people in the North provided a very different challenge. Highlanders lived in remote villages on the fringes of Thai society. They spoke their own languages, were not regarded as ethnically Thai and were often not naturalised. They were regarded by the state as a menace at worst and a nuisance at best. In general, they were misunderstood and looked down upon by lowland Thais—in part because the mainstay of many hill tribe villages was opium.

Opium had come back to haunt the West. Up until the Second World War the British, and to a lesser extent the French, had promoted the opium trade. The British had fought two wars with China in the 19th century to make money out of the drug and keep opium dens in business. By the mid-1960s, heroin was turning up on the streets of European and American cities and in the veins of hooked American GIs serving in Vietnam. Thailand made the trade in opium and heroin illegal in 1959. Western governments were pursuing an all-out war on the drug trade and were willing to fund research into alternatives for poppy growers.

The king was particularly concerned by a United Nations Development Programme (UNDP) survey in 1965 that showed Thailand as the producer of 145 tonnes of opium

Left *Opium poppies. Harvested opium was easily transported for trade and as a form of currency, and could also be used for pain relief and to dampen hunger pangs.*

annually—a very significant portion of the world supply. By the 1970s, northern Thailand, Laos and Burma, dubbed the "Golden Triangle" in an off-hand remark by an American diplomat that caught the imagination of the Western media, became known as the world's main source of opium and heroin.

State-sponsored efforts to relocate some of the highland villagers in the early 1960s had largely failed. The king took a different tack. Since his first visits to highland villages in 1963, he could see that what ailed the Hmong, Karen, Yao, Akha, Lahu and Lisu communities (who then numbered around 275,000 in total) was not drugs but poverty, poor health and a lack of education. The Golden Triangle was, according to the king, in fact a "poverty triangle" and the people who were making large profits were the dealers, not the farmers.

Thus, his approach to eradicating opium was in stark contrast to the "surround, search and destroy" tactics of the army and police. According to Chakhoy Pueatit, headman of the Muser village of Ban Kob Dong on Doi Ang Khang, when the king visited his village he would come into their houses, sit on the floor, ask how they lived and listen to their problems. But when soldiers came, the villagers would run into the forest to hide. "We'd go home only after they had destroyed our poppies and left," he said.

The king saw the hill tribe people as pawns in a web of international narcotics trafficking run by powerful people, according to Tuenjai Deetes, a well-known development worker who spent years working with the highlanders. "He also recognises the hill people's land rights, as many of them have lived in these forests since long before they were declared state properties." A visit to the village of Doi Pui by the monarch in 1968 was indicative of his approach. With a retinue of soldiers and officials, he walked to the village through the dense forest and over rocky outcrops a few kilometres northwest of Bhubing Palace in Chiang Mai. When he spotted the illegal poppies that the villagers were growing, his reaction was unexpected. Panya Laulee, who was 20 years old at the time, remembers the king, standing in the middle of the family's poppy field, advising the Hmong villagers to pile soil around the base of the poppies to help them grow better.

King Bhumibol's light-hearted comment helped ease any sense of confrontation. He then questioned the Hmong villagers about how much a family earned annually from the sale of opium. "The answer was 3,000 to 5,000 baht," the king later recalled. "When asked how much the annual selling of fruit might bring, the reply was that the local variety of peaches could fetch 4,000 to 12,000 baht. It was then that we thought we had the answer."

66 The Golden Triangle was, according to the king, in fact a 'poverty triangle' and the people who were making large profits were the dealers, not the farmers. 99

The idea was that they could improve the wild fruits, such as local peaches, through grafting, and grow other, more lucrative fruits. As lowlanders could not grow these crops successfully on the plains anyway, there would be little competition. Marketing them would also not be too onerous. But why give up a drug with sure-fire demand for an experimental fruit? Panya said that there were other incentives to make the change. "We faced problems from the armed Chin Haw drug traders who forced us to trade only with them and at a low price," he recalls. As a result of the opium trade, "people came to ask for money—police came, government people, too."

The Hmong farmers gradually cut back on opium. A road built to the village made it easier to transport fruit and vegetables to lowland markets. The king personally gave the village three lychee fruit trees. Twenty years later, Panya says grafts from the original trees have been taken and planted throughout the hills of northern Thailand.

Hearts and Minds

A year after his 1968 visit to Doi Pui, the Royal Project was established. Designed to improve the lives of hill tribe people and expand the crop substitution programme, the king chose his friend and sailing buddy, Prince Bhisatej Rajani, to run it. Prince Bhisatej was trustworthy and he was also tough. An experienced mountain walker, he had served with the British Special Operations Executive—known as "Winston's Irregulars"—charged with disrupting the Japanese war effort during the Second World War.

To launch the Royal Project, the king donated 200,000 baht to Kasetsart University to buy land he had scouted next to Doi Pui village and carry out research into alternative crops. His other main test site was on Doi Ang Khang, a mountainous area along the Burmese border—and an environmental disaster area to many. Much of the tree cover had been cut and burned down by Chinese migrants and Muser hill tribe people who grew poppies. Farmers were moving up the mountain and the slopes were becoming vulnerable to erosion.

For these very reasons, the Royal Project team saw this as a good place to test the suitability of fruit trees for the highlands and also to apply some of the king's ideas for reforestation. By the early 1970s, Ang Khang was established as the Royal Project's first agricultural research station. Teachers and local hill tribe leaders from villages in Chiang Mai, Chiang Rai and

Nan provinces were offered agricultural training. Today, the area continues to flourish and has become a popular tourist site known for its natural beauty.

Opium eradication was just part of the highland development equation. The Royal Project also encouraged the hill tribes to abandon the slash-and-burn practices that could be destructive to the environment. As the king said, "If all of us help the hill tribe people then we are indirectly assisting the country to develop and prosper, as the success of the hill tribe development programme means that they will live and farm in one area, thereby aiding the reforestation and watershed development projects for the future benefit of the country." In addition, the Royal Project was an indirect way to fight the spread of communism. Hill tribes generally lived in poverty in the borderlands close to Burma and Laos with little attachment to the Thai state at a time when Thai communist insurgents roamed the hills looking for recruits. Winning over the highlanders and defending the nation from local insurrection and invasion by foreign communist insurgents were among the government's top priorities.

The king did not like the suggestion that without the communist threat, he would not be undertaking such work. "We would be here anyway," the king retorted when a reporter once raised the issue. Although the king was not as interested in the politics of the Cold War as helping his people, Thailand's monarch did not deny that the growing insurgency was a concern. "Once water is adequately available, the people will not abandon their homes," said the king, responding to concerns that farmers might join the communists. "Attempts should be made to bring over the people to our side so that they will not join the United Front [the communists] … We must firstly provide protection and assistance to them in various ways, and this is the policy to push back the terrorists."

For the hill tribes, the appeal of communism was less alluring than meaningful improvements to their current welfare. By way of illustration, Prince Bhisatej recalled a trip to Doi Inthanon when it was a communist hotspot. After the Border Patrol Police had returned from a patrol, the prince realised he had a window in which the communists would likely be absent from a particular hill tribe village. "So I went up and talked with the Karen headman, and the people said they were poor and short of rice and asked if we could help them—like we had done in a neighbouring village. I asked them why they did not ask the communists for help. The villagers said those people [the communists] only help with their mouth."

Although the northern hills were a neglected backwater, there was no shortage of volunteers for the humanitarian mission of the Royal Project. Because a prince was working

Far left *King Bhumibol and his entourage inspect a poppy field in the North.*

Centre *The king meets with hill tribe villagers taking part in opium replacement projects. The programme involved identifying viable alternative cash crops for hill tribe farmers.*

Left *The village headman and shaman of Ban Khob Dong at Doi Ang Kang welcome King Bhumibol to the highlands in 1970.*

on a project launched by the king, it was easy, Prince Bhisatej said, to recruit help from the best and brightest academics. These included well qualified people from Kasetsart University, the only university researching highland agriculture, and Mae Jo and Chiang Mai universities. The volunteers often spent their days off travelling to hill tribe villages to help improve farming methods. Free of hierarchical procedures and red tape, many found working under the Royal Project less stressful than governmental work. The Royal Project also struck a chord with the diplomatic corps. There were offers of donations of temperate and semi-temperate fruits from Australia, France, Indonesia, Iran, Israel, Italy, Lebanon, New Zealand, the UK and West Germany.

No Overnight Success

In the early 1970s, the Royal Project garnered much publicity after it successfully grew peach trees. But as with the king's initial dairy project in the 1960s [*for more details of this project, see page 198*], the success resulted in excess supply and the market price for peaches plunged from eight baht to just two baht per kilo. Many farmers let the crop rot rather than take it to the market. Prince Bhisatej remembers on another occasion calling for volunteers in a mountain village on Doi Inthanon to grow strawberries. Only three farmers stepped forward. "We produced the plan and helped them put money in their pocket, and the year after a lot of people wanted to grow strawberries." It started with strawberries and then moved on to kidney beans, which became known as the "king's beans", as well as a number of other crops.

From the outset, King Bhumibol predicted it would take three decades to eradicate opium. Voicing his concern in a meeting with the king in 1982, Giuseppe di Gennaro, executive director of the United Nations Office on Drugs and Crime (UNFDAC), said, "No serious planning could be so long term." Donors would not take this seriously, he warned. The king listened in silence. "I was sure I had changed the king's mind," said di Gennaro afterwards. He hadn't.

The king had already recognised that it was a long-term project and believed that eliminating the opium trade was, in any case, only one aspect of the job. "The other task is to give these people a better way of life," the king told David Lomax of the BBC in 1979. "So this will continue even if—and I don't think it is in the very near future—if opium is

eradicated like smallpox has been. We have to continue this programme for a long time, so that we give these people a better life and also so that everyone will get the benefit of it." Citing the monarch's commitment, Prince Bhisatej recalls how he and the king walked for kilometres through the hills to check the Ministry of Agriculture's claim that the imported species of Arabica coffee bean would not grow well in Thailand because it was susceptible to disease. "We walked for two hours to see these three trees and the ladies of the court accompanying us complained like anything," he remembers. "But because we went to see the trees, the farmers were interested and persevered. And now Thailand has Arabica coffee."

Kerd Pankannerd, 59, says the king first came to his village of Khun Klang on Doi Inthanon in 1982—the Hmong villagers killed a cow and held a ceremony in his honour. At that time, the hills here were largely bare of trees and the people could see their cows at a distance on the hills, in contrast to today where the hills are covered in thick forest, punctuated by tight terraces of flowers and fruit. "When we began planting strawberries, flowers and fruit, the income was not as good as from the sale of opium," Kerd says. Over time, the areas devoted to opium slowly dropped and they began to earn more income from the sale of alternative crops. "It was better than trying to hide our opium crop from government officials," he admits.

Over the years, the Royal Project's success drew critics. Some lowlanders were jealous of the attention paid to highlanders. Conflicts arose over the use of resources, particularly water. Before the concerted move to more environmentally friendly methods, there was also controversy over the pollution caused by fertilisers and pesticides. Land-hungry lowlanders moved into the highlands pushing hill tribe villagers out, sometimes by burning down their homes. Non-governmental organisations working with the hill tribes also levelled some criticism at the programme. They claimed hill tribe people were only being further marginalised and losing their cultural identity through contact with a state intent on turning them into "good Thais".

The king was undeterred. To put what had grown into 38 Royal Development Centres under one umbrella, the Royal Project Foundation was established in 1992. The project's Doi Kham, or Gold Mountain, hill tribe agricultural product brand gradually grew in stature in Thailand and abroad. Today, top hotels happily serve the produce to their most discerning guests. The work in Thailand's highlands has also caught the attention of governments and NGOs around the world. Some of the Royal Project's proven strategies have been

Far left *Akha hill tribe women pick tea.*

Centre left *Cross-bred peaches. The fruit proved to be a breakthrough produce for the Royal Project.*

Centre right *Lettuces at a hydroponic farm. Hydroponic techniques allow for soilless cultivation and make optimal use of limited fresh water supplies.*

Left *The first outlet for Royal Project produce, at the royal factory in Chiang Mai's Fang district.*

reviewed by countries dealing with their own drug menace, including Bolivia, Colombia, Laos, Mexico, Myanmar, Pakistan, Peru and Vietnam. In addition, there is currently a UN-financed programme in Afghanistan.

The Rainmaker

In parallel with the growth of the Royal Project, the king continued to pursue solutions to the constant drought that plagued many provincial areas. Rainmaking, due in part to its novelty, would become perhaps the king's most famous initiative in this area. As early as 1952, the Thai government had looked into purchasing rainmaking equipment from the US. The equipment "seeded" clouds with special chemicals in order to trigger the release of water vapour and ultimately rain. Test projects had also been carried out by countries in other tropical areas, including the Caribbean and South and Central America. The results there had not been acted upon for agricultural application for reasons of cost effectiveness.

In the mid- to late-1950s, the king urged the Ministry of Agriculture and Cooperatives to begin experiments. In the 1960s, the government of Field Marshal Thanom Kittikachorn granted funding for the Artificial Rainmaking Research and Development Project to be set up under the Ministry of Agriculture and Cooperatives. The work was costly, but the results were considered satisfactory. By 1969, the Royal Rain Project was established and the king and Mom Rajawongse Debriddhi were conducting more intensive experiments. Explaining the process, the king observed: "Rainmaking is like a warship. You fire the missile far, then close in order to properly hit the target. Since we have facilities for rainmaking, we should be sure to use it properly to get rain in the right places." The results of the trials were hit-and-miss. The first test over Khao Yai National Park did not yield a clear result. Further tests were held over Khao Tao Reservoir and at Hup Kapong—also with mixed results.

The king was always realistic about the benefits as well as risks of the project. The "miraculous making of rain in the dry season" to provide enough water for cultivation was not possible, and the methods could not replace a well-organised expansive irrigation system, he warned. "Rainmaking is just one hopeful way for the season when rain should already be falling," the king said. "Artificial rainmaking is still novel, so care has to be taken because of the cost and potential to waste resources."

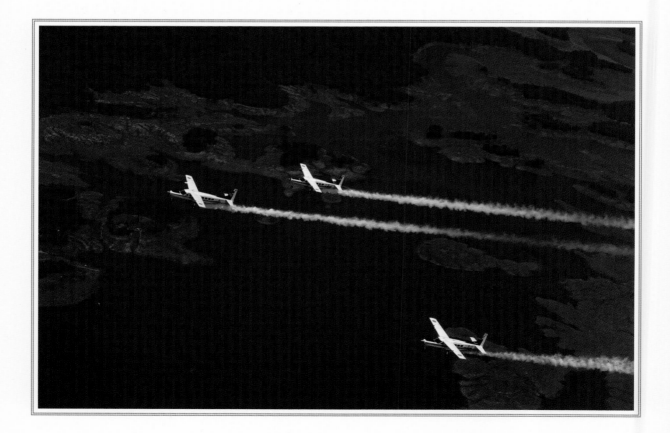

Opposite top left Chemicals for seeding the clouds are mixed in readiness for carefully judged aerial dispersal.

Opposite top right Rainmaking personnel from the Bureau of Royal Rainmaking and Agricultural Aviation load an aircraft at Hua Hin provincial airport, May 2011.

Opposite bottom Planes release chemicals in an effort to induce rain. During the 1980s, more than half of Thailand's provinces requested rainmaking flights each year.

Delegations from around the world, including the US, expressed interest in the project. In late 1972, at Kaeng Krachan Reservoir in Phetchaburi province, a team of Singaporean government officials were treated to a display. Singapore had difficulty providing enough water for its small but growing population and was dependent on water piped from neighbouring Malaysia. The king's reputation as a rainmaker was put to the test. After five hours of checking air humidity and talking by walkie-talkie with his team and aircraft flying sorties seeding the clouds with chemicals, rain fell on the reservoir.

During the early 1970s, the king received many requests for rainmaking and several successful missions were flown. Fruit growers in Chanthaburi province were so thrilled by the rain created during a period of drought in 1972 that they clubbed together and presented the king, along with baskets of fruit, money to help buy more aircraft. "All of you have witnessed that artificial rain revived trees which would otherwise [have] been lost," the king told the Chanthaburi orchardists.

Between 1977 and 1991, requests for artificial rain were received from an average of 44 of the country's 72 provinces each year. The royal rainmaking units responded when conditions allowed. During a drought in 1993, rainmaking over the Bhumibol and Sirikit dam catchment areas was used experimentally to try and raise water levels and increase flows for irrigation and electricity generation.

While Thailand's royal rainmaking was rooted in science, it also neatly dovetailed with ancient concepts of Thai kingship. A Thai king had historically been considered the Lord of the Land, a semi-divine being who could harness the environment and was responsible for ensuring strong harvests. The image of the king trying to bring rain to the farmers held much symbolic power. Indeed, later in his reign, images of the king looking down from the heavens or, in the case of cinema hagiographies, descending in rain drops, became commonplace in publicity materials and tributes relating to the reign.

Rights and Fights

By the early 1970s, the country's population had more than doubled since King Bhumibol's accession and stood at over 40 million. The issue of land rights was coming to a head as the government recognised that millions of farmers did not own the land they cultivated or lived

as tenants. Security of tenure and the right to farm ranked high among the burning issues of the day. "There have been great worries that Thai people would become landless and end up working as slaves, which is something we do not wish to happen," the king observed. "But if we could solve this problem by fairly allocating land to the people and setting up what you could call settlements, groups or cooperatives, it would give the underprivileged a chance to better themselves."

A telling example of the problem occurred when the government designated territory as forest reserves. As a result, farmers who had lived on the land for generations suddenly became trespassers. This presented a dilemma for those who wanted to preserve the forests without violating the rights of ordinary people. In a speech to lawyers in 1973, the king said, "They have human rights. It's a case of the government violating the people, not the people violating the law."

When the government of Mom Rajawongse Kukrit Pramoj sought to introduce a Land Reform Act in 1975, landless and tenant farmers from the newly created Farmers Federation of Thailand (FFT) rallied behind the idea. Since its inception in 1974, the FFT had lobbied for an increase in paddy prices, rent controls and land for the landless. The Land Reform Act would have eliminated landholdings over 50 *rai* (though plots of up to 1,000 *rai* could be retained if they were being farmed productively). A farmer who could prove that he was previously renting land was entitled to 25 *rai* to farm. King Bhumibol supported the government's idea and the Crown Property Bureau (CPB) divested itself of nearly 50,000 *rai* across eight provinces (close to half its upcountry holdings). The government bought the land from the CPB for distribution under the scheme. The CPB used the money from the sale to set up a special fund for supporting cooperatives in the model of Hup Kapong in the area of the relinquished holdings. The king offered start-up capital as well for these cooperatives. The Land Reform Act, however, faltered.

In retrospect, the timing of the 1975 initiative could not have been worse. Communist forces were sweeping to power in Laos, Cambodia and Vietnam—and Thailand's elite feared their country could be the next "domino" to fall. Although the struggle by farmers was in many respects non-ideological, conservative and right wing elements portrayed it as part of the communist menace. Under the banner of "Nation-Religion-King", various militia and Village Scouts were organised to violently quash the farmers' movement. Eighteen FFT leaders were assassinated during a seven-month period in 1975, including Intha Sriboonruang,

Far left King Bhumibol in casual military fatigues. The communist insurgency peaked in the 1970s. The king thought the best way to convince villagers to reject communism was to improve their livelihoods.

Left Villagers read anti-communist comic books in 1967.

> 66 Undeterred by the turmoil of the 1970s, King Bhumibol continued with his development work, insisting that alleviating poverty and improving people's livelihoods were the best ways to reduce support for communist insurgents. 99

the federation's vice-president. Given the violent rightist reaction, the government put the reform on hold and had to assuage landed interests. Landlessness remains an issue to this day, underlining the complexity of the issues involved.

Undeterred by the turmoil of the 1970s, King Bhumibol continued with his development work, insisting that alleviating poverty and improving people's livelihoods were the best ways to reduce support for communist insurgents. In an address to the Rajaprajanugroh Foundation in 1972, the king said, "People who are hungry and sick are receiving help from people who are neither government officials nor loyal to the country, but are terrorists. So we have to give help immediately. It is everyone's duty to give timely help so that people in danger feel comforted and remain loyal to the country."

In 1976, he initiated a project in the North in the Khao Kho–Tung Samo mountain range between Phetchabun and Phitsanulok provinces—areas that had been under insurgent influence. The army pursued a classic counter-insurgency programme, bulldozing roads through the mountains to open up the area. The king then followed with an agricultural and livelihood development programme featuring the construction of reservoirs, the cultivation of new vegetables and the use of *pla nil* (*Tilapia nilotica*) for fish breeding in ponds. Overall, an area of 44,000 *rai* was opened up and developed as the Khek River Basin Development Project. The king preferred that military veterans and reservists and their families were given priority in working and developing the area.

New Foundations

The 1980s ushered in a period of relative political stability and economic growth that allowed King Bhumibol to consolidate and expand his development work. The country's new prime minister in 1980, General Prem Tinsulanonda, pursued a conciliatory approach toward the much-diminished communists, offering amnesty to the remaining insurgents. He welcomed foreign investment and tourism, and launched numerous infrastructure projects. He was also keen to help the king with his development work through additional government funding and manpower. The bulk of the king's schemes fell under the Royal Development Projects. By the start of the 1980s these projects numbered over 1,000 and were peppered all across the kingdom, comprising a myriad of initiatives: water source development and protection;

agricultural development; environmental protection; livelihood development; transportation; public health and welfare; and training and awareness programmes. Organisation and coordination became increasingly challenging. The king kept extensive paperwork in his palaces and there were separate offices at the project sites. Various government ministries and departments also worked on the projects. With the growing number of organisations working towards the same aim, better overall coordination was needed.

With the king's support, the Prem government established the Coordinating Committee for Royal Development Projects in 1981, which was later renamed the Office of the Royal Development Projects Board. Dr Sumet Tantivejkul, who had been secretary-general of the National Economic and Social Development Board (NESDB), was put in charge. The board helped streamline the management of the projects and prevent duplication with work being undertaken by government ministries. This also offered a fast track for implementing some projects. Concerned that his ideas were going astray on occasion, the king was able to exercise more oversight with the improved administrative structure.

The government's floating fund for royally initiated projects was about 400 million baht (US$16 million) in the early 1980s—a budget that has since risen to about 2 billion (US$67 million). The king was sensitive about the costs and influence of his development work. Aware of the power of his words, he did not want his ideas to be considered orders. Thus, the early projects near his summer palace in Hua Hin were first called "Projects Initiated in Accordance with His Majesty's Wishes". He later decided the phrase "His Majesty's Wishes" was still too strong, so his activities were renamed "Royally Initiated Projects".

In tackling crucial water resource issues, it was natural that the king should rely heavily on the services of the Royal Irrigation Department. His main point man from 1984 onwards was Pramote Maiklad, the director-general of the department, who had been accompanying the king on his trips for several years. Pramote was put in charge of managing the king's field visits to water resource projects and thus gained close insights into the king's working style.

Trips were arranged at short notice, often only a day in advance, sometimes just hours. "The king doesn't like people to make a fuss, setting up tents and preparing," explains Pramote. On one occasion, Pramote's team received three hours' notice and rightly guessed that the king wanted to visit a village on the other side of a stream. They quickly built a makeshift bridge. "The king was surprised because there was no bridge on his map," Pramote recalls. "I had guessed he would need this to get to the village."

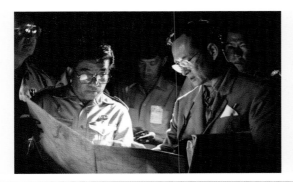

Far left *King Bhumibol speaks on a walkie talkie in a helicopter. The king often travelled to remote areas by helicopter, using a walkie talkie to stay in touch with officials on the ground.*

Centre *King Bhumibol, accompanied by Princess Sirindhorn, consults with local villagers on one of their many field trips.*

Left *King Bhumibol pores over a map with government officials on one of his many field surveys.*

Many trips and projects were inspired by petitions. Petitioning the king was a traditional form of communication that allowed a monarch to hear grievances and engage with the problems of ordinary people. The Office of His Majesty's Principal Private Secretary, which receives the petitions, would pass on those related to potential development projects to Sumet's office. After an assessment of the problem, information might be sent to the king. If needed, the king would prepare a 1:50,000-scale map and carry out initial research before travelling to the petitioner's area. In Bangkok, he would spend hours in his study at Chitralada Villa, surrounded by teleprinters and communication devices, poring over materials spread across the floor, using his radio to talk to officials, day or night, using his personal call sign. Every day he would receive weather forecasts from the Department of Meteorology. This was his operations centre—and pages were under strict instructions not to tidy up. Nobody but the king was allowed to throw anything into the bin.

The king would often drive himself to the location and walk through the farms, to get a feel for the place and also to show moral support to the farmers. Sumet's team helped collect information at the site. The king then held a public hearing on the spot—an approach which came to be known as "rapid rural appraisal". Sometimes people rejected the initial proposal and alternatives were considered. Once an agreement was reached with the villagers and local officials, the king would then turn to Sumet, who managed funding and say, "*Tung ngoen* (Moneybags), do you agree?"

On a tour of a project in 1992 with French journalist Jean-Francois Mongibeaux of *Le Figaro* magazine, the king spread his handmade maps on a table and explained his approach. "I draw these maps myself. Thus I know the names of all the villages I visit. One has to be simple. Simplify all things. If one entrusts a project to experts, they write up big files, which no one understands. Us, we like to go on the ground, to speak with people, to know about their problems." Thai society has a strong structure of hierarchy and patronage, and this working method tended to bypass the traditional order of doing business and contrasted with the way the government ran their ministries and departments. This hands-on work in the fields and highlands also contrasted dramatically with his formal duties in the capital, where the king, during some years, presided over more than 800 ceremonies and official engagements in a year. While court officials in Bangkok would normally speak to the king in the ancient royal language of *rajasap*, farmers and other commoners were free to talk to the king in whatever dialect of Thai they spoke. The king himself had a good memory for names

and faces. In an effort to create a sense of shared experience with people, the palace would send back photos of royal visits to the villages for people to hang on their walls. The visits helped increase a sense of attachment to the monarchy. For most farmers, like many others, an encounter with the king was considered a lifetime highlight.

The king was always keen to empower farmers and the poor by listening to their struggles, but he never advocated simply throwing money or new technology at problems. In a speech in 1975, he outlined his approach: "Heavy development of advanced and more efficient machinery creates joblessness because people are robbed of their jobs by machines…Therefore we should think of tools and plans that are easy and practical, making the most of the energy and other resources available in our country. Such plans may not look glamorous or modern and may not give us as much in terms of yield, but the produce obtained would be enough for consumption. More than that, most people will have jobs and be able to earn the decent living they wish for."

The king preferred communities to, as he put it, "explode from [the] inside"—to develop themselves. In this sense, he approached people and society in the same way he did nature— respecting intrinsic balances that should not be destroyed by excessive measures. In a 1986 site visit in Sakon Nakhon province joined by Derek Davies, editor of the *Far Eastern Economic Review*, the king explained, "No one really appreciates. They always want more. That's why they must be encouraged to make themselves self-supporting, to stand on their own feet. That is why it is important not to give too much and even more important not to promise too much. If your attempts are too ambitious, only one thing has to go wrong or be delayed and a whole programme is affected. And that causes disappointment. You must give the minimum. The minimum amount." Asked to define the minimum, the king replied: "The minimum includes water to drink and water to irrigate the fields. These basics are lacked by the villagers, and that is why we must give them."

Grounds for Debate

Since the early 1970s, the king has made visits to his southern residence, the Thaksin Ratchaniwet Palace in Narathiwat province. A particular problem in the area was brought to his attention in 1974: the large, unproductive swamp known as Pru Bajoh. The king called

Far left King Bhumibol spreads a map out across the bonnet of his four-wheel-drive vehicle during an inspection visit to a new weir on the Pai river with officials from the Royal Irrigation Department.

Centre King Bhumibol checks directions with a local. He is carrying one of his trademark maps, personally annotated and taped together.

Left King Bhumibol at the wheel of a left-hand-drive Jeep Wagoneer with Princess Sirindhorn in the passenger seat during a tour of royal projects in Ratchaburi province.

on government agencies to reduce flooding on the land so that it could be used for agriculture and otherwise developed. But the project did not work. When the king visited in 1981, he found crops were failing because of high acidity—the swamp soil included over a metre of organic matter underlain by mud with a high content of pyrite. This releases sulphuric acid as it oxidizes. Similar soil problems had been encountered in some parts of Malaysia.

Pisoot Vijarnsorn, a soil specialist, thought he might have an answer. A privy councillor with agricultural expertise, Prince Chakraband Pensiri Chakrabandhu helped arrange for Pisoot to be granted an audience with the king. The soil specialist was young and spoke frankly, explaining that the project was failing due to improper drainage. The king listened carefully. Pisoot recalls feeling honoured that his views were being taken seriously, but his ideas were at odds with the Royal Irrigation Department, which had been running the programme. After Pisoot spoke up, there was a dispute between the soil experts and water technicians in the two departments.

The king, however, was not looking for "yes men", and said it was important to ascertain the facts. Scientists should always tell the truth, he said—even if at times it was more diplomatic to avoid disagreement. "Dialogue is a constant process. Argument occurs all the time," says Sumet. "If you are close to him, you will see how charming he is. He constantly asks for opinions until he is satisfied with the answer."

After his dialogue with Pisoot, the king initiated the Klaeng Din Project—a term often translated as "tricking the soil". The new programme involved extensive experimentation. A team set to work on acidic swampland land at the newly established Pikun Thong Royal Development Study Centre near Thaksin Ratchaniwet Palace. They divided it into blocks and drained the water, making the soil dry as long as possible. They would then use liming and leaching techniques to neutralise its acidity and plant different crops to determine which ones would survive. They then went on to plant various species of rice. In time, rice grew where before there was just abandoned land.

As Pisoot knew, experimenting with soil was a decidedly unglamorous pastime. But, second to water, it was proving the crucial component in many of the king's agricultural projects. Protecting the soil and maintaining its natural properties is basic to protecting watersheds, preventing erosion and improving crop yields. The Klaeng Din Project had much wider implications beyond the marshland near the southern palace. Eight million *rai* of land in Thailand suffered similar problems.

Left *Farmers walk with their cattle inside Phupan Royal Development Study Centre.*

Right *The rugged vetiver grass, which has numerous landscaping and agricultural applications, is used to bind loose hillside soil threatened by subsidence.*

Far right *A farmer offers the king papayas at Pikun Thong Royal Development Centre.*

Living Museums

By the mid-1980s, the king had travelled far and wide around the country, and his understanding of the diversity of its problems was hard to match. The reign had witnessed many transformations. Infrastructure had improved so much that few villages remained beyond reach as they had been in 1946 when he came to the throne—and indeed in 1952 when King Bhumibol made his first tentative rural forays. Healthcare and access to education had also improved, and the economy had grown at more than seven percent each year for decades. But in many parts of the country, whether from logging or monoculture, the environment had been degraded. On a visit in 1983 to a plot of land at Huai Sai in Phetchaburi province with a group of Royal Forest Department officials, the king surveyed a dry and barren landscape. Instead of a variety of natural vegetation, endless lines of pineapple plants stretched to the horizon. "The place will become a desert," the king warned.

Armed with the sort of long-term vision acquired over many years, he announced that he wanted to restore the lush forest King Vajiravudh had set eyes upon when he designated the same area a reserve in 1924. "[King Bhumibol] described the forest he had in his mind and people didn't believe him," recalls Aree Suwanchinda, one of the officials present. Aree remembers the king saying it would take 20 or 30 years for their efforts to be rewarded.

Over a quarter of a century later, the Huai Sai Royal Development Study Centre is 11,212-*rai* of thick forest cut by streams, with abundant wildlife including hog deer and a plethora of agricultural, environmental and community projects, including family farms where farmers follow the king's methods. It is a living testament to the relevance of many of the king's theories. The dramatic improvement of the ecology of the area can be seen by simply comparing photographs of the project when it featured sparse tree cover to images of the dense forest and undergrowth today.

Huai Sai Royal Development Study Centre was the last of several centres the king established and put under the able leadership of Prince Chakraband Pensiri. The first centre, Khao Hin Sorn Royal Development Centre, was established on 1,895 *rai* of land in Chachoengsao province in 1979. This was followed by the Kung Krabaen Bay Royal Development Study Centre in Chanthaburi; Pikun Thong in Narathiwat; Huai Hong Khrai Royal Development Study Centre in Chiang Mai; and the Phupan Royal Development Study Centre in Sakon Nakhon. Each centre is situated in a different region of the country

and has its own focus based on the local conditions. Phupan, for example, suffers from sandy soil and a lack of rain and thus emphasises solutions to those problems. The centre at Kung Krabaen Bay focuses on aquaculture and mangrove conservation.

Pradab Kladkempetch, director of the Huai Hong Khrai Royal Development Study Centre in Chiang Mai, worked out what could be done with the right mix of reservoirs, weirs and water piping. "Before the king began this model project here on 8,500 *rai* of land in 1982, the area was very dry, the soil poor and there were many forest fires," recalls Pradab, a Royal Irrigation Department official. King Bhumibol arranged for eight reservoirs to be built as well as canals and small check-dams that slow the passage of the water and promote seepage into the ground. The project needed careful planning, with attention to altitude, gradient and the types of canals and small dams that would be appropriate.

According to the king's vision, each royal development study centre serves as a "living natural museum", providing lessons in development that people can see for themselves and then apply to their own lives and work. Explaining what the king and officials refer to as the "geo-social" approach, the king said: "Development must respect varying regional geography and ways of living. We cannot impose our ideas on the people. We can only suggest. We must go to meet them, find out what their needs are, and then fully explain to them [what can be done]. In order to work out a programme to help people, it's necessary that you know the people you intend to help … there is no short cut. One does not know a people merely by memorizing some research papers prepared by research centres. You must meet the people and like them."

At the start of the Huai Sai project in 1983, the king thought carefully about how to reforest the dry land, studying the natural environment and stressing the need for patience. The Royal Irrigation Department went to work building check-dams on the hills and the king also turned to a multi-tasking natural ally he greatly favours: vetiver (*Vetiveria zizanioides*). This hardy grass, once dismissed as no more than a weed, develops exceptionally deep roots, retains water and nutrients, stimulates soil regeneration, contains flooding and inhibits erosion—particularly on raw and denuded slopes. The ground at Huai Sai was so hard in places that hammers, chisels and bores were needed to make holes to plant the remarkable plant, which if used correctly can restore eroded hardpan terrain into productive arable land or young forest floor in a matter of years.

Vetiver can also be used to line canals, waterways and ponds, for boundaries and road

verges, irrigation control, landscaping and even for some woven handicrafts. Free and natural, vetiver grass also reflected the king's preference for sustainable solutions. Thailand has become a world leader in vetiver use, even hosting a number of international conferences. King Bhumibol's role in its promotion in Thailand has been central to its success. Huai Sai proved an ideal natural laboratory for vetiver's many applications. "It took 13 years to improve and turn bad soil into good soil," recalls Aree, describing an assisted process that was essentially natural from a botanical standpoint.

The deputy director of the centre, Police Lieutenant Colonel Noppakun Bamrungpong, said the project combined simple methods with some more advanced technologies. Progress was hard won. The aim was to build a mountain forest, or wet forest system, and this meant planting trees on the tops of the barren hills, pumping water up to the top using solar power and allowing the seeds from the trees to fall and grow further down the hills. "Some agreed with this approach to reforestation and some did not," he said, but in the end the forest did indeed grow from the top down.

The king often stopped by to monitor progress, sometimes on his own at night and even in the rain. He said he was not concerned if there were setbacks. Hoping the study centre would bring together officials and departments so that they would work effectively together toward common goals, the king offered encouragement. "Sometimes there are failures from the experiment which the centre should not be ashamed of," he said. "In a development study centre things that were done wrongly can be a monument to wrongdoing, which reminds us not to do it again."

At the same time that trees were being planted on the hilltops, parts of the land were put aside for experimental projects. Village Scouts arrived to teach agricultural development and to empower local farmers to form cooperatives and generally run their affairs better. Boonlom Panchang, 65, was appointed a local leader. "Maybe I was made leader because I was not afraid to speak up—or because I was the only person in the village who owned a motorcycle," he reflects. "When the king said there would be a project here that would provide roads, electricity and water, people said he was dreaming," recalls Boonlom of the first meeting. "The king said to me, 'Pi Lom, you have to convince the people here'." Boonlom became a fixer, liaising between the village and the Huai Sai centre—a tricky job. "Initially, it was dangerous for me because we had problems as various 'influential people' were involved and the government was going to take over land," he says.

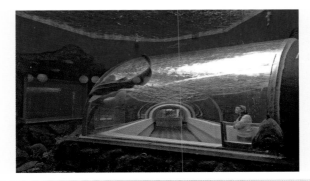

The major adjustment farmers were asked to make was to switch from the mono-cropping approach used in pineapple and sugar cane cultivation, which relies heavily on fertilisers, to mixed or integrative farming techniques. "We used to use chemicals a lot but we switched to an organic approach," Boonlom says. They began growing mangoes, lemons, jackfruit and vegetables. They also ditched the traditional middlemen in another move that ruffled feathers. Produce went direct to the market, bypassing wholesalers. Today, Boonlom's 40 *rai* yields his family close to a million baht each year.

Recognition and Reckoning

In 1988, Prince Bhisatej was invited to Manila to receive a Ramon Magsaysay Award for International Understanding on behalf of the Royal Project. The award recognised the success of the Royal Project in helping eliminate opium cultivation by providing suitable alternative livelihoods for the hill tribes and conserving the highland environment. The Royal Project was viewed in Asia and further afield as embodying important and effective principles for tackling the drug problem.

In the same year, the king set up the Chaipattana Foundation with himself as honorary president. Chaipattana means "Victory through Development". The name captures the notion of national development as akin to going to war. Princess Sirindhorn was made executive chairperson and Dr Sumet Tantivejkul secretary-general. The foundation relies on donations, and complements the efforts of both the Office of Royal Development Projects that works with government departments, as well as private sector projects to which the king had lent support. In general, the intention was for the foundation to operate like a non-governmental organisation, implementing projects quickly and bypassing red tape.

The Chaipattana Foundation was not exempt from having to register with the government. When Sumet went off to do the requisite paperwork, the official gave the form a cursory look. Then, after having not properly read it, he started asking testy questions: Why did the head of the foundation not come to register it himself? Did he know the office address and house number? Sumet did not know the house number of Chitralada Villa, irritating the bureaucrat still more. The official then belatedly noticed the name of King Bhumibol Adulyadej on the form and blanched. "Why didn't you tell me the king was registering this

foundation?" he demanded. Seven minutes later, the process was complete.

A disaster in late 1988 was another timely reminder of the battles that still lay ahead. Massive floods devastated 14 southern provinces, took 116 lives, and destroyed 16,000 homes and a million farms. After it became apparent that the disaster was due in large part to deforestation, there was a public outcry. The disastrous flooding and scale of the deforestation problem showed not only the prescience of the king but also the limits of his influence and power. In spite of his best efforts and many speeches, deforestation had been endemic for decades as illegal loggers and poor farmers decimated the green cover that had canopied more than two thirds of the land at the end of the Second World War. Influential politicians were among the beneficiaries from illegal timber proceeds. Comparisons of aerial photos with satellite photos over three decades revealed a shocking result: the country had lost half its forest cover, from 53 percent of land cover, or 273, 628 sq km in 1961 to 26 percent, or 133,521 sq km by 1993.

As early as 1971, the king warned about the dangers of deforestation. "Some people wonder why I became interested in irrigation and forestry," he said. "I remember when I was 10 years old, a science teacher who is now dead, taught me about soil conservation. We had to write: 'There must be a forest on the mountain or the rain will erode the soil and damage the mountain surface.' This is a fundamental fact of soil and forest conservation and of irrigation. If we fail to maintain the highland forest, we will have problems ranging from soil erosion to sedimentation in dams and in rivers. Both can lead to floods."

In 1974, in order to protect watersheds and fragile water resources, the king launched several reforestation projects. Poorly controlled logging concessions, overpopulation, infrastructure development, agribusiness and real estate speculation continued to make it very hard for the authorities to rein in the destruction. The slash–and–burn practices of some hill tribes drew much of the blame for what was in fact a countrywide problem. The Royal Forest Department had an extensive programme of protection and reforestation, but it was under–staffed and often criticised. Critics said the department's mission from inception had been to manage logging, not to protect trees.

Speaking about the issue, the king suggested that hill tribe people could help officials solve the problem. "There are three things in forests: firewood, fruit and wood for building houses. People—both highlanders and lowlanders—have knowledge about these things," he said. "They've been working for generations and have done it well. They're clever and know where to grow crops and where the trees should be kept. The damage was done by those who did not possess this knowledge—those who have long been away from farming. They've lived with modern comforts for so long they forget that life is [only] possible if they do proper agriculture."

The king's own approach to deforestation was generally to leave nature to its own devices. In 1987, for example, a policeman gave him a plot of land on which all the trees had been cut down. Left entirely alone, today it is thick with trees. The king also recommended that forestry officials try to "plant trees first in the hearts of the people". People might then plant real trees and care for them. Despite his efforts and influence, the king's message of protecting the environment has frequently fallen on deaf ears.

Water Works

While on a macro level King Bhumibol's influence was often limited, on the ground he could often wield real clout. By the 1990s, the overall number of the king's small-to-medium-sized projects—reservoirs, weirs and small dams—was adding up. By the beginning of the 1990s, 70 percent of the more than 3,000 Royal Development Projects focused on his overriding preoccupation: irrigation. "If we take proper care of the environment, there will be water for many hundreds of years," the king once said. "By that time our descendants might be thinking of some new ways to solve the problems. That would be their concern, not ours. But we have accomplished something."

While the royal projects tended to be grassroots, the government meanwhile launched large-scale dam building. Although the king often expressed his concern that new technology and grand schemes would not necessarily help farmers, he did not object to these projects. He recognised the high costs, including the displacement of people and flooding of valleys, but he also saw benefits from power generation and irrigation control.

In the 1990s, the king himself embarked upon some larger, more ambitious projects. Arguably, his most impressive water resource project is the Pa Sak River Basin Development Programme. The idea of developing the river basin to help regulate flooding and improve irrigation had been on the drawing board since 1965, but had been shelved due to high investment costs and other factors. In 1989, the king proposed reviving the project. He

Opposite *The Klong Lud Pho Watergate alongside the Bhumibol I Bridge, both of which were officially opened by King Bhumibol on 24 November 2010. Traffic mitigation and flood relief in Bangkok have become major preoccupations following the capital's exponential expansion in recent decades.*

stipulated that the site selected for the dam should achieve maximum benefit with a minimum of disruption to the people and the environment, displacing as few people as possible.

The Pa Sak Dam was completed in 1999 with a capacity of less than a tenth of the 13,462 million-cubic-metre Bhumibol Dam. It is the longest earth-fill dam in Thailand, with a lake stretching close to 25 kilometres. The dam can hold a maximum of 960 million cubic metres of water and helps irrigate over 130,000 *rai* of new farmland. It allows farmers in the region to grow two rice crops each year and aimed to improve their lives in other ways, promoting chemical-free agriculture, fisheries, reforestation and handicraft production. The lake also attracts thousands of Thai and foreign tourists each year.

Five years after the Pa Sak Dam was built, the king helped with the building of a dam on the nearby Nakhon Nayok River. He knew there would be some dissent. "People will probably start a hullabaloo when the Nakhon Nayok river is mentioned, since at present to obtain a piece of land for construction one must trespass on forests or national parks," the king noted when unveiling the plan for the Khun Darn Prakan Chol Dam.

Another royal project, the Klong Tha Dan weir, was submerged by the new dam project, and King Bhumibol used this as an opportunity to point out that royal projects were not exempt from evolution and future adjustment. "It has been said that royal initiative projects cannot be touched," he observed. "This line of thinking is wrong, or not quite correct. If royal initiative projects cannot be touched, Thailand will never progress. The initiative belongs to the king, and if the king's ideas cannot be changed, it means Thailand cannot improve. That royal initiative weir has served people for a long time and it has been worth the expense."

Old Challenges, New Solutions

By the mid-1990s, Thailand was widely regarded as riding high—an emerging Asian tiger economy. But on a 1992 trip to Khao Wong, a 1970s communist stronghold in Kalasin province in the Northeast, King Bhumibol noticed flaws in this picture of plenty. "They said they had got in the harvest and pointed to a heap of rice," said the king. "We went in for a closer look. The rice had grown well but did not produce many grains, only about two or three to an ear. The production could be estimated at about one bucket or less per *rai*."

The sight of the rice had a sobering effect. Thailand was one of the world's leading rice exporters, yet here was clear evidence that many farmers still struggled to grow crops properly—despite the efforts made by the government and the king over the previous decades. Farmers in the Central Plains typically managed two rice crops a year, while in Khao Wong they struggled with one poor one. While the king could see noticeable progress there compared to a visit a decade earlier, the problem still came down to water. The village suffered from the perennial problem in the region: unreliable rainfall.

"They had sowed the rice, but when it came to transplanting the seedlings, there was no water. They had to make holes in the sand and stick the seedlings in them. In the daytime the plant withered and drooped, but at night it straightened up with the dew. In the end it developed ears but not so many grains of rice," the king observed.

Khao Wong was a reminder that for many farmers life still hung on the vagaries of rainfall and the prayers of the local monks. Many young people had meanwhile left for Bangkok to try to find work and a less rustic way of life. Villages as viable farming communities were under threat. Better roads and a growing number of pick-up trucks, motorcycles and TV sets were superficial signs that life was improving. The king believed a new approach was needed to stimulate rural prosperity. He argued that it was not so much the amount of rain that was the problem, but its erratic timing. "When it rains, it is not needed; when it is needed, it does not rain. So rice is not plentiful," he commented. The king pondered a solution for non-irrigated, rain-fed areas of farmland such as Khao Wong.

One answer was the "New Theory". Announced in 1993, it came about partly by accident. As the secretary-general of the Chaipattana Foundation, Sumet had been asked to buy some land for the king next to a temple in Saraburi, north of Bangkok. The basic idea was to use the temple as a communal focus where people could also learn more about good farming techniques. The king suggested they dig a pond to store water for farming during the dry season. When he came to visit the Wat Mongkol Chaipattana Area Development Project, it struck him that the formula was a good balance. As it happened, the land had been split with 30 percent allocated to the pond, 30 percent for rice growing, 30 percent for mixed crops and 10 percent for other uses by the household.

The formula became the basis of his New Theory. As Sumet explains, with the king's New Theory you need to satisfy your stomach first. Using this approach, "You have your own 7-Eleven convenience store on your land." It can provide rice, fish, chicken and other

Far left *Crown Prince Maha Vajiralongkorn and Princess Srirasmi preside over a rice sowing ceremony at Chitralada Villa in May 2011.*

Centre *For the annual Royal Ploughing Ceremony at Sanam Luang, seeds specially cultivated on the grounds of Chitralada Villa are blessed in a Buddhist ceremony at the Chapel Royal, the Temple of the Emerald Buddha.*

Left *Agriculture officials don ancient attire to sow new rice in a newly prepared field in the grounds surrounding the Chitralada Villa away from public view.*

crops. Surplus products can be sold to build savings, and it is possible to earn some income all year from the various crops. Any excess land can be used for more cash crops. [*For more details of the New Theory, see page 271.*]

Plotting the Future

For many Thais, the image of their king that endures is of a simply dressed man perspiring slightly with a map in hand, a camera hanging from his neck, talking and listening to his people in the countryside. During King Bhumibol's record-breaking reign, the population of Thailand has more than tripled to over 67 million. Agriculture's portion of the country's GDP stands at 9.3 percent, compared with about 30 percent in the early 1960s. The king was always aware that his work in development would have successes and failures, gains and losses. His own ambition was thus, like his projects, appropriately measured. "When I was crowned, we launched royal development projects with the princess mother," he commented in 1992. "At first, spread over one year, then over five years. My objective was to improve peoples' lives without destroying their equilibrium, their traditional values, their identity. We hope that we have succeeded."

In 2011 there were 4,368 projects. Out of these projects, 1,770 focus on water resource development, 931 on the environment, including protecting forests, 559 on agriculture, 325 on developing vocational opportunities, 179 on social welfare, 164 on communications, 50 on public health, and 390 on other activities. The king's children are already carrying on with his work. The welcome mat is also out. Foreign governments and organisations have been keen to learn from the Thai experience. Over the years, learning forums promoting the king's ideas have been organised in Cambodia, China, Laos, Myanmar and Vietnam. Many foreign countries, including Indonesia, Oman and Swaziland have tapped the king and his experts for suggestions to improve the agricultural situation at home. The use of vetiver grass continues to be promoted through the Pacific Rim Vetiver Network hosted by the royal development projects board. In response to a request from the former President of the Lao PDR, Kaison Phomviharn, the king initiated the Huai Sonn-Huai Soie Agricultural Service and Development Centre in the Khong River Basin in Laos. Opened in 1994, the project is guided by Princess Sirindhorn and the Chaipattana Foundation.

Following the visit of the King and Queen of Lesotho to the Huai Hong Khrai Royal Development Centre in June 2006, a demonstration centre for sustainable agricultural development was set up in Lesotho on four hectares of land owned by the queen. The aim is to offer better agricultural models for a southern African country where current agricultural practices can still lead to poverty and malnutrition.

The United Nations presented its first UNDP Human Development Lifetime Achievement Award to King Bhumibol in 2006. UN Secretary-General Kofi Annan travelled down to Klai Kangwon Palace in Hua Hin, where the king was staying, to make the presentation. The award was timed to mark the 60th anniversary of the king's accession, and honoured his Sufficiency Economy thinking and promotion of a sustainable way of life that continues to elude so many in the world today. Crystallised and promoted in the wake of the 1997 Asian financial crisis, the Sufficiency Economy approach advocated a way of life that was moderate and secure, and rejected headlong dashes for profit and growth with no proper consideration for social wellbeing, sustainability, prudence or the environment.

"As a visionary thinker, Your Majesty has played an invaluable role in shaping the global development dialogue," Kofi Annan said at the presentation. "Your Majesty's 'Sufficiency Economy' philosophy, emphasizing moderation, responsible consumption, and resilience to external shocks, is of great relevance worldwide during these times of rapid globalization. It reinforces the United Nations' efforts to promote a people-centred and sustainable path of development." *[For more details of the Sufficiency Economy thinking, see page 266]*

Six decades on and the king's personal brand of people-centred development work is held in high regard by many around the world. Apart from the 2006 UNDP Award and the 1988 Magsaysay Award for the Royal Project, the king's work was honoured with the first International Rice Award in 1986 by the International Rice Research Institute based in the Philippines. In 1993, the king received the International Merit Award from the International Erosion Control Association for his promotion of vetiver grass in its many applications. The 1995 FAO Agricola Medal was awarded for the king's leadership in agricultural development and environmental protection; the 1999 Telefood Medal for his strong support in the battle against hunger and poverty; the 2003 Colombo Plan Award for the Royal Project; the 2004 Habitat Scroll of Honour Award for the royal development projects; and the first Dr Norman E. Borlang Medallion award by the World Food Prize Foundation in 2006 for exceptional humanitarian service in reducing hunger and poverty.

Far left *Villagers in Lesotho learn about the Sufficiency Economy. Lesotho adapted some of the lessons of the New Theory after its king visited the Huai Hong Krai Royal Development Study Centre in 2006.*

Centre *King Bhumibol discusses the Huai Sonn-Huai Soie Agricultural Service and Development Centre in Laos with Laotian president Nouhak Phoumsavanh during its opening in 1994.*

Left *Students from Chitralada School learn to grow rice at an experimental rice field in Chitralada Villa.*

King Bhumibol has received a string of other awards and honorary degrees recognising his contributions in a wide range of disciplines. He has also dispensed a few of his own, including the annual King of Thailand Vetiver Award to promote study of the resilient grass strain that offers so many environmental benefits. Winning awards was never an aim in itself, but they are evidence of the wider audience taking note of the king's projects. When Kofi Annan arrived in Hua Hin to present the UNDP award, it had been close to a decade since the king had ventured out personally to monitor his projects. Health problems had taken their toll. Personally visiting project sites, however, has become less of a requirement given the building blocks already put in place. Well-run organisations, such as the Chaipattana Foundation, the Office of the Royal Development Projects Board and the Royal Project, are capable of functioning autonomously. And with more than 4,000 projects under way, there is no shortage of work still to be done.

Today, much of the area surrounding Chitralada Villa better resembles a farm than the palace of a monarch. Day in, day out, the staff of what is now called the Royal Chitralada Projects lead groups of visiting farmers, government officials, uniformed school children and foreign visitors around the king's personal experiments. The king, meanwhile, continues to receive petitions from his subjects and monitor the progress of his life's work from afar.

Above *The Kok river winds through a classic northern Thai landscape in Chiang Mai province. Efficient water management, simple technology and sensitive manipulation of the environment have always been central to King Bhumibol's work in development, and are important foundations for his Sufficiency Economy thinking.*

MORE FROM LESS

Sufficiency Economy thinking was formalised in the aftermath of the 1997 financial crisis that rocked economies in Thailand and the region. Embracing Buddhist principles and drawing on King Bhumibol's many decades of hands-on research and work in development, the theory is a vision of sustainable development in the global era. Under the Sufficiency Economy thinking, the push for growth precipitated by capitalism is balanced by moderation and ethical behaviour. While focused on creating a model under which farmers may enjoy sufficiency, and which mitigates some of the risks posed by the environment and marketplace, its principles can also be applied on a larger scale in the public and private sectors.

Sufficiency Economy, or *Setthakit Pho Phiang*, is the title King Bhumibol Adulyadej gave in 1998 to his thinking on development. *Setthakit* is the Thai word for "economy", in the sense of the national economy; *pho* is the common word for "enough"; and *phiang* means "only" or "just". The linking of *pho* and *phiang* displays a typical Thai love for alliteration, and the result means "just enough". So the phrase means "a just-enough economy".

The spur to formalise, brand and publish the king's ideas on the economy came from the financial crisis of 1997, which had originated from the collapse of the Thai economy and spread throughout the global financial system. In his birthday speech in December 1997, the king argued that aiming to become a "tiger" economy was folly. He said it was much more important to develop "an economy where people are more self-reliant and have an adequate livelihood for themselves". Many Thais believed the crisis was the result of a reckless and extravagant pursuit of economic growth, so the king's call for moderation and restraint brilliantly captured the national mood at the time.

A working group of officials, academics and palace staff distilled the king's thinking on the economy from his public utterances over prior decades into a kind of manifesto, in both Thai and English, which the king reviewed. The government of the day adopted this statement as a guide to overcome the crisis. The national planning board made it the theme of the next three five-year economic and social plans. Major companies embraced the concept. Teaching on the principles of the king's ideas was incorporated into the school curriculum. Books, pamphlets, feature articles and websites were created to teach the principles of the Sufficiency Economy and publicise the successes of those who followed its dictates. In 2007, the United Nations Development Program (UNDP) devoted its *Thailand Human Development Report* to explaining the evolution and application of the Sufficiency Economy in the public and private spheres.

Sufficiency Economy is not an analysis of how an economy works or a blueprint for development planning. Rather it is a set of maxims for practical use in planning and implementing any project or human endeavour. At the heart of this approach are three principles: moderation; wisdom or insight—and the need for built-in resilience against risks which arise from internal or external changes. Although the term Sufficiency Economy was coined in 1997, the thinking had evolved over earlier decades. Its roots lie in the knowledge and practical experience the king had gleaned from his many development projects, and also in some basic tenets of Buddhist philosophy.

❝ Many Thais believe the 1997 financial crisis was the result of a reckless and extravagant pursuit of economic growth. The king's call for moderation brilliantly captured the national mood. **❞**

Lessons from Development

When the king ascended the throne, over four-fifths of his subjects were small agriculturists including both rice growers and hill farmers. His coronation oath to "reign with righteousness, for the benefit and happiness of the Siamese people" implied a commitment to them. Beginning in the early 1950s, he travelled widely in the countryside and hills, observing changes and asking people about their problems and hopes.

This was an era of rapid and jolting change as Thailand embraced the alluring idea of "development". The country was growing richer as never before but not without other costs that fell especially hard on small farmers. The farmers were often exploited by others who were better versed in the ways of an expanding capitalist economy, and they faced higher risks from market volatility. The natural environment on which the farmers depended was taking a beating—some felt they were losing control over their lives; and many were falling further and further into debt and becoming disgruntled as a result.

King Bhumibol's Sufficiency Economy maxims evolved in part from his personal efforts to address these problems. The king's early development projects had three main themes:

- Water management
- Simple technology
- Sensitive manipulation of the environment

The region around the king's seaside palace at Hua Hin is very dry because it lies in the rain shadow of nearby hills. When the king was surveying this area in the early 1950s, his jeep got stuck on a coastal mudflat and had to be pulled out by local villagers. He conceived the idea that a simple dam could turn this tidal marsh into a lake useful to the local villagers for fish farming, irrigation and drinking water. The lake, completed in 1953, serves these purposes to this day. In addition, it hosts an annual longboat competition which brings added income and entertainment to the locality. In nearby Hup Kapong, another simple bulldozed dam converted a poor village into a centre for growing high-value produce. These two projects became the model for hundreds of small-scale tanks and reservoirs over future years.

The king saw the benefit of simple technologies which small-scale farmers could understand and operate to great benefit. He founded projects inside the grounds of Chitralada Villa in

Bangkok to develop some devices such as a simple water aerator and a small-scale rice mill. He promoted the wider use of other technologies and practices such as buffalo banks, small tractors and methods to convert rice husk into fuel. Later, he discovered E. F. Schumacher's 1973 classic, *Small is Beautiful*, which gave the world the concept of "appropriate technology". Recognising a kindred spirit, he personally translated one of the book's chapters into Thai.

During this period there were glaring examples of how more intensive use of natural resources were changing the environment for the worse: soil erosion, deforestation, increased flooding and deterioration of the soil, among other problems. The king promoted simple methods to combat these changes by working in harmony with nature. Planting vetiver grass restrained soil erosion. Check-dams distribute water from rivers into nearby fields. Seeding hilltops hastened natural regeneration of forests. The king favoured techniques which were simple, economical, self-sustaining and already proven in traditional practice. In a speech on reforestation, he noted, "The farmers … have practised this for many generations, and done it well too. They are the experts."

Buddhist Basis

Besides learning from practical experience, Sufficiency Economy thinking drew on the ethical teachings of Buddhism. Two elements of these teachings have special prominence in the theory. The first is the idea of moderation or the middle way. Any action which deliberately aims for a middle course and avoids extremes on either side has a better chance of achieving success. The second idea is about intention and consequence. In Buddhist teaching every person accumulates *karma* through life as a result of good and bad actions, and the balance in this account helps determine that person's subsequent births and progress towards enlightenment. Behind this teaching is the idea that every action has a consequence that depends on the intention that willed the action. An action that is undertaken with good intent, founded on a basis of knowledge and pursued with honesty and perseverance has the highest chance of enjoying success.

The king explained these ideas to Chulalongkorn University students on several occasions in the early 1970s: "I want everyone to bear in mind the law of cause and effect. A result arises because of a cause, an action. Whether that result is good or bad depends on whether

66 The farmers … have practised this for many generations, and done it well too. They are the experts. 99

the action was good or bad. So to achieve any aim, you first have to study what is the appropriate means, and then proceed according to the law of causation with honesty and determination. Then everyone's work will have a good outcome, and taken together will result in the desired progress and security of our country."

"Everybody must continually subject their own actions to thorough analysis to ensure they are correct, based on rationality, wisdom, and self-awareness, in order to overcome all kinds of evil and to be able to achieve true success in both work and life."

Public Reflections

In pubic speeches, especially to students, the king conveyed the lessons gleaned from his projects. The learning he related was not about how to design a dam or regenerate a forest, but about the principles behind planning a project and bringing it to a successful conclusion.

One of the key principles concerned the importance of knowledge. No project was likely to succeed unless it was founded on a basis of knowledge. Development was not about new techniques but about equipping people with the knowledge to *use* new techniques. He set out this principle at length in 1974 at Kasetsart University: "One thing being strongly promoted at present is increase in production, in the belief that production is the source of income. Everybody should be able to see without difficulty that production is related to demand, distribution and business organisation as well as the extraction of income and profit to be used for consumption. Thus, the correct approach to increasing production is not through application of agricultural techniques to increase the value of production for its own sake. Rather, agricultural and other techniques should be applied to help the producer to receive returns for the labour, thinking and capital he has used in full measure, so he can use those returns to raise his standard of living to a more secure level."

A second principle was about prudence, working slowly, proceeding by stages, growing from an internal dynamic, achieving a level of competence and self-reliance before proceeding further, and taking care not to overreach one's capabilities. "It is extremely important to encourage and help people to earn their living and support themselves with adequate means, because those who are gainfully employed and self-supporting are capable of meaningfully contributing towards higher levels of development," he lectured the Kasetsart students. "As

regards the concept of gradual progress with caution and economy, it is to be followed if only in order to prevent failure and ensure certain and complete success; for if done without caution, it would be hard to expect any full benefit."

In 1975, he addressed Chulalongkorn University students on a third principle concerning the importance of perseverance, hard work, honesty and integrity: "The happiness and prosperity that people seek can be achieved, but by actions that are ethical in intention and execution, not by chance or by fighting and grabbing from others. True prosperity is something creative because it gives benefit to others and to people in general as well."

Macro Sufficiency

The king applied these principles not only to individual development projects but to the development of the national economy as a whole. "Development of the country must proceed in stages," he told Khon Kaen University students in 1973. "First of all, there must be a foundation with the majority of the people having enough to live on by using methods and equipment which are economical but technically correct as well. When such a secure foundation is adequately ready and operational, then it can be gradually expanded and developed to raise prosperity and the economic standard to a higher level by stages."

In his birthday speech at Dusit Palace in 1974, he wished everyone in Thailand "sufficient to live and to eat", and re-emphasised the need to sacrifice speed for prudence. "It is especially important to first build a foundation in which people have an occupation and the ability to make a living, as those who have an occupation and a reliable living can then progress upwards to higher levels of prosperity," he said. "The promotion of progress must proceed in stages with care, economy and foresight to prevent mistakes and disasters … if one focuses only on rapid economic expansion without making sure that such a plan is appropriate for our people and the condition of our country, it will inevitably result in various imbalances and eventually end up as [a] failure or crisis, as found in other countries."

The following year, speaking at the King Mongkut Institute of Technology, King Bhumibol pondered the growing enthusiasm for industrialisation on a world scale and the resulting pattern of unbalanced growth: "Economic and social conditions in many countries have changed; that is, a great deal of effort is harnessed to construct advanced technology

Far left *Fish are a valuable source of protein and the Sufficiency Economy idea encourages farming families to set aside part of their land as a pond for raising fish.*

Left *Farmers harvest rice using time tested, traditional methods.*

and great efficiency in the production process, leading to the rapid increase in products to the level of luxury. At the same time, unemployment increased because machinery has taken away jobs from humans. This caused economic downturns as the unemployed became poorer and the producers of goods went bankrupt because they were not able to sell their products. Thus, theoretical and practical adjustment to industrial development ought to be promoted to create a balance in other sectors in order to survive."

Model Farms

In 1994, the king revealed how his ideas should apply to agriculture. His scheme was based on a self-reliant family which through progressive stages was integrated with the local and national economies. The press promptly dubbed this the "New Theory". While the name was perhaps misleading, as several NGOs, academics and local wise men had advocated similar schemes, it stressed how much the king's scheme flew in the face of the orthodox quest for growth through higher investment and large-scale development.

The first stage of the scheme was a farm on a 15-*rai* holding, which is about six acres and the median for smallholders in much of the country. This holding was divided into four zones: 30 percent for digging a pond to store 19,000 cubic metres of water to irrigate cultivation in the dry season and to raise fish; 30 percent for rice cultivation sufficient for year-round home consumption; 30 percent for other crops and fruit; and 10 percent for housing, animal husbandry and other activities. Soil fertilisation, weed control and pest control used natural methods. The production system maximised synergies between livestock and crops in order to make the household self-reliant as well as provide some surplus for exchange on the local market. The king stressed that this was a basic model which could be easily modified to suit holdings of larger or smaller sizes, and to different regions where soil, water and cropping conditions varied. On this farm, a family could provide everything for themselves and avoid debt, excessive risk and exploitation by others. The king admitted that this model "was not easy to implement, because the one who uses it must have perseverance and endurance".

The second stage of the New Theory aimed to create self-reliance at the community level by increasing the production and availability of local goods and services through mobilising the surplus resources of households within a community. This might be done through

cooperative forms of production, community savings groups, community health centres and community forms of social safety nets. The idea was to increase the local provision of goods and services by introducing some division of labour to achieve economies of scale and scope, while still relying principally on the community's own capacity and resources. Exchange with the outside should increase, but local exchange was always preferable because it saved on transport and other transaction costs.

At the third stage, the community could then engage with the economy beyond the village to sell its excess products, to gain the technology for such projects as founding its own rice mill, to tap the services of banks and other economic institutions, and to negotiate with corporations for mutual advantage. Although the king presented this theory as just these three stages, progress towards an ever broader and more complex economy was implied. In another birthday speech, he explained: "Progress is not just about planting enough rice to eat. There must be enough to create schools, even works of art, so that Thailand prospers in every way, with no hunger or poverty, [enough] food for body and soul, and many other things."

The New Theory exemplified the king's conclusions about how to achieve real development with real benefits for ordinary people. Progress had to be achieved by stages, without unrealistic expectations. Before moving to another stage, there first had to be a firm foundation of self-reliance or else there was a strong chance of failure and loss of independence. The driving force for development had to come from within and be based on the accumulation of knowledge, honest commitment and perseverance. The New Theory model was welcomed by like-minded academics and development workers. Relevant government agencies undertook to provide support for such schemes. But the theory did not shift the government's agricultural policies or reorient the majority of farmers. On a broader level, it prompted only minimal debate. Thailand was in the throes of a spectacular economic boom based on industrial exports. Few paid much attention to agrarian economics.

Step Back to Progress

However, the economic crisis that hit three years later transformed the context of the debate. By December 1997, the currency had lost 40 percent of its value, consumption was dropping by a fifth, most of the nation's firms were technically bankrupt, and two million people had

Far left *A billboard near the Thai-Cambodia border advertises easy credit.*

Centre *A luxury car show near Bangkok. Moderation is a key principle of Sufficiency Economy thinking.*

Left *The urban sprawl of Bangkok. After the boom of the 1990s, a financial crisis brought the city back to earth and triggered more interest in the king's sufficiency economy ideal.*

fallen out of work. In this context, the king's words drew more attention.

In his birthday speech, he told a nationwide television audience: "Recently, so many projects have been implemented, so many factories have been built, that it was thought Thailand would become a little tiger, and then a big tiger. People were crazy about becoming a tiger ... I have often said to an audience such as this one that to be a tiger is not important. The important thing for us is to have a Sufficiency Economy. A Sufficiency Economy means to have an economy where people are more self-reliant and have an adequate livelihood for themselves ... It doesn't have to be complete, not even half, perhaps just a quarter, then we can survive ... Those who like modern economics may not appreciate this. But we have to take a careful step backwards."

The government immediately announced it would adopt the king's approach to guide the country out of the crisis. The central bank, armed forces and many private companies undertook to follow the king's approach. Quotations from the speech were relayed nationwide on television fillers and billboards. A year later, the king used his birthday speech to make clarifications and corrections. He stressed that his approach should be termed "sufficiency" rather than "self-sufficiency". He addressed some other misconceptions: "I may add that full sufficiency is impossible. If a family or even a village wants to employ a full Sufficiency Economy, it would be like returning to the Stone Age ... This sufficiency means to have enough to live on. Sufficiency means to lead a reasonably comfortable life, without excess or overindulgence in luxury, but enough. Some things may seem to be extravagant, but if it brings happiness, it is permissible as long as it is within the means of the individual..." He added: "Some people translate 'sufficiency' from English as: to stand on one's own feet ... This means standing on our own two legs planted on the ground, so we can remain without falling over, and without asking others to lend us their legs to stand on."

Crystallisation

Soon after this second birthday speech on sufficiency economy in 1998, a project was launched to make the king's ideas available in a more systematic and accessible form. A group of officials and academics helped to draft a formal exposition of the Sufficiency Economy, which the king officially approved in November 1999:

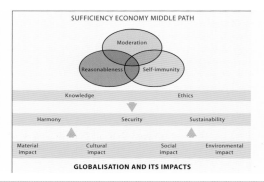

"The Sufficiency Economy is an approach to life and conduct which is applicable at every level from the individual through the family and community to the management and development of the nation.

"It promotes a middle path, especially in developing the economy to keep up with the world in the era of globalisation.

"Sufficiency has three components: moderation; wisdom or insight; and the need for built-in resilience against the risks which arise from internal or external change. In addition, the application of theories in planning and implementation requires great care and good judgement at every stage.

"At the same time, all members of the nation—especially officials, intellectuals, and business people—need to develop their commitment to the importance of knowledge, integrity and honesty, and to conduct their lives with perseverance, toleration, wisdom and insight so that the country has the strength and balance to respond to the rapid and widespread changes in economy, society, environment and culture in the outside world."

Another working group assembled all the relevant passages from the king's speeches and pronouncements over the prior three decades. They then subjected these writings to linguistic and content analysis to distil the key elements of the king's thinking. This group condensed the Sufficiency Economy down to three components:

- Moderation
- Reasonableness
- Self-immunity

The three components are explained here for greater clarity: "Moderation" is closely linked to the idea of sufficiency. In Thai, as in English, the word for sufficiency has two meanings: enough in the sense of not too little, and enough in the sense of not too much. It conveys the idea of a middle way between want and extravagance, between backwardness and impossible dreams. It implies both self-reliance and frugality. "Reasonableness" means both evaluating the reasons for any action, and understanding its full consequences—not only on oneself, but on others, the society and the environment; and not only in the short term, but the long term as well. This idea of reasonableness thus includes accumulated knowledge and experience, along with analytic capability, self-awareness, foresight, compassion and empathy. The need

Left *A community learning centre in Pho Tak district of Nong Khai province offers farmers a chance to learn more of the king's ideas.*

of "self-immunity" means having built-in resilience, the ability to withstand shocks, to adjust to external change and to cope with events that are unpredictable or uncontrollable. It implies a foundation of self-reliance, as well as self-discipline.

Besides these three components, two other conditions are needed to make these principles work: knowledge and integrity. "Knowledge" is almost akin to wisdom in English. It encompasses accumulated information, the insight to understand its meaning, and care or prudence in putting it to use. "Integrity" means virtue, ethical behaviour, honesty and straightforwardness, but also implies tolerance, perseverance, a readiness to work hard and a refusal to exploit others.

This formalisation of the Sufficiency Economy theory was disseminated through books, radio and television programmes, newspaper features on successful applications of the approach, websites and in other ways. In 2004, a sub-committee was set up within the planning agency to disseminate the king's ideas through seminars and various media. In parallel, a sub-committee in the Ministry of Education incorporated Sufficiency Economy ideas into the school curriculum on society, religion and culture, and it was taught at all levels from primary to higher secondary from 2009 onwards. In 2009, the army promoted a campaign under the banner Moderation Society ("a society of moderation where people live their lives just right") to propagate the king's ideas, especially among youth.

Appeal

Many different organisations publicly embraced the Sufficiency Economy. Each drew inspiration from a particular aspect of the theory. The managers of the national economy, for example, focused especially on the theory's call for prudence and built-in immunity against external shocks. Beginning in 1998, the authorities undertook a thorough overhaul of macroeconomic management with the aim of preventing another crisis like that of 1997. The national reserves were increased; inflation targeting was adopted to introduce more discipline into monetary policy; government debt was subject to strict controls; and a battery of risk indicators was compiled. Thailand's comparative success in surviving the international downturn of 2008 was cautiously attributed to this overhaul.

In 1999, the national planning agency, the National Economic and Social Development

> ❝ Reasonableness and moderation must be
> used to create a balance between material and
> mental dimensions, between self-reliance and
> competitive capability in the world market, and
> between rural and urban society. ❞

Board, adopted the Sufficiency Economy as the guiding principle for future plans. For this agency, the key message of the Sufficiency Economy was that Thailand had to move towards a more balanced, sustainable and inner-driven pattern of growth. The Tenth Plan for the years 2007 to 2011 set out the application of Sufficiency Economy principles in this way: "Thailand must reorient its development paradigm to have greater self-reliance and resilience by following the Sufficiency Economy philosophy in conjunction with a holistic approach to people-centred development. Development policy and national administration must follow a middle path which balances and integrates all dimensions of development, including the human, social, economic, environmental and political. Reasonableness and moderation must be used to create a balance between material and mental dimensions, between self-reliance and competitive capability in the world market, and between rural and urban society. A self-immunity system must be built into economic systems through risk management in order to handle the impact of changes both inside and outside the country."

For many people in business damaged by the 1997 crisis, the key message of the Sufficiency Economy was the need for prudence. Others focused on corporate social responsibility (CSR). In 2007, 100 businessmen pooled ideas on how the king's ideas could be used to stimulate CSR initiatives in *Sufficiency Economy: A New Philosophy in the Global World*. For others in government, business, agriculture or elsewhere the attractive element of the theory was its emphasis on the role of ethics. On 26 May 2006, the UN Secretary-General Kofi Annan presented a Human Development Lifetime Achievement Award to King Bhumibol. "His Majesty's Sufficiency Economy philosophy … is of great relevance to communities everywhere during these times of rapid globalisation," said the UN secretary-general. "The philosophy's 'middle way' approach strongly reinforces the United Nations' own advocacy of a people-centred and sustainable path toward human development. His Majesty's development agenda and visionary thinking are an inspiration to his subjects, and to people everywhere."

Crossed Wires

The most common misunderstanding of the approach is to read sufficiency as self-sufficiency, and to imagine the theory advocates independent family farms and a national economy shielded from the world as in Myanmar or North Korea. The misunderstanding has arisen

Right *United Nations Secretary-General Kofi Annan presents the Human Development Lifetime Achievement Award to King Bhumibol at Klai Kangwol Palace on 26 May 2006.*

in part because of some careless early translations. In the New Theory, even at the first stage, the farm is expected to create a surplus for sale. Also, this stage should not be read in isolation from the subsequent two stages which prescribe progressive integration with the outside world. At the national level, the king clarified that "*self*-sufficiency is not a Sufficiency Economy, but a Stone Age Economy ... There must be some gradual development, some exchange and cooperation between districts, provinces and countries, something beyond sufficiency."

Another common misunderstanding is that the Sufficiency Economy amounts to a rejection of globalisation. Again, King Bhumibol clarified his thinking. "As we are in the globalisation era, we also have to conform to the world," he said. The word globalisation was included in the formal statement of the approach to avert confusion.

A larger problem arises over interpretation. As the Sufficiency Economy is a set of maxims for practical action rather than a tightly reasoned and encompassing theory, these maxims can be used to support varying agendas. One example will illustrate this.

In 1999, Thailand's leading economists discussed the Sufficiency Economy over a two-day conference. They concluded that the approach was consistent with market capitalism based on competition and that the main result of adopting the approach would be to introduce more caution into economic management.

However, some proponents of Buddhist economics have proposed a very different interpretation. In their view the principles of competition and profit maximisation at the heart of capitalism are a source of anxiety rather than happiness. Buddhist economics aims to overcome selfishness by nurturing compassion, fairness and generosity. Advocates argue that the Sufficiency Economy, with its strong emphasis on moderation, amounts to a rejection of capitalist competition. They point especially to the king's birthday speech in 1998: "Sufficiency is moderation. If one is moderate in one's desires, one will have less craving. If one has less craving, one will take less advantage of others. If all nations hold this concept ... without being extreme or insatiable in one's desires, the world will be a happier place. Being moderate does not mean to be too strictly frugal; luxurious items are permissible, but one should not take advantage of others in the fulfilment of one's desires. Moderation, in other words, living within one's means, should dictate all actions. Act in moderation, speak in moderation; that is, be moderate in all activities."

The theory has come under criticism from many angles. Here are three examples: Some

believe the New Theory is simply irrelevant to the realities of rural Thailand today. They suggest that the vast majority of farmers have become so enmeshed with markets that the image of a relatively self-reliant smallholding can exist only in the imagination. A majority of farmers also no longer have access to large enough plots to attempt the allocation of resources the theory advises. To manage their risks, farmers prefer to diversify their activities, strengthen their links with the market and multiply their sources of credit, rather than retreating to greater independence.

At a broader political level, the approach has been criticised as an elitist attempt to diminish pressure for any change in the stark inequalities and injustices underlying Thai society. In this view, the underlying message of the theory is that "the wealthy can enjoy their wealth so long as they do so within their means. For the poor, the advice is to do better with what they have; [to] make do." These critics believe the theory encourages people to overcome their difficulties by exploiting themselves rather than by fighting for their rights and demanding greater justice from society at large. Some contend that Sufficiency Economy can be used to justify conservative opposition to government policies that help the underdog.

A third criticism is that the theory has simply failed to attract mass support because it does not offer people a clear and attractive benefit. Partly, this may be a matter of presentation. The theory is complex. Some of the concepts, especially the notion of self-immunity, use a Thai vocabulary which many people struggle to understand. But partly, this may be because the theory is not properly tuned to the ambitions and aspirations of most people.

Looking Forward

The Sufficiency Economy came to prominence in 1997 in the midst of the worst economic crisis for Thailand in the modern era. It helped to focus attention on switching to more prudent practices in economic management and business practice, though the crisis itself was education enough. It was adopted by the planning authorities as the touchstone for a decade of structuring the national economy. For many corporations, Sufficiency Economy helped to guide their corporate social responsibility projects. For many businesses and individuals, it provided a source of inspiration. For a core group of enthusiasts, Sufficiency Economy was a guide to a more ethical approach to business practice and public service.

Far left *"Sufficiency Economy For All"*
announces a promotional poster.

Centre *Inside the classroom of a provincial school,*
students are taught the basics of Sufficiency
Economy as part of the national curriculum.

Left *Students plant saplings as part of a school*
field trip. Sufficiency thinking promotes the idea
of sustainable development.

Yet, after the 1997 crisis eased and the cycle trended upwards again, the government returned to the policy of prioritising rapid growth, and managing the resulting social fallout through more government spending to help the vulnerable. Many businessmen rediscovered their old recklessness, leading to eccentric swings in speculative markets such as stocks and property. Corruption showed no sign of decline, and the building of a new international airport for Bangkok became a focus for accusations of malfeasance on a massive scale.

More than a dozen years after the Sufficiency Economy was launched as a kind of national agenda, it is questionable how much affect it has had on the major trends in economy and government. The economy has continued to become more open and hence more vulnerable to wayward outside forces—though the management of the economy has so far proved to be more prudent. There has been almost no shift towards a more balanced, inner-driven, and sustainable growth pattern. Instead, over-reliance on exports, inefficiency in the use of energy and damage to the natural environment have persisted. There has been no trend towards more sufficient agriculture. Indeed, there has been a net shift from food to cash crops, and from small-scale farms to large-scale plantations.

The call for people to be more self-reliant and less dependent on government welfare measures has faded into the background because the popular demand for better social provision has become too loud and the political risks of ignoring this demand too high.

The enthusiasm for consumption—especially of luxury goods—has not been noticeably blunted by any calls for moderation. Corruption persists in politics, business and the bureaucracy. Indeed, surveys consistently show that most people believe corruption to be on the increase. But perhaps a mere handful of years are too few to assess the impact of the Sufficiency Economy. Advocates of the theory stress that what is needed is a comprehensive change in the national mindset. That might already be under way, but it will have to await the rise of a generation educated in the Sufficiency Economy at school.

Part III: The Crown

More than seven centuries old, Thailand's monarchy is not always well understood by foreigners. This section contextualises and explains some of the key institutions and trappings of the crown, beginning with a detailed description of how the crown's assets have been managed in Crown Property. This piece is *followed by essays on the law of* lèse-majesté, *the Privy Council, and the process of succession. Many of the monarchy's rituals draw from ancient Buddhist and Hindu rites. In recent centuries, the crown has evolved to include more Western royal influences. This section concludes with an overview of the key regalia, ceremonies and traditions.*

Above *Ladawan Palace in Bangkok's Dusit District is home to the Crown Property Bureau, which is responsible for managing the crown's land holdings and assets.*

CROWN PROPERTY

During the days of absolute monarchy, the king was proverbially the Lord of the Land and, in principle, everything was crown property. In the late 19th century, the crown introduced a new institution, the Privy Purse Bureau—which later became the Crown Property Bureau—to manage its land holdings and wealth. The bureau has been instrumental in developing the country's infrastructure and remains one of the largest investors in the Thai economy to this day.

Since 1936, the law has made a clear distinction between property that belongs to the king as a person and that which belongs to the crown as an institution. The Crown Property Bureau (CPB) exists to manage the property of the crown. This property does not belong to the king in his private capacity, but to the monarchy as an institution which continues from reign to reign. This rather special category of property arose when an absolute monarchy, under which the king was lord over his realm and everything in it, both people and property, evolved into a constitutional monarchy that exists within a vibrant globalised economy.

By legal definition, the CPB is a juristic person. It is not part of the palace administration, nor is it a government agency, nor is it a private firm. It is a unique institution. It is also a rather mysterious institution. It is under no obligation to provide the public with details of its accounts or activities. However, in recent years it has responded to the need to provide more information of public interest.

The income of the CPB finances part of the day-to-day expenditure of the monarchy. As a result, the Thai monarchy differs in one key respect from many other monarchies which today are funded almost totally by allocations from the national budget.

The value of the crown property is considerable, but putting an exact figure on it is difficult. Part of the property is in the form of corporate investments, which can be easily valued. This part was worth around 200 billion baht (about US$6.7 billion) in 2010. But the other—and more valuable—part is in the form of land, around 8,300 *rai* in the capital and another 33,000 *rai* outside. (*Rai* is the Thai measurement for land area; there are roughly 2.5 *rai* in an acre.) There are various methods that can be used for estimating the value of the land. According to one estimate the Bangkok portion alone was worth almost one trillion baht (US$33 billion) at market prices. But the CPB itself books the value, based on cost, at less than a third of that figure.

Whichever method is used, the CPB is well established as one of the largest investors in the Thai economy. As a result, the CPB has a considerable impact on the Thai economy as a whole—and, conversely, the ups and downs of the Thai economy, in turn, have a major influence on the CPB.

The story of the CPB is partly a story about kings, and partly a story about Thailand's transition from a developing, agrarian country besieged by colonial powers to an open economy in the age of globalisation. When the CPB came into existence around three-quarters of a century ago, its properties had been accumulating over the preceding half century which saw Siam's transition from absolute to constitutional monarchy.

EARLY DAYS

The foundations of the crown property were laid in the two decades on either side of 1900. Until the late 19th century, Siam was an agrarian country ruled by an absolute monarch. The king was proverbially both the Lord of the Land and the Lord of Life. In principle, all the land in the realm belonged to him, and all the revenue from taxes and tolls was royal revenue. In other words, everything was crown property.

That situation changed dramatically in the second half of the 19th century. Siam became much more involved in overseas trade, exporting timber, tin and especially rice. Many people migrated from southern China to work as traders and labourers in the expanding commercial economy. The city of Bangkok was transformed from a picturesque but sleepy royal capital into a bustling port city. As part of this transition, a lot of the transportation and residence moved from water—the Chao Phraya river and connected canals—on to dry land. In the provinces, many new towns sprung up around tin mines and saw mills, and the waterways that were the thoroughfares of the rice trade.

This economic transformation greatly increased the potential for the government to raise revenues. But it also greatly increased the number of problems and projects for which the royal government needed money. First there was defence. One by one, all of Siam's neighbours fell under colonial rule, and

Siam itself was severely threatened. Next there was a demand for modern infrastructure—from roads to ports to telegraph systems—to sustain the growth of the new commercial economy. Next, the expanding population of the capital and provincial towns needed housing, roads and better sanitation.

Meanwhile, the government was still very traditional. Revenue collection depended on local nobles and tax-farmers who kept a large percentage for themselves. One of the major items of government expenditure was the upkeep of the royal family, and this expense was growing due to the expansion of the royal family. At his death in 1910, King Chulalongkorn had scores of children and grandchildren. These progeny resulted in ever swelling amounts of money spent on the construction of new palaces, maintenance of older ones, family ceremonies, and overseas education.

Modernising Finance

These pressures required a transformation in the way the country was governed. That transformation began with financial reforms in 1890. A Ministry of Finance was created for the first time. Modern methods of budgeting and accounting were introduced. Direct forms of taxation replaced old forms of tax collecting. As a result, the government's revenue grew spectacularly, from 15 million baht in 1892 to 50 million in 1905.

As part of this modernisation of government, spending on royal activities was separated and placed under a department within the Ministry of Finance named the Privy Purse Bureau (PPB). The Thai name, *phrakhlang khang-thi*, literally meaning "the store beside the bed", was taken from an old department that managed money allocated for the king's personal use.

Fifteen percent of government revenue was allocated to the PPB. As overall government revenue increased, so did the PPB's allocation, its staff and its activities. The revenue rose from 1.5 million baht in 1892 to 6.1 million in 1902 and 8.7 million in 1912. In 1895, the PPB had 26 officials in four divisions: revenue, palace expenditure, finance and shareholdings. By the late 1910s, the numbers had swelled to over two hundred with three additional divisions devoted to construction, accounting and central administration.

At first, the PPB's revenues were spent mainly on the upkeep of royal family members, maintenance of palaces and overseas education for royal children. But as the revenue grew, there was a surplus to these demands. The way this surplus was spent created the foundations of today's crown property.

Acquiring Land

Urban development was a subject of deep personal interest to King Chulalongkorn. The capital and provincial towns were growing rapidly without proper planning and management. The PPB began to acquire land. Some was previously unused. Some was acquired by purchase. Some fell into the king's ownership when debtors, often members of the royal family, defaulted on loans they had been granted by the king or the royal banking arm [which will be described later].

Some of this land in the capital was used for the palaces of royalty, but a large amount was used for building shophouses to accommodate the swelling numbers of Chinese labourers and entrepreneurs in the expanding port city. The rents charged for these shophouses were rather low. The PPB was more interested in providing accommodation for labourers and opportunities for business rather than maximising rental revenue. In major upcountry towns, the PPB concentrated on acquiring market areas so that the market dues could be used for improving sanitation and basic infrastructure in these new town centres.

By 1902, the PPB owned 4,083 *rai* in the capital, in three main areas:

- The old royal centre on Rattanakosin Island.

- Southward from Rattanakosin Island on the eastern bank of the Chao Phraya river from the Chinese quarter of Sampheng to the European area in Sathorn.

- Northward from Rattanakosin Island to the areas developing as the administrative nucleus.

These areas remained the principal centres of the city for the next century. Prior to the Second World War, the PPB was estimated to own one third of the land in the capital.

A Modern Entrepreneur

The second use of the PPB's surplus was to fund investments in the growing urban economy. The rationale was both economic and political. Most of the investment in this new commercial economy came from outside, especially from entrepreneurs of the European colonial powers. There were very few local entrepreneurs who had the funds or the incentive to invest. Most nobles were not interested. Several Chinese traders and former tax-farmers tried their hand at modern business but had neither the scale nor the skills and went bankrupt in the successive

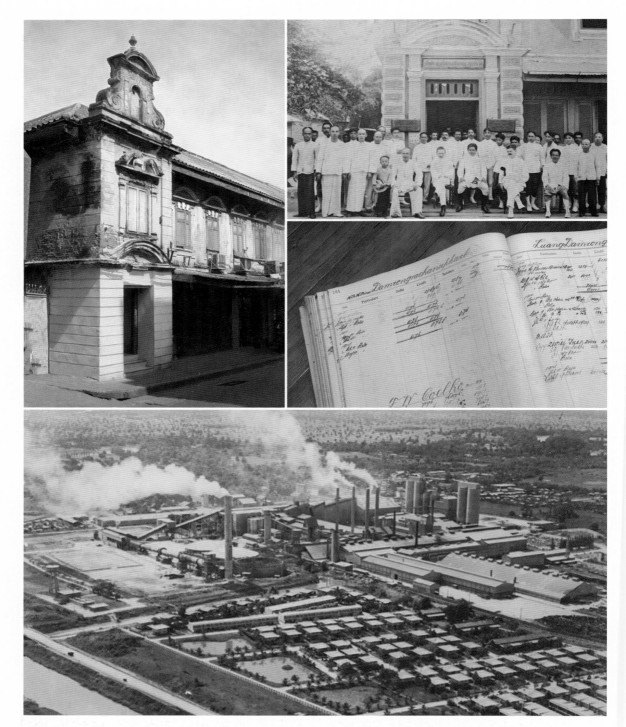

Top left The building occupied by the Book Club, the precursor of Siam Commercial Bank. *Top right* The multi-ethnic staff of Siam Commercial Bank in front of its Ban Moh office around 1907. *Right centre* A page of the Siam Commercial Bank ledger from 1913 containing records of Prince Damrong's account. *Above* An aerial photograph of a Siam Cement factory after the Second World War.

economic slumps of this era. The PPB was an exception to this rule. It had the funds and it also had a vision to prevent outsiders from utterly dominating the new urban commercial economy in Siam.

The PPB's major investments were in banking, cement and shipping. In 1906, the minister of finance, Prince Mahisara Rajaharudaya, proposed the founding of a bank to compete with foreign banks that "squeezed the blood from our traders". This idea was realised by first doing banking business semi-covertly through an institution named the Book Club, and then converting this into Siam Commercial Bank (SCB), which was established by a royal charter. The first years of the bank were rocky, but the PPB had the pockets to inject more capital and eventually the bank prospered.

In 1913, the PPB provided half the capital to fund the country's first cement plant. Almost from the beginning, the Siam Cement company prospered as a result of the demand generated by urban expansion. In 1918, the PPB also funded a shipping venture to compete against the European steamship companies, but this business proved more difficult

and the venture crumbled within a decade.

The PPB acquired around half of the 60 rice mills around Bangkok. It also invested in saw mills, tramways, importing, mining, electricity generation and the first railway line to Khorat (Nakhon Ratchasima), the gateway to the Northeast. Some of these ventures were acquired through foreclosure on loans made by PPB or SCB to local entrepreneurs who did not have the assets to survive sharp fluctuations in the economy caused by war, currency swings, weather patterns and other disturbing forces. As in the case of the banking and shipping ventures, the PPB was motivated to enter many of these areas to reduce the dominance of foreign business in the country.

By the First World War, the foundations of the PPB were laid on three pillars that remain to this day: land, banking and cement. The Japanese historian of the Thai economy, Akira Suehiro, described the PPB at this time as "a kind of proto-investment bank which exclusively served as the core organisation to undertake private business on behalf of the king."

ORGANISATION AND LEGAL STATUS

In 1899, the PPB was moved under the Royal Secretariat, becoming part of the palace administration under the direct control of the king rather than part of the evolving sphere of modern government. In 1932, absolute monarchy was abolished and a new era of constitutional monarchy began. As part of this change, the old Royal Secretariat was dissolved. In 1933, the PPB was placed under the Ministry of the Palace. Soon afterwards, this ministry was reduced to an office under the Bureau of the Prime Minister, and the PPB also became an office under the direct control of the prime minister.

After 1932, the allowances paid to various members of the royal family were abolished. Accordingly, the budget allocation for the PPB was reduced to 440,000 baht a year, 5 percent of the amount

flowing to the PPB a few years earlier. In 1935, King Prajadhipok abdicated, resulting in further reduction of the PPB's expenditure. Its outlays were now reduced to the upkeep of royal palaces, temples and other properties, and the continuation of some royal ceremonial.

These changes prompted a rethink about the nature and status of the PPB, and about the properties within its oversight.

Defining Crown Property

In 1935, an act was passed which classified royal properties into two parts: those that were the personal property of the king and would subsequently be subject to taxation, and those that belonged to the crown and would remain tax-free. A commission was then set up to allocate properties to these two categories.

In the following year, however, this arrangement was superseded by a more complex and thorough piece of legislation. The Crown Property Act of 1936 divided the properties into three categories.

• The first was labelled as the "king's private property" and included three elements, as described by the act: "property that belonged to the king before ascending to the throne; property conferred on the king by the state; or property acquired by the king by any means and at any time other than property acquired on account of kingship including any fruit accrued there from". Henceforth the income from this property was liable to taxation, but the other two categories remained tax-free.

• The second was labelled "public property" which the act defined as "property of the king which is used exclusively for the benefit of the state, e.g. palaces".

• The third category included the remaining property failing outside the first two categories. In practice, this meant land and corporate investments that had formerly belonged to the PPB. This third category defines what is now conventionally known as crown property.

The act laid down that income from the third category, after deduction of administrative expenses, was to be transferred to the king "for him to spend in his capacity as head of state". A board was created headed *ex officio* by the minister of finance with four other directors appointed by the king.

A year after the act, the government issued a decree establishing the Crown Property Bureau with the status of a department in the Ministry of Finance. The first director was Phraya Atcharasong-siri. Staff were transferred from the PPB. An Office of

His Majesty's Property was created under the Royal Household to manage the king's private property. The PPB survived as a separate organisation to manage 10 temples under royal patronage as well as Vajiravudh College, a secondary school founded by King Vajiravudh in 1910 and originally called the Royal Pages School, and a much reduced land bank mostly belonging to King Vajiravudh.

Improved Machinery

The legislation in the mid 1930s had created crown property as a distinct legal entity. In practice, however, the administrative arrangements did not work very well. As a result, an amending act in 1948 left the definition of crown property unchanged, but revised the machinery for managing it.

The Crown Property Act of 1948 reconstituted the CPB as a juristic person, independent of government and not placed under any ministry. The minister of finance remained as the *ex-officio* chairman of the CPB board. Other board members were to be appointed by the king. One of these would hold the post of director-general of the CPB and have full executive power.

During his reign, King Bhumibol typically selected board members who had worked in the Ministry of Finance or experienced bureaucrats with backgrounds in economics. He did not choose businessmen from the private sector.

The 1948 Act confirmed that the CPB's assets were tax exempt and could not be sold or transferred without the king's consent. Whereas the 1936 act had specified that the revenue from the crown property was "for the king to spend in his capacity as head of state", the new act specified that the revenue "may be disbursed only by the king, according to his disposition, in any way at all".

This new legislation made the administration of the crown property more independent than it had been before. In many areas, the director-general of the CPB could now act on his own, without depending on the legal status of the minister of finance, though the director-general was of course still answerable to the board, which had the finance minister as its *ex-officio* chairman. The 1948 Act paved the way for an era of much more active management of the CPB.

DOWNS AND UPS

Like any business, the investment body that began as the PPB and became the CPB has experienced both ups and downs. These have had two rather different determinants. First, as the PPB/CPB is so large and became so involved in many leading areas of the economy, it has always been uniquely vulnerable to the swings and roundabouts of the economy as a whole. Second, as the PPB/CPB is attached to the monarchy, it is affected by the politics surrounding the monarchy. Both these factors were at work during the period which followed the close of King Chulalongkorn's reign in 1910.

The PPB's rise from nowhere to become the country's largest investment body within two decades was followed by a period of stagnation and disorder. This was a period of great instability in the international economy. Two world wars, the Great Depression, failure to establish a stable system of international currencies, and the decline of Britain as the dominant power created recurrent disruptions which impacted especially hard on small, emerging economies such as Siam.

Besides, King Vajiravudh, Rama VI, did not share his father's vision of the relationship between commercial enterprise and the role of a monarchy. Although the PPB still received 15 percent of the government budget, it no longer generated a surplus for investment and in some years was in deficit. Between the start of the King Vajiravudh's reign and the Second World War, no new assets were added to the portfolio, while 293 plots of land were sold.

After the change of government in 1932 and the creation of the CPB under the Ministry of Finance in 1937, management of the properties suffered from a lack of direction. In 1943, a large plot of 1,300 *rai* which had been rented by the CPB to Chulalongkorn University was transferred to the ownership of the university by an act of parliament. Some politicians with influence in the government were found to have sold some CPB properties to themselves under suspicious circumstances. Others tapped the funds of the CPB to help finance some state enterprises founded in the late 1930s and 1940s as part of a war economy and economic nationalism. They also used CPB funds to finance private businesses. None of these ventures lasted very long. Most of the private projects disappeared during the political infighting and economic chaos immediately following the Second World War. State enterprises fared badly as a result of the post-war economic slump and poor management. They were closed down or sold off when the government abandoned the policy of economic nationalism in the 1950s.

As a result, the major assets of the CPB at the start of King Bhumibol's reign in 1946 were exactly the same three pillars as in the 1910s: landed property, Siam Commercial Bank and Siam Cement. One small addition was Deves Insurance, founded in 1947 to insure CPB assets.

New Reign, New Dynamism

The start of the new reign was also the start of a new, more profitable phase in the history of the Crown Property Bureau. Several factors contributed to this upturn. Under the Bretton Woods regime, the world economy experienced a long period of stability and growth. In this environment, the Thai economy grew without a break for four decades at an average of 7 percent a year, transforming the country from an agrarian backwater to a more complex, urbanised and partly industrialised economy.

The monarchy also discovered a new stability in contrast to the trials of the prior three decades. Especially after Field Marshal Sarit Thanarat became prime minister in 1958, the king began to play a larger public role. Through his royal projects and regular upcountry tours, he forged a closer bond with his subjects. As the monarchy as an institution expanded its scope, the CPB had the foundations to become more expansive.

The 1948 Crown Property Act created an indispensable legal basis for more positive management. The director-general now had greater independence to manage the CPB's assets. Moreover, while prior to 1948 there had been frequent changes of management, over the next six decades there were only three directors-general, providing exceptional continuity through the king's reign. In addition, in all three cases, the king appointed the director-general to serve simultaneously as the lord chamberlain or his deputy, the grand chamberlain. The lord chamberlain heads the Bureau of the Royal Household, which manages much of the day-to-day expenditure of the palace. This combination of roles undoubtedly ensured smooth administration.

Managing the Land Portfolio

The first of these three directors-general was Mom Thawiwong Thawansak. He served in the Ministry of Interior before joining the palace service as lord chamberlain in 1947. Mom Thawiwong concentrated mainly on management of the CPB's land portfolio. Over the period of weakened direction, many of the old properties in the old city, including shophouses, had ceased paying rents and become de facto private properties. Some vacant plots of CPB land had been occupied by squatters and become slum communities. Several new government buildings had been built on CPB land and often paid a token rent or sometimes no rent at all. Mom Thawiwong gradually improved the CPB's position. With government help, old shophouse properties were restored to CPB ownership. Slum communities were induced to pay rents, often at a minimal level. Levies on government departments improved, though still well below market rental rates. In a few areas, such as Saphan Khao, old Crown Property Bureau-owned buildings were pulled down and replaced by modern housing, shops and offices.

At the same time, Mom Thawiwong began to make profitable use of land in areas of the city that were prospering from rapid urban expansion. The CPB became a partner in many new ventures by providing land rather than monetary capital. One of the first such ventures was with a young, novice hotelier, Chanut Piyaoui. Her Princess Hotel was followed by the Dusit Thani luxury hotel, one of the city's first high-rise buildings, marking a new stage in the city's growth. The Dusit Thani expanded into an international hotel chain (though the CPB has since divested itself of its stake). The CPB went on to make similar ventures with several other hotels. The CPB applied the same model to joint ventures with shopping centres and commercial buildings.

Expanding Investments

Tentatively, the CPB also invested with entrepreneurs engaged in Thailand's first real wave of industrialisation. These included both domestic entrepreneurs such as the leading Sukri textile group as well as some foreign ventures such as Firestone Tires. In 1970, Mom Thawiwong was succeeded as director-general by Poonperm Krairiksh. Poonperm rose through the palace service to become grand chamberlain before his appointment to head the CPB. By this time, the CPB held shares in over 30 companies, which included the Dusit Thani, the Hotel Siam InterContinental, and the Thai Danu and Siam City banks. At the same time, the two pillars of Siam Commercial Bank (SCB) and Siam Cement Group (SCG) also began to develop into conglomerates in their own right with various subsidiaries.

By the mid 1980s the range of the bureau's interests had increased and widened substantially. It had acquired shares in prominent new hotels located on its land, such as the Oriental and Royal Orchid Sheraton, and many commercial projects on prime real estate, including the huge World Trade Centre. At the same time, due to its links with construction through Siam Cement, the bureau acquired holdings in the Sri Maharaja Company (plywood and other materials), and Christiani & Nielsen Thailand (a major construction company). In turn, Siam Cement, of which the CPB still owned 44 percent in the late 1970s, not only flourished in an era of building boom, but diversified into iron and steel manufacture in 1966, construction materials and ceramic floor tiles in the 1970s and later into electrical products and petrochemicals. By 1986, in Akira Suehiro's estimate, SCG was the largest industrial conglomerate not only in Thailand but also in Southeast Asia.

Similarly SCB, in which the CPB held a 50 percent stake in the late 1970s, also expanded and diversified. One authority estimated that the bank was one of the five largest financial conglomerates in Thailand by 1980. SCB had established various subsidiary companies, including finance and insurance companies. By the mid 1990s the bank had 77 subsidiaries and associated companies across the range of asset management, real estate, industry, warehousing, mutual fund insurance, mining, construction, entertainment, and vehicle production.

Not all the projects of the CPB and its two main subsidiaries flourished. The Firestone project soured. A venture into paper proved expensive. A venture into air travel flopped in an economic downturn. The CPB's role in most of its joint ventures was no more than a passive investor. The land portfolio delivered revenues far below its potential. But in this phase, the CPB recovered its status as one of the country's major investment bodies, and played a significant part in Thailand's transition to a new era of industrialisation.

In one momentous decision, the king dramatically reduced the CPB's landholdings. In 1975, the government launched a land reform scheme aimed at finding land for landless farmers. The king transferred 44,369 *rai* to this scheme, virtually all the rural land under the CPB's control, mostly in the central region. The compensation paid to the CPB was placed in a separate fund earmarked for supporting the development of the land.

Boom and Diversification

The next turning point came in the mid 1980s. Buoyed up by a flood of investment from East Asia and a spurt in the size of the labour force, Thailand entered a decade of galloping boom. The growth rate notched up to double digits. At the peak a million people a year were moving away from agriculture to urban employment, and a Japanese-owned factory was opening every three days. In one decade, the economy doubled in size and Bangkok shot up into the sky.

Right at the start of this boom, in 1987, Dr Chirayu Isarangkun Na Ayuthaya became director-general of the CPB. He had served as a university dean and government minister before his appointment as head of the CPB. As was convention, he was simultaneously appointed as grand chamberlain, the deputy head of the Bureau of the Royal Household. At this point, Chirayu did not overhaul the structure or reorient the policies of the CPB. As he explained later, the role of passive investor suited the special nature of the institution:

"The fact that the CPB is the investment arm for the monarchy, with a long-term and continuous reputation for reliability, induces Thai and foreign investors to seek joint ventures. Hence the CPB is invited to take a minority stake as a passive partner."

He continued his predecessors' policies of gradually improving the revenue from the land portfolio through a more commercial approach to property rents and land development. But he also initiated an important shift in the CPB's attitude to joint ventures, especially with overseas capital.

Many multinational companies flocked to Thailand after 1986 to take advantage of a liberalising environment and participate in the boom in export-oriented manufacturing. Most sought local partners, sometimes because investment regulations required it, but more often simply to find a way over the bureaucratic hurdles and gain some influence on political decision-making. Both SCB and SCG were attractive as partners because of their financial stability, their reputation for competent and honest management, and their unique political connections.

SCG became a partner in many joint ventures with multinationals, some in activities related to the group's petrochemical and construction businesses, but many others in the sub-sectors of electrical goods and automotive parts which boomed in this era. By the mid 1990s, SCG had around 120 subsidiaries and affiliates. SCG also invested heavily in new cement plants to keep up with the breakneck pace of urban expansion, and continued to diversify into other construction-related materials to meet larger and more sophisticated demand.

Siam Commercial Bank (SCB) was also caught

Above A chemical plant belonging to Siam Cement Group.

up in the wave of diversification associated with the boom, soaring foreign investment into Thailand and the financial market liberalisation which began in the later 1980s. By the eve of the 1997 financial crisis, SCB had 77 subsidiaries which ranged across asset management, real estate, industry, warehousing, mutual funds, insurance, mining, sugar, construction, entertainment and motor vehicle production.

As SCB thus evolved from a bank to a conglomerate, the CPB share was diluted, but remained 26 percent on the eve of the 1997 financial crisis. Similarly, the CPB stake in SCG declined from around half but remained a dominant 35 percent.

Besides the investments through its two main subsidiaries, the CPB expanded its own shareholdings using the surplus which its boom-era income delivered after deduction of royal expenses. Most of this surplus was reinvested through the Stock Exchange of Thailand which became more active from the mid 1980s. The CPB targeted new sectors of expansion in Thailand's maturing economy, especially media, manufacturing and energy. In 1996, the CPB became the major shareholder in iTV, the first television channel under private ownership, as well as ventures in press and radio. It also acquired stakes in oil refining, petrochemicals and electronics.

By the closing stages of the great boom, the CPB had become a sprawling conglomerate. According to estimates, the bureau had direct interests in around 90 companies, and indirect interests in another 300. Of these, 43 were listed on the stock exchange. Of 92 companies in which the CPB and its subsidiaries figured among the major shareholders (over 10 percent), 41 were in manufacturing, 18 in finance, seven in insurance, eight in hotels, six in property and construction, and 12 in media. The CPB's interests stretched across the spectrum of Thailand's modern urban enterprise.

In 1996, SCG had assets of 180 billion baht and annual profits of 6.8 billion baht, both figures having roughly doubled over the prior three years. SCB returned profits which averaged 6.4 billion baht between 1992 and 1996, and peaked at over 9 billion baht in 1996. These two pillars still contributed 60 percent of the CPB's total income. The land portfolio contributed an estimated 300 to 600 million baht a year, and miscellaneous other shareholdings contributed around 870 million baht. A study made by an officer of the CPB reported that the bureau's income had increased from 563 million baht in 1987, to nearly 2 billion baht in 1992 and 3 billion baht by 1997.

Over the great economic boom, the CPB had consolidated its position as one of the largest corporate groups in Thailand—if not the largest. It was deeply involved in the export manufacturing which now drove the Thai economy through a wide range of joint ventures. It was a pioneer in the rapidly expanding petrochemical sector. It was prominent in the financial sector which had grown as a result of financial liberalisation. It had ventured tentatively into the modern service sector which had begun to grow as the economy matured. Siam Cement Group was considered a model of good business management, and had become one of the first Thai companies to venture overseas.

Crisis and Restructuring

In 1997, the Thai economy fell into its worst crisis of the modern era, taking many other Asian countries down in its slipstream. The origins of the crisis lay in the heady atmosphere of the prior boom and the imprudent approach to financial liberalisation. On the upswing from 1986 onwards, everyone was making money and hoped the boom would go on forever. By the early 1990s, however, the phase of expansion spurred by the inflow of East Asian capital for industrial investment had topped out and begun to decline. At this point, goaded by the World Bank, Thailand liberalised its financial market. A new flood of financial capital arrived, this time from the West. Local entrepreneurs welcomed this flood because the cost of this money was less than they had paid earlier. But with industrial investment already on a down cycle, much of this flood flowed into speculative markets, especially real estate and the stock exchange. The government and central bank ignored the warning signs of rising debt and believed they could continue with a currency pegged to the dollar. When foreign investors began to withdraw funds, the currency peg could not be sustained. When it was removed, capital fled in panic and the value of the currency plummeted.

The vast majority of Thai firms had borrowed the new cheap foreign capital. They had also believed that the value of the currency would remain fixed, so had rarely hedged the borrowings. When the currency lost over a third of its value, their foreign borrowings soared by a similar ratio. Banks were especially hit because they had often borrowed in dollars and then lent to others in baht. A huge number of firms were technically bankrupt. The banks, buried in bad debt, ceased most of their lending, so business activity slumped. The IMF ordered the Thai government to spend less rather than more, so all sources of demand dried up, consumption plummeted by a fifth, two million people lost their jobs, and the economy shrank by around 15 percent in just 18 months.

Because the CPB had become so involved in the boom, it was now devastated by the bust. Both its major companies had been little more prudent than others in Thailand about their borrowing and investment. Around a fifth of SCB's liabilities came from borrowing in dollars. Many of its loans had been made to the real estate sector with the result that by 1998 over a third of the portfolio had to be classified as bad debt. SCG had invested heavily in expansion to meet the accelerating demand of the boom, contracting US$6.6 billion in debt, mostly in foreign currency and mostly unhedged. Many of the subsidiaries of these firms were in just as bad a state. So too were many of the listed firms in which the CPB had invested.

SCB paid no dividend for six consecutive years

(1998–2003) and SCG for four (1998–2001). The income from stock-market investments also vanished. To fulfil its role as the major shareholder of SCB, the CPB for the first time had to borrow money for the bank's recapitalisation—to the tune of 6 billion baht.

Inside the CPB in the eye of this storm, there was "no panic", according to Chirayu. "But we were concerned for the future of the two pillars." Ultimately, this crisis prompted a major overhaul which was probably long overdue. Over the prior decades, the scale and complexity of the CPB's activities had utterly changed but the management had not been reformed in parallel. Both SCB and SCG had become enmeshed in a more globalised economy but had not yet adjusted to cope with the dangers. Both of the companies and the CPB were now subject to major restructuring.

In SCB and SCG, this restructuring followed the classic pattern: refocus on the core business; divest peripheral subsidiaries; restructure management to suit the new pattern; add new talent. Many of the joint ventures with foreign capital contracted

during the boom were now sold off. In addition, both firms drew inspiration from the king's Sufficiency Economy thinking, particularly on the imperative to build in immunity against outside shocks.

The CPB formed two new companies. CPB Property, established in 2000, took over management of land and property projects. CPB Equity, established in 2001, oversaw the share portfolio and holdings in non-core companies. Both companies elected board members and appointed executives with expertise in their field. CPB Equity disposed of non-core investments and limited its exposure to the stock market, retaining just enough stake to have a feel for market movements that might affect the core business. CPB Property looked for solutions to large projects which had fared badly in the crisis. The prime example was the massive World Trade Centre where a new investor was found to take over the project. The company also identified plots which were unused or had potential to deliver better development combined with higher rental value. With the government agencies among its tenants, it introduced a graded programme of

Above *Siam Commercial Bank's Chaloem Nakhon branch on Bangkok's New Road was built in 1921. SCB, one of the key pillars of the Crown Property Bureau, delivered the CPB income of 2.5 billion baht in 2010.*

rental increases. With slum communities, the CPB prepared a fund to invest in improving the environment, employment opportunities and the quality of life to ease the burden of increased rents.

The CPB also established a reserve fund to guard against any financial crisis in the future.

SCG returned to profitability in 2001 and SCB in 2003. They were helped by the scale and speed of their restructuring, but also by the strong rebound in the Thai economy and by government policies for recovery. The government identified finance and property as two key areas for concerted action, with the result that both sectors revived by 2001. SCB took advantage of a government scheme to aid bank recapitalisation. SCG took a new interest in ex-port markets with the result that exports expanded from 5 percent of the company's total sales before the crisis to 40 percent by the early 2000s, helped especially by rising demand for cement and petrochemicals in China's booming economy.

In 2002, the CPB reported that it had paid off the over 6-billion baht debt incurred at the beginning of the crisis. By 2004, SCG's profits exceeded its pre-crisis level, and by 2005, the CPB's income had risen to 9.3 billion baht, around three times its pre-crisis level.

The 1997 crisis had been a massive shock, but the reaction of the CPB and its two key pillar companies to this shock allowed the group to emerge even stronger.

THE CROWN PROPERTY BUREAU TODAY

The experience of the crisis also prompted a shift in the public position of the CPB. In the past, the CPB had kept itself discreetly in the background. Since the crisis, it has begun to act rather more like a large investment group with many business partners, many stakeholders and a responsibility to the wider public.

Revenues

By 2011, the income of the Crown Property Bureau was still coming primarily from the old three pillars of Siam Commercial Bank, Siam Cement Group and land holdings.

The CPB has a 23-percent stake in SCB which delivered the CPB an income of 1.4 billion baht in 2008, 1.4 billion baht in 2009, and 2.5 billion baht in 2010.

The CPB has a 32-percent stake in SCG which delivered the CPB an income of 4.7 billion baht in 2008, 2 billion baht in 2009, and 3.4 billion baht in 2010.

The CPB owns a total of 41,000 *rai* of land. Of this, 8,300 *rai* is in Bangkok, virtually all in the historic centre. The upcountry holdings are by and large in urban areas, particularly in the major towns of the Central Plains such as Nakhon Pathom and Chachoengsao, but with some smaller holdings further afield in provinces such as Lampang in the North and Songkhla in the South.

In total, the CPB has 40,000 rental contracts, around 17,000 in Bangkok alone. Its tenants are very varied. The most important categories are government and semi-government offices, slum communities, shophouses and markets in the old centre, and prime commercial sites occupied by hotels, office blocks and shopping centres.

In the pit of the 1997 financial crisis, when income from the other two pillars shrank to nothing for several years, the CPB was under pressure to increase its income from land holdings. Since the other two pillars have returned to financial health, this pressure has eased.

For historical reasons, several public-sector organisations were paying the CPB only nominal rent or, in some cases, nothing at all. After the 1997 crisis, the CPB set a policy of raising the annual rents

Top Occupying premium CPB land on Ratchadamri Road, Thailand's largest shopping mall opened as the World Trade Center in 1990 and was relaunched as CentralWorld in 2005. **Above** Restored shophouses on Na Phra-Lan Road opposite the Grand Palace date back to the reign of King Chulalongkorn. A significant portion of CPB land in the old city centre is occupied by rows of shophouses.

on these properties by increments up to a target of 2 percent of the government's appraised value. With the easing of financial pressure, this target was revised down to 1.5 percent.

Around a hundred slum communities in the capital are located on CPB land. Earlier, the CPB had adopted a "land-sharing model" in an attempt to increase the low returns from this land. Under this model, residents were moved into multi-storey housing, freeing up a portion of the land for the CPB to rent out more profitably. In retrospect, this policy was not a success. Some communities openly objected, creating unfavourable publicity. Many families which used their residence for many things other than everyday living found it difficult to adapt their lifestyle to a multi-storey block. Maintenance was also a problem. The CPB abandoned this land-sharing model and instead joined hands with the government's Community Development Institute to develop these communities by strengthening community organisation, upgrading skills, increasing income-earning opportunities, and providing better housing security through long-term leases.

A significant portion of CPB land in the old city centre is occupied by rows of shophouses, many built in the late 19th and early 20th century. The majority still house shops and small businesses. Many rents have fallen way below market levels over the years. Here the CPB set a policy of raising rents according to the nature of the business and the tenant's ability to pay. An outside consultant recommended that 4 percent of the government's appraised value was a fair rate. However, as the financial pressures have eased, so too has this policy. The target remains but its achievement may take decades. The CPB's policy is to raise the rents only when leases change hands.

From the CPB perspective, 93 percent of its land is "not really commercial". According to Chirayu, with respect to these holdings, "our role is not to look at earnings as our major objective". In pursuit of income, the CPB concentrates on just 7 percent of its total land, meaning mostly large-scale projects on prime land in the centre of the capital. Here the policy is to raise annual rents to 4 percent of the property's market value.

Some projects to develop key sites are being pushed ahead despite some public controversy. One such site is the lower end of Wireless Road, which once housed the Armed Forces Preparatory School but for the past decade has been rented to the promoters of a tourist night market. Another is on Lang Suan Road, which has become a prime inner-city site for upmarket residences and retail enterprises, and where the CPB's properties have been literally overshadowed by massive commercial developments on adjoining roads.

The CPB's income from its properties was 2.5 billion baht in 2010.[1]

CPB Equity was established to manage all financial investments outside the three pillars (and the fourth minor pillar of Deves Insurance). These investments are now considered "non-core," and Chirayu stresses that CPB Equity has "no expansive role". Its major task has been to rationalise the scattered investments acquired in the pre-crisis boom years, but at a leisurely pace, taking advantage of market opportunities. The company's results, as reported to the government's Department of Business Development, show large changes in asset value from year to year, and big swings between profit and loss. The net result from 2000 and 2005 was that the company broke even.

Over the last three years (2008–2010), the CPB's total revenues have fluctuated in the range of 9–11 billion baht a year.[2]

According to the Crown Property Acts of 1936 and 1948, the bureau is exempt from all taxes. In the case of some new taxes introduced since these acts, such as VAT, local development tax, and house and building tax, the CPB has chosen to pay these taxes rather than seek a judicial ruling whether it is liable or not. The CPB pays no business tax. In connection with recent discussions on the introduction of a land or property tax, the CPB has sent a letter to the government supporting the proposal.

Expenditure

The CPB prepares an annual budget which is then reviewed by the CPB board under its chairman, the minister of finance, before being submitted to the king's secretariat to gain royal approval. The CPB then disburses funds against this budget, but only against the signature of the incumbent monarch. Even a regent has no authority to disburse CPB funds except "for royal public charity or religious or royal custom". According to convention, the CPB releases funds through two institutions: the Bureau of the Royal Household and the Office of His Majesty's Principal Private Secretary.

The funds are used for four main purposes: part of the expenses of the core royal family, meaning the king, his children, and grandchildren and their families; royal activities including public appearances, events and tours; part of the maintenance of palaces and other buildings owned by the crown (principally the newer upcountry palaces, as the older Bangkok palaces are defined as "public property", owned and maintained mostly by the state); and costs arising from the presentation of honours and the royal sponsorship of ceremonies. Additional expenditures require special approval by the king. The CPB also has a budget for social activities.

CPB funds are not used to pay the staff employed by the Bureau of the Royal Household or the Office of His Majesty's Principal Private Secretary. These costs, as well as the costs for security provided by the police and armed forces, are borne by the public budget. The royal development projects are also funded mainly from the government budget, and the CPB's involvement is only on the fringes, such as the building of museums for educational purposes and sponsoring visits by schoolchildren.

Explaining the king's role in the decision-making process at the CPB, Chirayu says, "Because of the strict protocol that His Majesty adheres to, he does not comment to me directly on CPB matters. Instead, he deliberates according to board recommendations, under the chairmanship of the minister of finance. When there are petitions to him mostly by small tenants of the CPB, we are answerable by communicating a written account to him through the Office of His Majesty's Principal Private Secretary in every single case."

Regarding the management of the CPB by its board, Chirayu says, "It is my opinion that the CPB has one of the best boards in the country. First of all, the CPB has the incumbent minister of finance as chairman. Then where else can you find a board comprising two former ministers of finance, one former communications minister, one former education minister, and a former long-serving secretary-general of the NESDB [National Economic and Social Development Board] who in his long and productive career in public service was also governor of the Bank of Thailand and deputy prime minister?[3] Why are all of these people helping to look after the affairs of the CPB? I think the main reason is their respect for the institution of the monarchy."

Administration

The CPB in 2011 has a staff of 1,200 divided roughly as follows: 500 engaged on property management, 400 on general administration and 300 on social projects, including community development. Of the total, two-thirds are stationed at the headquarters in Ladawan Palace and one-third at several provincial offices. The staffing has been increasing quite rapidly from only 735 in 1988, with the addition mainly for community and social development functions. Each year, some 50 or 60 people, mostly degree holders, are taken on as trainees. Remuneration policy and welfare provisions at the CPB use those established by the Bank of Thailand as benchmarks.

The bureau's accounts have always been audited by the government's Auditor-General's Office, but are not disclosed to the public. In 2011, the CPB for the first time produced an annual report, similar to that of a major corporation, but this report did not include any financial statements.

Corporate Presence and Activities

Since the 1997 financial crisis, the CPB has become much more aware of itself as a corporate entity. Perhaps because of the need to look outside for financial help, and perhaps because of sharper scrutiny by academia and the international press, the CPB has become more conscious of itself as a public institution of sorts with many different stakeholders.

Since the crisis, the CPB has set up a communications department with the responsibility for communicating both inside and outside the CPB.

The CPB's involvement in projects of corporate social responsibility has expanded to include a wide range of activities.

Several temples in the historic centre have been under royal patronage since their foundation, some two centuries ago. When Wat Makutkasattriyaram, which is situated close to the CPB's offices, needed restoration, the bureau became involved in the project which eventually took twelve years. The CPB's input was not so much funding as managerial help, in particular, arbitrating between the temple's community of monks on one hand and the Fine Arts Department and other government bodies on the other. As a result of this experience leading to a successful result, the CPB was invited to become involved in similar projects at other temples, and now has 22 such projects on its hands, including at Wat Bovornives, where the king was ordained in 1956, and Wat Ratchanatdaram. The budget for these projects in 2011 was 472 million baht.

The CPB is also involved in the preservation of buildings with royal associations in the vicinity of the Grand Palace. These buildings include its own head office of Ladawan Palace, and buildings on Phra Arthit Road and in the Yaowarat area.

Also in the old city centre, the CPB is involved in both preserving buildings and developing public facilities on some of its properties. In collaboration

Above *Students from various schools receive scholarships granted by the Crown Property Bureau. Human betterment and creating educational opportunities are the main thrusts of the CPB'S CSR activities.*

with the Tourism Authority, the CPB undertook the preservation of the Chalermkrung Royal Theatre. When a commercial building on Ratchadamnoen Road fell vacant, the CPB renovated it as the Rattanakosin Exhibition Hall, housing multimedia displays on the history, arts and culture of old Bangkok.

In concert with its pillar companies, the CPB has several projects geared to youth. These include scholarships, cultural performances and sponsorship of the national badminton team. In 2009, the CPB Foundation contributed 2 million baht to the first Thailand Youth Festival which organised workshops, exhibitions and a performance to showcase the achievements of youth. A second, expanded festival with the Crown Property Bureau as a sponsor was scheduled in 2011.

In cooperation with the National Science and Technology Development Agency, the CPB funds a chair professorship to enable top scientists to carry out research. The present incumbent, Dr Jumras Limtrakul, professor in physical chemistry at Kasetsart University, who is reckoned to be among the top ten in his field in the world, has a five-year tenure to pursue research on the application of nanotechnology in industry. The CPB also funds a radio station which provides traffic news and social broadcasting with the cooperation of the traffic police and the Bangkok Metropolitan Authority.

PUBLIC ACCOUNTABILITY

Over the last century, Thailand has changed from an absolute monarchy where the king in principle was lord over all the land in the kingdom to a constitutional monarchy where there is a clear legal distinction between the king's private property and the property that belongs to the crown.

At the beginning of this century of transformation, King Chulalongkorn developed a considerable portfolio of investments in urban property and modern business enterprises. Although that portfolio has experienced fluctuations as a result of the booms and busts of the economy and the politics surrounding the monarchy, it has survived largely unscathed. During King Bhumibol's reign, it has prospered due to the long-run strength of the economy and the political security of an exceptionally long, stable and happy reign. The CPB stands at the head of one of the country's largest capital groups.

At the point of the transition from absolute to constitutional monarchy, this portfolio was transformed into a fund for financing an important part of the expenses of the monarchy's upkeep and activities. Some funding still falls on the government budget. In the budget for 2011, the allocation to the Bureau of the Royal Household was 2.6 billion baht while that of the Office of His Majesty's Principal Private Secretary was 477 million baht.[4] Other expenses, primarily for security, are estimated to raise the total to 6 billion. Still, core expenses are covered by the revenue of 9–11 billion baht from the portfolio of assets managed by the Crown Property Bureau. The director-general stated, "It is my opinion that His Majesty's policy is to use taxpayers' money as little as possible."

This differentiates the Thai monarchy from most other monarchies which depend totally or heavily on budget allocations. In the UK, for example, the total budget allocation to the monarchy in 2009 was £41.5 million. This covered the expenses of the core members of the royal family, their staff, the maintenance of palaces and other properties, and the outlays incurred in public activities and overseas tours.

Taxpayers are of course keenly interested in the use of their money. The budget allocations to the UK and other similar monarchies have to be approved by parliament and published in annual reports. Anyone can view the UK royal family's income from public funds and the breakdown of its usage with a couple of clicks of a mouse.

Above *Wat Makutkasattriyaram, famous for its murals depicting Buddhist tales, was one of a number of temple restoration projects undertaken by the Crown Property Bureau.*

Royal finances are a focus of public fascination. In Thailand, estimating their magnitude was once the province of a few journalists working with imperfect information. More recently, better estimates have become available. The variation between different estimates is now largely a function of different methods for valuing land. The high estimate of the value of the assets under the CPB's control is around a trillion baht.

As the baht has strengthened against the dollar recently, this converts to around US$37 billion. If such wealth belonged to an individual, he or she would rank in the top six on the *Forbes* list of the world's billionaires. But this wealth does not belong to an individual. It belongs to the crown.

Several commentators have confused the difference between personal and institutional owner-ship. Partly this is because the whole subject has been shrouded in mystery. Ignorance is a breeding ground for imagination. The CPB has begun edging towards greater transparency but there remains some way to travel, and Thailand is part of a world where the inexorable demand for greater transparency and accountability needs to be addressed.

"I respect the right of the public for transparency of a public organisation and public officials," says Chirayu. "I also personally believe that I have the duty to judge on the nature and extent of the request for information from the CPB. Ignorance breeds suspicion—yes. But excessive curiosity, I believe, can also lower a dignified and trusting relationship. The increasing interest in the CPB in today's world makes me seriously think all the time about this appropriate balance."

Above On 5 December 2009, members of the public gather outside Siriraj Hospital where the king was hospitalised. Due to the reverence Thais have traditionally accorded their monarchs, some legal scholars argue that the lèse-majesté law, which protects the king from insult, is justified as a reflection of societal consensus.

THE LAW OF LÈSE-MAJESTÉ

Monarchs are typically protected from injury and insult by laws of lèse-majesté. *While the wording of such laws is usually quite similar, their actual application differs between kingdoms. In Thailand, a dramatic upsurge in the number of* lèse-majesté *charges within the last decade has brought new attention to the law, its origins and unique susceptibility to abuse.*

Ancient Siamese kings enjoyed an exalted status incomparable to monarchies almost anywhere. For a commoner to even gaze upon the king of Siam was considered a serious offence until the 19th century. Due to social, cultural and religious beliefs, teachings and customs, most Thais today retain an innate respect for the king and the monarchy. Indeed, a key difference between contemporary Thailand and other constitutional monarchies is that in the latter republican sentiment is legal—or at least tolerated.

In Thailand, according to Section 112 of the Criminal Code, "Whoever defames, insults, or threatens the king, the queen, the heir-apparent, or the regent, shall be punished with imprisonment of three to fifteen years." This law of *lèse-majesté* is the most robust and by far the most frequently used of its kind in the world today.[1]

Only in recent years, during a period of intense political upheaval, has discussion of the law of *lèse-majesté* really arisen. Previously, there was a common perception that any criticism of the law might itself be construed as an act of *lèse-majesté*. However, a major spike in the number of cases brought to trial has shone a light on a standing law that only a decade ago appeared to be falling into virtual disuse. This has made it one of the most contentious issues of the day.

In general, defenders of the law argue that problems do not lie with the law itself but rather with unscrupulous individuals who abuse it for ulterior motives. Opponents regard it as a remnant of absolute monarchy which does not conform to democratic principles.

ORIGINS IN THAILAND

A Siamese proto law of *lèse-majesté* was included in *The Three Seals Code* of 1805, a codification of laws from the Ayudhya period. Provision 7 of the Law on Revolt and Warfare prescribed the following by way of penalty: [2]

"Whosoever dares, without fear, to impudently speak of the king, disparages of royal acts, edicts or commands, that person has transgressed the royal criminal laws of the king and shall be punished with the Punishment of Eight Instances, namely:

1) Beheading and seizure of household.
2) Slitting the mouth and cutting off the ears, hands and feet.
3) Given 25 or 30 lashes with a leather whip.
4) Imprisoned for a month and then made to cut grass for elephants.
5) Fined fourfold and made into a serf.
6) Fined twice.
7) Fined once.
8) Pardoned from punishment on the promise of good behaviour. [3]

In the 19th century, Thai kings could, and did, sentence critics to long prison sentences for offences that could be termed *lèse-majesté*. [4] When King Chulalongkorn (r. 1868–1910) moved to centralise and modernise the Thai justice system, he reformed the law. In 1900, the king issued an edict that combined personal defamation, sedition and *lèse-majesté* into a single law. The new law was most likely inspired by his tour of Europe in 1897, when the king visited the last German emperor, Kaiser Wilhelm II, in Berlin. Given the prodigious number of *lèse-majesté* cases being prosecuted in the German Empire at the time, it is highly unlikely that the issue would have gone unnoticed by the visiting Siamese.

Featuring a mild maximum sentence, King Chulalongkorn's law placed Siam at the liberal end of *lèse-majesté* legislation for the time. Notably, it carried an exemption clause providing protection for those expressing an "honest opinion" and introduced some modern terminology to render archaic phrasing more precisely:

(1900) Defaming the king, the major concubine, royal progeny, ... Section 4.—Whosoever defames the reigning king of Siam or the major consort, or the princes or princesses ... with intemperate words which may clearly be seen as truly defamatory, this person has acted illegally. (Imprisonment of up to three years/fine of up to 1,500 baht.) [5]

After 1908, however, the punishment for *lèse-majesté*, which had been incorporated into the first modern legal code, placed Siam alongside the more intransigent absolute monarchies of the day, notably Russia and Spain—both of which imposed penalties of up to eight years' imprisonment. [6] Unlike many constitutional monarchies at that time, the law was drafted to protect a broader range of royals, added the legally ambiguous term "malice" into the mix and eliminated any exemptions.

(1908) Article 98.— Whosoever displays malice toward or defames the king, the queen consort, the heir apparent, or regent when he is carrying out his duties to the king, shall be liable to imprisonment not exceeding seven years or a fine of not more than five thousand baht, or both.

(1908) Article 100.— Whosoever displays malice toward or defames the princes or princesses from whichever reign, the punishment shall not exceed three years or a fine of not more than two thousand baht, or both. [7]

As the 20th century progressed, and the number of constitutional monarchies declined, *lèse-majesté* offences were prosecuted with increasing discretion. Spain and Japan were exceptions to this trend with militaristic governments disposed to applying the law. After the Second World War, European monarchs adjusted to constitutions which gave more protection to the rights of ordinary individuals. The development of international human rights frameworks also stifled *lèse-majesté* prosecutions. Indeed, over the second half of the 20th century globally, there have been only occasional *lèse-majesté* cases here and there, even though the law remains in almost all constitutional monarchies.

In the first half of the 20th century, Siam (which first became Thailand in 1939) followed the global trend. Although there are no known statistics on *lèse-majesté* prior to the end of absolute monarchy in 1932, scholars have remarked that Siamese kings appeared remarkably tolerant of criticism in the lively press of the day.[8] Instead, they preferred to exert influence over the public sphere by restricting press licenses, or amending and using other laws to limit freedom of speech, such as the 1927 revision of the Sedition Act. After 1932, some of the more repressive measures in the criminal code were reduced. The 1935 Sedition Act, for instance, forbade communicating or teaching anything that aimed "to bring into hatred or contempt the sovereign, the government or the administration of the state, by the people ..." More significantly, the revision provided an exemption clause:

"Provided that there shall be no offence under this section when the said words or writing or printed documents or means whatsoever will merely be an expression of good faith or amount to a critical and unbiased comment on governmental or administrative acts within the spirit of the constitution or for the public interest."[9]

Legal scholars have argued that the phrase "within the spirit of the constitution" ascribed special status to freedom of speech.[10] They cite the sole *lèse-majesté* case to come before the Supreme Court in the quarter century following the overthrow of absolute monarchy. In 1939, a local spirit doctor made the claim that he was powerful enough to call upon the king and the constitution to come and prostrate themselves before him. Such an outrage in previous times would have resulted in certain conviction, but on this occasion the Supreme Court acquitted the defendant. Although there was no change to the *lèse-majesté* law immediately following the 1932 revolution, the law could be—and was—read as indirectly allowing criticism of the monarchy.

As in other constitutional monarchies, application of Thailand's *lèse-majesté* law seemed to be on the wane in the 1950s, with less than one person charged each year from 1949 to 1956. Over the following decades, the trend reversed. The resurgence in the law dates from the late 1950s when the prestige of the monarchy was being actively restored. This was in part a bulwark against the spread of communism—which was clearly antithetical to monarchy.

When the Thai penal code was revised in 1956, the new *lèse-majesté* law no longer provided protection to other members of the royal family, but it did not reduce punishment for the crime. However, rather than providing greater precision, or

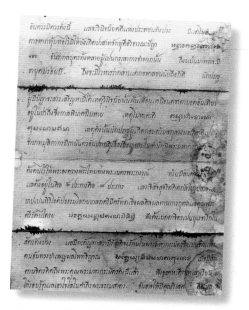

Above *The oldest collection of Siamese laws is in The Three Seals Code of 1805.*

adding exemptions, the law in the revised criminal code of 1956 added "insult" to the list of actionable offences:

Article 112.—Whosoever defames, insults or threatens the king, the queen, the heir apparent, or the regent shall be punished with imprisonment not exceeding seven years.

Lèse-majesté cases subsequently jumped almost five fold between 1956 and 1976 when there was an average of five arrests and prosecutions annually. After the violent suppression of student activists during the military coup of 1976, the punishment for *lèse-majesté* was increased from a maximum of seven years imprisonment to 15 years. A minimum of three years was introduced at the same time. The most significant spike in arrests for *lèse-majesté* prior to 2007 was in 1977 when jailed student leaders were charged with the crime. Most of those arrested, however, were never sent to trial. Between 1977 and 1992, the average number of cases rose to almost 10 each year. By

the mid-1990s, when the communist threat had essentially vanished, a scholar argued that *lèse-majesté* was becoming "a kind of cultural crime perpetrated against Thainess... the quintessential crime of cultural betrayal".[11]

Despite this increase, a deputy principal private secretary to King Bhumibol predicted in 1987 that the law would gradually fade into disuse as it already had in the UK.[12] Initially, this view appeared to be justified. From 1993 to 2004, the average number of new cases of *lèse-majesté* dropped by half, with no cases at all in 2002. In recent years, however, the number of *lèse-majesté* cases passing through the Thai judicial system has increased markedly. An all-time high of 165 charges of *lèse-majesté* were sent to the Court of First Instance in 2009.[13]

Thailand currently has the most severe *lèse-majesté* law seen anywhere in more than a century, comparable only to Japanese wartime legislation.[14] The minimum sentence equals the maximum sentence in Jordan, and the maximum sentence is three times that found in most European constitutional monarchies.

LÈSE-MAJESTÉ ABROAD

Lèse-majesté laws are common to constitutional monarchies. They are intended to protect the reputations of monarchs held in revered positions. The wording of *lèse-majesté* laws is largely similar, and typically linked to a constitutional provision proclaiming the inviolability of the monarch.

Although absolutist states of the 17th and 18th centuries in Europe differed in many ways from the absolute monarchy in Siam prior to 1932, they did have one legal mechanism in common: treason against the state and *lèse-majesté* were synonymous. On the whole, *lèse-majesté* laws rose and strengthened under absolutism, leading in many cases to indiscriminate use. Prior to the revolution in France, for instance, there was a spate of *lèse-majesté* cases, particularly in the 1750s.[15]

The German Empire in the late 19th century generated the highest concentration of *lèse-majesté* cases in modern history. Between 1885 and 1905, as many as 10,000 cases of *lèse-majesté* were prosecuted in Germany—an average of 500 per year. The law allowed a maximum period of imprisonment of five years, but sentences typically ranged from a month to three years, and averaged almost six months in the early 1890s.[16] Although these sentences might sound quite light, a newspaper calculated that in the 1890s German courts handed down a total of 2,600 years of imprisonment "as the price of the very limited amount of freedom of speech which exists in the empire". Some of the convicted were under 15.

A professor of history at Berlin University was

accused of *lèse-majesté* and threatened with demotion for his views on German history. One commentator argued that academics should have "the right to speak critically of historical events", further expressing a worry that:

"... it would appear that any citizen at the close of the nineteenth century (excepting in Russia and in uncivilised countries) should have the right to criticise the policy of the government, and still more so a professor of history, unless he consents, against all the glorious traditions of the German universities, to teach with a gag in his mouth."[17]

The severe application of *lèse-majesté* in the German Empire was ultimately counterproductive. One newspaper argued in 1897: "The law has been vigorously enforced, but it has been not only powerless to prevent offences of this nature—it has, to a large extent, created a condition of affairs it was designed to guard against."[18]

Even with an avowed republican party in the German parliament, the bizarre dynamics of the *lèse-majesté* law made it impossible for any force in German society to revise it. In the end, it was the emperor himself who took the matter in hand. In 1904, Kaiser Wilhelm II "directed the Ministry of Justice to deal liberally with all persons convicted of insulting him". In 1906, he apparently pardoned all those in jail for *lèse-majesté*.[19] Thereafter, it is difficult to find any international press reports of German *lèse-majesté* cases.[20]

Writing in a personal capacity, Tjaco Van den Hout, Holland's ambassador to Thailand, noted that *lèse-majesté* laws in Europe today "are hardly ever applied and if they are, the punishment is usually mild". In one case, two journalists were forced to pay monetary damages for publicly insulting a foreign head of state. The European Court of Human Rights found that protection of foreign heads of state from criticism "amounts to conferring on [them] a special privilege that cannot be reconciled with modern practice and political conceptions". In another case, a civil court ordered a member of parliament to pay 60,000 euros in damages to the president of Turkey. In both instances, the court indicated that regular defamation laws were sufficient "to protect heads of state and ordinary citizens alike from remarks that damage their honour or reputation or are insulting".[21]

In 2008, a Dutchman was charged for drunkenly screaming insults about his queen, and threatening to shoot her. The lower court ruled that he was inebriated and dismissed the case.[22] A year earlier, a Dutch court fined a man 400 euros for defaming Queen Beatrix and making lewd statements.[23] In Spain, a court imposed a fine of 200 euros on a defendant who had burnt a royal portrait.[24] Finally, Danish prosecutors in early 2011, once securing the necessary approval from the minister of justice, proceeded with prosecution of a *lèse-majesté* case against four Greenpeace activists who crashed a "royal gala dinner" in 2009 as part of a protest.[25]

In Norway, a law of *lèse-majesté* is in place, but cases never go to court. Section 101 in the Norwegian criminal code reads: "Any person who defames the king or the regent shall be liable to detention or imprisonment for a term not exceeding five years." But Section 103 provides a limitation on whether prosecution can proceed: "Prosecution of any defamation pursuant to sections 101 and 102 shall be initiated only by order of the king or with his consent." No Norwegian king has sued in his own name since 1878.[26]

THAI LÈSE-MAJESTÉ TODAY

Thailand's *lèse-majesté* law is not unusual in its wording which places the monarch in a revered and inviolable position. The difference lies in its applica- tion, the frequency with which it is invoked, the severity of the punishments, the absence of exemp- tions on constitutional or other legal grounds—and the force it exerts over the judicial system.

There is a growing body of literature on the subject, and a greater awareness about how the law operates, and the political and legal issues it raises.[27] Somchai Preechasilpakul of the Law Faculty of Chiang Mai University has argued that a law so easily and so often used as a political weapon deviates from accepted legal principles. As a whole, aspects of the language used in the law, the lack of procedural guidelines for arrests and prosecutions, and the right of any citizen to make a complaint—there have even been instances in which the complainants have been foreigners[28]—are all topics that have been raised in the widening discussion of *lèse-majesté* in Thailand.

Unlike regular defamation cases, which can only be initiated by a damaged party, *lèse-majesté* complaints can be made by anyone. In recent years, a young man was involved in an altercation after not standing for the royal anthem in a cinema, and a complaint was then lodged against him by the disputant; a foreigner was charged over a 103-word paragraph referring to the crown prince in a self-published novel; and a web master was arrested for violating Section 15 of the Computer Crime Act (which is sometimes called the Computer-Related Crime Act). She was charged with failing to remove "a forum topic that contains defamation of the monarchy posted by a forum member".

The Computer Crime Act, passed not long before a general election returned Thailand to parliamentary democracy in 2007, has led to an increase in the number of charges. Section 14 (2) prohibits electronic transmission of "false computer data in a manner that is likely to damage the country's security or cause a public panic". Section 14 (3) prohibits transmission of any material "related with an offence against the kingdom's security under the criminal code". Violators of the act may be imprisoned for up to five years and fined up to 100,000 baht per infraction.[29] Section 15 provides the same punishment for anyone who intentionally allows offensive material to remain available (such as on a forum discussion on a website).[30]

From 2007 through to the middle of 2010, there were 31 cases pursued under the Computer Crime Act relating to national security content. All four cases in which the courts have already handed down verdicts resulted in convictions. Nonetheless, in January 2011, a Thai court had dismissed a case in which the alleged offender was accused of posting *lèse-majesté* contents on a website, due to insufficient evidence. From 2008 through to the middle of 2011, more than 60,000 URLs (web pages) from more than 70 websites were blocked by court orders for what was deemed to be *lèse-majesté* content under the 2007 Computer Crime Act and *lèse-majesté* law. As a result of these blockings, Thailand was rated "not free" in a 2011 report on internet freedom by Freedom House, a US advocacy group.[31]

Regardless of the Computer Crime Act, complaints and charges have become more encompassing. They have been filed against individuals for comments made in regard to a daughter of the king, the institution of the monarchy itself, and to symbols or symbolic references that could be equated with the king. Although the institution itself is not protected by the *lèse-majesté* law, criticism of the institution and its accoutrements has been construed on some occasions as an insult to the king himself.[32] Complaints and charges have covered a widening number of other associations with the king—more distant members of the royal family, Thai history, royal development strategies, the Privy Council, the royal anthem and the status of the Crown Property Bureau. In particular, *lèse-majesté* complaints have been frequently used as a weapon against political opponents—especially in the polarised politics Thailand has fallen victim to since 2006.

There is no question that a significantly increased number of premeditated attacks have been made against the king, members of the royal family and the royal institution on the Internet and in public speeches—much of which are grounds for seeking legal redress. However, the king has never sued any of his subjects, or for that matter initiated a *lèse-majesté* charge.

As in any country, Thai police, judges and prosecutors are servants of the state, but they lack unambiguous guidelines for proceeding with *lèse-majesté* cases. As a result, the police in particular have reason to be fearful of being charged with malfeasance for not acting when a complaint of *lèse-majesté* is filed at their station. Prosecutors are similarly inclined to prosecute, and judges must of course hand down verdicts strictly within the framework of the law. With guidelines and open debate on the topic missing, the courts have tended to interpret the scope of *lèse-majesté* quite broadly and irrespective of context—making convictions almost certain.[33] It is difficult to have a *lèse-majesté* charge dismissed, and the judicial process usually takes years.

Compared to other countries, Thai prosecutors take a remarkably high 90 percent of all cases to trial. Kittipong Kittayarak, the permanent secretary to the Ministry of Justice, notes that there is very little "prosecutorial discretion" in Thailand, and there is even less discretion in taking up *lèse-majesté* cases.[34] The conviction rate for all criminal cases is already exceptionally high. In 2004, for instance, courts handed down a total of 388,566 verdicts, with a conviction rate of 98.64 percent.[35] While the conviction rate from 1993 to 2005 was slightly lower for the 50 *lèse-majesté* cases tested in court—94 percent—the odds against acquittal are still overwhelming.

Very few *lèse-majesté* cases reach the Supreme Court. In trial, most defendants confess to the crime and enter guilty pleas. There are two advantages to this strategy. The first is that in all court cases a confession generally reduces prison sentences by half. The second is that after a verdict has been reached at the lower court level and becomes final, the convicted person can begin the process of applying for a royal pardon.[36] All royal pardon requests go through the Privy Council, which

reviews some 100 to 150 applications each year for all types of convictions. Its recommendations are then forwarded to the king.[37]

The recanting and pardoning process has been characterised as a "reaffirmation of the defendant's loyalty to the king": the defendant confesses and recants his or her words, thus reaffirming loyalty to and reverence for the monarchy.[38] Of late, however, not all those convicted have chosen to take this path. From 2005 to 2010, at least 46 charges leading to conviction in the Court of First Instance were appealed.[39]

When foreigners are occasionally convicted, applications for a royal pardon are quickly granted, opening the way to permanent deportation.[40] A Japanese author, for instance, was charged in the northern city of Chiang Mai with insulting the queen and heir apparent in a Japanese-language book on rural life. The court halved the initial three-year sentence upon the defendant's confession, and suspended the remainder.[41] In 2007, a Swiss national, while in a state of extreme intoxication, defaced pictures of the king and was jailed. For showing contrition, the court halved his 20-year sentence, and two weeks later he was pardoned and deported.[42]

In Thailand, there are no exemptions available to defendants in *lèse-majesté* cases, unlike in common defamation suits. It is considered no defence if the offending statement is an honest opinion, an allegation that can be proved, or fair and reasonable comment on a public figure. Rights of expression guaranteed under the constitutions in most constitutional monarchies provide a form of exemption that in practice trump *lèse-majesté* laws. In Thailand, however, the *lèse-majesté* law trumps any such constitutional provisions.

The International Covenant on Civil and Political Rights (ICCPR), ratified by Thailand in 1996, and the Constitution of the Kingdom of Thailand guarantee freedom of expression. Sections 4, 5, and 30 of the 2007 constitution uphold the principle of equality of "all persons" who shall not suffer

Above *Nine judges of the Supreme Court sit in session in February 2010.*

"unjust discrimination" for differences in what is termed a "constitutionally political view". Section 45 guarantees that "a person shall enjoy the liberty to express his opinion, make speech, write, print, publicise, and make expression by other means". Sections 28 and 29 forbid the state to "affect the essential substances" of the "rights and liberties" that every person may exercise as long as it is not "contrary to this constitution or good morals".[43] In a similar manner, the International Covenant on Civil and Political Rights recognised in Article 19 that the exercise of the rights to freedom of expression may be subject to certain restrictions as provided by law and necessary to uphold the rights or reputations of others, or to protect national security or public order, or public health or morals. At the same time, it also recognises that the exercise of the right to freedom of expression "carries with it special duties and responsibilities".

Although the National Human Rights Commission of Thailand can take cases to the Constitutional Court, the commission has yet to act on numerous requests for assistance by those charged with *lèse-majesté*. Accordingly, the law has yet to be tested in the Constitutional Court for consistency with other provisions in the constitution.

CURBING ABUSE

When Abhisit Vejjajiva became prime minister in December 2008, he pledged to protect the monarchy and set up an oversight committee to look into *lèse-majesté* cases. In late 2009, the prime minister chaired the first meeting of the Advisory Committee on the Security of the Kingdom,[44] which was charged with examining violations of the *lèse-majesté* law (Article 112), the defaming or insulting of heads of state of other countries (Article 133), or representatives of other countries (Article 134). The committee also set out to review the Computer Crime Act and the use of computers in ways possibly detrimental to national security, including the circulation of content containing *lèse-majesté*.

In providing a rationale for the committee, the order states that such violations are of great importance and "may have adverse effects on the institution of the monarchy, security of the country and friendly relations with foreign countries". The committee was to review the handling of such cases by all state agencies, and to ensure the rights and liberties of those charged with such crimes are constitutionally protected.

The committee included the attorney-general, permanent secretaries of the ministries of justice, information and communications technology, defence, interior, foreign affairs and culture, as well as the heads of the judiciary, police, intelligence and the military. The committee has the duty to "consider, give advice and provide recommendations" concerning the manner in which these cases are handled with respect for the rights of those charged.

In a bid to reduce the damage associated with prosecutions, the committee was asked to forward other alternatives instead of criminal prosecution and to consider the intention and behaviour behind the commission of offences, the feelings of remorse of those accused, and to examine the overall effect a case might have on "security and peace and order of the country". Through research and examination of how such cases are handled, the committee is to provide advice and to propose direction and measures to prevent further violations. Moreover, the committee is authorised to consider the laws and legal proceedings and propose amendments to make them more proper.

Permanent secretary at the Ministry of Justice and chairman of the committee, Kittipong is careful to say that the committee's work does not focus simply on *lèse-majesté*, but a broader set of laws.[45] A key problem in his view is that insufficient "discretion" is employed by both police and prosecutors. *Lèse-majesté* is handled reflexively, he argues, like "an assembly line". In practice, once a complaint of *lèse-majesté* has been made at a police station, the police have to take action. They are very reluctant to use discretion at this point and dismiss a complaint "for fear they are going to be prosecuted for ignoring their duty".

Kittipong says the committee's work will ultimately focus on the prosecution side. While the remarkably high proportion of cases prosecuted may have little social and political effect in other types of crime, the virtually automatic prosecution of *lèse-majesté* cases may cause "alienation".

"We want them to strike a proper balance," says Kittipong. "We are trying to get the prosecution to weigh the pros and cons." He cites Holland where

prosecutors try to assess possible damage to the fabric of society.

In its first phase, the committee has been trying to set up a system for police and prosecutors to improve coordination internally and with each other. The committee eventually hopes to put in place a reliable process. With better coordination and more discretion, fewer complaints based on a broad interpretation of the law will be forwarded for prosecution—a process that is both time-consuming and costly to the public purse, as well as potentially inflammatory politically.

The committee has categorised *lèse-majesté* offences into various offender groups by considering the nature and intention behind the commission of the act charged, level of violence, and effect on security, peace and order of the country. The committee's position is that the *lèse-majesté* law is still justified for those intentionally conspiring to overthrow the monarchy.

Meanwhile, particular care is needed for those who just "go along with the crowd", passing on information they have heard, academics who critically examine the political and governmental system, implicating the monarchy and *lèse-majesté*, and foreign correspondents who do not understand Thai perspectives and the traditions of the Thai monarchy. Punishing these groups of people without considering the pros and cons to the society could alienate people.

The committee views that the monarchy should be left above politics, and anybody who uses the law against another for his or her own benefit damages the institution. This may include people who misguidedly think they are protecting the monarchy by accusing others of *lèse-majesté*. The committee is finding ways to deter them from using the law. "We have to let them know that by doing that they are hurting the institution," says Kittipong.

"Each case should be properly handled with more discretion," says Kittipong, who believes the best-case scenario rests with minimising the number of cases that go to court. The committee contemplates no changes to the *lèse-majesté* law itself since there is a real threat to the institution that cannot be ignored. "Once there's a threat, a large number of people—ordinary people, too—want to protect the monarchy, and so there's no move to change the law," says Kittipong.

The committee waits to be consulted by police and prosecutors, but has no executive authority. Those asking can decide whether or not to take the advice on offer. By early 2011, the committee had been asked to review fewer than a dozen cases, most of which are still in progress at the time of writing. No further action was taken in a complaint filed against the Foreign Correspondents' Club of Thailand, and another involving a prominent social commentator, Sulak Sivaraksa. In the latter case, it was evident that Sulak was not trying to overthrow the monarchy, although he was critical in some areas and was proposing certain reforms.

"If we can make the difference very clear," says Kittipong, "then it is good for our legal system, too, that we do not use the *lèse-majesté* law in such cases." The permanent secretary believes research should focus on "the adverse impact" that abuse of the law is going to have on the monarchy. "We have to make a very clear picture for everyone to see," he argues. A solution, he suggests, may be found through a comparative study with countries such as Holland which has stronger traditions of prosecutorial discretion, but Thai police and prosecutors still need to do more research to establish their own internal guidelines.

The results of the committee's work thus far are modest, and Kittipong concedes it still has very little clout. He believes many share the same concerns that abuse of the *lèse-majesté* law will ultimately hurt the institution itself, and describes the committee as "the voice of conscience" needed to help keep the monarchy above politics.

A THAI LEGAL PERSPECTIVE

A leading Thai legal mind, Borwornsak Uwanno, has laid out a key line of argument supporting *lèse-majesté*. The central premise of his detailed argument is that all countries place certain limitations on free speech due to their specific cultural and legal circumstances.[46] Thailand adheres to international legal standards in general, but limits freedom of speech when it may harm society. The Thai people's relationship to the monarchy is unique and an expression of the kingdom's particular ethical and cultural character. The *lèse-majesté* law exists as the result of a "societal consensus" and therefore Thailand, as part of its right to self-determination, should be allowed to use the *lèse-majesté* law without adverse judgment from abroad.

Borwornsak argues that the Thai monarchy's relationship to society is different from other constitutional monarchies with its "long history dating back to ancient times, [it] has an exalted religious and social status ... but has close bonds with the people, who love and respect [it] for the monarch's contributions to their well being".

"Thais have seen not only these images of magnificence, which reflect the continuity of Thai history and tradition, but also those of the king and queen and their children sitting on the ground and conversing in plain language with ordinary people in remote, harsh areas of the country where no one wanted to go. Royal development projects, which today number more than 3,000, were thus initiated, reflecting the monarchy's closeness to the people... The bond between the Thai monarchy and the Thai people is unique. It is not one between the head of state as a political institution and the people as holders of sovereign power. It is a special relationship with certain characteristics that may be difficult for foreigners to appreciate."[47] Borwornsak writes that the *lèse-majesté* law is thus "the effect of Thai culture and ethics, not the cause which coerces Thai people to respect the king as alleged by some". This position, he writes, could be termed "law as an expression of popular will".

In 2007, former prime minister Anand Panyarachun, speaking to the Foreign Correspondents' Club of Thailand, outlined a similar position: "You have to go by the will of the people ... I think you have to respect the thinking and customs of the people in this country ... I am sure that the king does not mind whether the law exists or not, but the Thai people never, never tolerate criticism of the king ... I believe that the Thais are more royalist than the king."[48]

On the other hand, some argue that, in the context of the troublesome political conditions facing Thailand today, the law itself is part of the problem.[49] Some legal scholars have called for repeal of the law in its entirety.[50] Since the law of lèse-majesté is connected to the constitutional provision holding the king as a revered person, abolition of the law would probably entail amending other parts of the constitution.[51]

A ROYAL PERSPECTIVE

Thailand's law of lèse-majesté has one very prominent critic: King Bhumibol. Because lèse-majesté laws are used so infrequently in most monarchies, it is rare for a monarch to express an opinion on the subject.

In 2005, after an increase in politically-inspired lèse-majesté complaints, King Bhumibol used his annual televised birthday address to convey three concerns:

- The king, he said, is a human being and as such should be subject to criticism.
- Charges against those accused of lèse-majesté should be dropped, and those held in jail for lèse-majesté should be released.
- The use of the lèse-majesté law ultimately damages the monarchy.[52]

King Bhumibol said that a British phrase, "The king can do no wrong," implied the king was not human. "But the king can do wrong," he said, arguing that when the king is not subject to criticism he is "in trouble". When criticism is prohibited and people are jailed for lèse-majesté, "the damage is done to the king". The king also said that in other constitutional democracies monarchs are criticised. "No one dares send people who insult the king to jail because the king [in that country] will be troubled,"

the king said. He reminded everyone that he had in fact never told anyone to send critics to jail—and neither had previous kings in the Royal House of Chakri. Indeed, no Thai king has sued one of his subjects using post-1900 lèse-majesté legislation.

"Actually, I do the same thing: do not send people to jail but release them. Or if they are in jail, release them. If they are not in jail, do not sue them because it would cause trouble," said King Bhumibol. He added that jailing people personally caused him "trouble" because he then had to give a royal pardon.

Although the king's observations were unambiguous, the authorities dropped few cases and freed none of those already jailed. Indeed, within weeks lèse-majesté accusations were flying in all directions. In the years following King Bhumibol's speech, the number of lèse-majesté complaints filed to the police actually increased.

Between 2005 and 2010, the appeals court handed down 41 lèse-majesté verdicts, and another 11 cases went to the Supreme Court.[53] This unprecedented spike played a part in the nosedive Thailand has experienced in comparative surveys on freedom of expression. The Reporters Without Borders' World Press Freedom Index, for example, ranked Thailand 59th in 2004, but the kingdom had dropped to 153rd among 178 nations by 2010.[54]

Above *King Bhumibol grants a rare private audience to the entire Privy Council at Piamsuk Villa,*
Klai Kangwol Palace, on 15 August 2003.

THE PRIVY COUNCIL

Thai monarchs historically had personal advisers who would counsel them on the kingdom's affairs. In the late 19th century, King Chulalongkorn created a formal advisory body called the Privy Council. In the 20th century, the role, size and makeup of the Privy Council has changed with each subsequent reign. What is the composition and what are the functions of the Privy Council today?

In 2004, King Bhumibol opened the new chambers of the Privy Council, the 19-member body that serves at his pleasure. The Privy Council is charged with providing advice the king may request or require on various matters relating to the discharging of his duties as constitutional monarch. In his address, the king pointed out that the "councillors are not advisers of other people, they are advisers only to the king. They do not have to give guidance to others. If they do so, they do it in a private capacity, not as a privy councillor ..."

The king further said that: "Any judgement made both in the Privy Council and with other people has great importance because people believe that you are knowledgeable, have experience and consider thoroughly all matters in a straightforward, loyal and honest manner ... Therefore, I request you to be cautious in conversation, in judgment, in opinions given in Privy Council meetings and outside as well, meaning that the general public, officials and people await to hear your views. But what is spoken is not the views of privy councillors but those of knowledgeable persons ... I therefore request you to be cautious in all that you think, say and do in order to set an example and be of benefit to all.[1]

The king's words were prescient. In the years following his speech, the perceived involvement of certain privy councillors in political matters became a subject of much controversy.

An institution previously of little note was thrust into the spotlight. As a result, the public and media have speculated about the role the council plays in national affairs, how it functions and even why it exists at all.

Above King Prajadhipok and Queen Rambhai, top row, and the members of the Supreme Council of State: Prince Bhanurangsri Savangwongse, middle row left; Prince Paribatra Sukhumbhand, middle row right; Prince Damrong Rajanubhab, bottom row left; Prince Narisara Nuvadtivongs, bottom row centre; and Prince Kitiyakara Voralaksana, bottom row right.

ORIGINS OF THE PRIVY COUNCIL

Privy councils in general originated from the period of European absolutist states when centralisation and bureaucratisation required the devolution of powers from the king to trusted ministers.[2] The term "privy council" as such dates back to 13th-century Britain where the council evolved into a nascent cabinet by the 16th century. By the 18th century, however, the Privy Council had ceded much of its power to the parliament.[3] Today, only a few countries still have privy councils: Bhutan, Brunei, Canada (it last met in 1981), Denmark, Norway, Thailand, Tonga and the United Kingdom. Of these, Britain's Privy Council is one of the most active. It facilitates the British monarch's relationship to government and its stated purpose is to advise on the exercise of prerogative powers and certain functions assigned to the queen and the council by act of parliament.[4]

An official publication of the Thai Privy Council states that it was originally set up following the English tradition, which was "the root of the current Privy Council". But it also states that at present the two privy councils are starkly different. In contrast to the large British Privy Council (as of 2011, it consisted of 593 members), in Thailand privy councillors are carefully and individually selected. Moreover, the Thai Privy Council is more involved in providing advice on judicial and legislative matters than the British Privy Council.[5]

The origins of the Thai Privy Council date to the reign of King Chulalongkorn (r. 1868–1910). Although Thai monarchs had always had personal advisers, the king institutionalised their function by creating the Council of State, whose members were mainly non-royal, senior officials, and in the same year, established a privy council, through which advice could be given to the king by the "privy councillor or personal adviser to His Majesty the King".[6] Its 49 members were chosen from the royal family, the Council of State and from the Thai nobility.[7] The 1874 Act establishing the body stipulated that members were to be chosen "in accordance with His Majesty's wishes, and they were to hold office till the end of the reign".[8] These two bodies were essentially the Siamese government that saw the kingdom through what has been called the great reform of the 1890s. One historian has stated that the purpose of the Thai Privy Council was "to guarantee a constant flow of information to the king and to provide a wide debating ground to discuss the ways and means for major reform".[9]

During the reign of King Vajiravudh (r. 1910–25), when the number of privy councillors was increased to 233, the council was more of a ceremonial than a working body.[10] Those who received the Most Illustrious Order of Chula Chom Klao automatically became privy councillors. When King Prajadhipok became king in 1925, there were increasing calls for a more representative system of government. To resolve the ongoing controversy and increasing public disillusionment over the administering of the state's affairs under absolute monarchy, King Prajadhipok created two new bodies. In the first month of his reign, he established the Supreme Council of State, which has been described by one scholar as "a five-man ruling cabinet of powerful princes". King Prajadhipok described in a letter to a foreign adviser the urgent need to rebuild faith in the monarchy: "On my succession to the throne it was thought absolutely necessary to do something at once to gain the confidence of the people, hence the creation of the Supreme Council. This had immediate effect and I really gained the confidence of the people in one day."[11]

In 1927, the king created the Privy Council Committee. The Privy Council Act of 1927 specified that this body of 40 members would be "a consultative body to assist His Majesty in carrying out the affairs of state".[12] Because it was intended to represent a wider range of opinion, the highest-ranking princes were excluded and the body was

Above *King Ananda, right, presides at an official function, accompanied by Prince Bhumibol with Prince Dhani in between.*

comprised instead of lesser-ranking royal family members and also senior officials.[13] However, even after five years of work, the committee, according to one historian, "had still not developed into a widely known forum nor did it appear to reflect public opinion".[14]

In 1932, when absolute monarchy in Siam was replaced with constitutional monarchy, both the Supreme Council of State and the Privy Council were disbanded. In 1935, following the abdication of King Prajadhipok, a three-person regent council was established to serve in the name of the new monarch, King Ananda. However, King Ananda (r. 1935–46), who was a minor living abroad at the time, instead depended on his family for advice.[15]

After King Ananda's premature death, Prince Bhumibol became king and returned to Switzerland to continue his education. His uncle, Prince Rangsit of Jainad, was made regent in the king's absence.[16] The coup of 1947 began a decades-long military dictatorship under which the monarchy was to see its renaissance, and along with it, the Privy Council. The provisional constitution of 1947

established the Supreme State Council made up of "elder statesmen" who "shall give him counsel in affairs of state" (section 9). Sections 13 and 14 of the constitution, respectively, specified that councillors were to "execute the personal affairs of the king and give him counsel" and "act as advisers to the king by submitting to him their true opinion in the general interests of the country".[17] To qualify, it was required that potential candidates for the Supreme State Council had at least 25 years in government service and had attained at least the level of director-general or government minister for a minimum of four years. The 1947 constitution also provided the king with the prerogative to appoint the senate that was equal in size to the House of Representatives.

The return of powers to the throne was carried forward by the 1949 constitution as well. Under this constitution, the Supreme State Council was replaced with the Privy Council. The restrictions on who could serve were tightened, but the number of councillors was increased from five to nine. The Privy Council was to provide advice to the king "on all matters concerning the exercise of his functions" and to carry out "such other duties as provided in this constitution".[18] Nominations for a new king if the throne became vacant still required parliamentary approval. The general framework of the Privy Council established by the 1949 constitution essentially defined the functions and structure under which it operates to this day.[19]

Building from the 1949 constitution, the 1952 constitution laid out the basic contours of the Privy Council's role, and that of the monarchy, until 1974. The constitution of 1974 increased the number of privy councillors to no more than 15 (including the president). A draft of this constitution also had senatorial appointments countersigned by the head of the council. However, King Bhumibol rejected this clause, warning that "it violates the principle that the king is above politics".[20]

The number of privy councillors was increased to a maximum of 19 members in 1991. The 1997 constitution listed in greater detail those who cannot serve. Excluded were anyone serving on the independent agencies created by the 1997 constitution, such as the Election Commission or the National Human Rights Commission. In deliberations amongst drafters of the 2007 constitution, there was discussion to forbid even rectors and members of university councils from serving.[21]

FUNCTIONS OF THE PRIVY COUNCIL

In a similar vein to the Thai constitutions since 1947, the more recent 1997 and 2007 constitutions describe how privy councillors are chosen and removed, their requisite qualifications, their official duties in a broad sense, the oath they take and their role if the king is absent from the country.

At his own pleasure, the king selects no more than 18 privy councillors and a president of the council, or removes privy councillors (as well as officials of the Royal Household and of the royal chief aide-de-camp); only the appointment or removal of the Privy Council president need be countersigned by the president of the National Assembly (sections 12, 13, 16, 18). The Privy Council's duty is to give "advice to the king on all matters pertaining to his functions" (section 12). Privy councillors are forbidden by the constitution to hold a host of positions in the government sector. Section 14 prohibits privy councillors from holding political office, being a member of an independent agency such as a member of the National Anti-corruption Commission, or being a member of a political party (section 14, see figure 1).

According to section 15, privy councillors must make a solemn oath before the king:[22]

"I, [name of the declarer], do solemnly declare that I will be loyal to His Majesty the King and will faithfully perform my duties in the interest of the country and of the people. I will also uphold and observe the constitution of the Kingdom of Thailand in every respect."[23]

According to the constitution, the Privy Council is routinely commanded by the king to perform the following functions:

• Deliberate and submit its views on all matters in which the government requests the king's signature or sanction, such as legislation, royal decrees or appointment of high officials.
• Consider petitions for clemency from prisoners as well as other petitions submitted by private citizens.
• Serve on behalf of the king's initiatives such as on the board of the Anandamahidol Foundation or in service to royally initiated development projects.
• Represent the king at special events—for example laying wreaths at funerals.[24]
• Attend court functions.

The constitution also provides that other duties be

Above *Veterans salute the president of the Privy Council General Prem Tinsulanonda who laid a wreath on behalf of King Bhumibol and Queen Sirikit at Victory Monument on Veterans Day, 4 February 2001.*

carried out by the Privy Council, such as:

- Submitting the name of a suitable person to hold the office of regent (section 19).
- The president of the Privy Council serving as temporary regent *pro tempore* (section 20).
- Drafting the palace law amendment (section 22).
- Submitting the name of the successor to the throne in the case that there is no heir designated

and the throne becomes vacant (section 23).

Dr Kasem Watanachai, a privy councillor since 2001, separates the work of the council into three categories.[25] The first set of duties are those designated by law and the constitution. Kasem says the privy councillors with a legal background review all legislation and provide the council with an overview and initial opinion. At its weekly two-hour meeting on Tuesdays, the council also considers petitions from those in prison seeking a royal pardon, a task forming the council's main function in Kasem's view.[26] Different councillors are assigned to particular cases as the council takes some of the initial steps of the royal pardon. The entire council reviews two or three petitions each week. An additional legal duty of the council is to vet the high official appointments submitted by every government ministry.

In most instances the councillors come to an agreement on a given law, petition or appointment and its opinion is then forwarded in written form to the king. Occasionally when the council cannot agree, both the majority and minority opinions are sent. Kasem emphasises that the Privy Council is merely an advisory body; it is the king who exercises his own judgment. In a 2004 speech to the Privy Council, the king noted: "Whether or not [the council's advice] is taken or acknowledged, do not take it to heart, because it is the king who must make decisions on the various matters."[27]

The second key area of the council's responsibility is to help oversee royal projects. Each councillor "is given a certain set of royal projects to look after", according to Kasem, who himself chairs a number of scholarship funds and a mobile medical programme.

Thirdly, the privy councillors are delegated to represent the king at various functions. When representing the monarch, the privy councillor will wear a white uniform and typically be provided with an official limousine from the Bureau of the Royal Household if a journey is required. Privy councillors travel throughout the kingdom to preside over annual events sponsored by each royal project, meet with foreign dignitaries, or serve other functions, such as attending royally sponsored cremations.

Privy councillors are appointed for life. Kasem recalled one case when a councillor was "allowed to step down" in order to stay with his children abroad. However, the king rarely meets with the council— although he did at the opening of the privy council's new chambers in 2004.

Privy councillors have recently been provided compensation for their service on a salary scale which is roughly equivalent to that of a government minister. As of 2011, the president of the council makes 121,990 baht per month while the members make 112,250 baht.

Although there is not any law forbidding a privy councillor from sitting on the board of a private company, Kasem says there is a "gentleman's agreement" among councillors not to do so. In the past, some members have held positions on the board of the Crown Property Bureau (which manages the assets of the crown), or on the boards of its associated companies, such as Siam Cement Group and Siam Commercial Bank. With regard to the latter, the bank has since 2003 discontinued the practice of having any privy councillors on its board. The fact that some privy councillors have also accepted positions on the boards of other large companies has opened the Privy Council to some criticism.[28] Privy councillors are not required to declare their assets nor are they provided any special legal protection as a result of their work on behalf of the monarch.[29]

COMPOSITION OF THE PRIVY COUNCIL

The Privy Council is described in a Thai government publication as "an august body of distinguished advisers who possess exceptional experience and knowledge of state affairs".[30] King Bhumibol, in his address to the Privy Council in 2004, said, "Your responsibility is to be knowledgeable, capable in all technical matters in official careers and in private life". The king went on to say that privy councillors "must be of good reputation, good knowledge, whose judgment people naturally want to hear".[31]

Accordingly, privy councillors boast a wide range of experience and positions. As of 2011, the Privy Council includes three former prime ministers: Tanin Kraivixien, who was named prime minister in October 1976 and then became a privy councillor in 1977, Prem Tinsulanonda, who served as prime minister for eight years in the 1980s before joining the council, and Surayud Chulanont, who stepped down from the council to become prime minister in 2006.[32] Former Privy Council president, the late Sanya Dharmasakti stepped down from the council to become prime minister in 1973.[33]

In 2004, five of the privy councillors came from a military background. Another five were from the field of law, eight were technocrats, state enterprise managers or from a civil service background, and one came from education.[34]

The king's frequent interactions with the military during his extensive travel throughout the country, especially during the Vietnam War era, may explain why such a relatively high number of military men have been appointed as privy councillors. In 2011, the average length of tenure on the Privy Council was 14.5 years, and the average age of privy councillors was 75. The oldest in 2011 was 92 and the youngest 62.[35]

The members of the council as of 2011 have previously held a host of appointed bureaucratic positions such as senator, secretary-general of the National Security Council, permanent secretary to the Ministry of Agriculture and Cooperatives, Ministry of Education and Ministry of the Interior, director-general of the Royal Irrigation Department, councillor of state, and elected positions within the judiciary such as president of the Supreme Court.[36]

All Privy Council members are members of the Anandamahidol Foundation which sponsors candidates for educational scholarships. Several serve on the board of the Chaipattana Foundation, which was created to oversee and systematise the king's development-related efforts.[37]

It is also worth noting that during the long reign of King Bhumibol, the Privy Council has experienced exceptional continuity, having been led by only three presidents: Prince Dhani Nivat (1949–74, except for a few brief intervals such as when he became regent in 1951), Sanya Dharmasakti (1975–98) and Prem Tinsulanonda (1998–).

PERCEPTIONS OF THE PRIVY COUNCIL

A leading member of the royal family, Prince Dhani Nivat, played a significant role in the promulgation of the 1949 constitution, which re-established many pre-1932 royal powers, including a new and more powerful Privy Council. Prince Dhani became its president in 1949.[38] After the occasionally bitter conflicts between the civilian and royal leaderships finally simmered down in the 1950s, the Privy Council played a relatively quiet role in Thai affairs. While privy councillors are typically seen as being removed from politics,[39] historians have argued that members of the Privy Council have not always maintained neutrality.[40] In a 1976 interview, the then-president of the Privy Council, Sanya Dharmasakti noted that privy councillors must "remain neutral in politics".[41]

Privy Councillor Kasem argues that the most prominent misconception the Thai public has about the council is that it possesses "high authority". On the contrary, he says, "We don't have any authority at all... We're just a kind of adviser to the king and that's it." The cause of this misconception, Kasem says, is that Thais attach a great deal of importance to the title of privy councillor. He says the title in Thai is very exalted, and Thais believe anything exalted has authority or power.[42]

There are additional points of confusion. Media and the public frequently interpret the public words and actions of privy councillors as reflecting the monarch's own wishes. Indeed, this distinction

Above *King Bhumibol grants an audience to Privy Council members and their spouses at Siriraj Hospital on 27 September 2010. The king has been receiving care at the hospital since September 2009.*

between a privy councillor acting or speaking in an official versus private capacity, or whether certain privy councillors have remained neutral (or "above politics") or not, has been blurred in recent years. In part this is because, even if their public words are predicated as a personal opinion, the privy councillor speaking is still designated in news reports as a privy councillor.[43] In addition, privy councillors, all of whom have held top positions in the government or military, are viewed by the public as retaining much of their former influence and connections. Thus they are perceived as having power to effect change behind closed doors.

The perception that privy councillors are involved in politics as "extra-constitutional" figures has deepened considerably since 2006, leading to unprecedented debate about the influence of the institution. For example, when two privy councillors, both speaking as former civil servants, made widely reported public speeches about corruption to civil servants on Civil Service Day, many observers interpreted it as high-level condemnation of the

government of the time by the Privy Council. More significantly, there have been sustained ongoing allegations that a number of privy councillors, acting in a private capacity, were involved in a military coup in 2006.[44]

The president of the Privy Council, Prem Tinsulanonda, has been accused of involvement in the removal from power in 2006 of the prime minister at the time, Thaksin Shinawatra. Protesters against the coup surrounded Prem's home and called for his resignation. As evidence of his alleged role in the coup, they cited speeches he made to units of the military in the months before the putsch, although these speeches were not made in his capacity as Privy Council president. In light of the contentious debates over the influence of members of the Privy Council and arguing that the council is not consistent with democracy, some have called for the reform or even abolition of the body altogether.[45] Rarely commented on throughout its history, the role and influence of the Privy Council has rather suddenly become the subject of much discussion.[46]

Above Crown Prince Maha Vajiralongkorn takes the oath of allegiance in the Chapel Royal, Temple of the Emerald Buddha, after his investiture as heir to the throne at the Grand Palace in 1972.

SUCCESSION

Successions prior to the end of absolute monarchy in 1932 could be contentious, especially during the Ayudhya period from the 14th to 18th centuries. In 1924, King Vajiravudh attempted to clarify the succession process by laying down the Palace Law of Succession. After Siam became a constitutional monarchy, various amendments relating to succession were introduced. The succession laws and protocols provide insights into the Thai crown's past and future.

Royal succession in Siam should not be confused with the simpler system of primogeniture common to other monarchies in which the oldest male heir automatically accedes to the throne by right of first birth. Complicated by ancient traditions, successions in Siam, as in other Southeast Asian kingdoms, have historically been less straightforward and characterised by what one historian referred to as a "vagueness of succession".[1] Traditionally, throughout Siamese history, this vagueness has been defined by the following tension: the desire to maintain hereditary continuity—and ensure a smooth succession—within a dynasty versus the desire to fulfil the ancient Buddhist ideal that the king should be the wisest and most meritorious of his subjects and thus reign with their assent as an "elected" king. Historically, both the Western and Eastern systems were prey to contention and intrigue, and neither could ever entirely guarantee there would be no competition for the throne.

SUCCESSION IN THE DAYS OF ABSOLUTE MONARCHY

The Palace Law *(kot monthien ban)*, which many scholars date to 1480 and is often wrongly referred to in English as the "Palatine Law", offers early evidence of how succession was determined in ancient Siam.[2] Derived from Sanskrit, *kot* means rules; *monthien* means royal residence, or the house of the king; and *bala* means protect. Therefore, *kot monthien ban* means "rules to protect the royal house".[3] This is a set of strictures concerning traditions and customs related to the royal court.

During the Ayudhya period (c. 1351–1767), the Palace Law defined the role and prescribed behaviour of court officials in relation, particularly, to the safety of the king and his possessions. It was a blueprint for Siam's "feudal" system that outlined in detail royal duties related to governing, social ranking (sakdi/yot) and designation of official positions— as well as the rules by which the court functioned. It also prescribed different levels of punishment for those violating the Palace Law; rajasap, the royal language used at court; and regulations for women living in the inner court.[4]

The original Palace Law relating to succession did not lay out a clear system for determining a successor upon a king's death. Rather, it provided a frame of reference from which the next king could be chosen. Typically, the new king would be either the late king's son born of a major queen or consort (nor phra phutta chao), or one of his brothers.[5] The law also provided rules by which someone who was neither a son nor a brother of the deceased king could accede to the throne, should the situation or circumstances require it.[6]

However, the Palace Law was not always followed and did not ensure smooth successions. At least one third of Ayudhya's royal successions involved bloodshed. Indeed, the history of the kingdom at that time is a chronicle of frequent usurpations and of ambitious men thwarting the final wishes of recently departed kings.

Above The complex of the Front Palace, or Wang Na, pictured here, is the National Museum today. It is generally believed that the structure pictured prominently in the front, which no longer exists, was used for mounting and dismounting elephants.

Historian David Wyatt observed that "virtually all successions to the throne of Ayudhya in the seventeenth and eighteenth centuries were, at the least, irregular, and in many cases either disguised or real usurpations".[7]

After the overthrow of King Taksin (r. 1767–82), the founder of the Royal House of Chakri, Rama I (r. 1782–1809), established a more effective system for royal succession. Rama I commissioned scholars to collect and revise laws from the Ayudhya era. The Palace Law was a constituent part of this new legal compendium called *The Three Seals Code,* which was needed, Rama I said, because old laws were often misinterpreted and this led to injustice. *The Three Seals Code* defined the titles and correct behaviour of what might be called the nobility; laid out the ancient belief system relating to kingship, succession, and royal duties; described royal regalia; and defined space, geography and even architecture hierarchically.[8] Succession under the *The Three Seals Code* took into account the potential of the next king to be, as prescribed by ancient Buddhist texts, a *dhammaraja* (righteous king). This was manifested in his upholding of the Ten Virtues of Kingship. Lineage, however, still played a very important role.

All of the transfers of power in the Royal House of Chakri that followed the introduction of *The Three Seals Code* were accomplished with almost no bloodshed—although they were not without some complications.[9]

In part, greater adherence to the idea that the wisest and most capable possible successor should be chosen has tempered the eight successions of the Royal House of Chakri during the Rattanakosin era. At a special council of senior members of royalty and officials, it was agreed that Rama II should succeed his father.[10] After the death of Rama II in 1824, a grand assembly of the royal family, high officers of state and members of the Buddhist monkhood led by the supreme patriarch was convened. The assembly chose a son born of Rama II and a royal consort, a prince who had a proven record, over the king's much younger and less experienced half-brother, Prince Mongkut, who had recently been ordained as a monk. Although as the son of a full queen, Prince Mongkut might have had a superior claim to the throne in terms of lineage, he remained in the temple. This averted a potential succession crisis and any conflict with Rama III.[11]

The nuances of all this were beyond the understanding of many European observers raised in the less complicated tradition of primogeniture in which the oldest male heir always succeeds by right of lineage. In the eyes of some Westerners, it appeared that the new king had usurped the throne.

Rama III's own succession nearly became a crisis. As his health continued to deteriorate in 1851 following months of fruitless discussions about possible successors, the heir to the throne remained unnamed. A foreign observer of the time recounted that: "All parties concerning the question of the succession were preparing themselves with arms and troops for self-defence and resistance." Before they could come to blows, "there was convened at the king's palace ... a meeting of all the princes, nobles, and chief rulers of the land to confer on the all engrossing question of who shall become the successor to the present king."[12]

One of the possible successors to the throne was Prince Mongkut again. Over the 27 years Rama III reigned, the royal monk had become the leader of a Buddhist reform order. When considering his heir, Rama III had reportedly expressed reservations about the princes who might succeed him. If Prince Mongkut became king, Rama III feared he might order the Sangha to dress in the style of the [Buddhist] Mons.[13]

To assuage such doubts, Prince Mongkut wrote a letter to the assembly to make his own case for succeeding to the throne. He also ordered monks in his order to discontinue any practices considered unorthodox or foreign.

According to historian David Wyatt, who cites an account given by Prince Mongkut to American missionary Dan Beach Bradley, about two weeks before

Above *Prince Yodyingyot, left, was nicknamed George Washington, and was not succeeded in the Front Palace after his death in 1885. His father, King Pinklao, right, served as the second king during the reign of King Mongkut.*

Rama III died the assembly resolved to protect the claims to the throne of Prince Mongkut and his talented younger brother, Prince Chudamani (or Phra Pinklao). As it came to pass, when Rama III passed away, Prince Mongkut became king and Prince Chudamani became "second king". King Pinklao lived in the Front Palace. He was the only second king in the history of the Royal House of Chakri.

King Mongkut left the position of second king open after Phra Pinklao died in 1865.[14] If King Mongkut had named a replacement second king, the throne could have passed to that person rather than to one of his sons.[15] When King Mongkut died in 1868, the Great Council was assembled again. It selected 15-year-old Prince Chulalongkorn, King Mongkut's oldest son, and Chaophraya Sri Suriyawongse, a leading member of the powerful Bunnag family, was appointed regent. The council also named the son of the former second king, Prince Yodyingyot (later known as Prince Wichaichan), as the *uparat*.[16]

As *uparat*, Prince Yodyingyot, who resided in the Front Palace previously occupied by Phra Pinklao, had 2,000 of his own troops and modern military equipment. In the Front Palace Crisis of 1875, the troops of King Chulalongkorn (r. 1868–1910) and Prince Yodyingyot nearly clashed when it appeared that Prince Yodyingyot was challenging the throne. Prince Yodyingyot sought refuge in the British consulate, and after lengthy negotiations, his troops were disarmed and the prince was allowed to return to the Front Palace.[17]

When Prince Yodyingyot died in 1885, King Chulalongkorn discontinued the Front Palace and *uparat* system entirely.[18] A year later, King Chulalongkorn elevated the oldest, full-blooded prince among his sons, Prince Vajirunhis, to the position of crown prince. The investiture came well ahead of any expected succession. It was not surprising that the king at this time should choose a modified system of primogeniture to designate his heir apparent. A succession crisis might have left Siam vulnerable to interference from predatory, encroaching Western colonial powers. As Wyatt noted: "By 1910 [the year of King Chulalongkorn's death] the Siamese had abandoned the old rules of succession to the throne and had adopted the Western pattern of designating the heir to the throne long in advance."[19]

The accession of King Vajiravudh (r. 1910–25) was the least problematic succession in the history of the Royal House of Chakri up to that point. After the premature death of Prince Vajirunhis, his younger full brother, Prince Vajiravudh was invested as crown prince in 1895 and, upon the death of his father King Chulalongkorn, acceded to the throne. Based on his own experience as heir, King Vajiravudh knew that his father had wanted to institute a more ordered system of succession based on primogeniture which unequivocally designated a crown prince. During his reign, however, King Va-

jiravudh, was unable to produce a male heir and, as a result, succession became an issue again. Of the 77 children fathered by King Chulalongkorn, only seven sons born of queens survived beyond 1910. In the early 1920s, two of King Vajiravudh's three younger full brothers died. By the end of 1925, only the youngest brother, Prince Prajadhipok, was still alive. As a result, Wyatt writes that, "the problem of succession to the throne came to prominence rather suddenly in the last few years of the reign".

This situation provided important impetus for drafting the Palace Law of Succession (*kot monthienban wa duai kansubsantatiwong*) in 1924. This law, which continues to provide the framework for succession today, confirmed the primacy of the lineage of King Chulalongkorn and Queen Saovabha, and the king's sole and authentic right to choose his successor. It also made the determination of succession as legally precise and binding as possible.[20]

THE 1924 PALACE LAW OF SUCCESSION

The 1924 Palace Law of Succession was, in part, an attempt to eliminate the vagueness relating to succession within the Thai monarchical system. In the first section, King Vajiravudh states that "according to royal tradition, Siamese kings have the sole power and prerogative to designate any descendant of the royal family as heir to the throne".[21] Explaining why this new law was needed, King Vajiravudh wrote: "But as it has been in the past, and could be in the future, the king cannot name his own successor … resulting in troubling events … When kings have died, the vying for royal power has opened an opportunity for persons … who have been obstructive to the prosperity of the kingdom. It has also been the opportunity for enemies, both internal and external, to think of doing harm to the royal family and the freedom of Siam. [Such a situation] has brought disaster to the Thai nation. The king has thus desired to have a law determining succession in order to reduce the

trouble of contending [for the throne] within the royal family."

This, King Vajiravudh said, was the result of the king not being able to name a successor "with certainty". The king felt that the monarch of Siam "must be someone who people throughout the realm could place their absolute respect and trust in". He admitted that there were members of the royal family who were "deficient" and "not up to standard". Such persons "caused a [a lack of] peace and order and were trouble to the people of the realm, even [capable of] bringing disaster to the royal family".

According to King Vajiravudh, it was his father's intention to bring Thai royal successions into closer line with those of other nations. The important principles established by the law concern the king's right to name or remove an heir apparent, the procedures to be used if the king has not named an heir apparent, and also a description of the suitable

Above *King Chulalongkorn with eleven of his sons at Taplow Court in Buckinghamshire, England in 1893.*

characteristics for an heir to the throne.

The reigning king has absolute power to name any royal male as heir apparent, and upon being announced publicly, the "position of such heir is secure and indisputable":

Section 5. The king has the sole power and prerogative to designate any descendant of the royal family as heir to the throne, depending on his judgment and trust placed on the ability of the said person to succeed him.

Section 6. Once the king has designated the heir to the throne and has had such designation proclaimed to members of the royal family, officials and the public at large, the position of such heir is secure and indisputable. When the necessary time comes, the said heir shall immediately ascend the throne to succeed the late king in accordance with the latter's wish.

The king also has absolute power to remove an heir apparent from the position. If he does so, "his entire lineage is removed from any claim to the throne":

Section 7. The king has the sole power and prerogative to remove the heir to the throne from his position. Anyone who has been removed from the position of heir to the throne shall be considered as broken from [excluded from] any claim to succession and his name shall be removed from the line of succession. His sons and his entire lineage of direct descendants shall also be excluded from the line of succession. The king has the sole power and prerogative to exclude any member of the royalty from the line of succession.

Section 8. and 9. lay out the processes by which a new king is determined when the king dies with no heir apparent designated. In such case, the chief state official is to invite the first in line of succession to be king. Section 9. was set out "to clear any doubt" as to "the order in the line of succession", delineated down to 13 levels. Below are the first five levels:

(1) The first-born son of the king and queen;
(2) The first-born son of the said prince and his royal consort;
(3) Younger sons, in order, of the said prince and his royal consort;
(4) The second-born son of the king and queen

when the first-born son is deceased and has no male children;

(5) The first-born son of the second-born son of the king and queen if the second-born son is deceased;

(6) Younger sons, in order, of the second-born son [and so on].

While Section 9. ranks those eligible for kingship, the law's next set of clauses entitled, "On those who must be excluded from the line of succession", describes what might disqualify a potential heir to the throne.

Section 10. addresses members of royalty in the line of succession who may be unsuitable to accede. This section is not really so much a law as a piece of advice. It states:

"Whoever is to ascend to the throne should be one whom the masses fully respect and can be contentedly taken as their protector. Therefore any member of the royalty whom the multitude holds as loathsome, such person should foreswear the path to succession in order to remove the worry from the king and the people of the realm."

Section 11. states: "Descendants of the royal family with any of the following characters shall be excluded from the line of succession:

(1) Insanity;

(2) Convicted of a serious crime under the law;

(3) Unable to serve as Upholder of Buddhism;

(4) Married to a foreign consort, i.e. a woman whose nationality is originally not Thai;

(5) Being removed from the position of heir to the throne regardless of during which reign such removal took place;

(6) Being proclaimed to be excluded from the line of succession.

The last exclusion, Section 13., pertains to accession by a princess:

"Section 13. As it is deemed to be untimely for a princess to ascend the throne as a sole sovereign of Siam, inclusion of princesses in the line of succession shall be categorically prohibited."

Other points in the law provide guidance for when the new king is a minor under 20 years of age (a member of the royalty is to be named as regent and the two most senior privy councillors are to act as advisers). Procedures were also put in place for future kings to amend the law. They are advised to keep in mind that the law was written to strengthen the dynasty, and that amendments required approval from two-thirds of the Privy Council.

The 1924 Palace Law of Succession was put into effect the following year with the accession of King Prajadhipok. He had never been groomed for the throne, nor had he ever expected to accede or aspired to doing so. Prince Prajadhipok had spent most of his adult life in military schools—the Royal Military Academy at Woolwich in England and L'École Supérieure de Guerre in France—and had only returned to Siam in 1924. When his older brother died late the following year, he was at the top of the succession list and became Siam's last absolute monarch.[22]

Although the Palace Law on Succession worked in 1925, there remained some underlying problems. King Prajadhipok wrote in 1926 that the law still embodied the two distinct and rather contradictory principles that had long characterised succession in Siam: "the principle of election and the principle of hereditary succession".

For example, if the king did not designate his own successor, the throne was to go to one of his sons. King Prajadhipok remarked, "This sounded straightforward enough, but a complication arises here owing to the habit of polygamy." The law specified that the next king was to be chosen according to the rank of his mother, the queen. But there were four ranks of queen, and this arrangement was complicated by the fact that the rank of a queen could either be raised or lowered "according to the whims of the king". Thus several people could still make competitive claims to the throne. King Prajadhipok observed: "This, to my mind, creates very great possibilities of complications."[23]

In addition, King Prajadhipok (r. 1925–35) was not convinced that the flexibility in the law, which allowed for a monarch to choose a successor who would please the people, could be properly applied. In a letter to a confidant, he wrote [original emphasis]: "The king has absolute power in everything. This principle is very good and very suitable for the country, *as long as we have a good king.* If the king is really an elected king, it is probable that he would be a fairly good king. But this idea of election is really a very theoretical one, and in reality the king(s) of Siam are really hereditary, with a very limited possibility of choice. Such being the case, it is not at all certain that we shall always have a good king. Then the absolute power may become a positive danger to the country... Some sort of *guarantee* must be found against an unwise king."[24]

SUCCESSION DURING THE CONSTITUTIONAL ERA

With the introduction of Siam's first constitution in 1932, the king was placed within a constitutional framework. Many of the 18 constitutions that have followed since 1932 contain provisions concerning succession and all of them have affirmed that choosing an heir apparent is a prerogative of the king. In the absence of a designated heir, these constitutions generally left the question of succession up to the Privy Council or members of the royal family working under the 1924 Palace Law of Succession. For example, in 1935, when King Prajadhipok abdicated without designating an heir, the cabinet took five days to consider possible successors within the Royal House of Chakri bloodline before settling upon Prince Ananda Mahidol. This choice followed the 1924 Law of Succession and was also approved by the National Assembly.

No debate was needed when the unmarried young King Ananda (r. 1935–46) died unexpectedly on 9 June 1946. His younger brother, Prince Bhumibol Adulyadej, was the undisputed heir.

In a special night session on 9 June, the parliament unanimously endorsed the younger brother of King Ananda as the country's new king, according to the Palace Law governing succession.[25] The only question was whether he would accept the throne. At an audience attended by the prime minister and the cabinet, the prince was asked by his mother if he would accept. The king nodded. Told by his mother that he must state his acceptance, the young prince said "yes".

King Bhumibol designated Prince Vajiralongkorn as the heir apparent in 1972 when he invested him as the crown prince.[26] As an heir apparent has already been designated, the process of succession is clear and uncomplicated. Section 23 of the 2007 constitution, for instance, states: "In the case where the throne becomes vacant and the king has already appointed his heir to the throne under the Palace Law on Succession [1924], the Council of Ministers [cabinet] shall notify the president of the National Assembly. The president of the National Assembly shall convoke the National Assembly for acknowledgement thereof, and the president of the National Assembly shall invite such heir to ascend the throne and proclaim such heir as king."[27]

A more complicated situation arises if no heir apparent has been designated by the king. A number of Thai constitutions provided some limits on the Privy Council in such a situation. The first constitution of Siam, for instance, left the matter of succession to the parliament and candidates for king would be put up for a vote. Similarly, the 1949, 1952, 1968, 1974, 1978, 1997 and 2007 constitutions all specify that the name of a successor when no heir apparent has been designated must be brought before the parliament for approval. According to the 2007 constitution:[28] "In the case where the throne

Above *King Bhumibol and Queen Sirikit appear with Crown Prince Maha Vajiralongkorn on a balcony of the Ananta Samakhom Throne Hall on 2 December 1999, shortly ahead of national celebrations for the king's 72nd birthday.*

becomes vacant and the king has not appointed his heir under paragraph one, the Privy Council shall submit the name of the successor to the throne under section 22 to the Council of Ministers [cabinet] for further submission to the National Assembly for approval. For this purpose, the name of a princess may be submitted. Upon the approval of the National Assembly, the president of the National Assembly shall invite such successor to ascend the throne and proclaim such successor king."

Since 1974, all full constitutions have included a clause affirming that "the name of a princess may be submitted" (Sec. 23).[29] However, this inclusion is only significant when no heir apparent has been designated. In part, owing to this amendment, the Buddhist ideal of "election" and the lack of certainty regarding who would assume the throne during some previous successions, there remains a sustained belief, still prevalent in some quarters today, that the next succession is not entirely decided.

While the successions of all monarchs from the Royal House of Chakri involved a process of endorsement, in some form, involving either elder royals, the Privy Council or the national government, there is nothing uncertain about the next succession. As things stand in 2011, the cabinet will inform the president of parliament who will invite Crown Prince Maha Vajiralongkorn to become king.[30]

Above *The Bhudthan Thom Throne in the Chakri Maha Prasat Throne Hall at the Grand Palace in Bangkok.*

CEREMONIES AND REGALIA

The ceremonies, regalia, iconography and other trappings of the Royal House of Chakri play a vital role in projecting the institution of the monarchy—and form part of the kingdom's heritage and Thai national identity. Borrowing from Buddhist, Hindu and Brahman traditions, among others, many arcane rites, rituals and symbols date from the kingdoms of Sukhothai and Ayudhya. Others, such as anthems, have been adapted or created in more modern times.

ROYAL CEREMONIES

Coronation

Ancient India's *Mahabharata* describes a coronation in the Vedic era in which Hindu deities crowned the god Indra. In the Sukhothai era (c. 1249–1350), Brahman and Hindu elements were incorporated into the coronation of Maha Dhammaraja I to demonstrate the monarch's divine powers. Many such rites have remained relatively unchanged through the centuries. Rama I (r. 1782–1809) had two coronations. The second was painstakingly planned to replicate the traditions of the previous kingdom of Ayudhya (c. 1351–1767) and to revive a sense of community and continuity among the Siamese in the early years of the Royal House of

Chakri. King Mongkut (r. 1851–68) included many ancient traditions in his coronation, and allowed foreign observers to attend the grand audience given later that afternoon. The king wanted the outside world, particularly the West, to be aware of Siam's unique culture and heritage. In 1873, King Mongkut's son, King Chulalongkorn (r. 1868–1910) commanded those present at the grand audience following his coronation to stand up and bow, thereby curtailing the ancient practice of prostration.

In modern times, grand audiences take place to mark the king's birthday at the Grand Palace. The king is revealed from behind a golden curtain enthroned, and is offered eulogies by the crown prince, the prime minister and the president of the

Above *King Bhumibol on his coronation day in May 1950 sits upon the Noble Throne of Bhadrapith as he receives the Great Crown of Victory from the chief court Brahman.*

House of Representatives before delivering his own address to those assembled.

Thailand's last coronation took place on 5 May 1950 when King Bhumibol Adulyadej crowned himself at the Grand Palace. While many of the royal and religious traditions in the ancient ritual were shortened or simplified, it was still a model coronation ceremony. Two days earlier, King Bhumibol had paid homage to the relics of his predecessors in the reliquary hall, the Hor Phra Tat Monthien. The next morning, a gold name plate, a plaque with an astrological chart and two seals were brought in proces-

sion from the Chapel Royal, the Temple of the Emerald Buddha, to the Baisal Daksin Hall. The golden name plate was inscribed with the king's full name and titles. His astrological chart was inscribed on a sheet of gold measuring 17 by 31.5 cm and weighing 192.5 gm. The two seals, one official and one personal, were traditionally carved from solid ivory. The present-day official seal, however, is made of solid gold.

On the morning of his coronation, King Bhumibol participated in an ancient ablution ceremony of symbolic purification. The rites mixed Brahman and Buddhist traditions. The ceremony took place in a pavilion erected for the occasion next to the Amarindra Throne Hall. The king, wearing a white robe and a gold-trimmed cloth which left his right shoulder bare, sat beneath a suspended gilded lotus pod that showered him with lustral waters mixed from the five most sacred rivers of India, and five great rivers and four significant lakes of Thailand. The combined waters had been blessed by Buddhist monks. The supreme patriarch proceeded to pour water from special receptacles on King Bhumibol's back and hands. After this, the mixed lustral water was poured from diverse gourd-shaped urns on to the king's hands by Prince Rangsit of Jainad, followed by the chief court astrologer. The chief court Brahman poured more mixed lustral water from other sacred receptacles and shank shells over the king's hands. King Bhumibol received three bael leaves on a stalk from the chief court Brahman, which he placed behind his right ear. The grand master of the court then poured more mixed lustral water from a right-circling sacred shank shell, again over the hands of the king. This ritual concluded the ablution ceremony.

At the auspicious time of 11.30 am, King Bhumibol appeared in the Baisal Daksin Hall attired in traditional regal attire and wearing the Ancient and Auspicious Order of the Nine Gems and a heavy gold embroidered outer robe. He ascended the backless octagonal Athadish Throne centred beneath a seven-tiered White Umbrella of State. The grand marshal of the court presented a ceremonial receptacle for the king to receive the water of coronation from representatives of parliament. The water had been collected from important water sources in 18 provinces and had been blessed by Buddhist monks from the most important temple in each province before being sent to be mixed and again ritually blessed at the Chapel Royal, the Temple of the Emerald Buddha. Sitting upon the Athadish Throne while facing east, King Bhumibol received the water of coronation from a member of parliament alternating with the chief court Brahman

followed by a court Brahman, who presented consecrated water to the king as he faced towards all the remaining points of the compass. When King Bhumibol again sat facing east, the president of the Senate, speaking in Pali, invoked blessings upon the king. This was followed by the president of the House of Representatives who invoked blessings in Thai and presented the king with more coronation water. Speaking in Pali and Thai, the chief court Brahman then invited the king to receive a symbolic nine-tiered White Umbrella of State emblematic of the king's protection and supremacy over all his dominion. King Bhumibol descended from the Athadish Throne and entered the western side of the Baisal Daksin Hall and ascended the Noble Throne of Bhadrapith, which is made of ficus wood and surmounted by a nine-tiered Umbrella of State. The chief court Brahman then announced the opening of the portals of Kailas––inviting the god Shiva to descend into the king from Mount Kailas, a Himalayan mountain located in northwestern Tibet where the god Shiva is said to dwell. For Hindus and Buddhists, Mount Kailas is the mythical Mount Meru, a cosmic font of wisdom that can defeat all poisons. The priest then brought various regalia to King Bhumibol, including the Golden Tablet of Style and Title engraved with his title. The chief court Brahman presented the Great Crown of Victory, which King Bhumibol raised with both hands to place upon his own head—thereby crowning himself. The king was then presented with four more of the five key royal regalia, plus royal paraphernalia, utensils and weapons. King Bhumibol acknowledged each of the 27 items brought to him.

Speaking to the assembly as a fully crowned monarch for the first time, King Bhumibol proclaimed: "We shall reign with righteousness, for the benefit and happiness of the Siamese people." As a libation was poured, King Bhumibol made a silent vow to rule by the ten virtues of kingship. According to the Tenfold Practice of Ten Duties of King-ship detailed in an ancient Buddhist scripture, the

Above *The quintet of key royal regalia comprises, clockwise from top centre, the Great Crown of Victory; the Royal Staff; the Royal Fan and Whisks (combined as one); the upturned Royal Slippers; and the Great Sword of Victory.*

Suttanta Pitaka, these are: generosity, moral behaviour, self-sacrifice, honesty, gentleness, austerity, non-violence, tolerance, public welfare and freedom from hatred.

During the ablution ceremony and during the presentation of the crown and other royal regalia—paraphernalia, utensils and weapons—to mark the ceremony of coronation, Buddhist monks chanted victory stanzas, while court Brahmans, astrologers and officials blew conch shells, played two-faced drums, struck gilt-bronze victory drums, sounded gongs and blew trumpets. A Thai court orchestra played traditional music and the Royal Thai Army band played the royal anthem. A 21-gun salute was fired during both ceremonies. During the coronation ceremony the Royal Thai Army and the Royal Thai Navy each fired 101 gun salutes while Royal Thai Airforce planes sprinkled flowers around the precincts of the Grand Palace. At this time, all the temple bells throughout the kingdom were struck in unison for a total of seven rounds.

In the afternoon, the king reappeared wearing the Great Crown of Victory and his heavily embroidered robes of state. Enthroned in a semi-divine state in the Amarindra Throne Hall beneath a nine-tiered umbrella, King Bhumibol was revealed in a grand audience to the gathered assembly of members of the royal family and senior officials as a crowned king for the first time. The impressive gilded wooden throne sits high upon a multi-tiered base carved with angels and garudas.

After the audience, the king went to the Baisal Daksin Hall where he conducted a ceremony for Queen Sirikit, anointing her with lustral water and elevating her to the full rank and title of queen. Later that day, borne aloft on the same throne set upon a palanquin, the newly crowned king progressed to the Chapel Royal, the Temple of the Emerald Buddha, where he publicly affirmed his Buddhist faith. He then proceeded with Queen Sirikit to the Dusit Maha Prasat Hall to honour the reliquaries of earlier kings which had been specially brought out. On the evening of the following day, Buddhist monks came to bless his symbolic residence in the Grand Palace, where King Bhumibol spent his first night as a crowned monarch before moving to the Chitralada Villa of Dusit Palace, the royal couple's residence at the time.

Regalia

Royal regalia affirm the elevated status of the king and symbolically project his rights, duties and powers. They also embody important elements in a nation's traditions and heritage, and lend continuity between reigns. The key regalia of the Royal House of Chakri were adapted from ancient India's Brahman and Buddhist traditions, and evolved from the practices of earlier Southeast Asian kingdoms.

The ceremonial act of presenting pieces of regalia to a monarch dates back to India's Vedic era (c. 1200–500 BC). Those rituals, transmitted orally, were eventually written down around 300 BC in the sacred Hindu theological text, *Satapatha Brahmana*. The text describes how a Vedic priest gave a bow and three arrows to a new king so he could kill the god Indra's enemy, Vritra—a gigantic, thirsty serpent capable of causing droughts. India's Hindu epic, the *Ramayana*, was also written around the same time and refers to King Rama's axe and other royal items. A Buddhist Jataka tale tells of a Jain prince, Bharata, who takes "five emblems of royalty" which scholars identified as a sword, an umbrella, a crown, slippers and a fan.

The Dvaravati and Khmer empires, which flourished directly before the emergence of the first Siamese kingdom of Sukhothai, provided inspiration for early Siamese regalia. An inscription at Sukhothai's Wat Sri Chum reveals that a Khmer king of the later Angkorean era crowned Prince Pha Muang of Tak with a royal headpiece in the mid-13th century—one of the earliest mentions of regalia in Siam. The same king also gave Prince Pha Muang a sword of victory. One hundred years later, in 1347, Sukhothai's King Lithai from Si Satchanalai was crowned. A Wat Sri Chum inscription and illustration described his coronation as involving five ornaments: a sword, a crown, shoes, a staff and a fly whisk. Similar regalia appeared during the Ayudhya era from the 14th to 18th centuries.

By retaining ancient regalia, the Royal House of Chakri kings linked the new dynasty to the earlier Siamese kingdoms of Sukhothai and Ayudhya. The five key regalia remain the Great Crown of Victory, the Great Sword of Victory, the Royal Staff, the Royal Slippers and the Royal Fan and Whisks—the latter items are taken together as one. Virtually all of these were fashioned predominantly from gold by artisans in the reign of Rama I.

The Great Crown of Victory is worn only on coronation day. The royal court's chief Brahman presents the headpiece to the king, who crowns himself. This unusual practice stems from the Khmer concept of the *devaraja*—a divine king— whereby the monarch personifies Hinduism's four most powerful deities: Indra, ruler of the heavens; Brahma, the creator; Shiva, the destroyer; and Vishnu, the protector. By placing the Great Crown of Victory upon his own head, amid Brahmanic chants, a king confirms his symbolically elevated and unique status as the link between the heavenly and earthly realms.

The Great Crown of Victory has featured in all Chakri coronation ceremonies. Weighing 7.3 kg and 66 cm in height, it rises in four circular tiers of diminishing diameter. The crown is made of gold which, like Chakri kings, does not easily tarnish. Decorated with diamonds, rubies and enamel, the crown features small shimmering flowers of diamonds set in gold on springy stalks at the four compass points, which are marked with gold settings embellished with diamonds. Each flower is inlaid with five diamonds. The pagoda-shaped crown peaks in an elongated, central spire which holds at its zenith a large diamond—the Phra Maha Wichian Mani. This was placed there in the mid-19th century by King Mongkut, who had sent a mission to India's Kolkata (Calcutta) to obtain the great gem. The crown's tall, circular shape symbolises Hinduism's Mount Meru, the abode of the god Indra. The mountain is situated at the centre of the celestial universe, according to Hindu and Buddhist beliefs. With such a crown upon his head, each Chakri king is symbolically enthroned at the heart of the universe. On each side, the crown has two ornate flaps which rest behind the ears and sweep down towards the shoulders. These stylised decorative elements in the crown have their ancient origins in earrings and hanging flower garlands. A separate jewelled, golden cord acts as a chinstrap, and is knotted in a bow beneath the chin.

The Great Sword of Victory imbues kings with special powers at all times. The appearance of a sword in the hands of a royal warrior was mentioned in the *Mahavamsa* chronicles written by Buddhist monks between the 6th century BC and 4th century AD in ancient Sri Lanka. The text tells how a mythical *yakkhini* appeared as a female horse, attracting the attention of Pandukabhaya, who reigned from 437–367 BC and wanted to capture the horse. "He seized her by the mane and [grasped] a palm-leaf that was floating down the stream. By the effect of his merit, this turned into a great sword ... She said to him: 'I shall conquer the kingdom and give it to thee, Lord! Slay me not!' Then he seized her by the neck and, boring her nostrils with the point of his sword, he secured her thus with a rope."

A sword was also among several objects which India's Emperor Ashoka presented to Sri Lanka's King Tissa over 2,200 years ago. The same Sukhothai-era inscription at Wat Sri Chum reveals that when the Khmer king crowned Prince Pha Muang of Tak, the Khmer ruler presented a sword at the coronation. A royal sword also appeared among regalia a century later when King Lithai from Si Satchanalai was crowned in Sukhothai—according to the same temple's ancient inscriptions.

The Great Sword of Victory is purely ceremonial and has never been used in war. It has a bevelled double-edged blade that is broadest towards the sharp tip and tapers in the Siamese style towards the handle. The double edge enables the monarch to defend the kingdom from internal and external threats. The sword was recovered from a lake in Pattabong in 1783 at the start of Rama I's reign. To contain the 64.5-cm-long blade, Rama I commanded that an ornate scabbard be created and a tapering, gold-and-enamel handle 28.4 cm in length be fashioned. The blade's waist above the handle has golden inlay depicting Vishnu, Rama and Indra, and a half-man, half-bird garuda. Sheathed, the entire piece is slightly more than a metre in length.

The Royal Staff is a long, slender rod made of cassia wood sheathed in gold sheet. A metal knob, inlaid with gold, sits at its top. Branching out from the staff's lower tip is a gold claw, comprising three small prongs—the same number of points on the flatter trident held by Shiva. Chakri monarchs use the staff to show their intention to reign correctly—walking along a straight path with unwavering justice and purpose.

Some historians consider royal staffs as akin to royal sceptres elsewhere. Whatever they are called—staffs, walking sticks, sceptres, canes—they have been linked to royalty throughout the ages. For example, in the late 1600s, the king of Sri Lanka had a small, multi-coloured cane which featured precious stones at its lowest end and was topped off with a golden knob.

King Bhumibol and earlier Chakri kings only wear the golden Royal Slippers during the coronation ceremony. The uppers are topped with diamond-studded enamelled gold and have pointed, upturned toes—said to be inspired by shoes from ancient India. The soft, faded slippers are lined with red velvet. They weigh 650 gm and date back thousands of years. The *Ramayana* mentions Rama's magical slippers, which he removed to give to Prince Bharata in the Indian kingdom of Benares. "For three years the slippers ruled the kingdom. The courtiers placed these straw slippers upon the royal throne

Above *The golden Royal Slippers with upturned toes.*

when they judged a cause. If the cause were decided wrongly, the slippers beat upon each other, and at that sign it was examined again. When the decision was right, the slippers lay quiet."

The Chakri dynasty's five main objects of regalia are rounded out with the Royal Fan and Whisks. One whisk is made from a yak tail and the other with hairs from the tip of a white elephant's tail. Fans and whisks appear throughout Southeast Asian history. For example, stone bas-reliefs at Java's 9th-century Borobodur temple complex and Cambodia's 12th-century Angkor Wat portray their ceremonial use around royalty.

The fan handles are slightly curved and topped with a gilded talipot palm leaf blade trimmed into an oval shape. The large leaf, its outer frame and the handle's shaft are all covered with enamelled gold. The joint, where the fan's handle secures the leaf, is colourfully decorated with gold, red, green, white and blue *rajawadi* enamelling. A lace pattern of small diamonds encircles the handle's shaft. The original yak hair whisk dates from the coronation of Rama I. King Mongkut added the second, reasoning that hair from a white elephant's tail was more appropriate than anything deriving from yaks, which are not native to Siam. Both Rama I's whisk and King Mongkut's are used in all royal coronations. These are the only items among the original five main regalia to have been updated in the past two centuries. All of the Royal House of Chakri regalia are kept in the Chakrabarti Bhiman Hall of the Grand Palace. The five most important pieces of regalia are venerated each year on the anniversary of Coronation Day.

Marriage

The concept of a Thai king having only one queen is a modern phenomenon. Even in the early 20th century, it was normal practice for a Siamese monarch to have many wives. Apart from helping secure successions, the custom enabled kings to form alliances with powerful families, many of whom offered their daughters to the monarchs. If he wished, a king could elevate a consort to the rank of queen. Siamese kings traditionally had multiple queens, consorts and other wives. They lived in an inner part of the palace that could only be entered by women and children, and were waited upon exclusively by their female servants.

King Vajiravudh (r. 1910–25) had a number of marriages during his reign. One of his wives, a commoner named Prueng Sucharitkul, was elevated to be Phra Sucharitsuda, the chief consort. As his bride, she dressed in Western style. This was the first royal wedding in Siam to feature such attire. In 1917, Prince Prajadhipok, the future king (r. 1925–35), signed a palace registry and had his wedding witnessed—as was normal. He personally believed in monogamy, but could legally have had multiple wives had he so chosen. In 1930, certificates were introduced for all marriages and divorces.

King Bhumibol continued with the precedent of monogamy set by his uncle, King Prajadhipok. In a simple ceremony on 28 April 1950 presided over by his paternal grandmother Queen Savang Vadhana at Srapatum Palace, the king married 17-year-old Mom Rajawongse Sirikit Kitiyakara. Queen Savang Vadhana poured lustral water and then anointed the couple during the simple ceremony, and the newlyweds signed two identical marriage registers specially made for the occasion by the Ministry of Interior. Each book was covered with yellow lambskin, embossed with the royal standard and a red royal garuda with gold lettering, and had a brown leather spine. The customary fee of 10 baht and 10 satang as required for the civil ceremony of the day was paid. King Bhumibol then bestowed the title of queen upon his young wife.

Barge Processions

Royal progresses traditionally were made on land upon an open palanquin, and on water by barge. These processions were rare occasions when the public had the opportunity to witness the majesty of their kings, and were thus accordingly grand.

The former capital at Ayudhya was set amid a network of canals at the confluence of three rivers. Royal barges essentially constituted the ancient navy. King Maha Chakkraphat (r. 1548–69) employed barges in wars against the Burmese, and installed cannon and animal figureheads on the larger vessels. The main barges were used for ceremonial purposes, such as welcoming foreign officials. In the time of King Narai (r. 1656–88), grand waterborne processions were frequent and could involve as many as 147 gilded vessels. The war barges in the royal fleet were sometimes used for racing. In 1767, Ayudhya hosted barge races between the king's barge, the queen's barge and those of several nobles. Fortune tellers claimed that if the king lost, his kingdom would enjoy prosperity. If his barge was victorious, calamity and famine would strike. Whatever the outcome of the race that year, the Burmese invasion resulted in the sacking of the old Thai capital at Ayudhya and the destruction of 400 ceremonial and war barges.

Rama I progressed by barge around Bangkok along the Chao Phraya river and various canals. King Vajiravudh and King Prajadhipok used royal barges in their coronation ceremonies. During the Second World War, the barges were damaged in allied bombing raids. In May 1957, the first, post-war royal barge procession was staged, with royal permission, by the government to mark the 2,500th anniversary of the Buddhist era. King Bhumibol did not participate in it.

In 1960, King Bhumibol began travelling in a royal barge procession down the Chao Phraya to Wat Arun, the Temple of Dawn, as part of the annual Royal Kathin Ceremony when he presented robes to senior monks. By doing so, he affirmed his commitment to Buddhism in a grand spectacle visible to the public. After 1967, despite their popularity, the processions were discontinued for 15 years before being staged again during the 1982 Bangkok bicentennial celebration at the

Above *The great Suphannahong (Golden Swan) Royal Barge, left, was first used in 1912 by King Vajiravudh. The Ananta Nagaraj Royal Barge is drawn up alongside on the Chao Phraya river.*

government's request. Royal barge processions are still only held on special occasions. In 1996, to mark the king's 50th year on the throne, a new Narai Song Suban royal barge was constructed for King Bhumibol's riverine procession to present *kathin* robes. The ancient fleet included 52 barges powered by 2,082 men from the Royal Thai Navy.

In 1999, a flotilla of barges to Wat Arun was a high point in celebrations marking King Bhumibol's 72nd birthday and completion of his sixth 12-year cycle. The 1999 procession included 52 barges, with the king riding on the Suphannahong, or Golden Swan—a barge first used by King Vajiravudh in 1912. The huge swan-like vessel replaced a barge from the reign of Rama I. It was carved from the trunk of a single massive *takhian* tree, a particularly hard tropical hardwood known as ironwood in English. Softer golden teak is also used in the construction of the ornate prows of these vessels. The god Brahma's steed is a *hong*—the Thai rendering of the Sanskrit word *hamsa*, a mythical swan. In October 2003, a magnificent royal barge procession was

held, with royal permission, during the Asia-Pacific Economic Cooperation (APEC) forum. Guests from 21 Pacific Rim countries attended. Three years later, in 2006, celebrations for the 60th anniversary of King Bhumibol's accession included a royal barge procession. Members of virtually all of the world's reigning royal families attended, along with other leaders and dignitaries who had arrived in Bangkok for the celebrations.

Significant Days

Most Thai public holidays honour significant events in the Chakri dynasty or the life of the Buddha, and typically are marked with special royal rites. Chakri Day on 6 April commemorates the founding of the dynasty on that day in 1782; Coronation Day, introduced by King Mongkut to match a similar event held by European royalty, is currently celebrated on 5 May, the date of King Bhumibol's coronation; and Chulalongkorn Day commemorates the death of King Chulalongkorn on 23 October 1910. On that day each year, thousands of people gather to pay respects at an equestrian statue of the former king by French sculptor George Saulo at the Royal Plaza in front of the Ananta Samakhom Throne Hall.

King Bhumibol and Queen Sirikit's birthdays are celebrated nationally on 5 December and 12 August respectively. Ancient Siam did not have a tradition of celebrating birthdays. In the mid-1800s, King Mongkut was inspired to follow some of the practices of other nations, and this included marking his own birthday. By the time King Chulalongkorn had acceded, royal birthdays were marked in an increasingly splendid manner, including the illumination of Bangkok's main streets and sites. These celebrations became grand spectacles. King Bhumibol's reign has seen the most elaborate and lavish displays organised by the government, and celebrations spread over several days. His birthday is also Father's Day in Thailand while Queen Sirikit's is Mother's Day. Other holidays mark significant dates on the Buddhist calendar such as Khao Phansa, the traditional start to the rainy season when all monks are expected to return to their temples for the Buddhist Lent, or "rains retreat".

The king presides over many other ceremonies throughout the year that do not involve public holidays but are nevertheless significant. For example, the national contributions by earlier Thai kings such as King Naresuan and King Taksin, are commemorated. Three times a year, the king or the crown prince changes the robes adorning the Emerald Buddha, the most revered Buddha image in the kingdom and the Royal House of Chakri's palladium. In May, to provide guidance to farmers for their upcoming season of rice planting, King Bhumibol presides over the Royal Ploughing Ceremony. This Hindu agricultural ceremony dates back more than 2,000 years and became popular among Buddhists in the Sukhothai era. The seeds are blessed ahead of the ceremony on Sanam Luang nearby at the Chapel Royal, the Temple of the Emerald Buddha. This practice was introduced by King Mongkut who was keen to introduce more Buddhist elements into the proceedings. According to the Buddhist concept of kingship, monarchs are responsible for the progression of the seasons, the soil's fertility and the productivity of crops. When the Royal Ploughing Ceremony concludes, there is a mad dash to collect as many of the sacred royal seeds as possible to take back to the countryside. A similar ceremony has also been revived in Cambodia in recent years.

Three days before his birthday, King Bhumibol takes the salute at the annual Trooping of the Colours. Battalions drawn from six regiments of the Royal Guards parade in brightly coloured uniforms at the Royal Plaza and reaffirm their oath of loyalty to the king in the presence of the royal family and other dignitaries. The ceremony can be traced back to an oath of allegiance taken by troops in the Ayudhya era. At that time, the event was held in Wat Phra Sri Sanphet or Wat Mongkhon Bophit as the ceremony was considered sacred. According to Palace Law, any member of the court who missed the ceremony was sentenced to death. Later, the punishment was eliminated, but the oath was retained by Rama I. Members of the extended royal family, military officers, court officials and some civil servants were expected to take the oath.

Milestones and Celebrations

During the exceptionally long reign of King Bhumibol, numerous special anniversaries and milestones have been celebrated. King Chulalongkorn provided a model in 1893 for later celebrations with the silver jubilee of his accession. There were also public celebrations in 1908 marking the 40th anniversary. Seventy-eight years after King Chulalongkorn, King Bhumibol celebrated his own silver jubilee in June 1971. The king cast two Buddha images—one for his reign and one to present to Wat Bovornives—and initiated construction of Ratchadaphisek Road, a ring road for the capital. Commemorative stamps and coins were specially issued by the post office and royal mint. King Bhumibol also honoured his ancestors in ceremonies and presided over a special military parade on Ratchadamnoen Avenue.

Other significant national celebrations were held when King Bhumibol turned 50 on 5 December 1977, and for the Rattanakosin Bicentennial in 1982, the 200th anniversary of the founding of the Royal House of Chakri and of Bangkok as the country's capital. There were also celebrations for King Bhumibol on 7 January 1985 when he attained the same age as his grandfather, King Chulalongkorn, who was 57 years and 33 days old when he died. The ceremonies honoured King Chulalongkorn's life and work for the nation.

Many Asians regard birthdays that mark the completion of a 12-year cycle as particularly auspicious. The most important of these is the 60th birthday at the end of the fifth cycle. King Bhumibol's fifth-cycle anniversary in 1987 was a major event celebrated across the kingdom. Ceremonies lasting several weeks included a royal barge procession.

On 2 July 1988, King Bhumibol had been on the throne longer than any previous monarch in the kingdom's history, again matching an achievement of his grandfather King Chulalongkorn. To mark 42 years and 23 days on the throne, three days of celebration included Buddhist and other ceremonies at or close to the Grand Palace. A special ceremony to pay homage to ancestors was held in a three-balconied pavilion in Ayudhya province that had been used by King Chulalongkorn for the same purpose when he surpassed the 40-year reign of a king in the former capital, Ayudhya.

Over the ensuing decades, King Bhumibol passed new milestones that were widely celebrated. At the reign's 50th anniversary in 1996, the kingdom's first ever golden jubilee was staged. The king bestowed another royal title on his late brother, King Ananda, and a golden jubilee pavilion was erected at Sanam Luang where the king and queen venerated past monarchs and received blessings. Live performances and fireworks were held to entertain the public, and a holiday was declared. In June, the Supreme Command mobilised Thailand's biggest-ever military parade, with 4,000 troops, 600 vehicles and 24 aircraft. Britain's Queen Elizabeth II and Prince Philip arrived in October after expressing a particular desire to visit. US President Bill Clinton made a state visit in November, the first since President Richard Nixon's in 1969. There was also a royal barge procession in November. In 1999, King Bhumibol reached 72, completing his sixth 12-year cycle. The king's 60th year on the throne in 2006 was marked by almost a week of celebrations and an immense outpouring of popular emotion. Tens of thousands of Thais gathered in front of the Ananta Samakhom Throne Hall on 9 June. The king appeared on a balcony, and gazed out at the massive gathering of people. Most of them wore yellow, which is the colour of the Royal House of Chakri and also symbolises Monday—King Bhumibol's day of birth. Foreign kings, queens and royalty from 25 other dynasties attended the events in Bangkok, which included fireworks, a royal barge procession and a state banquet.

ROYAL INFRASTRUCTURE

The Grand Palace

Construction of the Grand Palace commenced in 1782 with the founding of the Royal House of Chakri. It included the Chapel Royal, the Temple of the Emerald Buddha—the only temple in the kingdom with no monks in residence. Throughout the period of absolute monarchy, the palace served as the secular and religious heart of Siam. It was the official main residence for the Chakri kings—although they have actually lived elsewhere in the latter four reigns. The Grand Palace was created as a separate royal precinct protected by 1,900 metres of solid castellated walls with gates and guard towers.

King Chulalongkorn was the first Chakri king to reside outside the Grand Palace. He built the teakwood Vimanmek Mansion residence in 1901, a few kilometres away, and later the Ambara Mansion. King Prajadhipok lived at Sukhothai Palace before his accession, and moved to Ambara Mansion during his reign. Later, King Bhumibol and his family lived in Chitralada Villa, which is part of Dusit Palace. The Grand Palace remains the venue for many royal ceremonies, including coronations and royal anniversary celebrations. In recent decades, it has also become one of the kingdom's most popular tourist sites.

Among the most important buildings at the Grand Palace is the Chakri Maha Prasat Hall, which was erected in 1882 by King Chulalongkorn to mark the centenary of the Royal House of Chakri and designed by British architect John Chinitz. The relics of several Chakri kings and family members are kept in this building in two locations. In the middle of the hall are the relics of King Mongkut and Queen Debsirindra, and King Chulalongkorn, Queen Saovabha Phongsri and Queen Savang Vadhana. The site also houses the reliquaries of King Vajiravudh, King Prajadhipok, King Ananda, Queen Rambhai Barni, Prince Mahidol, Princess Srinagarindra and Princess Galyani Vadhana. The west side of the Chakri Maha Prasat Hall houses the reliquaries of other queens and the sons of previous kings with the rank of chao fa.

The Chakri Maha Prasat Hall has been the scene of many royal audiences given to diplomats, foreign royalty and other honoured guests. It houses the gold-niello Bhudthan Throne, which is no longer used, beneath a nine-tiered umbrella. The paintings hanging on the throne hall's walls depict Siamese diplomatic initiatives, such as King Louis XIV of France welcoming King Narai's ambassador at Versailles, and King Mongkut's ambassador being received in audience by Queen Victoria at Windsor

Castle. One depicts King Mongkut's ambassador meeting Emperor Napoleon III at Fontainebleau, and another the second French embassy to Siam in the reign of King Mongkut.

The Chakri Maha Prasat Hall is linked to the Mulsathan Borom Asana Hall, where other receptions are held. Guests are sometimes invited to dine in the stately Boromrajasathitmaholarn Hall, where the king or other members of the royal family propose toasts and give speeches during large banquets. These halls and chambers are linked to the Sommuti Dhevaraj Uppabat Hall, which is occasionally used for private audiences among members of the royal family and smaller gatherings.

Next to the Chakri Maha Prasat Hall, on the right side of the building, is the elegant Dusit Throne Hall. It replaced the Amarindra Pisek Thone Hall in 1789 which had burnt down after being struck by lightning. Its Ayudhya-influenced architecture features a tiered mondop-style roof. The early Rattanakosin-style spired roof symbolises Mount Meru, and creates an impressive silhouette. Rama I's teak throne, inlaid with mother-of-pearl, is kept inside under its own nine-tiered umbrella. Formerly used each year for Coronation Day rites, the Dusit Maha Prasat Hall has been used for lying-in-state ceremonies for deceased royalty, including Chakri kings beginning with Rama I. For this reason, the hall is never used for audiences.

Nearby, the small Aphonphimok Pavilion was built by King Mongkut as a disrobing area. It has mounting platforms, enabling a king to arrive and depart by palanquin. King Chulalongkorn liked its exquisite decor and classic Thai design so much that he built a replica at Bang Pa-in Palace near Ayudhya. In 1958, a replica of the Aphonphimok Pavilion was displayed at the Brussels Exposition.

To the left side of the Chakri Maha Prasat Hall stands the cluster of Phra Maha Monthien buildings, including the important Amarindra Throne Hall, built in the 18th century. This houses Rama I's boat-shaped, wooden Busabok Throne. The throne later became an altar for Buddha images, positioned

Above *The Grand Palace in Bangkok is now a major tourist attraction.*

behind the new throne beneath a nine-tiered Umbrella of State. Every Chakri monarch has used the Amarindra Throne Hall for important royal and state occasions, including coronations and formal appearances. An entrance to be used only by the king, queen and their children leads from the Amarindra Throne Hall to the Baisal Daksin Hall, an inner audience chamber used for coronations and decorated with murals depicting heavenly Hindu scenes. The hall was built not long after the Royal House of Chakri was founded in 1782 by Rama I, who died there in 1809.

Before King Vajiravudh's reign, the Chakri dynasty's royal womenfolk lived in the Grand Palace's female-only Inner Court area. Kings were the only adult males able to enter. Special rules applied, and it had its own entirely female police force. The inner area was originally cramped with wooden buildings, but Victorian-style residences were later built in brick. The Inner Court's residents included the king's unmarried daughters, as well as his sisters and unmarried aunts, surviving widows of his father and his *chao chom marnda* (wives who had borne him a child) and their infants. These women lived in separate households, each with their own ladies-in-waiting and female servants. Boys would have to leave the Inner Court after their top-knots were cut in a rite of tonsure at about the age of 11.

During King Bhumibol's reign, the Inner Court's Suan Kularb School was revived by Princess Sirindhorn as a kindergarten and to teach courtly crafts such as garland making, fruit carving, embroidery, cooking and perfume mixing, ancient skills that were once highly regarded. In King Chulalongkorn's reign, they were taught at Suan

Kularb, the original Royal Pages School, which had been installed in a former residence.

In a separate, walled-off area of the Grand Palace stands the magnificent Chapel Royal, the Temple of the Emerald Buddha. Its outer walls are illustrated with 178 panels portraying the *Ramakien* epic. This tale was adapted into Siamese from India's *Ramayana* in the late 18th century, during the first decades of the Royal House of Chakri. The panels encompass several buildings, including the Chapel Royal, which houses the Chakri dynasty's jade palladium image, the Emerald Buddha. Ancient accounts and legends speculate that the Buddha image's origins lie in West Asia, but it was officially discovered in 1434 in modern-day Chiang Rai when lightning struck an old chedi, revealing the statue beneath crumbling masonry. The Emerald Buddha was kept in Lampang and Chiang Mai, in modern-day northern Thailand, before being taken to Luang

Above *The Emerald Buddha in the Chapel Royal, Temple of the Emerald Buddha, at the Grand Palace in Bangkok.*

Prabang and ending up in Vientiane in 1564, where it remained until 1778, when Chao Phraya Chakri, the general and future Rama I, sacked the city. He brought the revered image back to the capital in Thon Buri to present to King Taksin. In 1784, two years after becoming king, Rama I had the Emerald Buddha brought across the Chao Phraya river to his new capital of Bangkok. The compound of the Chapel Royal, Temple of the Emerald Buddha, also contains the Hor Phra Nak, where the relics of royal children below the rank of *chao fa* are kept. The bell-shaped Phra Sri Rattana Chedi, built by King Mongkut, is said to contain a piece of the Buddha's chest bone. The temple contains other chapels, scripture halls and libraries of palm leaf scriptures. In the Prasat Phra Thep Bidon, a pantheon of life-size bronze statues depict the first eight Chakri monarchs.

Rama I displayed his great satisfaction with the Grand Palace when he gave Bangkok its official full title, which was later edited by King Mongkut: Krung Thep Mahanakhon Amon Rattanakosin Mahinthara Yuthaya Mahadilok Phop Noppharat Ratchathani Burirom Udomratchaniwet Mahasathan Amon Piman Awatan Sathit Sakkathattiya Vishnukam Prasit. The title can be translated as: "City of angels, the great city, the eternal jewel city, the impregnable city of God Indra, the grand capital of the world endowed with nine precious gems, the happy city, abounding in an enormous royal palace that resembles the heavenly abode where reigns the reincarnated god, a city built by Vishnukam according to Indra's command."

Bureau of the Royal Household

In the mid-14th century, King U Thong created a system to administrate his increasingly complex royal affairs. It was based on four sections: Krom Mueng, to ensure law and order were maintained among his subjects; Krom Wang, to adjudicate through various courts of law; Krom Klang, to keep accounts and run the kingdom's finances; and Krom Na, to provide oversight for agricultural production and the storage of food throughout the country. Later, during King Trailok's reign, two more departments were added to oversee the kingdom's southern and northern regions. This administrative system remained in place up until 1892 when King Chulalongkorn restructured the divisions into a dozen *krasuang*, or ministries. Each had a minister, most of whom were members of the royal family. The 1892 ministries were closely modelled on those of European governments, and even employed some European civil servants. In 1935, the government unveiled the new constitutional monarch's administrative system, which had a much reduced status as the Bureau of the Royal Household directly under the prime minister. As its workload gradually increased, it was brought more in line with the needs of a modern constitutional monarchy. After restructuring, a 1966 royal decree proclaimed ten divisions that reflected the growing and diversified requirements of modern Thailand's monarchy: the Secretariat Office; Royal Residences Division; Administrative Division; Treasury Division; Royal Pages Division; Palace Division; Ceremonies Division; Royal Staff Division; Royal Doctors Division; Royal Vehicles Division; Arts and Architecture Division; and the Privy Purse. An additional division was created in 1986: Crown Prince Maha Vajiralongkorn's Personal Affairs Division. In 1987, the Personnel Division and Palace Grounds Division were added. The most recent addition was King Bhumibol's Personal Affairs Division in 1998.

Office of His Majesty's Principal Private Secretary

King Chulalongkorn established a Royal Secretary Department to assist him with various written tasks, including communiqués, correspondence and confirmations. It later became known as the Office of His Majesty's Principal Private Secretary. Today, among other things, the office enables King Bhumibol to respond to the numerous letters he receives from people and organisations that ask for royal permissions, donations, recommendations, pardons and other assistance. The office also ensures that the king's speeches and other statements reach the intended recipients.

At its core, the Central Division and the King's Personal Affairs Division are concerned with private matters, individual requirements and overall planning. The Queen's Personal Affairs Division mirrors these functions. A separate Foreign Affairs Division deals with the monarch's state visits and foreign affairs both abroad and in Thailand, including ambassadors presenting their credentials. The Information Division enables the media to receive images of the royal family and information, and gain access to royal events. The Secretariat Office of the Privy Councillors coordinates with the Privy Council. The Legal Division oversees technical details concerning the workings of a constitutional monarchy. The Inter-Projects Relations Division ensures royal projects run without overlapping. Three Personal Affairs Division offices are assigned to Princess Sirindhorn, Princess Chulabhorn and Princess Soamsavali. The Administrative Division, Information Centre and Queen Sirikit Institute also assist the royal family with projects, displays and events designed for large public audiences.

Royal Gazette

Early Siamese kings employed court officials to announce new laws and other royal edicts at certain public places. Before printing presses were widely available, much had to be laboriously copied by hand, causing confusion through misspellings, poor handwriting and other lapses. In 1839, during Rama III's reign, an American missionary set up a printing house in Bangkok. Among its first publications in 1839 were 9,000 copies of the king's Decree Forbidding Opium Smoking and Sale. Later, King Mongkut, delighted by a printing press he himself had set up at Wat Bovornives while a monk, established a printing house inside the Grand Palace. It produced the *Royal Gazette* which contained various announcements and royal news for officials and the public. The first issue in 1858 was free. The Royal Command which announced the first *Royal Gazette* said the publication was needed because "forged documents, under [royal] seal and notices, are sometimes manufactured by the unscrupulous in the name of His Majesty ... as instruments of unjust extortion, thereby causing popular grievances as well as the loss of prestige on the part of the king ..."

After a shaky start, the *Royal Gazette* underwent an expansion during King Chulalongkorn's reign and by 1874 was published weekly with an annual subscription costing eight baht. It reported official promotions, appointments among the Buddhist clergy, significant births and deaths, and included weather information for farmers. Some foreign news was also included.

King Vajiravudh expanded the *Royal Gazette* to include laws, royal commands, news of royal ceremonies, company registrations and other developments of note. During the constitutional era, government bills passed as acts of parliament and signed by the king became law only after they had been published in the *Royal Gazette*. During King Bhumibol's reign, the *Royal Gazette* became an essential source for Thai and international investors, lawyers, consultants and others, for updates about laws, taxes, stock market rules, requirements for bidding on government contracts and other business-related information. The *Royal Gazette* remains a public document and is currently published by the Office of the Prime Minister.

Brahmans and Court Astrologers

Since ancient times, royalty in Asia have employed Brahman priests to organise and conduct important ceremonies as representatives of Brahma, a supreme god. In India, even before the Hindu religion emerged, Brahman priests provided ceremonial interpretations of Brahma's prescriptions for kingly acts. Brahmans are believed to have first migrated to Southeast Asia from India in the 5th and 6th centuries. By the time kings began ascending their various thrones in ancient Siam, Brahman rites had already been codified and passed on by Khmers and others to the country. The Chakri kings incorporated Brahman traditions into the major rites of passage, including coronations, cremations and ceremonies to honour ancestors. Brahman priests have always been rewarded by Siamese monarchs. Rama I, for example, built a small Brahman temple in 1784. King Chulalongkorn once noted that coronations should only be conducted by Brahmans.

"It will be sinful and cursed if conducted by others," he said. "Only the Brahmans can hold the king up on the throne. The king cannot go up there by himself. The Brahmans must present all ceremonial objects to the king and announce the king's honour and be the first to accept the king's first order."

After absolute monarchy ended in 1932, the Department of Brahman Ceremonies and the court astrologers were disbanded. The Royal Court Ministry was abolished and replaced with a bureau. This reduced the number of Brahmans connected to the palace, and also led to the cancellation of many ceremonies. When King Bhumibol sought to revive neglected Brahman rituals, it became clear that few people still knew how to conduct them or really understood the symbolism.

Thailand has only one Brahman temple—the Dhevasathan, or Bot Brahman in Thai—which all of the kingdom's handful of Brahmans regard as their spiritual headquarters. It stands next to the Giant Swing, which Rama I erected in 1794 to honour Shiva. The Brahmans of Thailand have lived in the country in an unbroken line through the generations. A Brahman priest must be the son of a priest—a requirement that greatly limits the number of candidates. The royal court's present chief Brahman is known as Phra Rajaguru

Above *Brahman priests perform rites at Sanam Luang during the annual Royal Ploughing Ceremony, which is held each May.*

Vamadevamuni, as was his father.

Astrology has played a major role in royal life since ancient times. Court astrologers produced horoscopes for Chakri kings, and fixed dates for many rituals according to the lunar calendar.

Brahman priests and court astrologers are maintained as part of the nation's cultural heritage. The Bureau of the Royal Household's Ceremony Division has a department which employs 12 priests and 13 astrologers.

RANKS, TITLES AND DECORATIONS

The title Rama has always been a part of the full titles of Chakri monarchs. The title recalls ancient India's King Rama who ruled the kingdom of Ayodhya. The Siamese capital of the same name hailed its first ruler as King Ramathibodi, Rama the Lord (r. 1351–69). King Vajiravudh introduced the system of numbering the Chakri kings by declaring himself Rama VI—and retrospectively renaming his ancestors. The founder of the dynasty was Rama I, and King Bhumibol is Rama IX. This form exists only in English and was unknown before the 1920s. King Vajiravudh's innovation was in some part made in the interests of clarity for foreigners. Prior to Rama III's reign, kings and elders were not referred to by personal names. When people wished to speak of the first Chakri king, they said, "His Majesty of the first reign." The next king was "His Majesty of the middle reign." Rama III was the "His Majesty of the present reign." With each successive reign, such references become more unwieldy.

In general, members of the royal family automatically receive their titles at birth and these titles denote their relationship to the king. Marriage does not automatically bestow a husband's rank on his wife. If a prince weds a royal woman, she remains at the rank she was born into. A female commoner, however, receives the courtesy title of *mom* when she becomes a prince's wife. The king, however, can exercise his own discretion and award titles to anyone he deems worthy.

Titles have been awarded by Chakri kings to various queens, consorts, royal family members and commoners as part of a seniority system that can be traced much further back to the mid-16th century. Over the centuries, these titles have created a complicated royal hierarchy. This became even more tangled and confusing when individuals received more than one title, new ranks were created or ranks were eliminated. Indeed, the Thai system of ranks and titles became so complicated, King Chulalongkorn wrote a treatise on the subject.

"It was hard to tell which was higher than which," King Chulalongkorn admitted, as he scrutinised the rankings during his reign. To clarify all the titles at birth, titles indicating family relationships, and titles bestowed by royal discretion, the king published *Thai Titles and Ranks with the Traditions of Royal Lineage in Siam*. Intricate Siamese titles created confusion when couples travelled abroad, even in modern times.

In the Royal House of Chakri, the most important royal ranks below the king are:

Somdet phra nang chao phra barom rajini. This title is given to a queen or royal consort. In Siam, a woman did not have to be born into royalty to become a queen, or *rajini*. She also did not have to be the king's first wife. On the other hand, marriage to a monarch did not automatically make a woman queen. The king had to elevate her to the rank. On occasions, a wife was elevated to the rank of queen after producing the king's highest-ranking son. A foreign woman could not become a queen.

King Chulalongkorn chose the title *somdet phra nang chao*, which he posthumously bestowed upon his beloved consort, Sunanda Kumariratana, who drowned in a boating accident. In 1881, when she was cremated, the grieving King Chulalongkorn posthumously added another rank by adding *barom* to her title, so she became Somdet Phra Nang Chao Sunanda Kumariratana Phra Barom Raja Devi. Affirming her new status in English, King Chulalongkorn wrote to the British consul in Bangkok and said she was to be described as a queen, and not as a princess. The king later elevated Phra Nang Chao Savang Vadhana to be the kingdom's first living *somdet phra nang chao*, after the birth of Crown Prince Maha Vajirunhis (1878–95). Her full title and name was Somdet Phra Nang Chao Savang Vadhana Phra Barom Raja Devi, and she was officially described in English as Her Majesty the Queen. After the death of Prince Vajirunhis, who was Siam's first crown prince, his half-brother Prince Vajiravudh (1881–1925) became crown prince, succeeding his father to the throne in 1910. Prince Vajiravudh's mother, Queen Saovabha Phongsri, the younger sister of Queen Savang Vadhana, became first queen following the elevation of her son, and was titled Somdet Phra Nang Chao Saovabha Phongsri Phra Barom Raja Devi.

In 1897, when King Chulalongkorn was preparing for his first visit to Europe, he elevated Queen Saovabha Phongsri with two new titles simultaneously. She was raised to be *phra barom rajini* as the mother of the new crown prince. The king also added the word *nat* to her title since she would act as regent during his time abroad. She became Somdet Phra Nang Chao Saovabha Phongsri Phra Barom Rajini Nat.

The longer title, *somdet phra nang chao* followed by *phra barom rajini*—without the *nat*—became the usual title for a queen during subsequent reigns. A queen regent was higher than a queen because she enjoyed amplified powers while ruling in a king's absence. In 1956, a transfer of duties to a queen regent occurred again when King Bhumibol appointed Queen Sirikit as his regent for the 15

Above *King Chulalongkorn poses with ten of his children from among his 32 sons and 45 daughters. In the middle behind the king and wearing a hat is Prince Mahidol, the father of King Bhumibol.*

days when he was ordained as a monk. After King Bhumibol emerged from the temple, Queen Sirikit's rank and title were elevated.

The title *somdet phra barom* became an extra part of an existing rank for certain high royalty who were entitled to possess a seven-tiered umbrella, which is one level lower than the king's nine-tiered umbrella. In King Bhumibol's family, four members have had this rank: Queen Sirikit, Princess Srinagarindra, Crown Prince Maha Vajiralongkorn and Princess Maha Chakri Sirindhorn. In 1970, the princess mother was elevated to the title of *somdet phra srinagarindra barom rajajonani*—"the mother of the king".

Chao chom was the title for a woman who was not a queen but a royal consort. If she gave birth to a child, she was elevated to *chao chom marnda*. Regardless of where a person was in the ranking system, their offspring would at birth invariably be slotted in at one level below their father. This system of descending layers served to reduce the overall size of the royal family over time because members of the fourth generation and below were not considered royal.

The top five birth titles for royal offspring in declining order are:

1. Chao fa—The first generation of sons and daughters of a king by a queen or a royal consort receive this high title at birth. They are considered "celestial" princes and princesses—*fa* means heaven. With their full title, they are called *somdet chao fa*, which in English would be: His/Her Royal Highness (HRH) Prince/Princess... All four children of King Bhumibol and Queen Sirikit were titled *somdet chao fa* at birth.

2. Phra ong chao—These are also first generation sons and daughters, but of a king and his non-royal *chao chom marnda*. In a following reign, they would be titled *phra boromwongse ter phra ong chao* and still be addressed as His/Her Royal Highness. *Phra ong chao* can also be the children of a celestial prince, making their children in turn third generation royalty. *Phra ong chao* children of a celestial prince are titled *phra chao voravongse ter phra ong chao* and are also addressed as His/Her Royal Highness. In 1927, King Prajadhipok created an exception and allowed children of a *chao fa* father and a non-royal wife who were titled *mom chao* to be elevated to *phra ong chao* as their grandmother was a queen. They were entitled to use the honorific His/Her Highness and the prefix *phra voravongse ter phra ong chao*. The king can also elevate a person of a lower rank or a non-royal *phra chao voravongse ter phra ong chao* if he so wishes.

3. Mom chao—The second generation grandchildren of a king, whose father was a *chao fa* or *phra ong chao*, are the last generation considered to be real princes or princesses. In English they can be called His/Her Serene Highness (HSH) Prince/Princess.

4. Mom rajawongse—As great-grandchildren of a king, these third generation offspring from a male *mom chao* have lesser status and are not considered royal—but neither are they commoners. It is difficult to translate their title into English since there is no direct comparison, but some have suggested referring to them as "honourable" or "lord" and "lady". A male *mom rajawongse* can be elevated to the title *mom* with a special honorific name. For example, Mom Rajawongse Chalermlarp Thawiwong became Mom Thawiwong Thawansak (the director general of the Crown Property Bureau in the 1940s).

5. Mom luang—These are the fourth generation, great-great-grandchildren of a monarch. They are children of a male *mom rajawongse* and are also commoners. The children of a male *mom luang* are fifth generation and may add *na Ayudhya* to their surname to indicate their royal descent. The particle *na* in a surname is similar to *de* in France or *von* in Germany.

In addition to titles, people can also receive decorations and medals from the king after performing good deeds or making donations to charitable causes and royal projects. Special titles are also conferred on some women to honour their status as a wife of a ranking royal, or to highlight a decoration they receive. All titles of nobility for males were abolished when absolute monarchy ended, but females were allowed to continue receiving decorations which accord them titles. King Bhumibol awards these titles annually on 5 May, Coronation Day. Although the king is not involved in the actual selection or promotion processes, military and police officers, palace officials and royal pages receive ranks and decorations that are technically bestowed royally. By receiving these, the recipients are honoured for their service to king and country, and the concept promotes loyalty to the royal institution.

Royal decorations honour public service and loyalty to the crown. The earliest decorations in Siam appeared in the Ayudhya era. Later, Rama I created his own system, and the number of orders and titles expanded in subsequent reigns. King Mongkut crafted a *dara* (star) decoration which became the model for many future awards. In 1861, he created The Most Exalted Order of the White Elephant which had a number of grades. The exalted orders were modelled on British decorations and were often bestowed on civil servants and diplomats.

Foreigners who aided the kingdom also received these decorations. King Chulalongkorn began dispensing The Most Exalted Order of the White Elephant to foreign monarchs for their help in international affairs. He added a conspicuous satin sash, 10 cm wide, to accompany the decoration. In 1909, The Most Exalted Order of the White Elephant was elevated to become Siam's highest decoration, and its name was lengthened to be the Knight Grand

Above *A sash belonging to the Most Illustrious Order of Chula Chom Klao*

Cordon (Special Class) of the Most Exalted Order of the White Elephant. In 1941, women were deemed worthy of also receiving a nearly identical version.

Other royal decorations could also be worn on a royal sash. King Chulalongkorn was also known as King Chulachomklao. In 1873, he created the Most Illustrious Order of Chula Chom Klao to recognise royal relatives, members of the armed forces and civil servants for their loyalty. Written upon it, for the recipient and future generations who inherit the decoration, are the words: "Keepsakes for those who have preserved our motherland in the past, and those who are preserving it today."

King Bhumibol has also presented decorations to foreigners, including foreign royalty. For example, when the Queen of England gave him a Royal Victorian Chain during his 1960 visit to London, he awarded her a Grand Cross and Collar of the Illustrious Order of the Royal House of Chakri.

Insignia

The Royal House of Chakri has a unique emblem, the Chakri. According to *The King of Thailand in World Focus*, "It combines the discus (*chakra*) and the trident (*tri*), the celestial weapons of the god Narai, of whom the Thai king is a personification. Narai is an incarnation, or avatar, of the Hindu god Vishnu. The conjoining of the *chakra* and *tri* denotes strength and power. The ancient title *Chao Phraya Chakri*, held for more than a decade by King Rama I before he became king, was given in recognition of battlefield prowess. In founding the dynasty, he chose both its name and symbol."

Rajasap

The language of the Siamese court, *rajasap* has traditionally been used when speaking directly to royalty, or when describing the world around them. The complicated royal language is split into

Above *King Bhumibol, Queen Sirikit and Crown Prince Maha Vajiralongkorn appear on the main balcony of the Chakri Maha Prasat Throne Hall. The Chakri insignia above the doorway combines a discus and a trident.*

five layers, and changes according to who is being addressed. The five levels were created to indicate the relative ranks of who is speaking to whom, and engender respect for royalty.

Rajasap dates from the Ayudhya era and uses words of Pali and Khmer origin. The word *raj* is Sanskrit for king. *Rajasap* appeared for the first time in the palace laws published during King Trailok's reign. It listed the words which were required when speaking to the king, and the prefixes and suffixes which must be added to normal nouns to make them exclusively royal. There are different levels of *rajasap* for addressing kings, queens, celestial ranks and monks. The highest category of *rajasap* is employed when talking to a monarch. A queen is usually considered to have a lower royal rank than a king, and thus would normally be one level lower in the vocabulary of *rajasap* as well. But Queen Sirikit retains the elevated status bestowed upon her after she acted as regent when King Bhumibol was ordained as a monk. As a result, the king and his queen are considered virtually equal in the etymological rankings of *rajasap*.

For example, when referring to oneself while addressing King Bhumibol or Queen Sirikit, a person would say, *"Kha Phra Phutta Chao,"* if they want to say "I" or "me". The phrase literally translates as "Slave of Lord Buddha". Common people are instructed not to speak to the royal couple directly, but instead literally talk to the dust beneath the soles of their feet. To do so, commoners preface their remarks with: "Under soles, coarse visible dust, fine invisible dust, gracious feet..."

When the king, queen or anyone else refers to the royal family in the third person, a separate group of words is used. King Bhumibol, in the third person, is traditionally described as *"phra chao yoo hua"*, which can be translated as "The supreme leader in our head." Many understand this as, "The supreme leader who we uphold above our head." Those who commonly use *rajasap*, such as members of the royal family, courtiers and palace staff are aware that its linguistic gradations instantly change, depending upon the social status of each person involved in a conversation.

The general public, however, is unfamiliar with many of the terms. Thus King Bhumibol does not require everyone to use *rajasap* when they speak to him. However, due to daily exposure to *rajasap* through television and newspapers, as well as classes at school, many Thais are able to understand much of the language.

White Elephants

Thai reverence for white elephants stems from the animal's ancient role as Erawan, the powerful mount of the Hindu god Indra. Thais and other Buddhists in Southeast Asia also revere the unique animals because, according to legend, Queen Maya, the Buddha's mother, dreamt of a white-coloured elephant entering her womb. Upon awakening, she found herself with child and her princely son grew up to become the Buddha.

Monarchs in ancient Siam, Myanmar, Sri Lanka and Cambodia have throughout history collected white elephants. A king's stature was often closely linked to how many he possessed. In Siamese history, white elephants have been heralded as far back as the famous Sukhothai Inscription One of 1293. Siam's national flag, designed by Rama II, featured a white elephant as the nation's symbol until 1917. To this day, whenever a white elephant is caught in the wild, the event is celebrated as auspicious for the kingdom, and by law the elephant should be offered to the reigning monarch.

Foreigners, meanwhile, have coined the term "white elephant" and given it negative connotations. In English, a white elephant can refer to a large investment requiring ruinous and unavoidable upkeep. While such elephants are commonly referred to as white, they are actually a full or partial albino. Ideally, their skin colouring should be light yellow, grey, red, purple or bluish, and the mouth's interior should resemble the pinkness of a lotus bud. White edges around the eyes, ears and trunk tip are especially admired. White toenails, and a sprout of red hair are also prized. The testicles should be close to a white colour. King Mongkut so admired the beasts that he wrote a guide to the physical features defining a perfect white elephant. On one occasion, the king gave permission for his son, Prince Chulalongkorn, to receive some distinguished visitors in an empty stall in the white elephant stables dating from the reign of Rama II. King Mongkut considered this a perfectly appropriate reception area since both the elephant and the prince held the same royal rank of *chao fa*. When the Chakri Maha Prasat Hall was built on the stable site in King Chulalongkorn's reign, statues of four elephants were included as visual reminders of

Above *King Bhumibol with Phra Savet Adulyadej Pahon, his most senior royal white elephant, which was found in the South in 1956.*

the old royal elephant stables once located there.

King Bhumibol has possessed nearly a dozen royal elephants of different ranks. The most senior full white elephant, Phra Savet Adulyadej Pahon, was captured in the southern province of Krabi in 1956. The royal elephants are attended by King Bhumibol's royal veterinary surgeon who ensures they are exercised, disciplined and fed grass, bananas, sweet potatoes and sugar cane. Royal elephants are not mated, so tasty green melons are offered to dampen their lust. In 1968, King Bhumibol poured lustral water over a new white elephant, Phra Savet Surakachatan. The monarch stood on a platform above while mahouts held the elephant still. The handlers then adorned the animal in a ceremonial costume, placing a golden chain around its neck bearing a royal cypher. Ornamental

head and howdah cloths were placed on the white elephant as decoration, and tufts of yak hair were dangled over its ears. During the feeding ceremony, as royal family members watched, Brahman priests blew conch shells and chanted stanzas of verse.

The Garuda

The earliest known use by Siamese royalty of the garuda image was in the 14th century during the reign of King U Thong, the first ruler of the kingdom of Ayudhya. His seal was a garuda carved in ivory. A large-winged garuda, surrounded by a circle, is part of King Bhumibol's Great Seal. "The seals bearing the sign of the garuda, or the so-called *Phra Khrut Phah*, are undoubtedly very old," observed King

Above *The garuda adorning Siam Commercial Bank's Chidlom building covers 81 square metres and is the largest in Thailand.*

Vajiravudh early in the 20th century. "They have been in use since the Ayudhya period. The seals of the kings of the Rattanakosin period are, as a rule, more personal and at each succession a new seal for the new king has to be redesigned and made according to his preference." The Thai government's stationery, uniforms and other important items also bear a garuda image because the government is considered to be in the king's service. On rare occasions, the king awards some businesses a garuda symbol, to acknowledge service to the crown. This allows some banks, offices, charities and companies to fix an impressive garuda crest over their entrances.

Siamese monarchs are traditionally thought of as incarnations of the god Vishnu whose mount was Garuda. According to Sanskrit texts, the mythical half-man, half-bird Garuda was allowed to perch physically higher than Vishnu when it was not transporting the god. This connection, in part, explains why, to indicate the personal presence of King Bhumibol, a flag emblazoned with a garuda is displayed, above his residence of Chitralada Villa, for example, or on top of other palaces and buildings when he is present. Even when King Bhumibol is being chauffeured in his ivory-coloured limousine, his car flies the royal standard—a yellow flag featuring a red garuda—from a small chrome pole on the front wing. A small garuda is also crafted by hand on the outside of the car's doors.

Anthems

In 1871, when the young King Chulalongkorn visited the British colony of Singapore, a military band struck up "God Save the Queen" during the welcoming ceremony. The same trip also took him to the Dutch East Indies (later Indonesia), where protocol officials asked what music should be played to herald his arrival. Returning to Siam, the king asked the kingdom's leading classical Thai musicians and songwriters to create a royal anthem. They originally chose a song written during Rama II's reign, but soon realised that traditional Thai music was not easily played by Western marching bands. Eventually, Russian composer Pyotr Schurovsky's music was selected, with lyrics written by Prince Narisara Nuvadtivongs. The words were later modified by King Vajiravudh and have, since then, remained untouched. The royal anthem is played on official occasions, royal birthdays and ceremonies at which the king, queen, crown prince or a representative of the king is present. A few minutes before any film is shown in any of the nation's cinemas, and before any form of major public entertainment or sporting event takes place, the royal anthem is played and the entire audience, including foreigners, must stand in silence to show respect. In cinemas, the anthem is accompanied by a visual hagiography of King Bhumibol, the queen and their children.

The royal anthem is in *rajasap* and a literal translation is nearly impossible. To begin with, it is not Thai but Pali in Thai characters. There is therefore no official translation, but there are numerous unofficial renditions in English along these lines:

We, subjects of His Great Majesty,
Prostrate heart and head
To respect a king
Whose merits are boundless.
Sole and supreme sovereign,
Siam's greatest,
Foremost in honour,
We are joyous because of his rule.

The fruits of his wisdom preserve
The people in happiness and peace.
May it be that
Whatever he wills shall be done
According to the hopes of his great heart
As we wish him victory. Hurrah!

Thailand also has a national anthem, created in 1932, after the end of the absolute monarchy. The music was composed by a German, Peter Feit, and the lyrics by Sa-nga Kanchanakphan—who was previously known as Khun Wichitmatra. The words were altered in 1939 by Colonel Luang Saranuprabhandi when the country's name was first changed from Siam to Thailand, but the music remained the same. It is played every day at 8 am and 6 pm when it is broadcast by television and radio, and via government-installed public loudspeakers, as well as on other occasions. The national anthem's lyrics are shorter than the royal anthem's, and can be rendered unofficially as:

Thailand unites all Thai people, every part of
Thailand belongs to the Thai people.
Our country forever maintains its sovereignty,
Because the Thais have always been united.
Thai people are peace-loving,
but do not shrink from fighting.
Nor shall they suffer tyranny.
Thai people are ready
to sacrifice every drop of
blood for the nation
And its victories.
Hurrah!

Right The score of Siam's first royal anthem, which was written after one of King Chulalongkorn's trips overseas.

NOTES:

A History of Kings

1   There are many theories and later writings concerning the nature of King Taksin's execution. Most suggest that, following the protocol regarding the taboo on the spilling of royal blood, he was placed in a velvet sack and killed by a single blow to the back of his neck with a sandalwood club. However, another 19th century account based on a letter written by King Mongkut says that the council of nobles and officials ignored this protocol and ordered him beheaded near Vichai Prasit Fort.

Crown Property

1   Data from the Crown Property Bureau.

2   Data from the Crown Property Bureau.

3   The current directors, in the order in which Chirayu refers to them, are Phanat Simasathian, Suthee Singsaneh, Chao na Sylvanta, Kasem Watanachai and Snoh Unakul.

4   Ngop praman doi sankhep 2554 (Budget in Brief 2011), table III-14, p. 77.

The Law of *Lèse-Majesté*

1   The term *lèse-majesté* is French. First used in the 16th century, it is derived from the Latin laesa majestas, meaning "injured majesty".

2   Thai conceptual categories in laws are retained. The term *kabot* is perhaps closest to the English "treason", which includes acts of rebellion and treasonous words—seemingly, anything that went against the king. The term *kabot* is still used in Thai legal parlance, although the translation into English seems awkward.

3   Khana Nitisat, *Pramuan kotmai ratchakan thi nung julasakarat 1166, phim tam chabap luang tra sam duang lem 2* (PKRI) [The Three Seals Law, Vol. 2] (Bangkok: Thammasat University, Rongphim ruankaew kanphim, 2529 [1986]), p. 375.

4   Craig J. Reynolds, *Sedition in Thai History: A Nineteenth-Century Poem and its Critics*, in, Manas Chitakasem and Andrew Turton, eds., *Thai Constructions of Knowledge* (London: School of Oriental and African Studies, University of London, 1991), pp. 28–31.

5   Thailand, Government, *Phraratchakamnot laksana min pramat duai kanphut ru khian thoi kham thet ok khotsanakan rattanakosin sok 118*, [Royal Edict on Defamation through False Spoken or Written Words Made Known [in] the Year 1900], PKPS, Vol. 17, r.s 118–19 [1898–1900], pp. 20–21.

6   *The New York Times*, 18 December 1910.

7   David Streckfuss, *Truth on Trial in Thailand: Defamation, Treason, and Lèse-Majesté* (London: Routledge, 2011), p. 420.

8   Matthew Copeland, chapter four, "Political Journalism" in *Contested Nationalism and the 1932 Overthrow of the Absolute Monarchy in Siam*, PhD dissertation, Australian National University, 1993.

9   Thailand, Government, *Phraratchabanyat kaekhai phoemtoem kotmai laksana aya ph.s.* BE 2478 *(chabap thi 3)* [Amendment to the Criminal Law Code of 1935], in, PKPS, Vol. 49, BE 2479 [1936] (20 Aug, 2478 [1935]), pp. 46–76. For some reason it does not seem to appear in the Royal Gazette until later. See, Thailand, Government, Ratchakitjanubeksa [Royal Gazette], Vol. 61, Part 6 (19 April BE 2479 [1936]).

10   Somchai Preechasilpakul and David Streckfuss, *Ramification and Re-Sacralization of the Lèse-Majesté Majesty Law in Thailand*, Paper presented at the 10th International Conference on Thai Studies (Bangkok: The Thai Khadi Research Institute/Thammasat University), January 9–11, 2008.

11   Streckfuss, *Kings in the Age of Nations*, p. 466.

12   "Democracy may end *lèse-majesté* law," *Nation*, 8 October 1987.

13   The Advisory Committee on the Security of the Kingdom reports that numbers peaked in 2009 with 165 cases before dropping off to 87 and 10 cases in 2010 and the first half of 2011 respectively.

It also indicates that the number of *lèse-majesté* complaints filed with the police shows a similar trend, peaking in 2009 with 104 cases before decreasing to 62 and 10 cases in 2010 and the first half of 2011 respectively. However, taking into account Sections 107 to 112 of the criminal code in 2010, 478 charges of *lèse-majesté* related charges were sent to the Court of First Instance. Because Sections 107 to 111 involve committing acts of violence or causing the death of the king, queen, heir apparent, or regent, or abetting such acts, and have not been used since the 1950s, we can assume that most, if not all, statistics derived from Sections 107 to 112 were referring to verbal references to the leading members of the royal family.

14   J.E. de Becker's 1916 study, *Elements of Japanese Law* (Transactions of the Asiatic Society of Japan 44:2 (December 1916) (Tokyo: Asiatic Society of Japan, 1916), reports that a conviction of *lèse-majesté* could bring a sentence of up to five years' imprisonment. At the time of its repeal in 1947, it was reported by *The New York Times* that the maximum punishment was 15 years (*The New York Times*, 8 October 1947).

15   Streckfuss, *Truth on Trial in Thailand*, p. 17.

16   *The New York Times*, 23 January 1898.

17   *The New York Times*, 3 January 1899.

18   *The New York Times*, 23 January 1897.

19   *The New York Times*, 11 November 1904, 26 August 1906.

20   The last reported case in Germany appearing in *The New York Times* was on 10 June 1906, when a newspaper was "confiscated" for poking fun at the relationship between Emperor Wilhelm II and Austrian Emperor Franz Josef.

21   Tjaco van den Hout, *Europe's Lèse-Majesté Laws and Freedom of Expression*, Bangkok Post, 21 May 2009.

22   <http://www.thecheers.org/news/Europe/news_17756_ A-man-has-been-jailed-for-four-months-for-insulting-Queen-Beatrix.html>

23   David Streckfuss, *Intricacies of Lese-*

NOTES:

Majesty: A Comparative Study of Imperial Germany and Modern Thailand, in, Søren Ivarsson and Lotte Isager, eds., *Saying the Unsayable: Monarchy and Democracy in Thailand.* Copenhagen: NIAS Press, 2010.

24 Achara Ashayagachat, *Public Support is Key to Royals' Survival*, Bangkok Post, 9 December 2009. <http://www.bangkokpost.com/news/local/28892/publicsupport-is-key-to-royals-survival>

25 <http://www.terradaily.com/afp/110301184219.kh4lhn79.html> [accessed 15 May 2011]

26 <http://www.legislationline.org/documents/section/criminal-codes> Bangkok Post, 9 December 2009. <http://www.bangkokpost.com/news/local/28892/public-support-is-key-to-royals-survival>

27 See Streckfuss, *Truth on Trial in Thailand*, pp. 325–26 for a short literature review; also the more recent, Janthajira Eammayura, ed., *Lak miti kotmail minphraboromdechanuphap* [Perspectives on the Lèse-Majesté Law] (Bangkok: Khrongkan prakatsaniyabat kotmail mahachon, khana nitisat, mahawithayalai thammasat, et al., 2553 [2010].

28 <http://asiancorrespondent.com/18471/foreign-defender-of-the-monarchy-update/>

29 Computer Crime Act, B.E. 2550 (2007), Government Gazette (Vol. 124, Section 27 kor. 18 June 2007, pp. 4–12.

30 Computer Crime Act, B.E. 2550 (2007), Government Gazette (Vol. 124, Section 27 kor. 18 June 2007, pp. 4–12.

31 Sawatree Suksri, Siriphon Kusonsinwut and Orapin Yingyongpathana, *Situational Report on Control and Censorship of Online Media, Through the Use of Laws and the Imposition of Thai State Policies* (Bangkok: iLaw Project, 2010); <http://www.boell-southeastasia.org/downloads/ilaw_report_EN.pdf> [accessed 15 May 2011]. Also see, <http://www.freedomhouse.org/images/File/FotN/Thailand2011.pdf> [accessed 15 May 2011]

32 Streckfuss, *Truth on Trial in Thailand*, pp. 195–202.

33 Somchai Preechasilpakul, *Konkai thi 'ayutitham' khaung krabuankan yuttitham Thai,*" Fa Diew Kan 4:2 (mesayon-mithunayon 2459 [April/June 1916), p. 72.

34 Interview with Dr Kittipong Kittayarak, permanent secretary to the Ministry of Justice, 28 December 2010, Nonthaburi, Thailand.

35 Thailand, Attorney General's Office, *Rai-ngan prajam pi, 2547* [Annual Report of the Attorney General's Office, 2004] (*Samnakngan aiyakan phiset fai sarasonthet, samnakngan wichakan*).

36 David Streckfuss, *Kings in the Age of Nations—The Paradox of Lèse-Majesté as Political Crime in Thailand*, Comparative Studies in Society and History 37(3) (July 1995), pp. 445–75.

37 Interview with Kasem Watanachai, 1 February 2011, Privy Council Chambers, Bangkok.

38 Streckfuss, *Kings in the Age of Nations*, p. 465.

39 Thailand, Office of the Judiciary, *Rai-ngan sathiti khadi tua ratcha-anajak prajam pi (ph.s. 2548–2553)* [English title provided is Annual Judicial Statistics, Thailand 2005–2010, respectively].

40 It is difficult to charge non-Thais credibly with a crime that could be construed as a betrayal of Thainess, and foreigners have in practice rarely been charged with *lèse-majesté*. But even if foreigners are unable to grasp the Thai view of monarchy, as is often claimed, they still remain subject to the laws of the kingdom—including *lèse-majesté*.

41 <http://quickstart.clari.net/qs_se/webnews/wed/bo/Qthailand-japan-crime.RXCk_DIN.html>

42 <http://news.bbc.co.uk/2/hi/asia-pacific/6547413.stm>

43 Office of the Council of State (Thailand), Constitution of Kingdom of Thailand 2007 <http://www.asianlii.org/th/legis/const/2007/1.html> The restrictions on the liberty described in Section 45 are rather extensive, allowing the state to restrict the freedom of expression when there is "law specifically enacted for

the purpose of maintaining the security of State, protecting the rights, liberties, dignity, reputation, family or privacy rights of other person, maintaining public order or good morals or preventing or halting the deterioration of the mind or health of the public".

44 *Khamsang samnak naiyokratthamontri thi 256/2552 ruang taengtang khana kammakan thi pruksa khadi khwam phit kieowkap khwammankhong haeng ratcha-anajak* (lap) [Order of the Prime Minister's Office No. 256/2009 concerning the appointment of the Advisory Committee on violations against the Security of the Kingdom (secret)], 18 November 2009 (3 pages).

45 Interview with Dr Kittipong Kittayarak, permanent secretary to the Ministry of Justice, 28 December 2010, Nonthaburi, Thailand.

46 Borwornsak Uwanno, *The Law of Inviolability in Thailand*, Bangkok Post, 7 April 2009. Available at: <http://www.bangkokpost.com/opinion/opinion/14660/the-law-of-inviolability-in-thailand> accessed 4 June 2009.

47 Borwornsak Uwanno, *Thai Culture and the Law on Lese Majeste*, Bangkok Post, 8 Apr, 2009. Available at: <http://www.bangkokpost.com/opinion/opinion/14766/lese-majeste-abuse-and-benevolence> accessed 4 June 2009. He counters the contention that there are no legal limits to the law, by stating that the courts can focus on the intent of a defendant in determining a suitable punishment, and the king has asked that the law not be applied "too liberally" as he "allows fair criticism".

48 *Nation*, 11 October 2007.

49 See, for instance, Thanong Khanthong's editorial, *The Law is not the problem*, (Nation, 6 March, 2009), and a rebuttal, David Streckfuss, *The Law is the Problem*, Seeds of Peace 25:2 (May-August 2552 (2009)), pp. 5–6.

50 Somchai Preechasilpakul, in section entitled, *Kotmai min kap khwam mankhong khong rat* [The lese majesty law and Security of the State, in, Janthajira Eammayura, ed., *Lak miti kotmail minphraboromdechanuphap*

[Perspectives on the Lèse-Majesté Law], pp. 55-105.

51   Jaran Cosananand, *Khwamrunraeng haeng thot thi mai pen tham lae kanpitkan "khwamjing" nai matra 112 haeng pramuan kotmai aya* [The Violence of Unjust Punishment and keeping out of "the truth" in Section 112 of the Criminal Code], ibid., pp. 163-70.

52   *Nation*, 5 December 2005.

53   Thailand, Office of the Judiciary, *Rai-ngan sathiti khadi tua ratcha-anajak prajam pi* (ph.s. 2548–2553) [English title provided is Annual Judicial Statistics, Thailand 2005–2010, respectively].

54   <http://en.rsf.org/press-freedom-index-2004,550.html>; <http://en.rsf.org/press-freedom-index-2010,1034.html>

―――――   **The Privy Council**   ―――――

1   The Privy Council of Thailand, *The Privy Council of Thailand* [2006], p. 7.

2   Paul Handley, "*Princes, Politicians, Bureaucrats, Generals: The Evolution of the Privy Council under the Constitutional Monarchy*," paper presented at the 10th International Conference on Thai Studies, Thammasat University, Bangkok, 9–11 January 2008, p. 2.

3   Hilaire Barnett, *Constitutional & Administrative Law* (Fifth Edition), London: Cavendish: 2004. p. 273.

4   <http://www.privy-council.org.uk/output/page2.asp> [accessed 17 January 2011]

5   The Privy Council of Thailand, *The Privy Council of Thailand*, p. 25-26.

6   The Privy Council of Thailand, *The Privy Council of Thailand* [2004] (Publication in commemoration of the Occasion of His Majesty the King Presiding Over the Opening Ceremony of the Privy Council Chambers at Saranrom Palace Gardens on Tuesday, 20 January, BE 2547 (2004), p. 24; Piyabut Saengkanokkul, *Phraratcha-amnat ongkhamontri lae phu mi barami nok ratthathammanun* [Royal power, privy councillors and charismatic,

extra-constitutional persons] (Bangkok: openbooks, 2550 [2007], pp. 66–67.

7   Terwiel writes that the 49 members were composed of "thirteen members of the royal family", two leading government ministers, "and many officials in less exalted positions". B.J. Terwiel, *Thailand's Political History* (Bangkok: River Books, 2011), p. 187; Rungrot Theplip, comp, et al, *Sang krung lae prawattisat kan borishan chat thai* [Building the city and history of administration of the Thai nation] (Bangkok: Thepphithak kanphim, BE 2521–22 [1978–79]).

8   *Privy Council, the Councillor of His Majesty the King Act*, 14 June 1874, Royal Gazette, Vol. 1, Sheet 17, p. 158, as quoted in Privy Council of Thailand, *The Privy Council of Thailand*, p. 24.

9   Terwiel, *Thailand's Political History*, p. 187; also see David Wyatt, *King Chulalongkorn the Great Founder of Modern Thailand*, in, Lauriston Sharp, ed., *Thailand since King Chulalongkorn* (*Asia Magazine* supplement No. 2, Spring 1976), p. 10.

10   Terwiel, *Thailand's Political History*, p. 253.

11   Sathaban Phrapokklao, *Phaen pattana kanmuang pai su kanpokkhrong rabop "Prachathipatai tam naew phrraratchadamri khong phrabat somdet phrapokklao jaoyuhua"* (ph.s. 2469–2475) [Phra Pok Klao Institute, Political development plan leading to a governance system "Democracy according to ideas of King Prapokklao" (1926–1932) (Nonthaburi: Sathaban Phrapokklao, BE 2545 [2002]), p. 171.

12   *Privy Council Act of BE 2470* [1927] as quoted in, Privy Council of Thailand, *The Privy Council of Thailand* [2004], p. 25.

13   Handley, *Princes, Politicians, Bureaucrats, Generals*, p. 4; Roger Kershaw, *Monarchy in South-East Asia* (London: Routledge, 2001), pp. 204-5.

14   Terwiel, *Thailand's Political History*, p. 254.

15   Terwiel, *Thailand's Political History*, p. 4.

16   Terwiel, *Thailand's Political History*, p. 4.

17   *Samnak kamathikan 3, Priapthiap ratthathamanoon haeng ratha-anajak thai ph.s. BE 2475–2548, lem 1* [Comparison of Constitutions of the Thai Kingdom 1932-2005, vol. 1] p. 15; Privy Council of Thailand, *The Privy Council of Thailand* [2004], p. 25.

18   *Samnak kamathikan 3, Priapthiap ratthathamanoon haeng ratha-anajak thai ph.s. 2475–2548, lem 1* p. 15.

19   The Privy Council of Thailand, *The Privy Council of Thailand* [2004], p. 25.

20   Kobkua, *Kings, Country and Constitutions*, pp. 46, 59, 141.

21   *Nation*, 1 July 2007, "CDA members Krisada Hai-wattanakul claimed that some private universities have been inappropriately exploiting 'the aura' of some privy council members for financial benefit." Also in Handley, *Princes, Politicians, Bureaucrats, Generals*, p. 7. For an overview of the constitutional provisions on the Privy Council, see Kanin Boonsuwan, *Phramahakasat kap rattathammanun* [King and constitution] (Bangkok: Poompunya, 2004) , pp. 29–32, 116, 128–29.

22   Constitutions of the Kingdom of Thailand, 1997 and 2007, <http://thailaws.com/; http://thailaws.com/law/t_laws/claw0002a.pdf>

23   Constitutions of the Kingdom of Thailand, 1997 and 2007, <http://thailaws.com/; http://thailaws.com/law/t_laws/claw0002a.pdf>

24   <http://www.thaimain.com/eng/monarchy/privy.html>

25   Interview with Kasem Watanachai, 1 February 2011, Privy Council Chambers, Bangkok. A similar description of privy councillor duties was made in 1976 by the then-president. Interview with Sanya Dhammasakdi, 11 January 1976 in Akarawat Osathanugroh, comp, *Nai Luang Kong Rao* [Our King] (Bangkok: Dokya Group, 1994), p. 45.

26   Other types of petitions may be addressed to the king as well. For the procedures and conditions surrounding submitting a petition for royal review,

NOTES:

see Borwornsak Uwanno, *Kanchai sitthi thun klao thawai dika tam kotmai lae prapheni* [Using the right to petition the king according to law and custom], unpublished paper, n.d.

27   The Privy Council of Thailand, *The Privy Council of Thailand* (Publication in commemoration of the Occasion of His Majesty the King Presiding Over the Opening Ceremony of the Privy Council Chambers at Saranrom Palace Gardens on Tuesday, 20 January BE 2547 (2004) [second printing 2006], p. 7.

28   One councillor currently serves on the Committee of the Bureau of the Crown Property and as an honorary chairman of the Siam Cement Public Company Limited. Also see <http://www.siamcement.com/en/01corporate_profile/board/chaovana_nasylvanta.html>

29   Members of a committee within the military-appointed legislative body in 2007 discussed the idea of providing special protection for privy councillors within the *lèse-majesté* law. This idea was rejected by the committee itself.

30   Office of the Prime Minister, 1979, pp. 123–4, as quoted in Handley, *Princes, Politicians, Bureaucrats, Generals*, p. 8.

31   The Privy Council of Thailand, *The Privy Council of Thailand* [2006], p. 7.

32   The only current privy councillor elected to a national-level position appears to be Kasem Watanachai, although Kasem felt there might have been others. Interview with Kasem Watanachai, 1 February 2011, Privy Council Chambers, Bangkok.

33   <http://www.ohmpps.go.th/privy/content_en.php?cg_name=Privy%20Councillor%20Name%20List> Not all appointed prime ministers, however, have been or become privy councillors. One notable example is Anand Panyarachun, who served as an appointed prime minister twice in the early 1990s.

34   Privy Council of Thailand, *The Privy Council of Thailand* [2004], pp. 36-72.

35   <http://www.ohmpps.go.th/privy/content_en.php?cg_name=Privy%20Councillor%20Name%20List> [accessed 5

Feb. 2011]; <http://www.ohmpps.go.th/privy/content_en.php?cg_name=Privy%20Councillor%20Name%20List> A similar range of backgrounds are described by the president of the Privy Council in 1976 who said, "Each privy councillor has expertise in different fields," while noting that the council at the time comprised three experienced in foreign affairs, two former military officers, two former presidents of the Supreme Court (one of whom had experience in land reform), two other legal experts, one expert in agriculture, one "educationist", and one engineer. Interview with Sanya Dhammasakdi, 11 January 1976 in Akarawat Osathanugroh, comp, *Nai Luang Kong Rao* [Our King] (Bangkok: Dokya Group, 1994), p. 53.

36   <http://www.ohmpps.go.th/privy/content_en.php?cg_name=Privy%20Councillor%20Name%20List> [accessed 5 Feb. 2011]

37   <http://www.ohmpps.go.th/privy/content_en.php?cg_name=Privy%20Councillor%20Name%20List> [accessed 5 Feb. 2011]

38   Nattapoll Chaiching, "The Monarchy and the Royalist Movement in Modern Thai Politics, 1932-1957," in, Søren Ivarsson and Lotte Isager, eds., *Saying the Unsayable: Monarchy and Democracy in Thailand* (Copenhagen: NAIS – Nordic Institute of Asian Studies, 2010), p. 165–68.

39   David Streckfuss, *Truth on Trial in Thailand: Defamation, Treason, and Lèse-Majesté* (London: Routledge, 2011), pp. 68–69, 152–4; also Thongchai Winichakul, *Toppling Democracy*, Journal of Contemporary Asia, 38 (1) (February 2008), pp. 28-29.

40   Nattapoll, *The Monarchy and the Royalist Movement*, pp. 170–71.

41   Interview with Sanya Dhammasakdi, 11 January 1976, in, Akarawat Osathanugroh, comp, *Nai Luang Kong Rao* [Our King] (Bangkok: Dokya Group, 1994), p. 45.

42   Interview with Kasem Watanachai, in Akarawat Osathanugroh, comp.

43   If Privy Councillor Kasem Watanachai is correct in saying that individual privy councillors rarely have audiences with the

king, then it is conceivable that any public statement of a privy councillor is made in a private capacity and thus should not be considered as representing the view of the king or palace.

44   Hewison and Kengkij, *Thai-Style Democracy*, p. 193; Terwiel, *Thailand's Political History*, p. 301. Also controversial was the privy council president's public support of the Democrat-led Abhisit Vejjajiva government. See Marc Askew, *Confrontation and Crisis in Thailand, 2008–2010*, and Pravit Rojanaphruk and Jiranan Hanthamrongwit, *Distorted Mirror and Lamp: The Politicization of the Thai Media in the Post-Thaksin Era*, in Marc Askew, ed, *Legitimacy Crisis in Thailand* (Chiang Mai: Prajadhipok Institute/Silkworm Books, 2010), pp. 45, 48, 177, 185–6. Paul Chambers, In the Shadow of the Soldier's Boot: *Assessing Civil-Military Relations in Thailand*, in, Marc Askew, ed, *Legitimacy Crisis in Thailand* (Chiang Mai: Prajadhipok Institute/Silkworm Books, 2010), pp. 211.

45   Somsak Chiamthirasakul, <http://www.thaimisc.com/freewebboard/php/vreply.php?user=midnightuniv&topic=10735> as quoted in Piyabut, *Phraratcha-amnat*, pp. 67-68.

46   Michael Montesano, et al, *Thailand in Crisis: The Twilight of a Reign or the Birth of a New Order? Proceedings of a Roundtable with a foreword by Anthony Reid*, Asia Research Institute Working Paper Series No. 114, p. 9

――――   **Succession**   ――――

1   Robert L. Solomon, *Aspects of State, Kingship, and Succession in Southeast Asia*, The RAND Corporation, unpublished paper, June 1970, p. 7. Drawing on the work of Robert Heine-Geldern, Solomon explained that the traditional models of kingship in Southeast Asia have been characterised by what he called a "vagueness of succession": "Southeast Asian practice—and ideal—regarding royal succession kept within the two poles of standardization of rules (which makes the transfer of office a smoother, more acceptable affair) and flexibility (necessary to maintain a minimal level of competence and adequacy)."

2   Solomon, p. 267, 273–4. King

Chulalongkorn, for instance, dated it to the reign of King Ramathibodi I; Damrong Rajanuphap placed it in the time of King Trailok. Some scholars have placed it even earlier to 1358. See Nongyao Kanjanajaree, *Sueb Rajasantativongse, Kot Monthien Ban B.E. 2467* (Law of succession, palace law 1924), in *Encyclopaedia of King Vajiravudh*, Vol. 2, Bangkok: King Vajiravudh Memorial Foundation under Royal Patronage, 2001.

3   Winai Pongsripien, ed, *Kotmai tra samduang: nahtang sungkom Thai* (three seals code: window to Thai society), p. 24. Another scholar defines it as "governance of the royal household". Voraporn Pupongpunt, *Phap luk sataban kasat nai kot monthien ban* (The image of the monarchical institution through Palace Law), p. 165.

4   Pridi Pispoomvithee, *Kot monthien barn: kwarm sumkan krongsang lae nuer ha.* (Palace law: significance, structure and content), pp. 261–3, 274, 276.

5   Voraporn, p. 211.

6   This could occur, for instance, when the god Indra provided such person with "the quintet of royal objects", or when someone sought out came from a rich Brahman family or possessed high abilities in warfare, Voraporn, p. 212.

7   David Wyatt, *Thailand A Short History*, (New Haven and London: Yale University Press, 1984), p. 105.

8   Winai. For a detailed description of the royal duties as specified in the Three Seals Code, see Voraporn, p. 250.

9   At the time of Rama I's death, a succession plot was uncovered that led to the execution of 40 people, including the contender for the throne, a son of King Taksin, and all of his male offspring. B.J. Terwiel, *Thailand's Political History* (Bangkok: River Books, 2011), p. 101.

10   Terwiel, p. 101.

11   Wyatt, pp. 166–67.

12   Letter by D.B. Bradley, dated 28 March 1851, to the *Singapore Straits Times*, as quoted in Terwiel, p. 147.

13   Terwiel, p. 143.

14   Terwiel, p. 167.

15   Terwiel, p. 167.

16   Terwiel, p. 180.

17   Terwiel, p. 193.

18   *Nuer glao chao Thai* (book from the Exhibition to Commemorate the 60th Anniversary of HM's Accession to the Throne), (Bangkok: Reed Tradex, 2006) p. 49.

19   Wyatt, p. 224

20   Wyatt, pp. 233–34.

21   The version of this law comes from the Council of State website. Translation of some articles was provided by an undated, unpublished version provided to a foreign journalist. All other articles are translated by David Streckfuss. <http://www.krisdika.go.th/wps/portal/general/!ut/p/c5/04_SB8K8xLLM9MSSzPy8xBz9CP0os3g_A2czQ0cTQ89ApyAnA0EIOAQGdXAwMLE30_j_zcVP2CbEdFAIfszEk!/dl3/d3/L3dDb0EvUU5RTGtBISEvWUZSdndBISEvNI9OMEM2MUE0MUIRQIJCMEIPVDBQUUNFMDBIMQ!!/>

22   Wyatt, pp. 234–35, 249; Terwiel, p. 251.

23   Sathaban phrapokklao, *Phaen pattana kanmuang*, op cit, p. 168.

24   Sathaban phrapokklao, Phaen pattana kanmuang pai su *kanpokkhrong rabop "Prachathipatai tam naew phraratchadamri khong phrabat somdet phrapokklao jaoyuhua* (ph.s. BE 2469–2475) [Phra Pok Klao Institute, Political development plan leading to a governance system, *Democracy according to ideas of King Prapokklao (1926–1932)]* (Nonthaburi: Sathaban Phrapokklao, 2545 [2002]), pp. 169–70.

25   The Associated Press, *Gun Kills Siam's Young King* in *The King of Thailand in World Focus* by the Foreign Correspondents' Club of Thailand (FCCT), (Singapore: Editions Didier Millet, 2008), p. 21.

26   FCCT, p. 88.

27   Constitution of the Kingdom of Thailand, 2007, <http://thailaws.com/law/t_laws/claw0002a.pdf>

28   *Samnak kamathikarn 3, priapthiap rattadhammanoon haeng raja-anajak Thai 2475-2548 lem 1* (Comparison of the Constitutions of the Kingdom of Thailand 1932–2005 Vol. 1), 2007 (Bangkok: The Secretariat of the House of Representatives).

29   Constitution of the Kingdom of Thailand, 2007, <http://thailaws.com/law/t_laws/claw0002a.pdf>

30   This is very carefully described in Roger Kershaw, *Monarchy in South-East Asia: The faces of tradition in transition* (London and New York: Routledge, 2001), pp. 152–3.

BIBLIOGRAPHY:

──────── **SOURCE MATERIAL IN ENGLISH** ────────

"80th Birthday Celebrations." *Bangkok Post* supplements, November–December 2007.

A Tale of Two Kingdoms. Bangkok: East Asiatic (Thailand), 1995.

Allman, T.D. "Bhumibol: Asian Phenomenon." *Far Eastern Economic Review* 17 December 1973.

Anand Panyarachun. *His Majesty's Role in the Making of Thai History*. 14th Conference of the International Association of Historians in Asia. Chulalongkorn University, May 20, 1996.

Anuman Rajadhon, Phraya. "Kingship in Siam." *Journal of the Siam Society* Vol. 42 (pt.1) 1954: 1–10.

Askew, Marc. "Confrontation and Crisis in Thailand, 2008–2010." Marc Askew, ed. *Legitimacy Crisis in Thailand*. Chiang Mai: Prajadhipok Institute/Silkworm Books, 2010.

Athada Khoman. *Siam: Days of Glory: 19th Century Photographers of Thailand*. Bangkok: Siam Renaissance, 2010.

Audric, John. *Siam: The Land and the People*. New York: A. S. Barnes and Company, 1970.

Barnett, Hilaire. *Constitutional & Administrative Law* (Fifth Edition). Cavendish, 2004.

Batson, Benjamin A. *Siam's Political Future: Documents From the End of the Absolute Monarchy*. Ithaca, New York: Cornell University, 1974.

Batson, Benjamin A. *The End of Absolute Monarchy in Siam*. Singapore: Oxford University Press, 1984.

Batson, Benjamin A., ed. *Siam's Political Future: Documents from the End of the Absolute Monarchy*. Ithaca, New York: Cornell University, 1974.

Bayly, Christopher and Tim Harper. *Forgotten Wars: The End of Britain's Asian Empire*. London: Penguin Books, 2008.

Bhumibol Adulyadej, King. *The Story of Mahajanaka*. Bangkok: Amarin, 1999 (2542).

Bhumibol Adulyadej, King. *The Story of Tongdaeng*. Bangkok: Amarin, 2004 (2547).

Borwornsak Uwanno. "Ten Principles of a Righteous King." *Bangkok Post* 12 June 2006.

Borwornsak Uwanno. "Thai Culture and the Law on Lèse-Majestè." *Bangkok Post,* 8 April 2009.

Borwornsak Uwanno. "The Law of Inviolability in Thailand." *Bangkok Post,* 7 April 2009.

Chaiwat Khamchoo and Bruce Reynolds. *Thai-Japanese Relations in Historical Perspective*. Bangkok: Chualongkorn University, Institute of Asian Studies, Innomedia Press, 1988.

Chaiyawat Wibulswasdi, Priyanut Piboolsravut and Kobsak Pootrakool. *Sufficiency Economy Philosophy and Development*. Bangkok: Sufficiency Economy Research Project, Crown Property Bureau, 2010. Humanities Textbooks Project, 2007.

Charoon, Pirayavaraporn. *Leprosy Control in Thailand*. Bangkok: Ministry of Public Health, 1996.

Chirayu Isarangkun na Ayuthaya. *His Majesty the King and the Royal Initiatives Towards Balancing Thailand's Development*. Bangkok: The Crown Property Bureau, 2010.

Chula Chakrabongse. *Lords of Life: The Paternal Monarchy of Bangkok, 1782–1932*. New York: Taplinger, 1960.

Chulalongkorn, King. *Thai Titles and Ranks: Including a translation of Tradition of Royal Lineage in Siam*. Translation by Robert Jones. Ithaca, New York: Cornell University, 1971.

"Commemorating HM the Queen's 5th Cycle Anniversary." *Ramkhamhaeng University Journal, Humanities Issue*, 1992.

Corbett, Ross, J. "The Extraconstitutionality of Lockean Prerogative." *The Review of Politics* 68, 2006: 428–448.

Damrong Rajanubhab, Prince. *Miscellaneous Articles Written for the Journal of the Siam Society by His Late Royal Highness, Prince Damrong*. Bangkok: The Siam Society, 1962.

Danai Chanchaochai. *King Bhumibol Adulyadej of Thailand*. Bangkok: DMG Books, 2006.

Dedications to HRH Princess Galyani Vadhana on her 80th Birthday. Bangkok: The Siam Society, 2003.

Dhani Nivat, Prince. "The Old Siamese Conception of the Monarchy." *Journal of the Siam Society*.Vol. 36.2, 1947: 91–106.

Dhani Nivat, Prince. "The Reconstruction of Rama I of the Chakri Dynasty." *Journal of the Siam Society* Vol. 43.1, 1955: 21–48. (Reprinted in *Collected Articles by HH Prince Dhani Nivat*. Bangkok: The Siam Society, 1976. 145–68.)

Dhani Nivat, Prince. "The Siamese Way of Life". SEATO Lectures. SEATO, Bangkok. 1960.

Dhani Nivat, Prince. *The Royal Palaces*. Bangkok: The Fine Arts Department, 1963.

Direk Jayanama. *Thailand and World War II*. Chiang Mai: Silkworm Books, 2008.

Dumaine, Betty and Layton, Dora H. *The Princess Mother*. Bangkok: Thai Watana Panich Press, 1972.

Dusdi Naiwattakul. "The Monarchical Institution and the People." *The Thai Monarchy*. Bangkok: The Public Relations Department, 2000.

Ellis, A. G. "The Service to Medicine in Siam: Rendered by His Royal Highness Prince Mahidol of Songkla." Reprinted from *Bulletin of the Institute of the History of Medicine*, Vol. IV, No. 2, February 1936.

Elphick, Peter. *Far Eastern File: The Intelligence War in the Far East 1930–1945*. London: Coronet, 1997.

Engel, David M. *Law and Kingship in Thailand During the Reign of King Chulalongkorn*. Ann Arbor: University of Michigan Center for South and Southeast Asian Studies, 1975.

Evans, Grant and Kevin Rowley. *Red Brotherhood at War*. London: Verso, 1984.

Evans, Grant. *The Politics of Ritual and Remembrance: Laos Since 1975*. Chiang Mai: Silkworm, 1998.

Faulder, Dominic. "The Royal White Elephants." *Sawasdee*, May 1987: 41–46.

Freeman, Michael. *The Grand Palace*. Bangkok: River Books, 1998.

Fry, Gerald W. "The Evolution of Educational Reform in Thailand." Second International Forum on Education Reform: Key Factors in Effective Implementation. Office of the National Education Commission.

Ambassador Hotel, Bangkok. 2-5 September 2002.

Galyani Vadhana, Princess. *As Mother Told Me* (English Edition) Bangkok: The Siam Society Under Royal Patronage, 1980.

Gerson, Ruth. *Traditional Festivals in Thailand*. Kuala Lumpur: Oxford University Press, 1996.

Gervaise, Nicolas. *The Natural and Political History of the Kingdom of Siam*. Paris: Claude Barbin, 1688. Rpt. Trans and ed John Villiers. Bangkok: White Lotus, 1989.

Gesick, Lorraine M. *Kingship and Political Integration in Traditional Siam, 1767–1824*. PhD dissertation. Cornell University, 1976.

Gray, Christine. *Thailand: The Soteriological State in the 1970s*. PhD dissertation. University of Chicago, 1986.

Gray, Denis D. and Dominic Faulder, eds. *The King of Thailand in World Focus*, 3rd Edition. Singapore: Editions Didier Millet, 2008.

Greene, Stephen L. W. *Absolute Dreams: Thai Government Under Rama VI, 1910–1925*. Bangkok: White Lotus Press, 1999.

Griswold, A. B. and Prasert na Nagara. "On Kingship and Society at Sukhodaya." *Change and Persistence in Thai Society*. William Skinner and A. Thomas Kirsch, eds. Ithaca and London: Cornell University Press, 1975. 29–92.

Grossman, Nicholas ed. *Chronicle of Thailand: Headline News Since 1946*. Bangkok: Editions Didier Millet and Bangkok Post, 2009.

Handley, Paul M. *The King Never Smiles: A Biography of Thailand's Bhumibol Adulyadej*. New Haven and London: Yale University Press, 2006.

Hanks, Lucien M. "Merit and Power in the Thai Social Order." *American Anthropologist*, 64, No. 6, December. 1962. 1247–61.

Haseman, John B. *The Thai Resistance Movement During the Second World War*. Bangkok: Chalermnit Press.

Heine-Geldern, Robert. *Conceptions of State and Kingship in Southeast Asia*. Ithaca, New York: Cornell University, 1956. First Published in *The Far Eastern Quarterly*, Vol. 2, November 1942. 15–30.

Hell, Stefan. *Siam and the League of Nations: Modernisation, Sovereignty and Multilateral Diplomacy 1920–1940*. Bangkok: River Books, 2010.

His Majesty the King and Water Resources Development. Amarin, 1987.

His Majesty's Photographic Portfolio. Thai Investment and Securities, 1989.

Hunter, Eileen and Narisa Chakrabongse. *Katya and the Prince of Siam*. Bangkok: River Books, 1994.

Ivarsson, Søren and Isager, Lotte, ed. *Saying the Unsayable: Monarchy and Democracy in Thailand*. Copenhagen: NIAS Press, 2010.

Iyer, Pico. "The Mystique of Monarchy." *Time*, June 2006.

Kemp, Jeremy. *Aspects of Siamese Kingship in the 17th Century*. Bangkok: Social Science Association Press, 1969.

Kemp, Jeremy. *Aspects of Siamese Kingship in the Seventeenth Century*. Bangkok: Social Science Review, Social Science Association Press of Thailand , 1969.

Kernfield, Barry, ed. *The New Grove Dictionary of Jazz*. London: Macmillan, 1988.

Kershaw, Roger. *Monarchy in South-East Asia: The faces of tradition in transition*. London and New York: Routledge, 2001.

Khwankeo Vajarodaya. "Twelfth Anniversary of the Distance Learning Foundation: Free and Open Low-Cost Distance Education via Satellite and Internet, the Wang Klaikangwon Model." Bangkok: 4th International Conference on eLearning, November 18–19, 2007.

"King Prajadhipok's Memorandum, Sukhodaya Palace, July 23rd 1926" (to Francis B. Sayre [Phya Kalyan Maitri], concerning the "Problems of Siam"). *Siam's Political Future*. Benjamin A. Batson. Ithaca, N. Y.: Cornell University, 1974. 13–22.

King Vajiravudh Memorial Foundation. *Dusit Thani: Muang prachathippatai kong Phra Bat Somdet Phra Mongkut Klao Chao Yu Hua* [Dusit Thani: King Vajiravudh's democratic city]. Bangkok: King Vajiravudh Memorial Foundation, 2010 (2553). King Vajiravudh Memorial Foundation. *Saranukrom Phra Bat Somdet Phra Mongkut Klao Chao Yu Hua* [The encyclopedia of King Vajiravudh]. Bangkok: King Vajiravudh Memorial Foundation, 1997(2540).

King, Allan W. *The Presentation of the Colours*. Sawasdee, N.p.: 16–20, 1987.

Kobkua Suwannathat-Pian. *Kings, Country and Constitutions: Thailand's Political Development 1932–2000*. London and New York: Routledge Curzon, 2003.

Korapin Taweta, ed. *Praisaniyabat Chotmaihet* [Royal Archival Postcards]. Bangkok: National Archive of Thailand, Fine Arts Department, 2010 (2553).

Kruger, Rayne. *The Devil's Discus: The Death of Ananda, King of Siam* (2nd edition). Hong Kong: DMP Publications, 2009.

Kukrit Pramoj, Mom Rajawongse. *The Role of Monarchy in Thailand*. Bangkok: American Chamber of Commerce. 21 August 1974.

Lazara, Leopoldo Ferri de and Paulo Piazzardi. *Italians at the Court of Siam*. N.p.: Amarin Printing and Publishing.

Lewis, Norman. *A Dragon Apparent*. London: Eland Books, 1984.

Leonowens, Anna. *The Romance of the Harem*. Charlottesville: University Press of Virginia, 1991.

Lingat, Robert. "Evolution of the Conception of Law in Burma and Siam." *Journal of the Siam Society* Vol. 38:, 1950. 9–3.

Lockhart, Bruce et al, *Thailand in Crisis: The Twilight of a Reign or the Birth of a New Order*. Singapore: Asia Research Institute, National University of Singapore, 2009.

Loos, Tamara. *Subject Siam: Family, Law and Colonial Modernity in Thailand*. Chiang Mai: Silkworm Books, 2006.

Manich Jumsai, Mom Luang. *Prince Prisdang's Files on His Diplomatic Activities in Europe, 1880–1886*. Bangkok: Charaenphol Press, 1977.

MacDonald, Alexander. *Bangkok Editor*. New York:

BIBLIOGRAPHY:

Macmillan, 1949.

Manyon, Julian. *The Fall of Saigon*. London: Rex Collings, 1975.

McBeth, John. *Reporter: Forty Years Covering Asia*. Singapore: Talisman Publishing, 2011.

Ministry of Public Health. *Public Health in Thailand*. Bangkok: Ministry of Public Health, 1963.

Moments in Southeast Asian Sport. Bangkok: Hattori Seiko-PRESKO Public Relations, 1985.

Morell, David and Chai-Anan Samudavanija. *Political Conflict in Thailand: Reform, Reaction and Revolution*. N.p: Oelgescglager, Gunn and Hain, 1982.

Mukhom Wongthes. *Intellectual Might and National Myth: A Forensic Investigation of the Ram Khamhaeng Controversy in Thai Society*. Bangkok: Matichon, 2003.

Naengnoi Panchaphan, Somchai Na Nakhon Phanom. *The Art of Thai Wood Carving: Sukhothai, Ayutthaya, Ratanakosin*. Bangkok: Rerngrom, 1992.

Naengnoi Suksri, Mom Rajawongse and Michael Freeman, *Palaces of Bangkok: Royal Residences of the Chakri Dynasty*. Bangkok: River Books, 1996.

Office of His Majesty's Prinicipal Private Secretary. *Illustrated Handbook of Projects Undertaken Through Royal Initiative*. 1982

Office of the Prime Minister. *Efficient Land and Water Management According to the Royally-initiated New Theory*. Office of the Royal Development Projects Board.

Office of the Prime Minister. *Fifty Years of Development Work According to the Initiatives of His Majesty King Bhumibol Adulyadej of Thailand*. Office of the Royal Development Project Board, 1996.

Office of the Prime Minister. *His Majesty the King and Water Resources Management*. Office of the National Water Resources Committee, 1996.

Office of the Prime Minister. *King Bhumibol Adulyadej and His Englightened Approach to Teaching*. Public Relations Department.

Office of the Prime Minister. *King Bhumibol: Strength of the Land*. National Identity Office, 2000.

Office of the Prime Minister. *Museum for Life*. Office of the Royal Development Projects Board.

Office of the Prime Minister. *Royal Activities: and International Cooperation*. National Identity Foundation, 2011.

Office of the Prime Minister. *Thailand in the 80s*. Bangkok: National Identity Office, 1984.

Office of the Prime Minister. *Thailand in the 90s*. Bangkok: National Identity Office, 1995.

Office of the Prime Minister. *The Chakri Monarchs and the Thai People: A Special Relationship*. Bangkok: National Identity Board, 1984

Office of the Prime Minister. *The Developer King*. Office of the Royal Development Projects Board, 2005.

Office of the Prime Minister. *The Royal Ceremonies Past and Present*. Bangkok: National Identity Board, 1990.

Office of the Prime Minister. *The Thai Monarchy*. Public Relations Department, 2000.

Osborne, Milton. *Southeast Asia: An Introductory History*. Sydney: George Allen and Unwin Australia, 1979.

Pasuk Phongpaichit and Baker, Chris. *A History of Thailand*. N.p.: Cambridge University Press, 2005.

Pasuk Pongpaichit and Chris Baker, eds. *Thai Capital after the 1997 Crisis*. Chiang Mai: Silkworm Books, 2008.

Pavin Chachavalpongpun. *A Plastic Nation: The Curse of Thainess in Thai-Burmese Relations*. Oxford: University Press of America, Inc, 2005.

Peleggi, Maurizio. *Lords of Things: The Fashioning of the Siamese Monarchy's Modern Image*. Honolulu: University of Hawaii Press, 2002.

Peleggi, Maurizio. *Thailand: The Worldly Kingdom*. Singapore: Talisman Publishing, 2007.

Pichai Chuensuksawadi, ed. *King Bhumibol Adulyadej: Thailand's Guiding Light*. Bangkok: The Post Publishing, 1996

Prabha, C. *Buddhist Holy Days and State Ceremonies in Thailand*. Bangkok: Prae Pittaya Publishing Company, 1964.

Pravit Rojanaphruk and Jiranan Hanthamrongwit. "Distorted Mirror and Lamp: The Politicization of the Thai Media in the Post-Thaksin Era." Marc Askew, ed. *Legitimacy Crisis in Thailand*. Chiang Mai: Prajadhipok Institute/Silkworm Books, 2010.

Prem Tinsulanonda. "Thailand: A Monarchy in a Globalized World." Washington D.C: Asia Society, May 24, 2001.

Prime Minister's Office. *Royal Activities and International Cooperation*. Bangkok: National Identity Foundation, 2011.

Prince Mahidol Award 2009. Siriraj Medical Textbooks Project.

"Prince Prisdang's Constitutional Dream." *Bangkok Post*, 9 December. 2010.

Privy Council. *The Privy Council of Thailand*. Bangkok: Amarin Printing and Publishing, 2004.

Reynolds, Bruce E. *Thailand's Secret War: OSS, SOE and the Free Thai Underground During World War II*. Cambridge: Cambridge University Press, 2004.

Reynolds, Frank E. "Sacral Kingship and National Development: The Case of Thailand." *Tradition and Change in Theravada Buddhism*. Bardwell L. Smith. ed. Leiden: Brill, 1973. 40–50.

Reynolds, Frank E. and Mani B. Reynolds, eds. *Three Worlds According to King Ruang: A Thai Buddhist Cosmology*. Berkeley, California: Asian Humanities Press, 1982.

Reynolds, Frank E. *Sacral Kingship and National Development: The Case in Thailand*. Contributions to Asian Studies, Vol. IV. University of Chicago, 1973. pp. 40–50.

Roberts, Edmund. *Embassy to the Eastern Courts of Cochin-China, Siam and Muscat During the Years 1832–3–4*. New York: Harper & Brothers, 1837.

Rolnick, Harry. *The King of Jazz*. Sawasdee. March, 1987: pp. 56–59.

Rosarin Smitabhindu, ed. *Penthi tha thotlong Kitpongkorrayrieng*. Bangkok: The Royal Chitralada Projects.

"Royal Jubilee." *Bangkok Post* supplement, June 2006.

Royal Remarks. Amarin Printing and Publishing, 1997.

Royal Thai Scholars – A Program Description. Global Development Studies Institute. <http://www.ts47.org/

download/TSProgramDescription.pdf>

Sayre, Francis B. "Siam." *Atlantic Monthly,* June 1926. 841–851.

Sayre, Francis B. *Glad Adventure*. New York: Macmillan, 1957.

Sayre, Francis B. "Siam's Fight for Sovereignty." *Atlantic Monthly,* November 1927. 674–689.

Schumacher, E.F. *Small is Beautiful: A Study of Economics as if People Mattered*. London: Abacus, 1974.

Seagrave, Sterling. *Lords of the Rim*. London: Bantam Press, 1996.

Segaller, Denis. "Royal Language." *Bangkok Post*, 5 December 1974. 39–40.

Seidenfaden, Erik. *Guide To Bangkok: With Notes on Siam*. Singapore: Oxford University Press, 1984.

Seni Pramoj, Mom Rajawongse and Mom Rajawongse Kukrit Pramoj. *The King of Siam Speaks*. Bangkok: The Siam Society Press, 1987.

Seni Pramoj, Mom Rajawongse. "King Mongkut as a Legislator." *Journal of The Siam Society* Vol. 38:1 1950. 32–36.

Sharp, Lauriston, ed. *Thailand since King Chulalongkorn*. New York: The Asia Society (Asia Supplement, No. 2), 1976.

Sharp, Lauriston. "King Chulalongkorn's Century." *Thailand since King Chulalongkorn*. Ed. Lauriston Sharp. New York: The Asia Society (Asia Supplement, No. 2), 1976.

Simpson, Keith. *Forty Years of Murder: An Autobiography*. London: Harrap, 1978.

Siriporn Dabphet. *The Coronation Ritual and Thai Kingship Since the Mid-Nineteenth Century*. Masters thesis. National University of Singapore, 2008.

Skinner, William G. and Kirsch, Thomas A. *Changes and Persistence in Thai Society*. Ithaca and London: Cornell University Press, 1975.

Solomon, Robert L. *Aspects of State, Kingship and Succession in Southeast Asia*. Santa Monica: The Rand Corporation, 1970.

Sombat Plainoi. *Sorties into Thai Cultural History*. Bangkok: Office of the National Cultural Commission, Ministry of Education, 1982.

Somkid Kaewsonthi, Harding, Alan G. and Somchai Peerapakorn. *The Economics of Early Leprosy Case Detection in Thailand*. Bangkok: Chulalongkorn University, Ministry of Public Health, 1995.

Sri Limpichat, Mom Rajawongse and Mom Rajawongse Putrie Viravaidya, eds. *Concepts and Theories of His Majesty the King on Development*. N.p.: United Nations, Department of Technical and Economic Cooperation and United Nations Development Programme, 2004.

Stengs, Irene. "Celebrating Kingship, Worrying about the Monarchy." 10th International Conference on Thai Studies. Bangkok: Thammasat University, January 2008.

Stengs, Irene. *Worshipping the Great Moderniser: King Chulalongkorn, Patron Saint of the Thai Middle Class*. Singapore: NUS Press, 2009.

Stevenson, William. *The Revolutionary King*. London: Constable, 1999.

Stevenson, William. *A Man Called Intrepid*. Guildford: Macmillan, 1976.

Streckfuss, David, ed. *Modern Thai Monarchy and Cultural Politics: The Acquittal of Sulak Sivaraksa on the Charge of Lèse-Majesté in Siam 1995 and its Consequences*. Bangkok: Santi Pracha Dhamma Institute, 1996.

Streckfuss, David. *Truth on Trial in Thailand: Defamation, Treason, and Lèse-Majesté*. London and New York: Routledge, 2011.

Streckfuss, David. "Kings in the Age of Nations—The Paradox of Lèse-Majesté as Political Crime in Thailand." *Comparative Studies in Society and History* 37(3), July 1995.

Studwell, Joe. *Asian Godfathers: Money and Power in Hong Kong and Southeast Asia*. London: Profile Books, 2008.

Sudaporn Luksaneeyanawin. *Portrait of a University: Chulalongkorn University at 75*. Bangkok: Chulalongkorn University Press, 1995.

Sugimori Hisahide. *Tsuji Masanobu*. Tokyo: Bungeishunju Shinsu, 1963.

Sufficiency Economy: 100 Interviews with Business Professionals. Bangkok: Amarin Publishing Services / Thai Chamber of Commerce, 2010.

Sunait Chutintaranond, ed. *The Immortal Art of Ayutthaya Gold*. Bangkok: Plan Motif, 2003.

Supaporn Chalapati. *Sufficiency Economy as a Response to the Problem of Poverty in Thailand*. <http://www.ccsenet.org/journal/index.php/ass/article/view/1362/1326>

Tambiah, Stanley J. "The Shaping of Thailand by the Chakri Dynasty." His Majesty King Bhumibol Adulyadej's Seventy Second Birthday. Thammasat University. 1999.

Tanin Kraivixien. *His Majesty King Bhumibol Adulyadej: Compassionate Monarch of Thailand*. Bangkok: The Katavethin Foundation, 1982.

Teddy Spha Palasthira. *Addresses*. Bangkok: Postbooks, 2010.

Temsiri Panyasingh, ed. *Buddhism in Thai Life*. Bangkok: National Identity Board, 1981.

Terwiel, B. J. *Thailand's Political History: From the 13th Century to Recent Times*. N.p.: River Books, 2005.

Terzani, Tiziano. *Saigon 1975*. Bangkok: White Lotus Press, 1997.

Thailand: A Traveller's Companion. N.p.: Editions Didier Millet, 2002.

"Thailand's Best Practices and Lessons Learned in Development." Thailand International Development Cooperation Agency. <www.tica.thaigov.net/tica/resources/Bestpractice1.pdf>

Thak Chaloemtiarana. *Thailand: The Politics of Despotic Paternalism*. Bangkok: Social Science Association of Thailand, Thai Khadi Institute, 1979.

Thammasat University. "The Chronicle of the Thai Junior Encyclopedia Project By Royal Command of His Majesty the King." <http://kanchanapisek.or.th/kp6/GENERAL/history/his-sara-en.htm>

Thak Chaloemtiarana. *The Sarit Regime, 1957–1963: The Formative Years of Modern Thai Politics*. PhD thesis.

BIBLIOGRAPHY:

Cornell University, 1974.

Thant Myint-U. *The River of Lost Footsteps: Histories of Burma*. New York: Farrar, Status & Giroux, 2006.

"The King Who Cares: The King and Education." *Bangkok Post* March 23, 2006.

"The Role of His Majesty." *Sunday Post* (Bangkok), March 12, 1995.

Thawatt Mokarapong. *History of the Thai Revolution: A Study in Political Behavior*. Bangkok: Chalermnit, 1972.

The King of Hearts. Bangkok: Kurusapa Business Organization, 2000.

The Music of His Majesty King Bhumibol Adulyadej. Bangkok: The Katavethin Foundation, 1987.

Thongchai Winichakul. *Siam Mapped: A History of the Geo-Body of a Nation*. Honolulu: University of Hawaii Press, 1994.

Thongthong Chandransu. *A Constitutional Legal Aspect of the King's Prerogatives*. MA dissertation, Chulalongkorn University, 1985.

Tsuji Masanobu. *Senko sanzenri*. Tokyo: Mainichi Wanzu, 2008.

United Nations. *The Royal Chitralada Projects*. N.p.: Food and Agriculture Organization, Regional Office for Asia and The Pacific, 1995.

Van Beek, Steve and Vilas Manivat, eds. *M.R. Kukrit Pramoj: His Wit and Wisdom, Writings, Speeches and Interviews*. Bangkok: Editions Duang Kamol, 1983.

Vasit Dejkunjom. *In His Majesty's Footsteps: A Personal Memoir*. Bangkok: Heaven Lak Press, 2008.

Vickery, Michael. "The Constitution of Ayutthaya: An Investigation into the Three Seals Code." Fifth International Conference on Thai Studies. SOAS, London, July 1993.

Vickery, Michael. "The Constitution of Ayutthaya: the Three Seals Code." *Thai Law: Buddhist Law. Essays on the Legal History of Thailand, Laos and Burma*. Andrew Huxley, ed. Bangkok: White Orchid Press, 1996. pp. 33–210.

Wales, H. G. Quaritch. *Siamese State Ceremonies*. London: Bernard Quaritch, 1931.

Wan Waithayakon, Prince. "The Thai Idea of Freedom." Meeting of the American Association, Bangkok, 26 January 1954.

Wan Waithayakon, Prince. *Collected Articles in Memory of HRH Prince Wan Waithayakorn, Krommun Naradhip Bongsprabandh, President of The Siam Society 1944–1949 & 1969–1976*. Bangkok: The Siam Society, 1976.

Warren, William. *Jim Thompson: The Legendary American of Thailand*. N.p.: Jim Thompson Thai Silk Co, 1989.

Warren, Willam, ed. *Thailand: King Bhumibol Adulyadej Golden Jubilee*. N.p.: Archipelago Press,1996.

Watson, Keith. *Educational Development in Thailand*. Hong Kong: Heinemann Asia, 1982.

Wilson, David A. *Politics in Thailand*. New York: Cornell University Press, 1962.

Wilson, David A. *The Evolution of Foreign Relations*. In *Thailand since King Chulalongkorn*. Lauriston Sharped. New York: The Asia Society (Asia Supplement, No. 2), 1976.

Woraporn Poopongpan. *Thai Kingship during the Ayutthaya Period: A Note on Its Divine Aspects Concerning Indra*. Silpakorn University International Journal, Vol. 7. (2007). pp.143–171.

Wright, Joseph J. *The Balancing Act: A History of Modern Thailand*. California: Pacific Rim Press, 2004.

Wright, Michael. "A Pious Fable Reconsidering the Inscription I Controversy: A 'Domonic' View." *Journal of the Siam Society* Vol. 83.0, 1995. 91–106.

Wyatt, David K. "King Chulalongkorn the Great: Founder of Modern Thailand. *Thailand Since King Chulalongkorn*. Ed. Lauriston Sharp. New York: The Asia Society (Asia Supplement, No. 2), 1976. 5–16.

Wyatt, David K. *Thailand: A Short History*. Chiang Mai: Silkworm Books, 2003.

Ziegler, Philip. *Mountbatten: The Official Biography*. London: Guild Publishing, 1985.

SOURCE MATERIAL IN THAI

Akarawat Osathanugroh. *Nailuang kongrao* [Our king]. Bangkok: Dokya Group, 2002 (BE 2545).

Anake Nawigamune. *Thayrub muangthai samairaek* [Early Photography in Thailand]. Bangkok: Saengdad, 1998 (BE 2541).

Aw Saw Ambhorn Satharn Radio Station and the Government Savings Bank. *Nailuang kab prachachon* [The King and the people] Bangkok: Dusit Palace, 1999 (BE 2542).

Bhumibol Adulyadej, King. *Kampauson: pramuan phrabarommarachowat lae phraratchadamrat kiewkub dek lae yaowachon* [The teachings of the father: collection of royal teachings and addresses about children and youth]. Bangkok: Rongpim Krungthep, 2009 (BE 2552).

Bhumibol Adulyadej, King. *Kampauson: pramuan phrabarommarachowat lae phraratchadamrat kiewkub setthakit paupieng* [The teachings of the father: a collection of royal teachings and addresses about Sufficiency Economy]. Bangkok: Rongpim Krungthep, 2010 (BE 2553).

Board of Directors of His Majesty the King's 50th Reign Anniversary Celebration. *Phra maha karunathikhun tor phasa wannakham lae hongsamut* [His Majesty's kindness to the works in language, literature and libraries]. Bangkok: Board of Directors of His Majesty the King's 50th Reign Anniversary Celebration, 1996 (BE 2539).

Chanida Chitabandit. *Krong karn anneangmajak phra ratchadamri: kan satapana phra racha amntjnam nai Phra Bat Somdet Phrachao Yu Hua dan* [The royal projects: the establishment of the royal prerogatives]. Bangkok: The Foundation for the Promotion of Social Science and Humanities Textbook Project, 2007 (BE 2550).

Chulalongkorn University. *Kwam pen kru sathit nai hathairat* [The teaching spirit embraced in Thai people's hearts]. Bangkok: Institute of Thai Studies, 1996 (BE 2539).

Chulalongkorn University. *Phra atchariya barami: kan prathomsuksa lae kan suksa prathomwai*

[The king's virtuous mastery in primary and early childhood education]. Bangkok: Faculty of Education, Chulalongkorn University, 2000 (BE 2543).

Chulalongkorn University. *Praisaniyabat chao fah BE 2466–2551* [Postcards Games BE 2466–2551]. Bangkok: Wongchorn, 1992 (BE 2535).

Crown Property Bureau. *Munpattana bon sentang kong kwamyungyun* [A Moral Compass Towards Sustainability]. Bangkok: Crown Property Bureau, 2009 (BE 2552).

Crown Property Bureau. *Rai-ngan prajampi 2553 ongkon hangkanrienru mungsukunnapab radablok* [Annual Report 2010 of the Crown Property Bureau: Learning organisation for world-class quality]. Bangkok: Crown property Bureau, 2010 (BE 2553).

Cultural Center Board of Directors. *Akkara sinlapin* [Supreme Artist]. Bangkok: Fine Arts Department, 1987 (BE 2530).

Faculty of Law, Thammasat University. *Pramuan kotmai ratchakan thi nung chulasakarat 1166, phim tam chabap luang tra sam duang lem 2 (PKRI)* [The Three Seals Law, Vol. 2]. Bangkok: Ruankaew kanphim, 1986 (BE 2529).

Fine Arts Department. *Phra rajaphithi lae ngan phra raja kusol prachampi* [Annual royal ceremonies and charitable activities]. Bangkok: Fine Arts Department, 2000 (BE 2543).

Galyani Vadhana, Princess. *Mae lao hai fung* [As Mother Told Me]. Bangkok: Bunnakij, 2007 (2550).

Galyani Vadhana, Princess. *Chaonai leklek yuwakasat* [Little princes, young kings]. Bangkok: Darnsutha, 1988 (BE 2531).

Genlong Snidvongs, Thanphuying. *Tham pen Dhamma* [Following the Dhamma path]. Bangkok: Katavetin Foundation, 1998 (BE 2542).

Kasetsart University and the Thai Military Bank. *Keeta maha racha sadudi* [A tribute to the musician king]. Bangkok: Kasetsart University, 1987 (BE 2530).

King Vajiravudh Memorial Foundation. *Dusit Thani: Muang prachathippatai kong Phra Bat Somdet Phra Mongkut Klao Chao Yu Hua* [Dusit Thani: King Vajiravudh's democratic city]. Bangkok: King Vajiravudh Memorial Foundation under Royal Patronage, 2010 (BE 2553).

King Vajiravudh Memorial Foundation. *Saranukrom Phra Bat Somdet Phra Mongkut Klao Chao Yu Hua* [The encyclopedia of King Vajiravudh]. Bangkok: King Vajiravudh Memorial Foundation under Royal Patronage, 1997(BE 2540).

Loubère, Simon de la. *Chotmaihet la Loubère ratcha-arnachak Siam* [Chronicle of Siam by Monsieur de la Loubère]. Bangkok: Sripunya, 2005 (BE 2548).

Ministry of Agriculture and Cooperatives. *Krongkan tamphraratchaprasong Hup Kapong Changwat Phetchaburi* [Hup Kapong project according to His Majesty's wish, Phetchaburi province]. Bangkok: Cooperative Promotion Department.

Ministry of Agriculture and Cooperatives. *Phra bat somdet Phra chao yuhua kub kanpattanakaset Thai* [His Majesty and Thai agricultural development]. Bangkok: Amarin, 1996 (BE 2539).

Ministry of Culture. *Phra raja phitee nai ratchakan Phra Bat Somdet Poramintra Maha Bhumibol Adulyadej* [Royal ceremonies of His Majesty King Bhumibol Adulyadej]. Bangkok: Fine Arts Department, 2000 (BE 2543).

Ministry of Culture. *Ruephraratchapithi* [Royal Barges]. Bangkok: Fine Arts Department, 1996 (BE 2539).

Ministry of Education. *Dut dung rom phothong khong kan suksa Thai* [The golden pho tree of Thai education]. Bangkok: Ministry of Culture, 2009 (BE 2549).

Nakkarin Mektrairat. *Phrapusong pokklao prachathipatai Thai* [The protector of Thai democracy]. Bangkok: Thammasat Press, 2006 (BE 2549).

National Archive of Thailand, Ministry of Culture. *Pramuanpab prawatsat Thai phra ratchapithi baromrachapisek samai Rattanakosin* [A collection of photographs of the coronation ceremonies of the Rattankosin era]. Bangkok: Fine Arts Department, 2007 (BE 2550).

Nongyao Kanjanajaree. *Sueb Rajasantativongse. Kot Monthien Ban BE 2467* [Law of succession, palace law 1924], in the *Encyclopaedia of King Vajiravudh*, Vol. 2. Bangkok: King Vajiravudh Memorial Foundation under Royal Patronage, 2001 (BE 2554).

Office of His Majesty's Principal Private Secretary. *Samut phap hetkan samkhan khong krung Rattanakosin* [Collection of photographs from significant events of the Rattanakosin kingdom]. Bangkok: Bangkok Printing, 1982 (BE 2525).

Office of His Majesty's Principal Private Secretary. *Krasae phra ratchadamri Phra Bat Somdet Phrachao Yu Hua dan* [Royal remarks by His Majesty the King]. Bangkok: Bangkok Printing, 1987 (BE 2535).

Office of His Majesty's Principal Private Secretary. *Pramuan phrachayalak lae pabphraratchakorraniya-kit Somdet Phra Nangchao Rambhai Barni Phra Baromrajini nai ratchakan ti 7* [A collection of photographs of King Prajadhipok's queen, Queen Rambhai Barni]. Bangkok: Icarus, 1985 (BE 2528).

Office of the Higher Education Commission. *Ek kasatra atchariya* [The king's ingenuity]. Bangkok,: Office of the Higher Education Commission, 1997 (BE 2540).

Office of the National Board of Education. *Nai luang kab karn suksa Thai: ha totsawat siriratchasombat* [The king and education: five decades of his reign]. Bangkok: Working Committee for organizing events for His Majesty's 50th anniversary on His accession to the throne, 1997 (BE 2540).

Ph. N. Pramuanmak. *Chewit chunchun*. Bangkok: Nanmee, 2000 (BE 2553).

Phanumas Thaksana, ed. *Royyim kong nailuang* [Smiles of the King]. Bangkok: Chaopraya News, 2009 (BE 2552).

Piyabutr Saengkanokkul. *Phra ratchaamnat ongkamontri lae pumibarami nok rattathammanoon* [Royal prerogative, the Privy Council and extra-constitutional figures]. Bangkok: Openbooks, 2007 (BE 2550).

Poramintra Krouethong. *Phra Chomklao* [King Mongkut: Photographs from the Reign of King Mongkut].

BIBLIOGRAPHY:

Bangkok: Matichon, 2004 (BE 2547).

Poramintra Krouethong. *Riakpaupittongnai* [What's wrong with saying father?]. Bangkok: Art and Culture, Vol 2., December 2010 (BE 2553): pp. 66–115.

Pridi Pispoomvithee. *Kot monthien ban: kwam samkan krongsang lae nueaha* [Palace Law: significance, structure and content], in *Kot monthien ban chabab chalerm phrakiet* [Palace law: Commemorative version]. Bangkok: Thailand Research Fund, 2005 (BE 2548).

Queen Savang Vadhana Foundation. *Srisavarintiranusorani: nomrumluektung Somdet Phra Panwatsa Ai-yikachao* [In memory of Queen Savang Vadhana]. Bangkok: Amarin, 2010 (BE 2553).

Raerai Naiyawat. *Ngan chung khong nai luang* [The King's craftwork]. Bangkok: Amarin, 1997 (BE 2540).

Rajabhat Institute, Nakhon Sawan. *Khru khong phandin: atchariyaphap hang pasa Thai nai Phra Bat Somdet Phrachao Yu Hua* [The nation's teacher: the king's mastery of the Thai language]. Bangkok: Thanarat Printing, 1998 (BE 2543).

Rosarin Smitabhindu, ed. *Penthi tha thotlong Kitpongkorrayrieng*. Bangkok: The Royal Chitralada Projects.

Rungrot Theplip, comp., et al. *Sang krung lae prawattisat kan borishan chat Thai* [Building the city: a history of the administration of the Thai nation]. Bangkok: Thepphithak Kanphim,1978–1979 (BE 2521–22).

Sakda Siriphun. *Kasat lae klong: Wiwatthanakan kanthaypab nai pathet Thai* BE 2388–2535 [King & Camera: Evolution of Photography in Thailand 1845–1992]. Bangkok: Dansutha, 1992 (BE 2535).

Secretariat of the Cabinet. *Kruang ratcha-itsariyapon Thai* [Royal Thai Orders and Decorations]. Bangkok: Amarin, 1992 (BE 2535).

Secretariat of the House of Representatives. *Priapthiap rattathammanoon haeng ratcha-anajak Thai* BE 2475–2548 lem 1 [Comparison of the Constitutions of the Kingdom of Thailand 1932–2005 Vol. 1]. Bangkok: Secretariat of the House of Representatives, 2007 (BE 2547).

Secretariat of the House of Representatives. *Ratthaasapha Thai tai rom phra barami 60 pi song krongrat* [The Thai National Assembly under his graciousness' 60th year reign]. Bangkok: Secretariat of the House of Representatives, 2006 (BE 2549).

Silpakorn University. *Phra bida hang karn anurak moradok thai* [The father of the preservation of Thai culture]. Bangkok: Roongsin (1977) Printing, 2007 (BE 2550).

Sirindhorn, Princess Maha Chakri. *Somdej mae kab karn suksa* [the queen and education] Bangkok: Chitralada School, 1992 (BE 2535).

Somchai Phongpattansilpa and Phaopun Chobnamtarn, eds. *Rattathamamnoon hang ratcha arnajak Thai phutta sakkarat* BE 2550 [The 2007 Constitution of the Kingdom of Thailand]. Bangkok: Charoenrat Kanpim, 2007 (BE 2550).

Somchai Preechasilpakul. *Konkai thi "ayutitham" khaung krabuankan yuttitham Thai* [The "unfair" mechanism of the Thai judicial system] Fa Diew Kan 4:2(mesayon/mithunayon BE 2549 [April/June 2006]).

Sonthiyan Chuenrurtainaitham, ed. *Phra ratchadamrat dub vikitchat* [The royal addresses that end national crises]. Bangkok: Green-Panyayan, 2010 (BE 2553).

Sports Authority of Thailand. *Phra maha kasat nak keela* [His Majesty the king, the athlete] Bangkok: Sports Authority of Thailand, 2006 (BE 2549).

Suan Sunandha Rajabhat University. *Nai luang khong rao* [Our king]. Bangkok: Amarin, 1987 (BE 2530).

Sumet Tantivejkul. *Taibuang phra yukonlabat* [Beneath His Majesty's footsteps]. Bangkok: Matichon, 2000 (BE 2543).

Supparat Lertpanichakun, ed. *Phra mamalai soklaluasuk*. Bangkok: Rongpim Krungthep, 1998 (BE 2541).

Teera Ramasootra. *50 Pi Rajprachasamasai hangkansanong phraratchapanitan* [50 years of Rajprachasamasai in responding to His Majesty's ideas]. Bangkok: Rajprajasamasai Institute, Ministry of Public Health, 2010 (BE 2553).

Thanachai Phadungthiti. *Phra maha kasat nak pokkrong nak kodmai* [The king, the magistrate, the legal expert]. Bangkok: Nitirut Publishing, 2006 (BE 2549).

The Prime Minister's Office. *50 Pi hang kanpattana tamkrongkan aunnuangmajakphraratchadamri kong Phra Bat Somdet Phra Chao Yu Hua* [50 years of development according to King Bhumibol's royally initiated projects). Bangkok: Office of the Royal Projects Development Board, 1996 (BE 2539).

The Prime Minister's Office. *Krut* [Garuda]. Bangkok: The Office of the Permanent Secretary. 2000 (BE 2543).

The United Nations Conference Center. *Phraratcha atchariyapab khong Phra Bat Somdet Phrachao Yu Hua dan technology sarasontet* [His Majesty's remarkable talent in information technology] Bangkok: National Information Technology Committee Secretariat, 1995 (BE 2538).

Uraiwan Sawasdisarn, Khunying, et al, eds. *Sirirattanarin Nawamintrathirat*. Bangkok: Amarin, 2006 (BE 2549).

Vilas Maniwat. *Phra ratcha aromkhan* [Royal humour]. Bangkok: Dokya 2000, 2010 (BE 2553).

Vimonphun Peetathawatchai. *Ek kasatra tai rattathammanoon* [The great constitutional monarch]. Bangkok: Rongpim Krungthep, 2010 (BE 2553).

Voraporn Pupongpunt, "Phap luk sataban kasat nai kot monthien ban" [The image of the monarchical institution through Palace Law]. *Kot monthien ban chabab chalerm phrakiet* [Palace law: Commemorative version]. Bangkok: Thailand Research Fund, 2005 (BE 2548).

Winai Pongsripien ed. *Kotmai tra samduang: nahtang sungkom Thai* [The Three Seals Code: window to Thai society]. Bangkok: Thai Research Fund, 2006 (BE 2549).

Wit Pinkhanngern. *Kruang ratachaphan* [Royal utensils]. Bangkok: Amarin, 2008 (BE 2551).

Woranuch Usanakorn. *Nai luang kub krongkan aunnuang majak phra ratchadamri* [The king and projects initiated by His Majesty]. Bangkok: Odeon Store, 1997 (BE 2540).

INDEX:

INDEX:

INDEX:

INDEX:

INDEX:

PICTURE CREDITS:

Every effort has been made to trace copyright holders of images in this book. In the events of errors or omissions, appropriate credit will be made in future editions of *King Bhumibol Adulyadej: A Life's Work*.

Abbas: 170

Agence France-Presse/ Getty Images: 171

American Chamber of Commerce: 318

Anake Nawigamune: 116, 232 left

Angelo Cavalli/Photolibrary: 20

Associated Press: 89, 95, 141, 185 below, 277, 351

Athit Perawongmetha: 173, 177 below left, 178, 181, 218 all, 219, 244 all, 260 all, 261, 271, 272-273, 282

Athit Perawongmetha/ Getty Images: 302

Bangkok Post: 10, 13, 14., 63 below, 83, 87, 93 below right, 100, 107, 115, 124, 125 right, 126, 128, 131-134, 136-137 top, 138 all, 145, 147, 151, 157 all, 159, 163, 166, 167, 169, 172, 176 all, 179, 182, 200 left, 210, 220 left, 222, 226 left, 236, left, 243, 251, 256 left, 320, 323, 355

Bank of Thailand: 70 top

Bettmann/Corbis: 135

Bowater Peter/Photolibrary: 343

British Broadcasting Corporation: 140

Bureau of the Royal Household: 8, 90, 108, 109, 110 all, 111 all, 113 all, 118, 149, 177 below right, 183 below

Crown Property Bureau: 278 right, 279, 296 all, 299, 301

Dallas and John Heaton/ Corbis: 7

Dean Conger/Getty Images: 246 right

Dmitri Kessel/Getty Images: 74, 91, 105

Dominic Faulder: 156, 162, 256 right

EDM Archive: 23 left, 26, 28, 76 top left & right, 93 top, 102 below

Faculty of Medicine, Siriraj Hospital: 48, 54, 55, 56 top, 57, 59 all, 70 below, 192 left

Getty Images: 177 top and centre

Horace Bristol/Corbis: 212 right, 230 left

Howard Sochurek/Time Life Pictures/Getty Images: 98, 104

Huai Hong Krai Royal Development Study Centre: 262 left

Hulton Archive/Getty Images: 330

Igna Spence/Photolibrary: 264

James Marshall/Corbis: 224 right

Phillippe Lissac/Godong/ Corbis: 225

Jim Thompson Foundation: 19

John Dominis/Getty Images: 42

Kevin R. Morris/Corbis: 347

Kraipit Phanvut/UPI: 137 below

Luca Tettoni/Photolibrary: 16

Luca Tettoni/Robert Harding/ World Imagery/ Corbis: 334

Manit Sriwanichpoom: 238

Marie Hensen/Getty Images: 96

Michael Freeman/Corbis: 23 right, 33

Ministry of Foreign Affairs: 262 right

National Archive in Commemoration of HM the King's Golden Jubilee: 40, 68 below, 114, 125 left, 127

National Archive of Thailand: 5, 24, 34 below, 39 all, 47, 49 all, 50, 51, 53, 58, 71, 76 below, 78, 79 all, 80, 82 top, 85, 92 all, 97, 101, 103, 143, 190 left, 196 all, 212 left, 305, 316, 328 all, 336, 338, 341, 353

National Library of Thailand: 56 below, 61, 62, 68 top right, 86, 99, 119, 122, 326

Office of Anand Panyarachun: 152

Office of His Majesty's Principal Private Secretary: 102 top, 175, 184 top, 192 right, 200 right, 204 left, 249, 324

Office of the Royal Development Projects Board: 188, 202 below, 205, 208, 214 right, 215, 216, 220 right, 224 left, 226 right, 228, 248 right, 252, 253 all, 254 all, 255, 258, 266 all, 270, 278 left

One Clear Vision/ Getty Images: 242 left

Paula Bronstein/Getty Images: 268 left

Poonnatree Jiaviriyaboonya: 158

Popperfoto/Getty Images: 34 top left

Pornchai Kittiwongsakul/ Agence France-Presse/ Getty Images: 310, 333

Pranburi Irrigation Project: 237

Royal Project Foundation: 240 all, 241, 242 centre & right

Privy Council Chamber: 314

Queen Savang Vadhana Foundation: 190 right

Rajaprajanugroh Foundation: 202 top, 206 all, 207, 209 left

Rajprachasamasai Institute: 194 -195 all, 214 left

Reg Speller/Fox Photos/ Getty Images: 65

Relief and Community Health Bureau, The Thai Red Cross Society: 193, 209 right

Richard Harrington/Three Lions/Getty Images: 230 right

Robert McLoed/Lantern Photography Co. Ltd.: 286 centre, 294, 358

ROHA/Photolibrary: 348

Romeo Gacad: 268 right

Satakun Boonsing: 93 below left

Serge Kakou: 31

Siam Cement Group: 286 below, 292

Siam Commercial Bank: 164, 186

Silpakorn University: 121, 123

Thai Bank Museum: 286 top left & right

Thanphuying Tasna Valaya Sorasongkram: 46, 52, 63 top, 66, 67, 68 top left, 73, 183 top

The Chaipattana Foundation: 148, 150

The Royal Chitralada Projects: 44, 198 all, 199, 233, 234 all, 263

The Royal Elephants Museum: 357

The Royal Irrigation Department: 232 right, 236 right, 248 left, 250 all

The Royal Photographers Society of Thailand: 246 left

Topical Press Agency/ Getty Images: 37

Wanee Banomyong: 81

W&D Downey/Getty Images: 34 top right

Royal permission for royal paintings and photographs: 82 below, 84, 88, 112, 120 all

EDITORIAL CONTRIBUTORS:

EDITORIAL ADVISORY BOARD

Anand Panyarachun served as Thailand's prime minister twice in the early 1990s. Before that, he spent over two decades in the foreign service, which included serving as Permanent Representative of Thailand to the United Nations, and ambassador to Canada, the United States and Germany. He has also held important posts with academic institutions such as the Thailand Development Research Institute. He is currently chairman of Siam Commercial Bank.

Thanphuying Putrie Viravaidya is one of King Bhumibol Adulyadej's deputy principal private secretaries. She is also director of the Co-ordinating Office of the Anandamahidol Foundation.

Dr Dhiravat na Pombejra taught at the Department of History, Faculty of Arts, Chulalongkorn University from 1985 until 2006. He has written and edited several works on the Ayudhya period.

Dr Duangtip Surintatip is the president of the Thai Association of Conference Interpreters. Having completed language studies in the UK and France on government scholarships, Dr Duangtip joined the civil service.

Pramote Maiklad is the former director-general of the Royal Irrigation Department. He has served as a Bangkok senator and is currently a committee member of the Chaipattana Foundation.

Dr Pisoot Vijarnsorn is a senior specialist on land development and adviser to Her Royal Highness Princess Sirindhorn's projects.

Dr Sondhi Tejanant is a former governor of Songkhla province. He has a personal interest in writing about contemporary Thai political history.

Dr Sumet Tantivejkul is a committee member and secretary-general of the Chaipattana Foundation. He is a former secretary-general of both the National Economics and Social Development Board and the Royal Development Projects Board.

Theerakun Niyom is the Ministry of Foreign Affairs' permanent secretary. He joined the foreign service in 1982 and has served in various positions at the ministry in Bangkok and overseas in New York, Ottawa and Seoul.

Dr Wissanu Krea-ngam is the chairperson of Law Committee No. 2. He has served as deputy prime minister and cabinet secretary.

EDITORIAL TEAM

Nicholas Grossman (Editor-in Chief) is the managing editor of Editions Didier Millet (Thailand). He was the editor of *Chronicle of Thailand: Headline News Since 1946*.

Dominic Faulder (Senior Editor) is a former special correspondent for *Asiaweek*. His recent editing projects include *The King of Thailand in World Focus* for the Foreign Correspondents' Club of Thailand, of which he is a former president.

Grissarin Chungsiriwat (Deputy Editor) is an editor at Editions Didier Millet. Grissarin, a freelance translator and interpreter, was assistant editor of *Chronicle of Thailand: Headline News Since 1946*.

Satakun Boonsing (Graphic Designer) graduated in graphic design from Platt College, California. He was the creative director for the branding agency Creative-Inhouse before joining EDM.

Ismail Wolff (Proofing Editor) is a Bangkok-based freelance journalist and writer. His work has been published in *The New York Times*, the *Guardian* and *National Geographic* (Thailand).

Chris Baker (Contributor) taught Asian history and politics at Cambridge University. He is the author of several books on Thai history and politics, including *A History of Thailand*.

Joe Cummings (Contributor) has authored several books about Thailand, including *Buddhist Temples of Thailand* and *Sacred Tattoos of Thailand*.

Richard S. Ehrlich (Contributor) is based in Bangkok and reports for *The Washington Times*, BBC radio, CNN's website and other international media.

Julian Gearing (Contributor) has covered conflicts, politics, religion and the environment in Asia and the Middle East for 25 years. He is a former staff correspondent in Bangkok for *Asiaweek*.

Robert Horn (Contributor) has worked as a reporter in Thailand for *Time*, the Associated Press and contributed articles for *Fortune*, *Businessweek* and *Institutional Investor*.

Dr Porphant Ouyyanont (Contributor) is an associate professor of economics at Sukhothai Thammathirat Open University. His reserach focuses mainly on Thai economic history and development.

David Streckfuss (Contributor) is an independent scholar and the author of *Truth on Trial in Thailand*. His work focuses on human rights, and political and cultural history.

Paul Wedel (Contributor) is president of the Bangkok-based Kenan Institute Asia and previously worked as a journalist for United Press International in Asia. He has served as president of the Foreign Correspondents' Club of Thailand.

Robert Woodrow (Contributor) is a former assistant managing editor of *Asiaweek*. Earlier, he worked for the *Bangkok Post*, *Reader's Digest* and the Economist Intelligence Unit. He also contributed articles to the *Encyclopaedia Brittanica* for many years.

Athit Perawongmetha (Assignment Photographer) is a Bangkok-based freelancer who works for Getty Images News Agency. His work has appeared in *The New York Times*, *Time* and the *International Herald Tribune*.

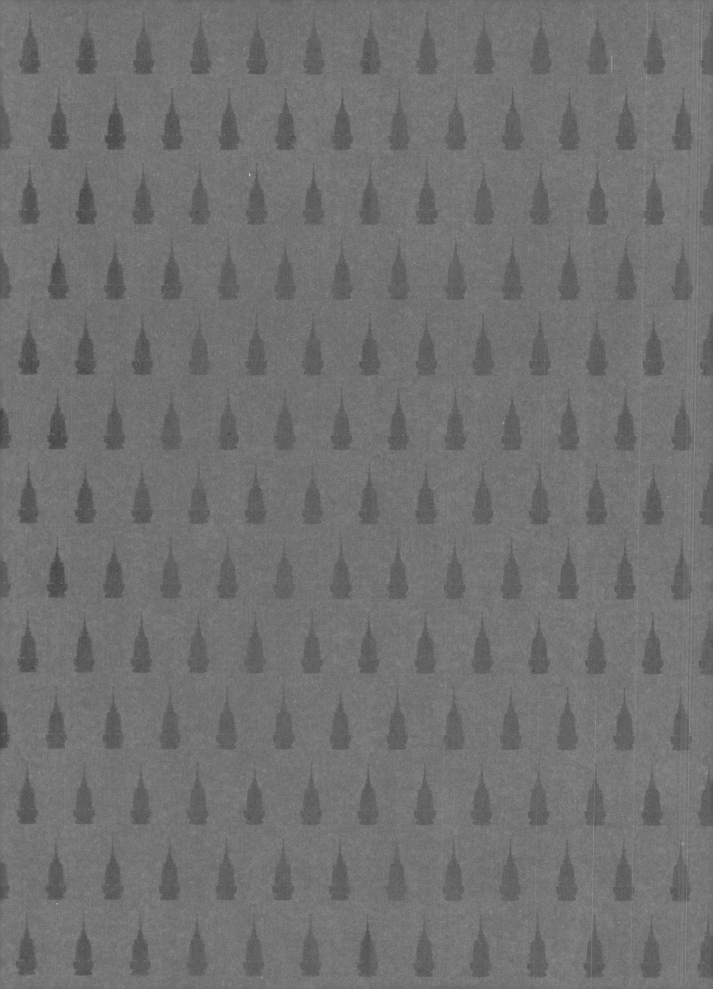